Transformations of the Welfare State

Transformations of the Welfare State

Small States, Big Lessons

Herbert Obinger, Peter Starke, Julia Moser,
Claudia Bogedan, Edith Gindulis, and
Stephan Leibfried

OXFORD
UNIVERSITY PRESS

2010

OXFORD
UNIVERSITY PRESS

Great Clarendon Street, Oxford OX2 6DP

Oxford University Press is a department of the University of Oxford.
It furthers the University's objective of excellence in research, scholarship,
and education by publishing worldwide in

Oxford New York

Auckland Cape Town Dar es Salaam Hong Kong Karachi
Kuala Lumpur Madrid Melbourne Mexico City Nairobi
New Delhi Shanghai Taipei Toronto

With offices in

Argentina Austria Brazil Chile Czech Republic France Greece
Guatemala Hungary Italy Japan Poland Portugal Singapore
South Korea Switzerland Thailand Turkey Ukraine Vietnam

Oxford is a registered trade mark of Oxford University Press
in the UK and in certain other countries

Published in the United States
by Oxford University Press Inc., New York

British Library Cataloguing in Publication Data
Data available

Library of Congress Cataloging in Publication Data
Data available

Typeset by SPI Publisher Services, Pondicherry, India
Printed in Great Britain
on acid-free paper by
MPG Books Group, Bodmin and King's Lynn

ISBN 978–0–19–929632–3

Contents

Acknowledgements

Transformations of the Welfare State: Small States, Big Lessons presents the findings of work undertaken by one of the sixteen interdisciplinary research groups at the University of Bremen's Collaborative Research Centre 'Transformations of the State' (TranState). At TranState some hundred scholars in political science, law, sociology, and economics are analysing how pressures from internationalization and privatization over the past 30 years have affected the core institutions and functions that define the classical nation state.[1] Without the continuing support of the German Research Foundation (DFG), which has provided generous funding for TranState since its founding in 2003, this book would not have been possible. We are also grateful to the University of Bremen for its commitment to the enterprise, with special thanks to its president, Wilfried Müller and vice president, Gerd-Rüdiger Kück. Their enlightened leadership has made it possible for the University of Bremen Social Science Department and institutions to realize their full potential, gaining international stature and, in recent years, rising to the top of the academic rankings for German universities.

Many people contributed their time and expertise to writing this book: without them it would never have been completed. We thank Carolin Echt, Lynn Meyer, Sarah Ryglewski, Nico Nobilis, Jendrik Schröder, and Janis Vossiek for research support, and Gitta Klein at the Centre for Social Policy Research (CeS) for her patient and good-humoured secretarial support. Bob Stephens, Susan St John, and Mike O'Brien generously shared their knowledge of the New Zealand welfare state and provided much practical help during the research trip of Peter Starke to that country. Christoffer Green-Pedersen, Asbjørn Sonne Nørgaard, and Jon Kvist supported Claudia Bogedan during her research stay in Denmark. Jon also provided valuable comments on Chapter 2. Special thanks go to Francis G. Castles. Frank, then a fellow at the Hanse Institute for Advanced Study in Delmenhorst, offered detailed comments and advice on the whole volume. We are particularly grateful to Dominic Byatt, our editor at Oxford University Press, for his encouragement and patience with a project that took 2 years longer than he had expected.

---

[1] See, for example, Leibfried and Zürn (2005) and Hurrelmann et al (2007); see also http://www.state.uni-bremen.de

Frank Castles, now back in Australia, is also responsible for transforming this small treatise from its original Teutonic English to intelligible, academically acceptable English. To comprehend the magnitude of this accomplishment, one must imagine entire chapters where a fluent, sophisticated English vocabulary has been subjected to German logic and sentence structure.[2] An excerpt from Mark Twain's 1880 essay on the German language may be helpful to the uninitiated:

> An average sentence, in a German newspaper, is a sublime and impressive curiosity; it occupies a quarter of a column; it contains all the ten parts of speech — not in regular order, but mixed; it is built mainly of compound words constructed by the writer on the spot, and not to be found in any dictionary — six or seven words compacted into one, without joint or seam — that is, without hyphens; it treats of fourteen or fifteen different subjects, each inclosed in a parenthesis of its own, with here and there extra parentheses which reinclose three or four of the minor parentheses, making pens within pens: finally, all the parentheses and reparentheses are massed together between a couple of king-parentheses, one of which is placed in the first line of the majestic sentence and the other in the middle of the last line of it — *after which comes the VERB*, and you find out for the first time what the man has been talking about; and after the verb — merely by way of ornament, as far as I can make out — the writer shovels in *'haben sind gewesen gehabt haben geworden sein,'* or words to that effect, and the monument is finished. . . . We have the Parenthesis disease in our literature, too; and one may see cases of it every day in our books and newspapers: but with us it is the mark and sign of an unpracticed writer or a cloudy intellect, whereas with the Germans it is doubtless the mark and sign of a practiced pen and of the presence of that sort of luminous intellectual fog . . .

With English taking over as the language for international communication, and various simplified English-as-a-second-language dialects emerging around the world (Mydans 2007, and references therein), academic Teutonic English — a sub-dialect of what we like to call 'Northern European Conference English' or Neclish — seems to have found acceptance in scholarly circles on the European continent. But to most educated Brits, Americans, and Australians, it is, at best, a foreign language, and at worst, as Mark Twain quips, a sign of 'a cloudy intellect'. We offer our most effusive and heartfelt thanks to Frank for saving us from this fate.

That said, the responsibility for any errors, false interpretations, or intractable Teutonisms remains, as always, entirely ours.

[2] This note of thanks is, we hope, no example, but here we had help from an American friend, writer and translator, Susan M. Gaines.

List of figures

List of tables

The Authors

Claudia Bogedan is a senior researcher at the Institute of Social and Economic Research (WSI) of the Hans Böckler Foundation, Düsseldorf. She has formerly been a researcher at the Collaborative Research Center 'Transformations of the State'.

Edith Gindulis is a postdoc researcher at the Collaborative Research Center 'Transformations of the State'.

Stephan Leibfried is Professor of Public and Social Policy at the University of Bremen and Director of the Collaborative Research Center 'Transformations of the State'.

Julia Moser is Project Manager 'Human Resources Development' at the Rationalisierungs- und Innovationszentrum der Deutschen Wirtschaft e.V., RKW Kompetenzzentrum, Eschborn. She has formerly been a researcher at the Collaborative Research Center 'Transformations of the State'.

Herbert Obinger is Professor of Comparative Public and Social Policy at the University of Bremen and directs two projects in the Collaborative Research Center 'Transformations of the State'.

Peter Starke is a postdoc researcher at the Collaborative Research Center 'Transformations of the State'.

List of abbreviations

ACT	Association of Consumers and Taxpayers
AHBs	Area Health Boards
AHV	*Alters- und Hinterlassenenversicherung*
ARF	*Amtsrådsforeningen*
ASVG	*Allgemeines Sozialversicherungsgesetz*
ATB	*Arbejdstilbudsordning*
ATP	*Arbejdsmarkedets Tillægspension*
BDP	*Bürgerlich-Demokratische Partei Schweiz*
CHEs	Crown Health Enterprises
CTC	Child Tax Credit
DA	*Dansk Arbejdsgiverforening*
DB	Defined Benefit
DC	Defined contribution
DF	Danish People's Party
DPB	Domestic purposes benefit
DRG	Diagnosis-related group
ECA	Employment Contracts Act
EEA	European Economic Area
EEC	European Economic Community
EES	European Employment Strategy
EL	*Ergänzungsleistungen*
EMU	Economic and Monetary Union
ERA	Employment Relations Act
EU	European Union
GMFI	Guaranteed Minimum Family Income
GMS	General Medical Services
GP	General Practitioner
GST	Goods and Services Tax
HFA	Health Funding Authority

List of abbreviations

IFTC	Independent Families Tax Credit
IHP	Individual Action Plan
IPAs	Independent Practitioner Associations
ISI	Import Substitution Industrialization
IV	*Invalidenversicherung*
IWTC	In-work tax credits
KL	*Kommunernes Landsforeningen*
KV	*Krankenversicherung*
LO	*Landsorganisation i Danmark*
MMP	Mixed-member proportional
NZBR	New Zealand Business Roundtable
ØD	*Økonomisk Demokrati*
OECD	Organization for Economic Cooperation and Development
PDEP	Personal Development and Employment Plan
PHO	Primary Health Organization
PR	Proportional representation
PAYG	Pay as you go
RHA	Regional Health Authority
SKOS	*Schweizerische Konferenz für Sozialhilfe*
SOE	State-Owned Enterprises
SP	*Særlig pensionsopsparing*
SUVA	Swiss Accident Insurance Agency
UV	*Unfallversicherung*
WFF	Working for families

Introduction

Small open economies are like rowing boats on an open sea. One cannot predict when they might capsize; bad steering increases the chances of disaster and a leaky boat makes it inevitable. But their chances of being broadsided by a wave are significant no matter how well they are steered and no matter how seaworthy they are.

(Joseph Stiglitz, 'Boats, Planes and Capital Flows',
Financial Times, 25 March 1998)

This book examines whether or not the recent transformation of the international political economy has triggered a fundamental change in the welfare state as a core dimension of the modern twentieth-century state (Leibfried and Zürn 2005). Focusing on Austria, Denmark, New Zealand, and Switzerland, we study the process of welfare state restructuring in four small developed economies between the early 1970s and the advent of the global financial crisis in 2008. We selected these cases because small nations represent crucial test cases exemplifying the ways in which countries respond to the challenges of the world market, including those imposed by deepening globalization and by a broad set of challenges generated by socio-economic modernization. Small states may be seen as inherently vulnerable (Easterly and Kraay 2000) and likely to experience such challenges more intensely than other nations. From this viewpoint, they may even constitute a kind of 'Sinatra case': if the welfare state can make it there, it can make it anywhere (see Bennett and Elman 2006: 462).

Even though the academic pay-off for researchers specializing in studying small countries is low (Katzenstein 2003), we are nevertheless convinced that big lessons can be drawn from the experience of small nations. Do smaller boats really face a higher probability of being capsized in the gusty ocean of globalization? Or do they, on the contrary, benefit from a greater mobility which helps them navigate a route through the storm? In the past, many scholars were inclined to the latter notion. Smallness was celebrated by economists and philosophers alike and scholars such as Leopold Kohr (1957) and Ernst Friedrich Schumacher (1973) even coined the slogan 'small is beautiful'.

1 Economic vulnerability in the past: coping strategies between 'domestic compensation' and 'domestic defence'

Smallness did indeed have its virtues in the past. The world's most advanced welfare states emerged in the small democracies of north-western Europe, combining economic wealth with a degree of equality never hitherto achieved in human history. Economically, small countries always face certain constraints from the small size of their domestic markets; but some of them also learned to turn vice into virtue in a number of ways. Through one of two alternative strategies, economic vulnerability was turned into economic prosperity.

The first strategy, 'domestic compensation', emerged in Scandinavia and some of the smaller Continental European countries and was based on a combination of trade openness and a generous welfare state.[1] Trade dependency and perceived economic vulnerability enhanced the domestic power of labour and generated an ideology of social partnership.[2] This constellation was highly conducive to the formation of comprehensive welfare states serving as a sort of safety valve against the fluctuations of world markets (Cameron 1978; Katzenstein 1980, 1985, 2003; Rodrik 1998; Rieger and Leibfried 2003). The structure of the welfare state was, at least in some of these countries, based on the inclusion of all citizens. Benefits were generous and often earnings-related. Extensive social services supplemented the system of income transfers, most notably in the Nordic countries. Strong Social Democratic and Christian Democratic parties as well as corporatism were among the main political driving forces. Moreover, the small size of the political elite in those countries fostered a strong sense of community and high adaptability to new problems, namely those requiring cooperation amongst the 'social partners' of labour and capital (Kuznets 1963: 29; Eisenstadt 1985). The economies of all these countries were strongly export-oriented specializing in industrial niche products typically supplied by small- and medium-sized companies.

The alternative coping strategy of small vulnerable countries during the *trente glorieuses* was to be found in New Zealand and Australia. Its defining characteristic was 'domestic defence' rather than 'domestic compensation' and was based not on openness but on trade protectionism, restrictive immigration

---

[1] Switzerland was, for a long time, something of an outlier since welfare state generosity was considerably lower than in the other nations adopting this strategy. In addition, protective arrangements shielded some domestic sectors from international competition (Bonoli and Mach 2000).

[2] Cameron (1978: 1255–8) emphasizes the role of the industrial structure in many of the small economies in Europe, arguing that a high degree of industrial concentration leads to high unionization rates and structures of industrial relations that favour neo-corporatist policy-making which, in turn, leads to higher levels of public expenditure.

policies, and 'social protection by other means' (Castles 1989). Privileged access to the British market, by virtue of their former colonial status, allowed Australia and New Zealand to concentrate export production on a small range of primary products. Income from these products — meat and wool in the case of New Zealand; originally, wheat and wool in Australia — cross-subsidized a range of industries that developed under the protective umbrella of tariffs and import licences. While these industries generated significant employment, they were usually not competitive in world markets. For New Zealand, the strategy worked only as long as the British market remained open and prices paid for the primary products were high and stable, conditions that began to disappear from about the late 1960s onwards. For Australia, it has been longer in disappearing, with minerals extraction replacing agricultural production for export, and markets in Asia — first Japan and, more recently, China — replacing the former British connection. The welfare state that developed in the context of this specific political economy of the small Australasian states was particular and, at least in the post-war era, in many ways the opposite of the comprehensive north-western European model (Castles 1985). The so-called wage earners' welfare state (see below) was small in terms of expenditure and residual in terms of benefit design. That is because 'social protection', in the widest sense of the word, was provided also through state intervention in the primary distribution of market incomes — institutionalized in a state-led system of wage arbitration — and not only through the ex-post redistribution of incomes.

In both cases, however, economic prosperity was the result of economic specialization as small countries found niches in world markets where their comparative advantages fully came to fruition (see Robinson 1963; Easterly and Kraay 2000; Armstrong and Read 2002 on the political economy of small states). The type of specialization differed, however, from country to country: labour-intensive industrial goods (with a comparatively low share of high-tech products) and raw materials in Austria; agricultural products, machines, pharmaceuticals, electronics, and furniture in Denmark; a highly efficient and innovative agricultural sector in the case of New Zealand; and financial services, chemicals, pharmaceuticals, watches, and machines in Switzerland.

Irrespective of the differences in the structure of the economy and the design of the system of social protection, for small countries, economic and social security during the golden age was intimately tied to the state. With the exception of Switzerland, private solutions in social provision remained marginal. Because of their high trade dependence and vulnerability, 'laissez-faire' was politically not an option for small nations during the immediate post-war decades. Indeed, domestic markets were highly regulated and sheltered from competition with the state controlling public utilities and, in some cases such as Austria, much of heavy industry.

2 Increasing external pressures: the advanced welfare states meet the global economy

In retrospect, however, the small boats floated in an unruffled sea. Both strategies of coping with economic vulnerabilities, that is, domestic compensation and domestic defence, had their heyday during the three decades following the Second World War against a backdrop of an international political economy that was increasingly open to trade but still based on national economies and relatively closed borders in other important respects. While the prosperity of small economies was always dependent on trade with other countries (Alesina and Spolaore 2005: chapter 6), relative trade openness in many of these countries did not go along with deregulated financial markets and fully fledged cross-border capital mobility. In this environment, monetary and fiscal policies could effectively be used by governments to practice Keynesian policies of macroeconomic stabilization and to extract the resources necessary for welfare state expansion.

Over the past two decades, however, a sequence of fundamental changes in the international political economy has made the economic seas more difficult to navigate. The demise of the Bretton Woods system of monetary relations, the two oil shocks of the 1970s, the deregulation of financial markets in the 1980s, and the deepening of European integration in the 1990s may all be seen as exposing advanced welfare states to greater pressure (Scharpf 2000). One of the most salient features of the political economy of recent times has been the emergence of a more truly global economic system. The deregulation of financial markets and the formation of a single market in Europe have offered easily exploitable profit opportunities abroad. One indicator reflecting the increased intertwining of economies is the growth of cross-border corporate investment since the 1990s (Figure 1).

An ever increasing process of economic denationalization inevitably leads to the question of whether the virtuous circle of economic specialization and high state-led social protection that characterized the first post-war decades has now turned into a vicious circle for small states. Many scholars — including those that formerly saw smallness as advantageous in welfare state building — now contend that smallness may be dangerous in a world that has undergone a fundamental economic and political transformation. For New Zealand, at least, the end of privileged access to the British market meant the end of an exceptionalism premised on the possibility of shutting out the influence of the world economy, and although Australia found new Asian markets for a different range of products, the price for these products was increasingly determined by world markets. The strategy of domestic compensation has also been under increasing threat. Critics (e.g. Lindbeck 1997) have argued that increased capital mobility and competitive pressures may force small boats — to pick up the metaphor once

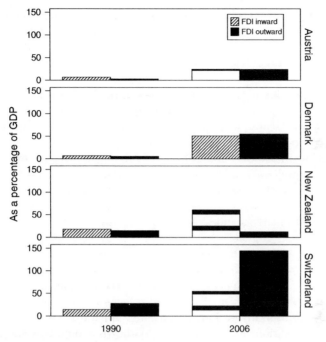

Figure 1: Foreign direct investment (stocks as a percentage of GDP) in Austria, Denmark, New Zealand, and Switzerland, 1990 and 2006

Source: UNCTAD World Investment Report 2007.

again — to jettison parts of their welfare state cargo to avert capsizing. Paulette Kurzer (1993: 251), for instance, argues that

> [t]ruly open, integrated small economies cannot sustain a politics of redistribution and consensual deliberation. Thus, in small countries that carefully filter their involvements and linkages with international markets, domestic compensation schemes function in the way in which they are supposed to operate. But in small countries with numerous international and cross-national linkages, social arrangements are pointless endeavours, unable to protect society against the repercussions of economic vulnerability.

Put more generally, this argument is known as *efficiency hypothesis* in the literature (e.g. Busch and Plümper 1999; Glatzer and Rueschemeyer 2005) and is sufficiently well known as to require only brief summary. The core proposition of the efficiency hypothesis is that that deregulation of financial markets, trade liberalization, decreasing transport costs, and improvements in the information technology have together fuelled the free and global exchange of capital, goods, and services. The resulting higher exit options for capital not only make it more difficult for nation states to maintain the tax burdens required to finance generous welfare states, but also weaken the bargaining position of labour. Competition for footloose capital and foreign investment will, therefore, force countries to lower tax rates, reduce regulatory standards, and seek to contain public debt in order to avert negative reactions by financial markets.

According to this thesis, the imperatives of financial discipline will almost certainly spill over to the realm of social policy as the welfare state represents the biggest single component of public spending in advanced Organization for Economic Cooperation and Development (OECD) countries. In the core OECD member states in 2005, the share of social spending in total government outlays amounted to well over 50 per cent (OECD 2008*a*). Many mainstream economists argue that the level of social security previously achieved cannot be retained, since small economies are forced to expose themselves to the chill winds of world markets and global competition given the small size of their domestic markets. Arguably the same applies to the countries formerly practising a strategy of 'domestic defence', where, of course, social spending levels started out lower than in north-western Europe. Moreover, national governments have lost autonomy in fiscal and monetary policy-making in the course of globalization and deepened European integration. For the majority of EU states, this has been institutionalized through the formation of the Economic and Monetary Union (EMU), while fiscal policy is additionally subject to the debt limits imposed by the Stability and Growth Pact. Neither Denmark nor Switzerland is a member of EMU, but these small nations are likely to be similarly constrained by the fact that they must compete in a financial and fiscal environment in which national autonomy is far more limited than in the immediate post-war era. For the most part, except perhaps in the context of crises like the financial meltdown of 2008–9, countries are therefore no longer in a position to practice Keynesian policies, but have to adopt a supply-side-oriented course in economic policy and, so the thesis suggests, downsize their welfare states accordingly.

An extreme version of the efficiency hypothesis therefore assumes that unleashed market forces will induce a downward spiral in benefit provision and regulatory standards which is paralleled by policy convergence towards a 'liberal' model of social provision. The predicted scenario is thus one of 'a race to the bottom' in social protection. Interestingly, it is a scenario depicted by neo-liberal and neo-Marxist scholars alike, even though the normative assessments of the two camps differ markedly (see Narr and Schubert 1994; Ohmae 1995; Strange 1996; Altvater and Mahnkopf 1999; Siebert 2000; Jessop 2002; Sinn 2002; Tanzi 2002).

Given its high prominence in the academic and political debate, it is perhaps surprising that very few scholars report findings that support the efficiency hypothesis (Garrett and Mitchell 2001; Busemeyer 2009). There are probably more studies that find no (robust) globalization effect (Castles 2001, 2004;

Brady et al. 2006). The same goes for analyses of convergence. Most studies find very little empirical evidence of welfare state convergence and, if they do, it is usually evidence of a catch-up process rather than the hypothesized race to the bottom (e.g. Castles 2001, 2004; Alasua et al. 2007; Starke et al. 2008). This evidence suggests that other factors are perhaps more important in explaining the developmental trajectories of mature welfare states. We will now turn to some of the theoretical alternatives in the literature on the present and future of the welfare state.

3 The limits of the efficiency hypothesis

The race to the bottom scenario is not the only game in town. Three bodies of theoretical argument which deny such negative welfare state effects are worth mentioning. The first argues that openness and social security may in fact be positively related through a 'new' logic of compensation, the second refers to the role of domestic politics, and the third theoretical strand claims that globalization is not the main driving force triggering contemporary welfare state changes. First, we summarize these theoretical arguments and then move on to discuss how the different arguments may be combined.

3.1 Compensation theories

There is a long-standing line of argument claiming that openness to foreign competition may not be as harmful to the welfare state as often assumed, but is, on the contrary, positively associated with the level of social security and state intervention in the domestic economy. This body of literature partly overlaps with the 'small states' school (see e.g. Cameron 1978; Katzenstein 1985, 2003; Rodrik 1998; Garrett 1998; Burgoon 2001; Rieger and Leibfried 2003, but see Manow 1999 for a critical discussion of the compensation argument). The compensation thesis is based on the empirical observation that, in the past, openness was positively correlated with corporatism and higher levels of state spending. The authors belonging to this school argue that this is the case because high levels of trade openness are only politically acceptable in democratic polities when the higher level of economic risk that automatically comes with greater openness (e.g. income volatility due to terms of trade volatility) is politically buffered through state intervention.

One of the most common means protecting against economic vulnerability is social security. According to this logic, cash-transfer programmes and active labour market policies may be used as a sort of 'lubricant' for liberal trade policies, since they provide a means of compensating the potential losers while at the same time reaping the overall benefits of foreign trade. Obtaining the consent of potential losers is the main motivation in this strategy and, consequently, welfare state retrenchment may eventually endanger globalization (Adserà and Boix 2002; Rieger and Leibfried 2003). The theoretical affinity to the 'domestic compensation' argument made with reference to small European states is obvious. Yet, the compensation school takes the argument further in that it applies the same logic to all countries, not just small states. The only difference is that, due to insufficient market size, small states really do not have any choice about opening up to world markets — and, in order to sustain openness, of compensating potential losers — unless they are blessed with relatively secure access to a larger market as Australia and New Zealand were in the past.

The empirical evidence in supporting the compensation argument is, as in the case of the efficiency literature, relatively limited. There is evidence supporting its micro-foundations, that is, that people whose jobs are more exposed to the world market feel more insecure and are more in favour of redistributive policies (Scheve and Slaughter 2004, 2006) and that parties supporting political-economic openness tend to fare better when compensatory welfare state politics are in place (Burgoon 2009). At the macro level, there is also some limited evidence supporting the compensation argument (Burgoon 2001; Ha 2008).

3.2 The neglected role of politics

An implicit assumption underlying the efficiency hypothesis is that politics is subordinate to market forces, which pressurize governments to adopt similar policies. Only under such circumstances will a race to the bottom and policy convergence occur. Many scholars argue that, because of the mediating and filtering effect of domestic politics, the negative impact of globalization on welfare states is much exaggerated and that politics continues to enjoy substantial autonomy in shaping public policy (Boix 1998; Garrett 1998; Garrett and Mitchell 2001; Huber and Stephens 2001; Swank 2002, 2005; Castles 2004; Ellison 2006; Glatzer and Rueschemeyer 2005; Zohlnhöfer 2009).

Cross-nationally distinct actor constellations and opportunity structures shaped by institutional configurations are seen as potential sources for different adaptation pathways for welfare states even where countries face similar problem pressures. Since these constellations tend to be either historically inherited and relatively stable, or, at least, non-convergent, it is highly probable that the differences between welfare regimes and the variety of social expenditure levels will persist in times of austerity and global competition. In consequence, no 'substantial convergence around a market-confirming model of minimal public social protection' is to be expected (Swank 2002: 5).

What is being emphasized here are two things: First, the importance of power resources in general and the partisan complexion of government in particular and, second, institutional variation. Even if recent economic and political transformations have forced the advanced democracies to abandon the post-war Keynesian consensus, governments of different partisan complexion can still choose between different supply-side-oriented strategies associated with distinct consequences for redistributive outcomes (Boix 1998). Some scholars contend that the forces underlying the expansion of the welfare state are still relevant for explaining welfare state changes in hard times. Hence, the 'old politics of the welfare state', that is, the classic middle-range theories developed to explain welfare state expansion (see Skocpol and Amenta 1986; Castles 1998; Myles and Quadagno 2002; Siegel 2002; Schmidt et al. 2007 for overviews) are still seen as having explanatory power in the 'silver age of the welfare state' (Taylor-Gooby 2002). Policies adopted are likely to be shaped by the distribution of powers resources. In this scenario, left parties and unions take on the role of the main defenders of the welfare state, while liberal and secular-conservative parties represent the spearhead of those who seek to dismantle it (Garrett 1998; Korpi and Palme 2003; Starke 2008).[3]

Institutional variation is the second factor seen as being of great theoretical significance, since institutions shape actor constellations, policy options, and strategies of and interactions between actors (Scharpf 1997). Relevant factors include state structures, electoral rules, and the system of interest mediation as well as the constraints imposed by the policy legacy of the past, including both structures of welfare provision and of economic production (Pierson 1994; Bonoli 2001; Huber and Stephens 2001; Swank 2002). Cross-national differences in numbers of veto players, different types of welfare regimes, and varieties of capitalism are seen as crucial factors structuring policy trajectories and, in consequence, as sources for non-convergence. The varieties of capitalism approach, for example, explicitly rejects the notion that globalization drives all economies towards a uniform market model. Instead of a run towards deregulation, Hall and Soskice (2001: 58) rather predict 'a bifurcated response marked by widespread deregulation in liberal market economies and limited movement in coordinated market economies'. Similar arguments are made with regard to the impact of welfare regime patterns on national adaptations to economic circumstances (Esping-Andersen 1996; Scharpf and Schmidt 2000). The (relevant) keyword here is path-dependency which may be seen as amongst the most potent of mechanisms impeding strong convergence in social policy (Pierson 2000, 2004).

The most elaborate and influential version of the path-dependency argument made in welfare state research is Paul Pierson's 'new politics' thesis.

---

[3] There is no clear consensus on the assumed role of Christian Democratic parties in recent decades. Yet, since Christian Democratic parties were among the forces of welfare state expansion during the 'golden age', it seems reasonable from the point of view of partisan theory to count them as among the pro-welfare parties even today.

He argues that welfare state reform in times of permanent austerity follows not the old, partisan way of the post-war decades but a new logic or what he describes as the 'new politics of the welfare state'. Pierson's main argument is that existing levels and structures of welfare state provision are to a great extent protected by democratic politics. Since support for the welfare state is strong and welfare state clienteles now constitute a very substantial share of the electorate, politicians who attempt to rollback the welfare state risk electoral retaliation. Politicians seeking office or re-election thus either refrain from welfare state retrenchment or pursue 'blame avoidance' strategies of retrenchment by stealth to reduce the visibility of painful cuts (Pierson 1994, 1996). According to this line of argument, neither systematic convergence nor a rollback of the (welfare) state is considered likely.

If changes take place nonetheless, they are assumed to be heavily shaped by political institutions. But the role of political institutions may be more ambiguous when it comes to retrenchment than during the era of 'old politics' (see Pierson 1994). The policy decisiveness conferred by the lack of veto points in Westminster-style polities, may well be offset by the higher accountability to which decision-makers are exposed in such a setting. Where the electorate can identify those responsible for unpopular policies, it is that much easier to punish them. In contrast, institutionally fragmented polities offer many veto points for opponents to obstruct policy change, but, thanks to the diffusion of decision-making sites, also provide many opportunities to practice blame avoidance strategies such as 'passing the buck' between different branches of government and, hence, afford more opportunities for retrenchment by stealth. The same goes for welfare state structures. The complex politics of contribution-based pension systems offer myriad opportunities for blame avoidance, while cuts to simple, tax-financed flat-rate benefits could be much more difficult to conceal from voters.

Despite these differences in the imputed impacts of political factors, these approaches agree that the filtering impact of domestic politics provides a set of strong forces impeding policy convergence towards a liberal welfare model and a downward spiral in benefit provision and regulatory standards. Instead, these approaches basically agree that we should expect policy persistence — 'business as usual' — or even divergence.

As with the efficiency and the compensation thesis, there is some empirical evidence that politics matter, but more in line with the old politics school. For instance, comparative analyses focusing on the development of benefit levels — rather than social expenditure — over the past decades reveal a picture with many countries having imposed significant benefit cutbacks in recent decades (Korpi and Palme 2003; Allan and Scruggs 2004; Montanari and Palme 2004). Moreover, these studies also demonstrate a great deal of cross-national variation in retrenchment attributable to differences in the partisan complexion of government, economic problem pressure, state structures, and welfare state patterns (Korpi and Palme 2003; Swank 2005). Because that is so, these studies, no more than those focusing on social expenditure, cannot be adduced as providing strong evidence for a downward convergence of benefit levels across countries.

Qualitative comparisons also provide evidence that politics still matters in the process of welfare state adaptation. This holds not only for the affluent OECD countries (Scharpf and Schmidt 2000; Huber and Stephens 2001; Swank 2002, 2005; Ellison 2006), but also for mid-income economies in other world regions (Glatzer and Rueschemeyer 2006). A recent literature review of welfare state retrenchment research arrives at a similar conclusion (Starke 2006). Apart from some limited comparisons (often based on single policy areas and a very limited number of countries), there is little qualitative research on welfare state convergence. Some researchers have, however, found limited convergence in the structural make-up of social policy, for instance in the fields of public pensions (Hinrichs 2009) and health care (Rothgang et al. 2005).

3.3 Endogenous challenges

The third objection raised against the efficiency hypothesis argues that globalization is far from being the only causal factor triggering contemporary welfare state transformation and may well not even be the most important one. Instead, many scholars contend that the pressure to which contemporary welfare states are now exposed have emerged quite independently of globalization (Pierson 1998, 2001). According to this line of argument, the most important strains to which mature welfare states are subject are a consequence of the transition of industrial to post-industrial and knowledge-based societies.

Deindustrialization and the resulting rise of the service economy are accompanied by decreasing productivity rates (Iversen and Cusack 2000; Iversen and Wren 1998) and, in consequence, declining economic growth and mounting unemployment (see Figures 2 and 3). Weaker economic performance driven by domestic structural transformation has been accelerated by a series of exogenous shocks affecting Western economies in the 1970s and the early 1990s. As a consequence, advanced welfare states have been increasingly confronted with an environment of 'permanent austerity' (Pierson 1998). Declining tax revenues consequent on reduced rates of economic growth make for budgetary strain, while the rising number of unemployed increases the pressure to augment public spending. The resulting theoretical expectations are ambiguous. Rising expenditure could eventually lead to a backlash against the unemployed and to cutbacks in (passive) benefits. At the same time, the increased attention that the problem of mass unemployment receives should also lead to new initiatives in labour market policy, for example, through various activation measures.

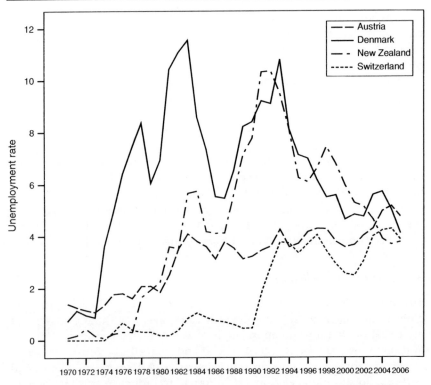

Figure 2: Rate of unemployment as percentage of civilian labour force, 1970–2006
Source: OECD Labour market database.

In addition, a fundamental transformation of society and economy has simultaneously engendered new social needs which have had to be addressed by the state. To begin with, profound changes of employment and family patterns induced by societal and economic modernization have created a series of needs and new social risks not catered for by contemporary social programmes (Kaufmann 1997; Alber 2002). Increasing numbers of single parents, rising divorce rates, and erosion of standard employment contracts have created new poverty risks, which, in general, have shifted demographically downwards from the elderly to younger cohorts and families. The transition from the industrial and manufacturing-based economies of the immediate post-war decades to the knowledge-based society of the early twenty-first century has meant that low-skilled workers have been increasingly marginalized, experiencing much greater risks of unemployment and poverty than in the golden age of the welfare state. Moreover, the massive entry of women into the labour market (see Figure 4) has increased the demand for childcare and eldercare. Since care work is typically delivered by women, the increase in

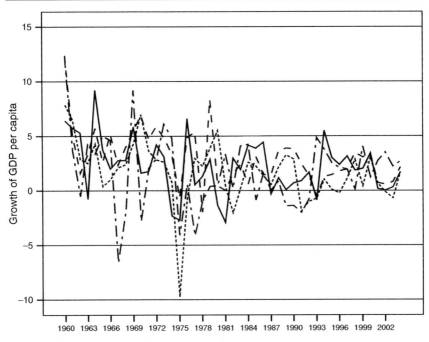

Figure 3: Growth of GDP per capita, 1960–2004

Source: Alan Heston, Robert Summers, and Bettina Aten, Penn World Table Version 6.2, Center for International Comparisons of Production, Income, and Prices at the University of Pennsylvania, September 2006.

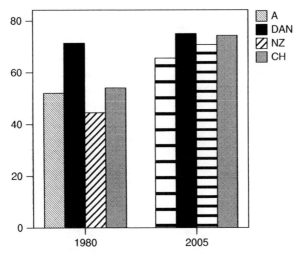

Figure 4: Female labour force as percentage of female population (15–64), 1980 versus 2005

Source: OECD Labour Force Statistics.

13

Table 1: Share of the elderly (65+), children (0–14), and the economically active (15–64) people

	Age	Total population (%)		
		1980	2000	2050
	65+	15.4	15.4	29.5
Austria	15–64	64.2	67.5	58.3
	0–14	20.4	17.0	12.2
	65+	14.4	14.8	22.2
Denmark	15–64	64.7	66.8	62.4
	0–14	20.8	18.4	15.4
	65+	10.0	11.8	26.2
New Zealand	15–64	63.3	65.5	58.2
	0–14	26.7	22.8	15.6
	65+	13.8	15.3	23.8
Switzerland	15–64	66.4	67.3	61.2
	0–14	19.7	17.4	15.0

Source: OECD population pyramids in 2000 and 2050 (own calculation); http://www.oecd.org/LongAbstract/0,3425,en_2649_33933_38123086_1_1_1_1,00.html

female labour market participation has fuelled demands for measures to reconcile work and family life such as parental leave schemes and the provision of institutional care facilities for children and frail elderly.

Perhaps the most dramatic challenges result from population ageing and the maturation of welfare states (Pierson 1998). The greying of society in inter-action with mature social programmes leads, ceteris paribus, to higher expend-iture devoted to the two biggest programme categories of advanced welfare states, that is, pensions and health care.

Since the ratio between the population aged 65 and over and the population aged 15–64 will become less favourable in the future (Table 1), the financial burden imposed on economically active cohorts will increase very considerably in coming decades. At the same time, the significant decline in fertility rates (Figure 5), other things being equal, will also reduce the size of the economically active cohorts. However, there are sizeable differences between OECD coun-tries, as also shown by the figure and the table. New Zealand has a significantly more favourable demographic profile than the other countries in the sample. The situation is probably most serious in Austria and Switzerland, while Denmark is able to offset some of the pressure stemming from greater longevity through persistently high fertility rates.

Taken together, the socio-economic transformations briefly described here have generated new social needs making welfare state restructuring and per-haps even welfare state expansion more likely than a race to the bottom. The underlying argument is neo-functionalist in nature. Societal and economic

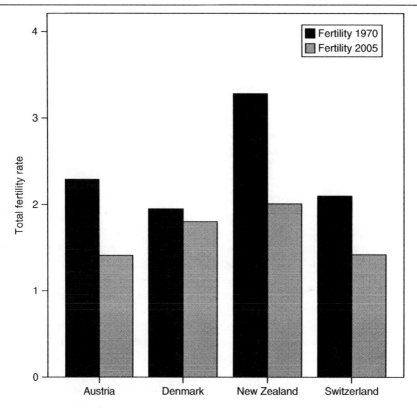

Figure 5: Total fertility rate 1970 versus 2005
Source: OECD Family Database.

modernization have undercut the functioning of previously existing social arrangements and created new risks and social needs to which governments must respond (Taylor-Gooby 2004; Armingeon and Bonoli 2006). Large and small states alike are confronted with these kinds of pressures. However, as the figures and data presented in this section make clear, these challenges vary in size and scope across countries.

A number of scholars assume that endogenous problem pressure interacts with the existing welfare states structures. It is claimed in the literature that these cross-national differences in socio-economic problem constellations are to some extent shaped by the institutional design of the welfare state (Esping-Andersen 1996; Pierson 1998, 2001; Scharpf and Schmidt 2000). Moreover, negative feedback effects generated by existing policies may undermine the political, fiscal, or social feasibility of a particular set of policies and therefore trigger social policy change (Weaver 2006). Yet it is plausible, as noted in the previous section, that national responses to such pressures are also shaped by domestic politics, notably actor preferences.

The quantitative literature on the determinants of social expenditure provides ample evidence that social spending trajectories are strongly shaped by rising social needs and economic structural change. In addition to the catch-up by welfare state laggards, the dynamics of social spending is largely driven by deindustrialization and rising dependency ratios, while political influences are either weak or non-existent (Iversen and Cusack 1998; Huber and Stephens 2001; Kittel and Obinger 2003; Potrafke 2007).

4 Scenarios and hypotheses

The scenarios depicted so far are not necessarily competitive. While the efficiency and the compensation theses are by and large incompatible, it is possible to combine either of these two bodies of theory in a meaningful way with theoretical accounts stressing the importance of domestic politics and socio-economic pressures. In fact, the compensation thesis has always emphasized a causal relationship between economic vulnerability, domestic politics, and social policy. But even the efficiency thesis can be combined with theories which claim that politics and socio-economic pressures play a decisive role in terms of welfare state adaptation in hard times. Only the most radical version of the efficiency thesis expects a race to the bottom irrespective of significant cross-national variation in domestic politics and welfare state patterns.

By relinquishing this extreme position, however, one could argue that the transformation of the international political economy together with deep domestic socio-economic changes have put mature welfare state under heavy strain and, as a consequence, forced policy-makers to adopt major revisions in the policy principles and the objectives that guided social policy during the *trente glorieuses*. More specifically, it is conceivable that a broad set of exogenous *and* endogenous challenges have fuelled a supply-side-oriented transformation of the conventional welfare state paradigm. The post-war Keynesian paradigm was based on 'politics against markets' (Esping-Andersen 1985). The goals of the welfare state included the stabilization of demand in periods of economic slowdown through social transfers compensating for loss of income, employment protection, and a crowding-out of markets from social provision. In contrast, the emerging new paradigm may entail a shift to 'politics with markets' which would not necessarily mean a roll-back of social protection, but rather the streamlining of social programmes in accordance with the imperatives of employability, flexibility, and cost-effectiveness. The result could well, for example, resemble the 'enabling state' which, according to Neil Gilbert, 'is captured by the tenet of public support for private responsibility — where "private" responsibility includes individuals, the market, and voluntary organizations' (Gilbert 2002: 16; see also Gilbert and Gilbert 1989). At a more macro level, Bob Jessop has argued that the post-war Keynesian welfare state is going to be replaced by what he calls the 'Schumpeterian workfare state', which is based on (*a*) the promotion of product, process, organizational, and market innovation; (*b*) the enhancement of the competitiveness of open economies mainly through supply-side intervention; and (*c*) the subordination of social policy to the demands of labour market flexibility and structural competitiveness (Jessop 1993: 9). This is not to say that policy-makers no longer have any choice or that political institutions and welfare state patterns are irrelevant. It rather means that a realignment of social policy has taken place. Partisan differences may still matter in this respect and institutions are likely to remain important in structuring this adjustment process.

In sum, we are left with three scenarios:

1. 'Business as usual': No sign of welfare state convergence. Strategies of compensation and domestic defence are still possible options.

2. 'Race to the bottom': Strong welfare state convergence towards welfare state residualism.

3. Transformation of the welfare state: Supply-side-oriented adaptation of national social security arrangements but no dismantling of the welfare state.

It is, therefore, an empirical question to find out what has happened over the last decades and how whatever changes have occurred can be explained. Our *starting assumption* is that politics matters. Relying on the main theories of comparative public policy research we therefore generally expect the following:

1. Socio-economic problem pressure, which includes the challenges caused by economic globalization as well as by domestic challenges, is an important trigger for far-reaching social policy changes.

2. The policies adopted to address these problems are contingent upon the distribution of power resources in general and the partisan complexion of government in particular.

3. A government's room for manoeuvre is conditioned by (*a*) the configuration of veto players, (*b*) the constraints imposed by supranational influences and the international economic environment, and (*c*) by the (social) policy legacy of the past.

5 Case selection, method, and period of investigation

In order to discover the ways in which small nations have responded to these challenges, our strategy is to conduct a small-*N* study and trace welfare state reforms over a period of more than 30 years.[4] We focus on the four policy sectors which take up the bulk of social expenditure in advanced welfare states. More specifically, we analyse the reforms implemented in pensions and labour market policy, health care, and family policy. We provide a fine-grained qualitative analysis of important legal changes in terms of generosity and structures of benefit provision, funding principles, patterns of regulation, and instruments of governance. In order to identify major long-term trends in these areas and to measure the magnitude of policy change, we focus on two aspects in particular:

1. We compare the current welfare state configuration with the welfare state patterns at the end of the so-called golden age. The idea is to examine whether our four countries still belong to the same welfare regime as in the early 1970s. If the efficiency hypothesis is correct, then we should be able to identify a 'blurring of regimes' (Goodin and Rein 2001) and a convergence to the liberal model over time.

2. As a heuristic yardstick for the extent of policy change in the four programme areas, we use Peter Hall's threefold classification of policy change (Hall 1993). First-order change refers to a modification of policy settings (e.g. adjustment of benefit level), whereas second-order change also includes the adoption of new instruments (e.g. new funding mechanisms). A third-order change denotes a paradigmatic policy shift characterized by new policy goals and underlying ideas (e.g. a shift from status preservation to basic security in pensions).

Since we are particularly interested in the nexus between economic globalization and the role played by domestic politics, we have selected four small countries which, on the one hand, are — by virtue of being small states — particularly vulnerable to and at the same time dependent on world market developments, and, on the other, show maximum variation in terms of their political and institutional settings.

As the small states literature has shown, small countries, owing to their lack of power, are rule-takers rather than rule-makers when it comes to the international economic order. Hence, they have to find a *modus vivendi* to cope with their economic vulnerabilities. The post-war record of such countries suggests that most accomplished this mission both in a flexible and successful way, either through a strategy of domestic compensation or a strategy of domestic defence. The question neo-liberal scholars now raise is whether these mutually reinforcing constellations are still sustainable in a markedly changed international political economy. If globalization threatens mature welfare states and heavy state intervention in general, as it is claimed by the efficiency hypothesis, then major welfare state transformations should be most readily

---

[4] The actual *N* is, of course, much higher than the number of countries studied, since a wealth of overtime as well as within-case evidence is used throughout the course of this book.

apparent in small countries, since they usually lack the choice of 'shutting out the world market'. In other words, their small size[5] and relative vulnerability to world markets 'makes them a kind of "leading indicator" of changes likely to occur later in relatively more sheltered economies' (Schwartz 1994: 530). Methodologically speaking, small countries are 'most-likely cases' of globalization-induced policy change. The 'big lessons' mentioned in the title of this book derive from this special status small states can justly claim in the research literature on world markets and the welfare state.

There are, moreover, good reasons to believe that small countries are able to respond swiftly to changes in the international environment. Since policy-learning capacities are high due to the small size of the political elite, while decision-making costs are lower for the same reason, there are reasons to think that small nations will be capable of reacting quickly to new challenges.[6] Therefore, not only do small countries face big pressures for policy change, but they are also, other things being equal, in a position to respond to these challenges in a rapid and flexible way. We therefore anticipate that the effects of globalization suggested by the efficiency hypothesis should, if at all, first and foremost become apparent in small open economies.

The other dimension that underlies our case selection is institutional and addresses the theories which put the domestic drivers of change at the centre of their analysis. First of all, our sample covers four different welfare regimes types (Esping-Andersen 1990). At the end of the golden age, Denmark was typically classified as a social democratic welfare state, whereas Austria was across the board categorized as a conservative welfare state. Switzerland, in contrast, showed strong affinities to the liberal welfare model at least during the immediate post-war period. Even though New Zealand's welfare state also exhibited strong liberal traits, it has been suggested that the countries of the Antipodes had, in the early post-war decades, established a separate regime type that could be variously described as a 'radical' or 'wage earner's' welfare state (Castles and Mitchell 1993).

Furthermore, the choice of cases is also designed to demonstrate the potential explanatory power of theories rooted in the old politics tradition. Our four countries show remarkable differences in terms of state structures, the partisan complexion of government, party systems, union density, and the patterns of democracy and interest mediation. This is not surprising if we take into account that these cross-national differences are seen as the main driving forces for the emergence of different welfare regimes, which, in turn, are also embedded in

[5] A country is considered small if its population was less than 15 million in the mid-1970s. Note that the size of the state territory is irrelevant since the size of the domestic market is exclusively determined by population figures.

[6] This argument was emphasized by Katzenstein (1985) and repeated more pointedly in a recent article: If 'you give a party in the capital, you can easily invite all the important political players. This makes a difference to both politics and policy' (Katzenstein 2003: 11).

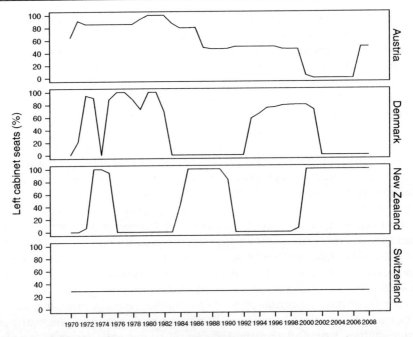

Figure 6: Cabinet seats of left parties, 1970–2008

Source: Klaus Armingeon, Sarah Engler, Marlène Gerber, Philipp Leimgruber, Michelle Beyeler. Comparative Political Data Set 1960–2007, Institute of Political Science, University of Berne 2009, figures for 2008 were amended by the authors.

distinct varieties of capitalism. Austria and Switzerland, for example, are federal systems, while the other two countries are unitary states. Switzerland is a prototypical consensus democracy, while New Zealand, for much of the post-war era, was an exemplar of majoritarian or Westminster-style democracy. Austria is the country with the most developed system of corporatism, while, at the national level, Switzerland has the greatest referendum experience in the world. Other than in Switzerland, all the countries in our sample have witnessed significant changes in the partisan complexion of government over the past 30 years (see Figure 6).

Comparing welfare reforms enacted by different cabinet constellations allows us to trace the impact of parties on welfare state change. Since governments of different ideological orientation typically operate under similar institutional constraints, variation over time is mainly restricted to changes in the socio-economic environment.[7] We can therefore examine the ways in which different partisan constellations respond to socio-economic

---

[7] An important exception in our sample is New Zealand, which changed its electoral system in 1993. This change led to changes in the nature of the party system and the pattern of government formation that may well have had an impact on social policy as well.

transformations and/or exogenous challenges, while simultaneously holding institutional influences constant. The case study evidence is used to trace the processes leading to welfare state change.

There is also variation in terms of membership in supranational organizations, with Denmark and Austria being members of the European Union, Switzerland choosing to stay outside and New Zealand being as geographically separated from Europe as it is possible to be.

As noted above, these differences in domestic politics and varieties of welfare regime patterns may be regarded as potential sources for non-convergence. Yet, their impact in the 'silver age of the welfare state' is disputed. We employ *intra-national* and *cross-national comparisons* to detect the influences of domestic politics on welfare state change. However, welfare state changes typically extend over a long time horizon. Welfare state reform initiatives only take effect in the long run and social policy change typically occurs in an incremental fashion with welfare states behaving like 'elephants on the move' (Hinrichs 2001; Hinrichs and Kangas 2003). Hence, to analyse welfare state transformation properly requires a research design capable of focusing on social policy changes over longer spans of time: It is only in the long run that continuous small changes are likely to add up to transformative institutional change and lead, in consequence, to path departures and discontinuities in public policy (Streeck and Thelen 2005a). Starting with the first oil shock in the early 1970s, this study therefore covers a period of over 30 years.

This case selection and time frame should help us to gain a deeper understanding of the ways in which globalization and domestic politics shape national trajectories of welfare state adaptation. The substantial variety of political and institutional settings in the countries constituting our sample allows for an empirical test of the aforementioned three scenarios. We have already argued that welfare state transformation should be most readily apparent in small states. If no convergence whatsoever has taken place, we are entitled to conclude that political actors still have full autonomy in public policy-making, irrespective of economic globalization ('business as usual'). If, however, initially distinct welfare states have to some degree converged towards a liberal model of social provision ('race to the bottom'), despite substantial variation both in domestic politics and the nature and incidence of new social risks, this would signify that the external forces of globalization are driving welfare state change.

However, our findings support neither of these scenarios. There is no evidence supporting a 'race to the bottom' in terms of social expenditure and benefit levels nor is there a convergence towards a liberal welfare regime. Likewise, the notion of 'business as usual' is also unwarranted. Everywhere economic policies have shifted to supply-side-oriented solutions which, in addition, have spilled over into particular areas of the welfare state. In consequence, one of the two coping strategies practised up to the 1970s, the strategy of domestic defence, has become unsustainable. Nevertheless, the welfare state has weathered the storm. It has seen restructuring, but, with one exception, no radical retrenchment. Welfare state restructuring has entailed some convergence, but national policy-makers have left their marks on the ways in which the supply-side-oriented paradigm was put into practice. Overall, and with reference to the quote cited at the beginning of this introduction, small states found a route through the agitated sea by steering a downwind course and, as we will see, they did so with surprising success.

6 Contents

The book is structured as follows: Chapters 1–4 are the four country studies which are presented in alphabetical order. The case studies follow a similar structure. The first part provides information concerning the political system as well as a brief summary of the historical development of the welfare state up until the 1970s. The status quo in social affairs at that time is the point of reference for evaluating whether or not subsequent welfare reforms have contributed to a transformation of the welfare state over time. To carry out intra-national comparisons, all case studies proceed chronologically. Thus, we distinguish between different phases demarcated by changes in the partisan complexion of government.[8] For each phase we provide a brief overview of the government agenda, socio-economic problem pressures, the related problem diagnoses of political actors, and changes in the international environment. In a next step, we analyse the politics of reform and trace the policy changes adopted in the four programme categories under scrutiny. By repeating this procedure for other governmental constellations, we can thereafter compare the welfare reforms adopted by different cabinets to gauge the impact of parties on welfare state change. Moreover, by tracing reform trajectories over the entire period of investigation and comparing the contemporary welfare state make-up with the status quo ante, that is, the state of the welfare state at the end of the 'Golden Age', we are finally in a position to judge the scope and direction of welfare state change in each of the four countries under consideration.

In Chapter 5, we use the material embodied in our historical narratives to undertake a cross-national comparison. We start with an overview of macro-developments in areas such as social spending and benefit generosity and move

---

[8] Due to the absence of variation in government composition, the Swiss case study is subdivided into decades.

on to a comparison of the reform paths and outcomes in the four countries in order to assess which of the three scenarios fits the empirical evidence best. Next, we examine the extent to which political factors can explain this scenario. In a final step, we derive some big lessons from the experience of small states and speculate on future developments.

1

Austria: the 'Island of the Blessed' in the Ocean of Globalization[1]

Austria's fundamental political transformation from an economically backward and multi-ethnic superpower to a small and wealthy democracy at the centre of Europe involved phases of democratic (1918–34), pre-fascist (1934–8), and Nazi rule (1938–45). Despite several regime breakdowns during the first half of the twentieth century, the welfare state established in the Habsburg era survived political upheavals by and large unscathed. Post-war Austria, by contrast, was characterized by a considerable economic, societal, and political stability between the 1950s and the mid-1980s. Two major parties, the Christian Democrats (ÖVP) and the Social Democrats (SPÖ), almost exclusively controlled the political arena throughout the post-war period: They either formed coalition governments (1945–66; 1987–99; 2007–?) or were able to govern alone (ÖVP: 1966–70; SPÖ: 1970–83). Despite proportional representation, the Austrian party system was virtually dominated by a duopoly of parties during the four decades following the Second World War.

Political decision-making followed consociational practices and was thus based on compromises rather than on the use of majority rule. Consociational democracy was mirrored by a pronounced corporatist system of interest mediation usually described as 'social partnership' (*Sozialpartnerschaft*). Core features of corporatism have been cooperation and the concertation of interests between a few organizationally privileged[2] peak associations of employers and employees, and the federal government. This framework provided the interest organizations of labour and capital with strong leverage to influence wages as well as the economic and social policies. In this system, industrial conflicts and strikes played a marginal role. Impressed by social peace and political stability,

[1] This chapter emerged from a cooperation with Professor Emmerich Tàlos (University of Vienna) and is dedicated to him on the occasion of his 65th birthday in 2009.
[2] Membership in the Chamber of Commerce (employers), the Chamber of Labour (employees), and the Chamber of Agriculture (farmers) is compulsory. Membership in the Austrian Trade Union Federation is voluntary. Together with the federal government, these four interest organizations are the key players of Austrian social partnership.

Pope Paul VI called Austria an 'island of the blessed' when Federal President Jonas paid the Vatican a state visit in 1971.

Even though the political system at first glance appears veto-ridden given the country's federal polity, bicameral system,[3] and directly elected president, in fact the Constitutional Court is virtually the only institution holding real veto power according to veto-player theory (Obinger 2001). Partisan veto players became only relevant in 1983 when a 17-year period of single party cabinets ended. Since then, coalition governments have been in the rule.

In retrospect, a duopoly of pro-welfare state parties, consociational democracy, and highly developed corporatism, as well as a Federal Constitution lacking institutional veto points, provided a political configuration highly conducive to welfare state expansion during the post-war period. Rapid economic growth provided the economic means for funding the expansion of the welfare state and smoothed distributional conflict between the social partners and their allied parties. As long as the economy was growing rapidly, both political camps shared the resulting productivity gains more or less equally. In addition, the relatively closed capital markets at that time secured a balance of power between both camps. Private business was small business, while large parts of big industry and the major banks had been nationalized since the late 1940s (Pelinka 1998: 151). The overall situation has changed remarkably from the 1980s onwards. Before the resulting social policy changes are examined, we provide a very condensed account of the historical evolution and design of the Austrian welfare state in order to map the status quo ante, that is, the state of the welfare state at the end of what today is in a somewhat misty-eyed manner referred to as 'Golden Age'.

1.1 Historical development of the Austrian welfare state until the early 1970s

The origins of the Austrian welfare state date back to the late nineteenth and early twentieth centuries when core branches of social insurance such as accident insurance (1887), health insurance (1888), and old-age pensions for white-collar workers (1906) were introduced in the western part of the Austrian-Hungarian monarchy in an attempt to settle the 'labour question' (*Arbeiterfrage*). As in Germany, social insurance was enacted under the auspices of a conservative autocratic elite in order to gain political loyalty in exchange for social privileges. Early public intervention in social affairs was not only seen as a vehicle to quiet an emerging labour movement and to stabilize the ancient

---

[3] The Austrian parliament consists of the National Council and the Federal Council. The latter can only suspend ordinary legislation and can be easily overridden by a simple majority in the lower house.

political and economic order, but should also contribute in containing the centrifugal forces resulting from the multi-ethnic make-up of the Habsburg monarchy (Hofmeister 1981). The main objective of social insurance was to protect wage earners against losses of income in case of sickness, occupational injury, unemployment, and old age. The legacy of paternalist authoritarian policies was mirrored in occupationally fragmented and mandatory social insurance with the major dividing line running between blue-collar and white-collar workers on the one hand and private sector employees and civil servants on the other. The statutory pension system is a case in point since pensions were restricted to white-collar workers in the beginning. The introduction of pensions for this occupational group in 1906 was a clear example of social policy from 'top-down' and clientele-oriented social policy (Tálos 1981; Alber 1982). Even though a pension act for blue-collar workers was passed in 1926, it was never implemented. It was Austria's *Anschluss* to Nazi Germany in 1938 that finally provided blue-collar workers with an entitlement to old-age pensions. In practice, however, the benefit level for most recipients remained meagre (Tálos 2000).

In 1920, unemployment insurance was introduced representing the final step in early welfare state consolidation.[4] This programme was a response to the appalling economic conditions in the aftermath of the First World War and was embedded in a broad range of social reforms[5] initiated by the Social Democrats and Christian Socials (today: Christian Democrats) which formed the first democratic cabinet after the demise of the Habsburg monarchy in 1918. Almost faced with a financial ruin during the Great Depression, unemployment insurance became the subject to considerable retrenchment during the 1930s.

While social insurance was pre-empted by the central state, poor relief was a responsibility of the municipalities and the *Länder*. Since occupational groupings such as peasants and agricultural workers were not covered by social insurance and the benefits offered by social insurance remained meagre in the beginning, poor relief continued to play an important role in social provision until the advent of the 'Golden Age' of the welfare state.

The basic objectives of public intervention in social affairs, the organizational principles of social insurance (self-administration), the mode of financing (social security contributions), the distribution of policy jurisdiction between different levels of government, and the structural make-up of the welfare state laid down in the late nineteenth and early twentieth centuries provided the guiding principles that underpinned the expansion of the welfare state in the twentieth century (Hofmeister 1981; Tálos 1981). The expansion during

---

[4] Long-term care allowance is the most recent major programme and was introduced more than 70 years later.

[5] Examples include the introduction of the eight-hour working day, the introduction of workers' holidays, and the adoption of a health insurance scheme for civil servants.

the *trente glorieuses* mainly affected the degree of coverage and the level and spectrum of benefits offered by the various social insurance programmes. In political terms, the fierce conflicts between the Christian Socials and the Social Democrats characteristic of the interwar period were replaced by a compromise-based cooperation between the two party camps. While the immediate post-war period was characterized by efforts to cope with war-induced social repercussions, the reinstatement of Austria's full sovereignty in 1955 signalled the triumph of the welfare state on all fronts.

A crucial step was the adoption of the General Social Insurance Act (*Allgemeines Sozialversicherungsgesetz*, ASVG) in 1955, which combined health and accident insurance and old-age pensions for blue- and white-collar workers into a single system. With this bill as a model, but regulated by separate laws, peasants, self-employed, artists, and other occupational groupings, such as veterinarians and notaries, were subsequently included into the various branches of social insurance from 1958 onwards. As a consequence, the share of the employed labour force covered by old age, health, accident, and unemployment insurance increased from 50 per cent in 1950 to 82 per cent in 1975 (Alber 1982: 152). In addition to the expansion of social insurance, family benefits and new schemes based on the principle of compensation were introduced in the post-war period. Examples include income support to victims of war and Nazi rule (1947) and compensation to members of the armed forces in case of injuries related to military service. The increasing inclusiveness and expansion of social policy was paralleled by an increase in public social expenditure from 15.9 per cent of GDP in 1955 to 24 per cent in 1975 (Butschek 1998: table 4.1).

The expansion of the welfare state during the 'Golden Age' can be exemplified for the four programmes analysed in more detail in this book. The three decades following the Second World War witnessed an unprecedented expansion of *public pensions*. With the General Social Insurance Act of 1955 as a blueprint, pensions were extended to peasants, the self-employed, and artists in 1958. Pensions for federal civil servants were restructured in 1965. In addition to the extension in coverage, the scope and level of benefits has been steadily improved. Benefits were linked to the development of wages in 1965 and a form of minimum pension (the equalization supplement or *Ausgleichszulage*) was introduced, which is a means-tested supplemental benefit to top-up very low pensions to a certain floor. Early retirement benefits in case of unemployment (1957) and for persons with long insurance records (1960) were added. Since 1960, pensioners receive fourteen pension payments a year,[6] while a supplementary allowance for disabled survivors was established one year earlier. Moreover, contribution-free periods were credited for the

---

[6] In Austria, the annual pension amount is paid as twelve equal payments with the addition of two bonus payments.

calculation of old-age pensions in periods of military service and tertiary education.

In the mid-1970s, entitlement for a standard old-age pension required a minimum of 15 insurance[7] years. In addition, claimants must have reached the statutory retirement age which was fixed at 65 years for men and 60 years for women.[8] Pensions were calculated on the basis of the average salary (up to the contribution ceiling) earned during the 5 years preceding retirement. The old-age pension was made up of a base amount equivalent to 30 per cent of the assessment base and a progressive increment factor. Persons with an insurance record of less than 24 years were entitled to draw a supplement to the base amount.

It is worth mentioning that markets in the field of pensions were largely crowded-out as an alternative route to benefit provision. Until the 1990s, 90 per cent of all pension benefits were provided by the statutory public pension scheme.

Public interference in the realm of the *family* dates back to the late 1940s when family allowances were established at the federal level. Initially restricted to employees and introduced on a provisional basis only, the introduction of family allowances exemplifies the corporatist style of social policy-making characteristic of the post-war period as public transfer payments to families with dependent children were offset by trade union wage restraint in a period of high inflation.

From the very outset, family policy was designed along male breadwinner model lines (Mairhuber 2000). Salient features of this model are weakly developed social services, a strong reliance on cash benefits and free co-insurance of family members in several social insurance branches (e.g. medical provision, widows' and orphans' pensions). One reason for this familialist policy profile is certainly a strong Catholic legacy (Kreisky and Löffler 2003). Deep-rooted Catholic sentiments among the population strongly influenced female labour market behaviour and reinforced traditional gender roles during the immediate post-war decades. The division of powers between different levels of government was a second factor accounting for this policy outcome. Jurisdiction in family affairs is divided between the federal government and the nine *Länder*. Cash benefits are provided by the federal government, whereas the provision of formal childcare is the responsibility of the *Länder* and municipalities. Incongruent political majorities at different tiers of government, pronounced ideological differences between the Social and Christian Democrats in this policy sector, and territorially fragmented policy jurisdictions all turned out to be

---

[7] Insurance years could be earned by contributory periods and fictitious qualifying periods, that is, periods of secondary and tertiary education, military service, parental leave, and spells of unemployment and sickness.

[8] The retirement age of females was reduced from 65 to 60 years in 1948.

major impediments to comprehensive social service provision. Hence, the lowest common denominator has been to enhance cash benefits. In 1960, for example, a parental leave scheme was introduced for 12 months. The benefit level was contingent upon family status and household income and was funded through unemployment insurance contributions. It has to be emphasized, however, that family-related benefits were also offered by other social insurance branches and through the tax system. Examples include the aforementioned free co-insurance of children and spouses in social insurance, family supplements in unemployment insurance, tax credits for children, or the maternity benefit regulated by health insurance.

Health care was, along with social assistance and the provision of social services, the programme where the impact of federalism was most pronounced. The *Länder* and municipalities were responsible for running and co-financing hospitals (investment and operating costs), while in-patient medical costs were reimbursed by the various social insurance carriers. Territorially fragmented jurisdiction in the hospital sector was traditionally a major source of duplication of effort and of overcapacity provision. Typical modes of governance in this field were temporary state treaties between the federal government and the nine *Länder* according to section 15a of the Federal Constitution. These treaties are valid for 4 years and regulate financing as well as the planning of hospitals and major medical equipment.

Health insurance was mandatory, occupationally fragmented, and funded through income-related social security contributions paid by employers and employees. As in the field of pensions, the legal basis of provision for blue- and white-collar workers was the General Social Insurance Act passed in 1955, while health insurance for civil servants, peasants, and self-employed was regulated by separate laws enacted in the mid-1960s. Contributions, contribution ceilings, co-payments, and cash benefits differed not only between these occupational groups, but also between blue- and white-collar workers. There was no possibility of the better-off taking out private medical insurance,[9] nor any competition between different sickness funds. The insured were free to select physicians, but could not select their insurance carrier. Given the increase in coverage during the post-war period, health insurance more and more became a universal system including almost the entire population. In addition, the scope of benefits was enhanced in the 1960s. Examples include the introduction of rehabilitation benefits and a maternity benefit for 12 weeks. In terms of cash benefits, the maximum duration of the sickness cash benefit was enhanced from 52 to 78 weeks. However, considerable differences between different occupational groupings remained.

---

[9] Private insurance is only possible to cover special services and additional comfort in hospitals.

Unemployment insurance has been regulated by a separate law since 1949. Labour market policy was largely transfer-oriented during the post-war period, while the first active labour market programmes were adopted in the late 1960s. Eligibility conditions for unemployment compensation were relaxed (e.g. abolition of waiting periods) and the level and duration of unemployment compensation were increased. In the mid-1970s,[10] eligibility required an insurance record of 52 weeks within the 2 years prior to unemployment. The benefit was granted for 12 weeks on a regular basis and for a maximum of 30 weeks for unemployed persons with a long insurance record. The benefit was calculated on the basis of wage scales and increased, as a general rule, with the salary. In addition, family supplements were provided. Once the entitlement was exhausted, the long-term unemployed were entitled to draw a means-tested emergency benefit (*Notstandshilfe*), which could be received for an unlimited period. In the 1970s, this benefit was available for Austrian citizens and long-term residents only and household income was fully taken into account. The benefit could vary between 75 and 100 per cent of the previous unemployment compensation. In practice, however, it was equivalent to 92 per cent of the unemployment compensation for a single person.

Social assistance as the social safety net of last resort remained under control of the *Länder* despite a constitutional provision that empowered the federal government to enact framework legislation in this field. However, its role declined with the expansion of the various social insurance programmes in the 'Golden Age'.

1.2 Patterns of the welfare state

Given this structural make-up, the standard account in the comparative welfare state literature depicts the Austrian welfare state as a prototypical Bismarckian or corporatist-conservative welfare regime (Esping-Andersen 1990). Social insurance is by far the most important pillar of the Austrian welfare state. Social insurance-related expenditure accounted for 15 per cent of GDP in the mid-1970s. Given this dominance of social insurance, benefits are tied to labour market participation, while non-employed spouses and dependent children are entitled to free co-insurance and survivors' benefits. Wage-centred social security is strongly imbued with the principle of equivalence, demanding a close relationship between the contribution record and the level of benefits. This is in particular true for cash benefits offered by health insurance, unemployment insurance, unemployment assistance, and pensions. Status preservation via earnings-related transfer payments (most pronounced in the realm of old-age pensions) and occupationally fragmented social security schemes, a lack of

---

[10] See §§14, 18, 20, and 36 *Arbeitslosenversicherungsgesetz* 1977 (BGBl Nr. 609/1977).

social services, and the preservation of the male breadwinner model are core elements of the Austrian welfare state giving rise to strong stratification effects in terms of gender and occupational status.

Social assistance, in contrast, is based on subsidiarity principle and tied to a means-test. Public assistance in case of hardship can only be claimed if all other sources of income maintenance such as employment, family support, and existing social benefits either have been exhausted or are not sufficient to guarantee a decent standard of living. Due to the allocation of jurisdiction in this field, benefits significantly vary across the nine *Länder*.

The Bismarckian character of the Austrian welfare state is also evident from the mode of *financing* and the organization of the Austrian welfare state. Social insurance is primarily funded through earmarked contributions paid by employees and their employers on a pay-as-you-go (PAYG) basis. Only pensions and health care (mainly hospitals) are to some extent co-financed by the public purse. Other sectors of the welfare state beyond social insurance show different funding patterns. Benefits delivered by the various compensation schemes are entirely tax-funded as are social assistance benefits. Family cash benefits are financed by employers and the public purse. In the 1970s, two-thirds of total social expenditure was financed from contributions, while the remaining share was funded from the general revenue.

The pronounced occupational fragmentation of social insurance characteristic of Bismarckian welfare states is mirrored in the *organization* of social insurance, which, from the very outset, has been based on the principle of self-administration. Unlike Germany, however, the representatives of the insured are not directly elected. Board members of the agencies and funds providing insurance cover are nominated by the Austrian Trade Union Federation and the so-called chambers, that is the statutory interest organizations of labour, capital, and farmers — in standard Austrian usage, 'social partners'. Implementation of social insurance affairs is the responsibility of the respective insurance carriers which are organized along territorial (health care) and occupational principles (pensions). Unemployment insurance, by contrast, was, until the mid-1990s, directly administered by the Ministry of Social Affairs.

1.3 Welfare state change since the early 1970s

1.3.1 Social Democratic hegemony, 1970–86

In 1970, a Social Democratic single party cabinet under Chancellor Bruno Kreisky came to power. Initially, Kreisky had to form a minority cabinet which was supported by the (then) liberal Freedom Party. The general election of 1971, however, provided the Social Democrats with an absolute majority in the National Council which lasted until 1983. In programmatic terms, the new government was committed to the idea of societal and political modernization (Kriechbaumer 2006), which included not least plans to expand and remodel the welfare state. The implementation of these plans was facilitated by the Social Democrats' absolute majority in parliament, lacking institutional veto points, as well as by a prospering economy. Austria was at that time still in a process of economic catch-up and thus experienced rapid economic growth resulting from a comparatively low level of economic development and war-induced destruction. In addition, the free-trade agreement of 1972 between European Commision and European Free Trade Association (EFTA) opened new export opportunities. Increasing trade openness, however, did not coincide with deregulated capital markets. Against this backdrop, the reach of the welfare state was considerably enhanced in the ensuing years with the effect that its Bismarckian character was enriched with some Social Democratic elements. However, this expansion of the welfare state, which characterized social insurance and labour law[11] alike, was mainly restricted to the first half of the 1970s.

A remarkable attribute of this period was that most reforms were based on compromises between the social partners. The negotiation-based style of *politics* did of course not rule out sporadic political conflicts in social policy, with collective labour law (e.g. *Arbeitsverfassungsgesetz* 1973) as the prime example. Nevertheless, the compromise-based pattern of decision-making prevailing in this period demonstrates that social partnership was widely practiced even in periods dominated by a single party government. Only about 15 per cent of all government bills drafted by the Ministry of Social Affairs between 1971 and 1975 were adopted with the Social Democrats' absolute majority in parliament; 76 per cent were actually passed unanimously (Tálos 1981: 328). Hence, the major role of parliament was more or less to ratify the compromises agreed upon in the pre-parliamentary decision-making process. Corporatist policy-making was institutionally facilitated by highly centralized and encompassing interest organizations of labour and capital. In addition, corporatist interest concertation benefited from the small size of the political elite. The inner-circle of social partnership consisted of no more than twenty to thirty persons (Farnleitner 1974). Its stability and functioning was guaranteed by a dense horizontal and vertical network between the two major political parties and the four major interest organizations. For example, many MPs were recruited from the various interest organizations, with the share, in 1978, amounting to no less than 56 per cent (Karlhofer 1999: 33).

In structural terms, a balance of power between the interest organizations of employers and employees contributed to a considerable problem-solving

---

[11] Collective labour law was codified under a single law in 1973 (*Arbeitsverfassungsgesetz*). In addition, wage compensation in case of bankruptcy (1977) and severance pay for workers (1979) were introduced. Moreover, working hours were reduced, while holiday leave was extended to 4 weeks in 1976. All these measures aimed at harmonizing labour law regulations between white- and blue-collar workers (see Tálos 1981: 329–38).

capacity of social partnership. Employers could not threaten exit because the free movement of capital was restricted at that time and the outsourcing of production sites was not a real option. The iron curtain then separated the country from Eastern Europe, while unit labour costs in western neighbour countries significantly exceeded the domestic level. Not surprisingly, the internationalization of production of goods and services was low as indicated by a very low-level of Austrian direct investment abroad (Breuss 1989: 399). Employers therefore had to rely on voice, not exit. Given the presence of a leftist government holding an absolute majority in parliament, it was rational for employers to take part in corporatist negotiations, while rapid economic growth and full employment facilitated compromises in public policy-making. In the 1970s, Austria still benefited from its belated economic modernization (Rothschild 1985; Maderthaner et al. 2007: 29). While most western democracies had already achieved full employment in the 1960s, Austria's post-war 'Golden Age' peaked only in the early 1970s.

1.3.1.1 FAMILY POLICY

Family policy was considerably restructured and expanded under the Social Democratic single party government. This was, in particular, the case for benefits under the aegis of the federal government, that is, cash benefits. The main objectives of reform were to increase redistribution, to adopt women-friendly policies, and to create equal opportunities for children from low-income families. The approach taken to increase vertical redistribution was to rollback family-related tax allowances in favour of tax deductions, benefits in kind, and new or higher transfer payments such as family allowances, the birth allowance, and a marriage allowance.[12] Family allowance and various kinds of tax credits (e.g. tax credits for children, single earner's tax credit) were repeatedly increased in subsequent years. The tax credit for children was converted into a transfer payment in 1978 in order to support low-income families more effectively (Bundeskanzleramt 1979, vol. 1: 177). Moreover, an upgraded family allowance was introduced for disabled children.

The maternity benefit was extended from 12 to 16 weeks, while the parental leave scheme was restructured in 1974. The partner's income was no longer taken into account and the insurance-based benefit was provided as a lump-sum payment. Single mothers were entitled to an upgraded parental leave allowance. Since 1976, an advance on alimony payments has been provided, which is then recovered from the person responsible for alimony. The introduction in 1977 of childcare leave for a spell of 1 week aimed at reconciling work and family life. However, no progress was made in respect of social service

---

[12] The marriage allowance was introduced in 1972. This generous transfer payment is a clear example for the continuation of traditional familialist policies. It was designed as a measure of support for household formation.

provision. Social Democrats neither launched major initiatives nor were they able, unilaterally, to expand the provision of childcare facilities, since these services fall within the sphere of competence of the *Länder*, which for the most part have been controlled by the Christian Democrats in the post-war period.

New benefits in kind included free school books and free transport for school children and apprentices. Social Democrats also abolished the system of household taxation with the aim of increasing the level of female labour market participation. Finally, gender equality was promoted by an overhaul of outdated legal provisions concerning family, marriage, divorce, and abortion. A state secretary for women affairs was established in 1979.

1.3.1.2 HEALTH CARE

In terms of health care, the Social Democratic single party government introduced general medical check-up examinations (1972), and mother and child examinations (1974) to strengthen preventive medicine. The thirty-second amendment of the ASVG (1976) made it possible for those not mandatorily covered by statutory health insurance to take out insurance on a voluntary basis. Students had already become entitled to take out voluntary health insurance in 1972. Likewise, the coverage of accident insurance was considerably enhanced when school children and students were integrated into this programme in 1976.

1.3.1.3 PENSIONS

The benefit spectrum of the pension system (ASVG) was also enhanced. Widows' pensions (1970) and minimum pensions (1973) were raised, while spells of tertiary education, parental leave, sickness, and unemployment were considered for benefit calculation (see Tálos 1986: 99). In 1978, the government made it possible for all those who had raised children to purchase insurance periods at a reduced rate.

Moreover, social insurance for peasants and the self-employed was restructured in the late 1970s. Health, accident, and pension insurance for peasants were combined into a single system (Farmers' Social Insurance Act, 1978). The same was true for the health and pension insurance of the self-employed organized in the Chamber of Commerce (Traders' Social Insurance Act, 1978). Social insurance for freelancers and other categories of the self-employed was regulated under a separate act adopted in the same year.

1.3.1.4 THE OIL SHOCKS: SUCCESSFUL CRISIS MANAGEMENT
IN THE SHORT RUN

The occurrence of the oil price shocks marked a turning point as it brought rapid welfare state expansion to an end. Moreover, the appreciation of the Austrian schilling in the wake of the demise of the Bretton Woods System imposed a burden on the export industry. In 1975, GDP declined by 1.5 per cent, while the budget deficit went up to almost 5 per cent of GDP. In consequence, the government shifted the priority from welfare state expansion to efforts aimed at maintaining full employment (Tálos 1981, 1986). The political strategy to cope with the repercussions of the oil shocks is captured in a famous quote by Bruno Kreisky who said in the run-up to the general elections of 1979: 'A few billion Schillings more debt gives me fewer sleepless nights than would a few hundred more unemployed'. The political response was an unorthodox set of policies labelled as Austro-Keynesianism. Recently, the then Minister of Finance described the measures adopted as a policy-mix without a patent remedy (Androsch 2005: 42). This policy package included coordinated wage policies, labour hoarding and investment in state-run industry, labour shedding via early retirement programmes, anti-cyclical deficit spending, and public promotion of investment and exports. In addition, the government adopted a hard currency policy. In 1976, the Austrian schilling was pegged to the Deutsche Mark for the first time so that the price stability resulting from monetarist policies of the German Bundesbank was imported in subsequent years. Macroeconomic management was based on strong cooperation between the government, the social partners, and the Central Bank (Nowotny 1986; Scharpf 1987). Highly centralized and encompassing interest organizations as well as a small circle of policy-makers provided the institutional foundations for efficient and effective crisis management.

1.3.1.5 LABOUR MARKET POLICY: SUCCESS AND CONSEQUENCES

Even though macroeconomic performance had worsened in the wake of the first oil shock, Austria outperformed most Western democracies in terms of macroeconomic and labour market performance in the crisis of the 1970s (Rothschild 1985; Scharpf 1987). Full employment was declared as the overriding goal and one which was successfully achieved, albeit at the expense of fiscal discipline. The government adopted various supply-side measures to downsize the labour force. The stock of the foreign labour force was continuously reduced from 1973 onwards (Tálos 1981: 340; Christl and Potmesil 1984: 282), while early retirement served as an instrument of labour shedding and, therefore, helped, together with an overstaffed nationalized industry sector, to cushion the mounting labour market problems in the short run. In addition, the repertoire of active labour market policy was repeatedly enhanced in the 1970s (Tálos 1986: 100–1). As a result, spending on active labour market policy tripled between 1974 and 1983 (Christl and Potmesil 1984: 290).

The government also relied on a strategy of 'domestic compensation' as the economic crisis was buffered by the welfare state, which was seen as an automatic stabilizer of demand. Unemployment compensation as well as family supplements (1978) were raised, while eligibility was relaxed through the

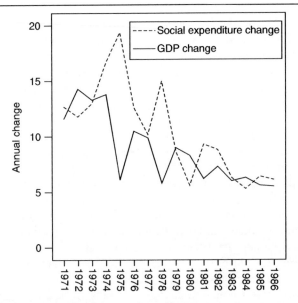

Figure 1.1: Annual change in nominal GDP and social expenditure, 1971–86
Source: Butschek (1998: table 4.1).

abolition of waiting days (1976). A special cash payment (*Sondernotstandshilfe*) was introduced for unemployed single mothers who had exhausted their parental leave entitlement. Already in 1973, a special benefit (*Sonderunterstützung*) for the elderly unemployed was established to bridge the spell until retirement. This programme was extended in the late 1970s. Overall, the aim of maintaining full employment was achieved. While the unemployment rate reached double digit-levels in a number of European countries, it remained under 3 per cent in Austria until 1981.

Austro-Keynesianism in general and the goal of maintaining full employment in particular had its price, however. The annual change in social spending exceeded GDP growth almost throughout the 1970s (Figure 1.1), so that the social expenditure GDP ratio went up from 21.1 per cent of GDP in 1970 to 27.1 per cent in 1983. The level of public debt skyrocketed from 20.4 per cent of GDP in 1970 to almost 50 per cent in the early 1980s. Labour hoarding in and subsidies provided to the state-run industries[13] contributed to economic inefficiencies in this sector which became fully apparent in the mid-1980s. The spread of early retirement programmes led to a remarkable decline in the effective retirement age from the mid-1970s onwards (see Figure 1.2) creating a time-bomb for pension policy in the longer run. In sum, the government

---

[13] While the number of jobs declined in the private sector, employment in nationalized industries increased by 2 per cent between 1973 and 1980 (Nowotny 1986: 48).

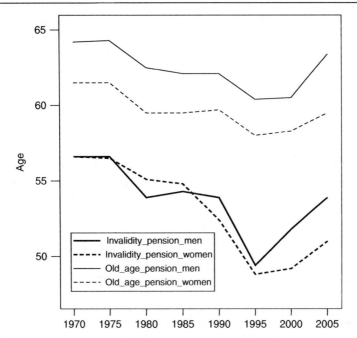

Figure 1.2: Development of the effective retirement age contingent upon pension type and gender, 1970–2005 (5-year intervals)

Source: Hauptverband der österreichischen Sozialversicherungsträger: Handbuch der österreichischen Sozialversicherung 2007, Vienna, p. 88.

practised a strategy of muddling through, while far-reaching structural reforms were postponed until a later time (Rothschild 1989: 121–2).

1.3.1.6 LOOKING FOR FRESH REVENUES AND A SECOND OIL SHOCK

A further policy response to the crisis of the 1970s, initially regarded as a temporary phenomenon, was to increase revenues. Given deteriorating public finances, the left government lifted the value-added tax (VAT) levied on durable consumption goods to 30 per cent in 1977. This so-called luxury tax was an attempt not only to tax the better-off but also to cope with a mounting trade deficit. In the second half of the 1970s, the government also attempted to contain public social expenditure by shifting welfare costs from the budget to social insurance. For example, the Social Democratic single party government established a so-called Hospital Cooperation Fund in 1978, which served as the main body for regulating hospital financing until 1996 and obliged social insurance carriers to co-finance hospitals. The government also reduced the federal grant to the pension scheme from 34.8 (1975) to 21.4 per cent in 1980 (Butschek 1998: table 4.8). This decline in public pension funding was compensated for by higher contribution rates in pension insurance (ASVG), which increased from 17.5 to 21.1 per cent between 1977 and 1981. In a similar vein, the contribution rates for farmers and the self-employed were also raised. Moreover, the government lifted the contribution ceilings for all occupational groups and social insurance branches (Tálos 1981: 360–1) and relied on equalization payments between different social insurance branches to cope with the financial problems of particular insurance schemes — most notably, pension insurance. Finally, the government discovered co-payments as a funding source for health care. The deductible for medical prescriptions was raised by 150 per cent in 1976. In sum, an important instrument of coping with the follow-up consequences of the crisis was to increase social insurance contributions.

The second oil price shock caused a further decline in economic growth paralleled by a slight increase in unemployment. Bruno Kreisky wrote in 1982[14] that Austrian Social Democracy 'attempts to practice a third way, which, in the face of the global economic crisis in the west and the economy of scarcity in the communist countries, offers the only realistic alternative'. Yet the leeway for policymakers to practise such policies declined in the 1980s. The attempt of the Austrian Central Bank to stimulate investment by lowering the interest rate below the German level in 1979 caused a massive outflow of capital that forced the Bank to renounce this course (Unger 2001). Once again, however, the government responded to this exogenous shock with expansive budgetary policies. In addition to labour shedding, it increasingly relied on demand-side-oriented labour market measures (Christl and Potmesil 1984: 284, 288).

Whereas the Social Democrats and the trade unions advocated the continuation of Keynesian economic policies, the deteriorating economic situation also increased scepticism concerning the welfare state, particularly among employers. Leading representatives argued, for example, that 'the welfare state has reached its outer limits if it has not already crossed them' (Stummvoll 1977). Moreover, the welfare state was blamed for having contributed to a financial calamity, since its expansion continued regardless of economic capabilities. The political remedies suggested by those offering such critiques included a moratorium on additional financial burdens imposed on employers, cutbacks in benefits (widows' pensions), the enhancement of individual responsibility in social affairs (co-payments), and measures to increase the efficiency of the social administration. In addition, the government was urged to adopt a much harder line in policing benefit fraud.

The left single-party government, however, did not respond to these claims as no welfare state retrenchment occurred until 1983. Nevertheless, mounting anti-welfare rhetoric in combination with increasing economic difficulties triggered a trend reversal in social policy. When taking stock of their economic policy agenda, Social Democrats argued that 'the mission of a comprehensive quantitative and qualitative expansion of the social security system is by and large accomplished.

---

[14] See SPÖ (1982: 4), translation by the authors.

It is now essential to ensure past achievements' (SPÖ 1982: 136). As a result, welfare state expansion virtually came to an end, while the ballooning budget deficit forced Federal Chancellor Kreisky and finance minister Salcher to launch an austerity package. This so-called Majorca-package, named after Kreisky's secondary residence where this plan was drafted, included significant tax increases and contributed not a little to the Social Democrats' loss of their absolute majority in 1983 and, in consequence, to the resignation of Bruno Kreisky.

1.3.2 A short period of transition: the SPÖ–FPÖ government (1983–6)

From 1983 to 1986, the SPÖ formed a coalition with the small Freedom Party (FPÖ), which then under its chairman Steger was inclined to liberal positions in societal and economic affairs. The SPÖ–FPÖ coalition was not only a transitional period in political terms (Pelinka 1993), but this was also true in terms of social and economic policy. Austro-Keynesianism was gradually renounced in this era of transition (Unger 2001; Lauber and Pesendorfer 2006), while the welfare state was subject to moderate benefit cutbacks for the first time in the post-war period. Mounting public debt and rising interest rates shifted the government's priority to balancing the budget.

1.3.2.1 PENSIONS

Since the unemployment rate went up continuously in the 1980s, the reform debate initially focused on labour market policy (Tálos 1986, 1987), but increasingly also on pensions. Rather than demographic problem pressure it was the swelling budget deficit and unemployment growth that put pensions at the centre of reform efforts. The federal grant devoted to pension insurance increased by 76 per cent between 1981 and 1985. The resulting budgetary pressure was the major reason why the first departure from the expansionist course occurred under the SPÖ–FPÖ government. In 1984, a restrictive pension reform was adopted which aimed to curb expenditure through changes in the pension formula. The base amount was abolished, while the progressive increment factor was replaced by a linear increment factor. Measures also included the extension of the assessment period to 10 years and the postponement of the introduction of widower's pensions legislated by parliament in 1981 in response to a ruling of the Constitutional Court. The government also increased contributions for pension insurance and facilitated early retirement in case of unemployment and invalidity (thirty-nineth and forty-nineth ASVG revision).

1.3.2.2 LABOUR MARKET POLICY

Irrespective of the fact that labour market performance in the early 1980s was still quite favourable as compared with most other countries, full employment effectively ceased to exist in 1982/3 and went up to more than 5 per cent over the next few years. The resulting rise in expenditure devoted to this programme (Tálos 1987: 153) evoked mounting criticism by employers. The tipping point towards retrenchment occurred in 1983, when the SPÖ–FPÖ government suspended unemployment compensation in case of compensation payments after dismissal. Nevertheless, the government responded to the rise in unemployment mainly with higher contribution rates and various supply-side-oriented measures rather than with large-scale benefit cutbacks. Moreover, the coalition established public employment programmes tailored to groups at the margins of the labour market. As already mentioned, the strategy of labour shedding by means of early retirement was continued.

1.3.2.3 HEALTH CARE AND FAMILY POLICY

Changes are also visible in family policy and health care, albeit to a lesser degree. The policy strategy in health care to cope with rising health expenditure was to extend co-payments. This policy has a long-tradition in Austria as particular occupational groups such as civil servants, peasants (until 1998), and the self-employed have to bear 20 per cent of medical treatment costs themselves. Moreover, a deductible for medical prescriptions and the hospitalization of close relatives had already been introduced in 1956. The SPÖ–FPÖ government relied on this tradition and introduced new out-of-pocket payments for in-kind benefits such as glasses or prostheses in 1982.

The expansion of family-related benefits virtually came to an end under the SPÖ–FPÖ government. Some benefits such as the birth allowance were even subject to moderate cutbacks. However, the coalition established a separate Ministry for Family Affairs for the first time (1983) and raised a special fund to support families in financial distress (Gisser et al. 1989: IX–XX).

In sum, the early 1980s witnessed a trend reversal in social policy which was mainly triggered by increasing economic problem pressure. The expansion of the welfare state not only came to a halt in this period, but was also, in some measure, put into reverse gear. As a result, social expenditure growth was brought into line with GDP growth (see Figure 1.1). However, the political response to this crisis was mainly based on a strategy of 'muddling through' which included, once more, higher social security contributions. The government was still committed to maintain full employment, but the leeway for pursuing this goal was meanwhile significantly constrained by the mounting public debt and rising interest rates that Austria experienced in the 1980s. Labour market problems were therefore papered over by means of the pension system, while some first-order policy changes aimed at financial stabilization were implemented in pension and unemployment insurance. By slightly changing the pension formula and imposing moderate benefit cutbacks, the government dabbled with explicitly retrenchment-focused strategies for the first time. Motivated by the idea of securing the status quo in social provision, however, these measures were not designed to undercut the traditional core principles underpinning the welfare state. Neither its basic objectives nor its fundamental structures were contested in this period.

Austria's economic performance further deteriorated, however. The budget deficit reached almost 5 per cent of GDP in 1985. In addition, state-run industry — due to inefficiencies and a slump in the market for steel — de facto collapsed in that year and could, in parts, only be rescued by huge public subsidies. The disaster of state-run industry, which employed about 20 per cent of the industrial labour force, caused the crumbling of an important pillar of traditional employment policies. Between 1980 and 1992, 55,000 jobs were shed and various finance ministers had to provide a total of €4.4 billion to cover the accumulated losses (Obinger 2006: 156). The implosion of the nationalized industries was just one episode among a series of economic and political scandals that shattered Austria in the mid-1980s. Federal Chancellor Fred Sinowatz stepped down in the wake of the controversy about the role of former UN Secretary General — and later Austrian Federal President — Kurt Waldheim during the Second World War. In 1986, Sinowatz's successor, former finance minister Franz Vranitzky, ended the coalition with the Freedom Party and called for new elections when right-wing populist Jörg Haider took over as chairman of the FPÖ. The general election of 1986 brought losses for both of the two major parties, while Haider's FPÖ gained almost 10 per cent of the vote. In addition, the Greens entered parliament for the first time. In this situation, a coalition between the Social and Christian Democrats resumed office for the first time since 1966.

1.3.3 The Grand Coalition: adaptation to a remarkably changed environment (1987–99)

The development of social policy from the mid-1980s until 1999 was presided over by the renewed Grand Coalition. The Grand Coalition saw itself as a 'restructuring partnership' for solving the major economic problems Austria faced and, from the late 1980s onwards, taking the country into the European Union. Debt containment and modernization of the economy were prime goals of the cabinet and were to be realized by means of structural reforms (Müller 1988). Economic growth was significantly lower compared to previous decades, while the rate of unemployment increased from 5.2 (1986) to more than 7 per cent in 1999. This development was paralleled by an increase in the number of the long-term unemployed and a spread of atypical work (Tálos 1999, 2005a: 44ff; Stiefel 2006: 77f). Budgetary pressure and labour market problems grew more acute with the de facto bankruptcy of large parts of state-run industry in the mid-1980s. Under these circumstances, the policy route of incremental adjustment and financial stabilization practised since the early 1980s was not only continued by the Grand Coalition, but actually pushed forward with greater speed and intensity (Tálos and Wörister 1998).

Both governing parties underwent a programmatic change of course around that time. This was not least the result of a generational change in politics and social partnership.[15] The pragmatic modernizers led by Chancellor Franz Vranitzky got the upper hand in the Social Democratic camp. Vranitzky, a former bank manager and minister of finance under the SPÖ–FPÖ coalition, initiated a change of policy which marked a break with the Kreisky era and which was only hesitantly accepted by the unions and party traditionalists (cf. Vranitzky 2004). The ÖVP got into the maelstrom of economic neo-liberalism and therefore increasingly advocated deregulation, flexibilization, tax as well as expenditure cuts, and privatization (Seeleib-Kaiser et al. 2008: 107–11). Along with a new moral conservatism with respect to societal affairs the party's programmatic platform became more and more neo-conservative since the mid-1980s (Müller 2006: 357).

As a result, no longer full employment at any price, but rather fiscal discipline and moderate supply-side-oriented economic modernization became the new leitmotifs of reform. The sound waves of the paradigmatic change in economic policy initiated by conservative governments in the United States and Great Britain hence reached Austria with the customary delay. The realignment of the left in economic policy brought the Social Democrats closer to traditional ÖVP positions (Müller 1988: 322–3). The policy shift initiated by the Grand Coalition was triggered by mounting economic problem pressure with public debt as the most important reform impetus, policy learning connected to the collapse of the nationalized industries and a profound recalibration in economic policy at the international level, and, finally, by the cabinet's intention to join the European Economic Community (EEC). More specifically, soaring public debt plus high real interest rates in the 1980s increased the pressure to impose austerity policies. Since the 1990s, intended EEC membership worked in the same direction given the fiscal criteria required for accession. As a result, deficit spending virtually ceased to be a possible policy option. Together with the full liberalization of capital markets in 1987, these developments sounded the death knell of Austro-Keynesianism (Winckler 1988).

The application for EEC membership was filed in 1989 and accession was finally accomplished on 1 January 1995. Even though it was clear that EEC accession would imply the demise of the historically grown mixed economy with its large public enterprise sector, a significant role of price regulations and various sheltered sectors, EEC membership was backed by the social partners. More specifically, they saw no real alternative to western economic integration and, therefore, strongly emphasized the economic advantages resulting from

---

[15] Leading representatives of social partnership like Anton Benya and Rudolf Sallinger, who had witnessed (civil) war and practised social partnership on a handshake basis, stepped down in the late 1980s and were replaced by a younger generation committed to a technocratic approach (see Pelinka 1998: 154).

participation in the common market. The main argument was that it would be better to be involved in making the rules as a full EU member rather than to take them from outside (Karlhofer and Tálos 1996: 50–63). As will be demonstrated in this section, however, EU accession marked not only a watershed for social partnership, but also for the welfare state.

After resuming office, the SPÖ–ÖVP government initiated a reorientation in economic policy by adopting a moderate supply-side strategy committed to debt containment, liberalization, deregulation and the privatization of state-owned enterprises. One of the first measures launched by the coalition was a major tax reform. Marginal income tax rates were lowered in accordance with international developments (e.g. the top income tax rate was reduced from 62 to 50 per cent), while the tax base was simultaneously extended by removing tax loop holes. The tax on interest, introduced as part of Kreisky's Majorca package, was abolished. Instead, capital yield tax, levied on profits and dividends, was raised from 20 to 25 per cent, while a 10 per cent tax rate on bonds and savings deposits was introduced. The corporate tax rate was lowered and fixed at 30 per cent, while some indirect taxes (e.g. tobacco and insurance tax) were increased (Genser 1989). In 1991, the special tax rate levied on durable consumption goods in the late 1970s ('luxury tax') was abolished. Corporate tax was raised to 34 per cent, while trade tax and property tax were abolished in 1994. The government also restructured the public enterprise sector and started to sell off public enterprises from 1987 onwards. While smaller companies were sold off entirely, the big state-owned enterprises remained under public control as the government did not wish to reduce the public share below the 50 per cent threshold (Obinger 2006).

The SPÖ–ÖVP government also significantly increased the reform intensity in the welfare state ambit. Despite mounting fiscal problems, however, the government did not immediately embark on a strategy of welfare state retrenchment.

1.3.3.1 FAMILY POLICY

With just one exception[16], family policy was considerably enhanced during the first legislative period of the Grand Coalition. As in most other continental countries, Austria has experienced a dramatic decline in fertility rates over the last three decades. Given significant ideological differences between the Social and Christian Democrats in this area, the lowest common denominator was to increase cash benefits. Based on the coalition agreement of 1987, the two parties also decided to lower the tax burden for families with dependent children. This goal was realized in the wake of the tax reform of 1988. The single earner's tax deduction was raised and the supplements provided for children

---

[16] The marriage allowance was abolished in 1988. This measure caused a huge run of applicants to civil registry offices in 1987.

(introduced in 1986) were tripled. A negative income tax was introduced under circumstances in which wage earners with low incomes could not benefit from tax deductions. In an effort to reconcile work and family life, the government drafted a so-called family package in November 1989. Once more, however, the measures proposed focused mainly on cash benefits and longer leave periods, while the government did little to increase the availability of childcare facilities. The parental leave allowance was enhanced from 12 to 24 months and extended to fathers in 1990. Moreover, the government increased family allowances and introduced an extra supplement for low-income families. The only measure taken to reconcile work and family life was to permit the parental leave allowance to be combined with part-time work.

Family policy has traditionally been shaped by the political parties, with the social partners playing only a minor role. In the 1990s, however, family policy was considerably influenced by the Constitutional Court. In 1991, a Court judgement ruled that family maintenance costs for the better-off were not adequately compensated by the tax system. The Grand Coalition responded to the Court ruling with various measures including increased tax deductions for families with dependent children as well as higher transfer payments. In 1992, family allowances were raised again, while a new supplement for children aged 19 and more was introduced. Overall, these measures caused extra costs of €430 million (Bundesministerium für Umwelt, Jugend und Familie 1999: 453–54).

1.3.3.2 LABOUR MARKET POLICY

While family policy was clearly a field of expansion through until the mid-1990s, the reform process in the area of unemployment insurance was neither linear nor exclusively restrictive, since, until 1993, a mixture of retrenchment and expansive measures was adopted (Tálos and Wörister 1998). Benefit enhancement or improvements included the abolition of a clause discriminating against women with regard to unemployment assistance (females were not entitled to unemployment assistance if the spouse or partner was in full-time employment), the introduction of a uniform net replacement rate of 57.9 per cent (i.e. the abolition of wage scales), and the integration of foreigners into the unemployment assistance scheme (as a result of a Constitutional Court ruling). In addition, particular measures were taken for problem groups in the labour market. These included the extension of benefit duration for the older unemployed with long insurance records, the retention of the assessment base for males aged 50 + and females aged 45 + in situations in which an unemployed person accepted a lower paid job, a higher exemption for older recipients of unemployment assistance and, finally, the reduction of the qualifying period for unemployed persons under 25 years of age from 52 to 20 weeks. On the other hand, the government increased the pressure on the long-term unemployed receiving unemployment assistance for more than 3 years. Thus, in the early 1990s the expansion of benefits actually outweighed benefit cutbacks.

1.3.3.3 PENSIONS

Balanced reforms, that is, measures that combined elements of retrenchment and expansion, also characterized pension policy until the mid-1990s. In contrast to the unemployment insurance scheme, however, retrenchment measures prevailed. Problem pressure in this field is apparent from the shorter intervals between the various pension reform activities initiated by the SPÖ–ÖVP government. The various pension reforms were largely triggered by increases in federal funding of the pension system on the one hand and by mounting pressure to contain budget deficits on the other. The various early retirement programmes were a particular source of expenditure growth. In terms of the expenditure/GDP ratio, the Austrian pension system was, in the 1990s, one of the most expensive in the world (OECD 2008a), not least because the effective retirement age was one of the lowest. The pressure to impose austerity policies resulting from ballooning budget deficits led to various retrenchment measures and higher contribution rates.

Already in 1987 (forty-fourth ASVG amendment), the assessment base was extended from 10 to 15 years. Moreover, spells of higher education were no longer considered for benefit calculation. The government also raised contributions rates for white- and blue-collar workers which, however, remained unchanged thereafter. Finally, the government introduced a temporary widow's/widower's pension for survivors under 35 who had been married for less than 10 years.

The pension reform of 1993 included more balanced measures. In an effort to contain costs, the Grand Coalition changed the indexation of benefits (adjusting them to net rather than gross wages). Moreover, the standard replacement rate of survivors' pensions (60 per cent) was reduced to 40 per cent for those survivors receiving other kinds of income. These restrictive measures were counterbalanced by the upgrading of spells of time devoted to child-raising for benefit calculation (up to 4 years per child) and a modification of the assessment period in 1993 (with the 'best' 15 years as the basis for benefit calculation).[17] Despite severe fiscal problems, the government continued and adopted new programmes that facilitated early retirement. These programmes included early retirement due to reduced ability to work and the introduction of a part-time pension (*Gleitpension*). In consequence, the effective retirement age further declined until 1995 (see Figure 1.2). Pension policy in the early 1990s was also influenced by the Constitutional Court. In 1990, the Court declared

---

[17] For the most part, it is the insured with a full insurance record who have benefited from this measure.

the difference in the retirement age between men (65 years) and women (60 years) unconstitutional. Policy-makers, however, decided on a long transition period for implementing this ruling. From 2024 onwards, the retirement age of females will be gradually raised in order to bring it fully in line with the retirement age of males by 2033.

1.3.3.4 HEALTH CARE

Cost containment and expansion of benefits also characterizes the reform trajectory in the health-care sector until the mid-1990s. Demographic change, medical and technological progress, and an increasing numbers of doctors made for an increasing expenditure trajectory after 1970. Concerns about rising cost along with the deficits accumulated by many sickness funds increasingly dominated the political discourse. The Grand Coalition primarily adopted measures to increase revenues. One approach to cope with rising health-care costs was to raise health insurance contributions and contribution ceilings for most occupational groups as well as retirees. The major exception was the contribution rate for blue-collar workers which remained remarkably stable over time (see Bittner 2005: 378). Despite the increase in contribution rates, health-related social security contributions have remained low in comparative perspective. For example, contribution rates are about 50 per cent lower than in Germany. Major reasons for this outcome involve the inclusion of the better-off in the health insurance system, higher out-of-pocket payments and a greater share of public grants in health-care financing (Wendt 2003). The second reform approach for addressing the problem of ballooning health-care costs was to increase co-payments and deductibles. In 1988, the Grand Coalition imposed a co-payment to cover parts of the so-called hotel costs of hospital treatment.

The early 1990s, however, also witnessed the introduction of new benefits. Since 1992, health insurance, for example, includes medication offered by psychotherapists, while differences in sick pay levels for blue- and white-collar workers have virtually disappeared. The most important expansive measure in cost terms, however, was the introduction of a federal long-term care allowance in 1993. Strongly pushed by various organizations of disabled people, the adoption of this universal programme has anchored a structurally unique pillar as part of the Austrian social security system. In contrast to the German system, which was introduced a year later and assumed a traditional social insurance character, the Austrian programme is entirely tax-funded. The new programme is designed to cover additional care-related costs and has replaced special supplements for handicapped people previously offered by pension insurance and other programmes. Entitlement is independent of income and the benefit is paid regardless of the cause of the need for long-term care. The care allowance is a lump-sum benefit that is staggered (has seven levels of payment) contingent upon the extent of the care required. Based on a state treaty, the *Länder* have agreed to guarantee nationwide provision of social services until 2010 and to provide a similar care allowance for people not qualified for a care benefit under federal law.

Overall, the pattern of welfare state adaptation until the mid-1990s was one of balanced reforms. It, therefore, comes as no surprise that the coalition's main objective of containing public debt totally backfired in this period. The budget deficit increased continuously and finally reached 5 per cent of GDP in 1995. In consequence, the level of public debt increased from 49.8 per cent (1985) to 69.2 per cent of GDP in 1995. Austria, therefore, actually exceeded the critical 60 per cent Maastricht threshold at precisely the time of its accession to the European Union. Obviously, this meant a ratcheting up of the pressure to stabilize public finances.

1.3.3.5 EU MEMBERSHIP AS A WATERSHED: THE LATE 1990S

Tensions between the coalition parties increased under these circumstances. Former Federal Chancellor Vranitzky reports in his memoirs that Vice-Chancellor Wolfgang Schüssel (ÖVP) ripped up a budget paper submitted by the Social Democratic minister of finance during a coalition meeting (Vranitzky 2004: 220). In late 1995, the coalition eventually split during negotiations on the federal budget as a result of severe partisan conflict over the appropriate measures to rein in the budget deficit. However, the Grand Coalition was restored after the general election in late 1995, in which the SPÖ gained seats. Nevertheless, the coalition partners became increasingly obstructive in subsequent years. Christian Democrats as well as employers called for more radical reforms to rollback the state in economic affairs and adapt the welfare state to a more competitive international environment. While the ÖVP and the interest organizations of employers advocated (neo-liberal) measures aimed at deregulation, privatization, containment of non-wage labour costs, and tax reductions, the Social Democrats and trade unions took a far softer line and devoted most of their energies to defending the status quo.

Tensions also spilled over to the social partners who could not reach an agreement on the budget stabilization course. More important, however, the balance of power between the peak associations became more asymmetric in the 1990s. EU accession provided employers with greater exit options which in turn improved their bargaining position. At the same time the mounting fiscal imbalances increased the pressure for debt containment in the shadow of the Maastricht Treaty. It was therefore no longer the distribution of productivity gains that was on the agenda of corporatism as in the past, rather the distribution of losses resulting from the imperative of budget consolidation. Moreover, EU membership has generally undercut the influence of the social partners, since traditional bargaining instruments were either restricted or became, like price regulations, entirely obsolete. In consequence, tripartite interest mediation became less important as compared to the heyday of corporatism, as it was not only practised less frequently, but also restricted to fewer policy sectors (cf. Tálos 2005*b*). Instead, the government more and more became the leading actor in social policy-making. Given the deteriorating economic performance and the fiscal constraints imposed by the Maastricht Treaty, the government adopted a strict austerity course immediately after EU accession. More specifically, the Grand Coalition launched two so-called austerity packages in 1995 and 1996. Officially labelled as Structural Adaptation Acts (*Strukturanpassungsgesetze*), both acts were umbrella laws by which dozens of federal bills were amended. Beside measures designed to increase public revenues, both austerity packages entailed significant expenditure cutbacks, which also affected the welfare state and, therefore, led to alienation between the interest organizations of labour and the Social Democrats. In a nutshell, EU membership marked a turning point not only in social policy, but also in terms of social politics.

1.3.3.6 LABOUR MARKET POLICY

To begin with, the mid-1990s witnessed a turnaround in labour market policy. While the contribution rate of unemployment insurance was stabilized at 6 per cent in order to freeze non-wage labour costs, from 1993 onwards, the government increasingly relied on benefit cutbacks and the activation of the unemployed. The replacement rate of unemployment compensation was lowered to 57 per cent. The restrictive course is apparent from the *Beschäftigungssicherungsgesetz* (1993) and the two austerity packages launched in 1995 and 1996. Qualifying conditions for unemployment benefits as well as sanctions were again tightened (cf. Tálos and Wörister 1998: 270–3). Finally, a bill aiming at working-time flexibilization was passed by the parliament in 1997. In this respect, Austria was a latecomer (Unger 2001: 354). On the other hand, in the second half of the 1990s, the Grand Coalition extended spending on active labour market policy and was also concerned with the social protection and employment rights of atypical employees (see below). Already in 1992, a bill stipulating the non-discrimination of part-time work and marginal employment was passed (Tálos 1999).

1.3.3.7 PENSIONS

The pension system became a permanent site of reform as evident from reforms adopted in 1995, 1996, and 1997. The austerity packages passed after EU accession included various measures to contain eligibility to all types of early old-age pensions. In addition, pension adjustment was suspended for one year. In 1997, the assessment base for pension calculation was extended to 18 years. Moreover, the increment factor was reduced and fixed at 2 per cent for old-age pensions and the government introduced a 'bonus–malus' or merit rating system in order to contain early retirement. A deduction of 2 per cent per year was imposed in case of early retirement, while postponement of retirement was honoured with a bonus. In addition, the contribution rate for the self-employed and farmers, which was lower compared to other categories of wage earners, was raised in 1997. In a similar vein, the contribution rate for civil servants, which was already higher compared to the contribution rate for the insured covered by the General Social Insurance Act (ASVG), was increased once more. Finally, the Grand Coalition enacted measures to harmonize the calculation of civil servants' pensions with that of general pensions in the long run. While the pensions of civil servants were traditionally calculated on the basis of the last salary prior to retirement, the government decided to gradually extend the assessment base in line with the ASVG regulations to 18 years.

The mandatory inclusion of the so-called new self-employed in the health, accident, and pension insurance systems (1996) was, on the one hand, an attempt to manage problems related to the 'new social risks' resulting from the spread of atypical jobs, but was also motivated by financial considerations on the other, that is, to secure an increase in contribution payments in the short- and mid-term. In 1998, so-called marginal employees (*geringfügig Beschäftigte*) were given the entitlement to take out voluntary pension and health insurance.

1.3.3.8 FAMILY POLICY

In the mid-1990s, even family policy experienced a backlash, albeit only for a relatively short time. The two austerity packages for the first time imposed major cutbacks in family-related benefits. Measures included the abolition of birth allowances and free public transport for students, the introduction of co-payments for school books, cutbacks in family allowances, and a reduction of parental leave entitlement for one parent from 24 to 18 months (Bundesministerium für Umwelt, Jugend und Familie 1999: 414–18).

A second ruling of the Constitutional Court in 1997 returned family policy back to its expansionary course. The Court ruled that policy-makers had not adequately responded to its ruling of 1991 on the costs of family maintenance. In consequence, this second judgment led to a further expansion of cash benefits in the late 1990s clearly offsetting the cutbacks of the mid-1990s. In 1999, the Grand Coalition responded to the Court's ruling with a comprehensive family policy package which included increased tax credits for families as well as providing higher transfer payments. In consequence, the present system of income support to families is again based on a more balanced dual system consisting of transfer payments and a variety of tax breaks.[18]

---

[18] Recall that the Social Democrats had attempted to rollback tax breaks in the 1970s on grounds of equity.

In addition to the strong impact of the Constitutional Court in the 1990s, a second novelty in family policy is worth mentioning. The late 1990s witnessed increased efforts to overcome massive shortcomings with regard to the provision of day-care facilities for children. As in virtually all advanced democracies, female labour market participation has increased markedly over recent decades. Since childcare (and nursing) work is typically delivered by women, their massive entry into the labour market has increased the pressure to adopt measures aimed at reconciling work and family life. Austria, however, has traditionally been an extreme laggard in terms of the provision of public childcare facilities, especially for very young children. In 1995, the proportion of children aged 0 to 2 in childcare was a meagre 3 per cent (Badelt and Österle 1998: 156). Income support to families, by contrast, was generous and, as already demonstrated, repeatedly expanded. Despite generous transfer payments, however, fertility declined steadily. In the mid-1990s, the coalition, therefore, for the first time, took serious steps to bolster family-related social services.

Given the jurisdictional split in the field of social services, the Grand Coalition provided special grants to sub-national governments in order to increase the number of childcare facilities at the local level. This financial assistance, provided in the period from 1997 to 2000, increased the number of slots provided by institutional childcare facilities as well as coverage rates for all age cohorts. Nevertheless, the coverage rate for toddlers is still very low from a comparative perspective. In addition, there is a substantial divide in coverage between rural areas and urban agglomerations. Of all crèches, 63 per cent are located in Vienna, whereas *Länder* such as Burgenland or Vorarlberg did not offer any institutional childcare facilities at all for this age cohort prior to the 1990s (Statistik Austria 2002: 9, 23, 26).

1.3.3.9 HEALTH CARE

Cost containment was the major impetus for health-care reform. One approach to curbing public health expenditure was to increase the public control of the health-care system and to reorganize both the organization and financing of the hospital sector. Given the territorial fragmentation in this field, the reform trajectory adopted was to strengthen health-care planning in order to reduce the oversupply of hospital beds and large-scale medical equipment. The main idea was to rein in duplication of effort and to reduce overcapacity in hospitals. In fact, the number of hospital beds has been considerably reduced over the past two decades. Given the distribution of competencies in this sector, all these efforts had to be negotiated between different branches of government and were formally based on a state treaty according to section 15a of the Federal Constitution. Based on such a state treaty, the Social Democratic single party government already had established a so-called Hospital Cooperation Fund in 1978, which served as the main body for regulating hospital financing and planning until 1996. In 1997, the system was considerably restructured on the basis of a new state treaty. The Hospital Cooperation Fund was abolished and replaced by nine regional funds located at the *Länder* level. In addition, the reimbursement for medical services provided in hospitals was fundamentally restructured, when a payment system based on diagnosis-related groups was introduced in that year. As in many other countries, the main idea was to shorten periods of hospitalization by adopting a performance-related reimbursement system.

The government also continued to enhance co-payments in case of sickness. In 1996, the coalition imposed new co-payments for attending spas and other forms of rehabilitation. As of 1997, patients had to pay a deductible for each health insurance certificate obtained (*Krankenschein*). The deductible for prescriptions was repeatedly raised.

Finally, the government also changed the eligibility to health insurance as the age limit for contribution-free co-insurance for children was reduced from 26 to 25 years.

1.3.3.10 SUMMARY

With the exception of the long-term care allowance, the various reform activities launched by the SPÖ–ÖVP government did not result in any fundamental departure from the traditional character of the welfare state. Fiscal stabilization and adaptation to a remarkably changed international political economy together with societal changes were the driving forces of these reform activities. However, both the scope and the speed of reform has increased compared to the early 1980s, when only some first-order policy changes (Hall 1993) were legislated. Austrian EU membership marked a watershed in this respect. While a mixture of expansive and restrictive reform measures were adopted until the mid-1990s, reforms in the wake of EU accession were overwhelmingly restrictive in character and associated with several second-order changes in social policy. Examples from pension insurance are the efforts to contain early retirement and to harmonize the pensions of civil servants with standard pension provision. Yet, the government did not deviate from status preservation as the overriding objective guiding the statutory pension system. Moreover, pressure by interest organizations of employers and the ÖVP to encourage private pensions were addressed only to a limited extent. A bill regulating occupational pensions was adopted in 1990 (Tálos and Wörister 1998: 263ff.), but did not do anything to diminish the predominance of statutory public provision. The health-care system was subject to one second-order reform, when the reimbursement of medical provision delivered by hospitals was restructured in the mid-1990s. As in other sectors, cost containment was the most important impetus for this policy change. In the field of labour market policy, reforms in the wake of EU accession were overwhelmingly restrictive in character.

In addition, cutbacks of cash benefits were accompanied by stronger activation measures marking a clear second-order change in this policy field. The pressure to rein in the budget deficit in the aftermath of EU membership also affected family policy with some transfer payments reduced or abolished in 1995/6. However, the late 1990s also witnessed second-order policy changes in this field. Due to rulings of the Constitutional Court, the dual model of income support for families was restored, while the Grand Coalition attempted to enhance the service orientation of this policy sector through expansion of formal childcare facilities. With hindsight, however, this latter effort must be regarded as something of a last hurrah.

Where the politics of social policy-making is concerned, the federal government increasingly dominated the policy-making process, while the traditionally strong influence of the peak associations of labour and capital steadily declined (Karlhofer 1999, 16ff.). The social partners' difficulties of agreeing on a joint course of action in a context of austerity and Europeanization were clearly recognized by both coalition parties (cf. Khol 2001: 38–44; Vranitzky 2004: 132, 154). Even though the influence of the social partners declined with mounting economic problem pressures and the resulting diminished scope for (re)distribution, the interest organizations of labour remained powerful enough to block far-reaching retrenchment (Tálos and Kittel 1999: 162). Tensions between the social partners nevertheless spilled over to the coalition parties which, given the considerable ideological differences between the two governing parties, became increasingly obstructive — something the general public saw as producing a 'reform jam'. Along with the benefit cutbacks imposed in the second half of the 1990s this contributed to the rise of right-wing populist Jörg Haider. The general elections of 1999 brought painful losses for both coalition parties, while Haider's FPÖ gained almost 27 per cent of the vote.

The lesson learnt by the ÖVP in the 1990s was that a major welfare state transformation could only be implemented *against* but not together with the Social Democrats. For leading representatives of the ÖVP (cf. Khol 2001), it was the informal veto power of the unions that was impeding policy change. Although the People's Party only ranked third in the 1999 general election, ÖVP chairman Wolfgang Schüssel exploited the window of opportunity opened by the election outcome and formed a coalition with the Freedom Party. Accompanied by fierce national and international protests, a centre-right government came to power for the first time since 1945.

1.3.4 'A good day begins with a balanced budget': the centre-right coalition (2000–6)

In February 2000 the new ÖVP–FPÖ coalition, constituted by parties with rather similar preferences in respect of both social and economic policy, took office. Given the small ideological distance between the partisan veto players and the permissive constitution, the window of opportunity to enact major policy changes stood wide open. The overriding goal of the centre-right coalition was to achieve a paradigm shift in economic and social policy. More specifically, the ÖVP–FPÖ coalition sought to accomplish the shift towards supply-side oriented economic policies, which had already been tentatively initiated by the Grand Coalition in the late 1980s. The ÖVP–FPÖ government stepped into the arena with an ambitious programme in order to 'halt a misunderstood Keynesianism, presented as Austro-Keynesianism, that had served as a smokescreen for soaring debt, and to free the nation of debt altogether'.[19] Strong emphasis was put on a largely expenditure-based restructuring of state finances with a balanced budget as the prime objective. 'A good day begins with a balanced budget', a slogan coined by finance minister Karl-Heinz Grasser in his 2000 budget address to the Austrian National Council, became the government's new leitmotif in fiscal policy.

With a view to taking a new approach in social policy (labelled as *Sozialpolitik neu*), which was mainly committed to improved targeting and to combating the misuse of social benefits, the coalition announced far-reaching welfare state changes including a neo-conservative recalibration of family policy (see Obinger and Tálos 2006: 25–34). In order to improve the competitiveness of the Austrian economy, which, located on the fringes of Eastern Europe, was now surrounded by low-wage economies about to join the European Union, the government announced tax cuts, a freeze in non-wage labour costs and planned various measures aiming at deregulation and flexibilization. In the beginning, however, the government had to raise taxes in order to balance the budget, making for a tax/GDP ratio in 2001 that reached an all-time high. In subsequent years, however, the government repeatedly failed to present a balanced budget (Marterbauer 2005). The announced tax reform was finally enacted in 2005 and included — not least in response to the low tax rates of the eastern transition countries[20] — a reduction in the corporate tax rate to 25 per cent. Along with the lack of any property tax in Austria, this reform triggered a significant influx of German capital.

The government aggressively sold its agenda to the public and there was neither an attempt to hide benefit reductions nor any effort to avoid confrontation with employee organizations. It was clear from the very outset that this neo-liberal programme would not be backed by the peak associations of labour. Hence the government adopted a strategy that envisaged a shift in the traditional balance of power. In order to bypass the informal veto powers held by the unions within the system of social partnership, the government changed the traditional rules of the political game. In an effort to remove the informal

---

[19] Stenographisches Protokoll des Nationalrates, XXI. GP, 40. Sitzung, p. 18.
[20] It should be emphasized, however, that Austria has significantly benefited from the EU eastern enlargement.

veto positions of labour, the centre-right coalition launched an onslaught on the self-administration of social insurance. In particular, the government changed the composition of the Federation of Austrian Social Insurance Carriers, abandoning thus a more than 100-year-old lasting tradition. More specifically, the traditional over-representation of labour in this body was replaced by a formally balanced representation of labour and capital. In practice, this reform changed the balance of powers in favour of the ÖVP and the employers' representatives. This can be exemplified in more detail for the newly established Federation's Executive Board. This body consists of twelve members with voting power and two nonvoting members. Employers and employees nominate five delegates each. The remaining two members with voting power are delegates of the chambers of agriculture and the union of public sector employees. Since the latter typically are strongholds of the ÖVP, the employers and the ÖVP-affiliated representatives now hold a majority on this steering board. Last but not least, the Social Democratic president of the Federation of Austrian Social Insurance Carriers was replaced in spectacular circumstances.

Even more important was that labour's former quasi-institutional role in the pre-parliamentary decision-making process ceased. Relying on a bigbang strategy (Starke 2008) the coalition utilized majority rule procedures to pursue its neo-liberal agenda. Based on the slogan 'speed-kills' coined by the ÖVP party whip Andreas Khol, reforms were literally pushed through in the coalition's first office term so that the opposition and the unions were repeatedly confronted with a series of *faits accomplis*. As a consequence, consociational democracy and corporatism virtually came to an end at the turn of the new millennium (Tálos 2005*b*; Karlhofer and Tálos 2006; Obinger and Tàlos 2006). The Social Democratic opposition was left with the Constitutional Court as the sole effective means of redressing unpopular reforms. The SPÖ, supported by its strong National Council mandate, took various restrictive social policy bills passed by the centre-right majority before the Constitutional Court. Success was mixed, however. The opposition also made use of popular initiatives which allow for federal bills to be initiated from below. Though this instrument is nonbinding, since parliament has complete freedom in handling a popular initiative, it lends itself to political mobilization and agenda-setting. However, the centre-right coalition once more relied on its majority and did not respond to any of these initiatives (Obinger and Tálos 2006).

1.3.4.1 PENSIONS

Pensions were again a main target of reform in the government programme. More specifically, the government envisaged the transformation of the pension system into a multi-pillar system and announced the abolition of existing early retirement programmes. Several factors were used by the government to justify this turnaround in pension policy. The most important was the need for a strict austerity course in order to achieve a balanced budget. Pension reform was also motivated by efforts to make the system sustainable in light of prospective demographic changes and to improve the fairness of the system, in particular, to level out differences resulting from occupational fragmentation as well as between generations (i.e. to reduce the financial burdens on the economically active generation). In order to realize these goals, the ÖVP–FPÖ government changed the rules of the political game. In contrast to traditional practice, the new government strongly relied on majority decisions rather than on negotiations. During the government's first term in office, which ended ahead of schedule because of a severe crisis within the Freedom Party in 2002, the changes implemented, however, markedly resembled those earlier contemplated by the Grand Coalition. The main goal of the pension reform of 2000 was to rein in early retirement. The retirement age was raised for various types of early retirement pensions, while deductions in case of early retirement were further increased. In addition, the government reduced the replacement rate of widows' pensions so that they now vary between 0 and 60 per cent.

The restructuring of the pension system was finally realized from 2003 onwards. Relying on majority rule and in accordance with the 'speed-kills' strategy, the reform was literally pushed through. More specifically, the transformation of the pension system occurred in three steps.

The first step was the so-called Pension Reform 2003. This reform abolished part-time pensions, early retirement in case of unemployment, and early retirement for persons with long contribution record (effective from 2017 onwards), while the annual pension deductions imposed for those taking early retirement were raised to 4.2 per cent of the gross pension. From 2004 onwards, the assessment base was to be gradually lengthened to 40 years (effective from 2028 onwards), implying that pensions would henceforth be calculated on the basis of a lifetime work record. Moreover, the increment factor was reduced from 2 to 1.78 per cent and the number of years required to qualify for the maximum pension (equivalent to 80 per cent of the assessment base) was extended from 40 to 45 years. In addition, the first benefit indexation will now only take place after 2 years of retirement.

This reform led to massive and, at least for Austria, atypical protests which were initiated by trade unions, societal organizations, and the opposition. Since even the government was divided on this reform, the coalition watered down the proposed changes to some extent by imposing a cap on the losses resulting from the reform. More specifically, total individual losses should not exceed 10 per cent during a transition period until the late 2020s. A further compensatory measure was to credit 24 instead of 18 months devoted to child-raising as contribution periods (with an upgraded rate). Finally, a special fund was established to provide assistance in case of hardship, while workers in heavy industries were exempted from some of the restrictive measures.

The second step in redesigning the pension system was the harmonization of the different occupational pension schemes. As in the case of the Pension Reform Act of 2003, the long-term fiscal solvency of the PAYG-based system as well as efforts to strengthen the trust of younger cohorts in the system were major factors motivating this far-reaching reform. The General Pension Act was enacted in 2005 and included the following measures: with the exception of civil servants employed by the *Länder* and municipalities, the new unified pension law would apply to all employees born in 1954 or later. An individual pension account was established for every insured person showing the contribution record and the accumulated claims. In contrast to initial plans proposed by the government, a defined benefit rather than a defined contribution pension account was established. The basic formula stipulates that the insured are entitled to a pension level of 80 per cent of average lifetime income at the age of 65. For each pension account a unified rate of 1.78 per cent of the annual contribution base was determined. The valorization of earned claims is based on the development of the average annual contribution base which, by and large, is in accordance with the development of average income.

Existing pensions will no longer be adjusted to net wages but rather to the consumer price index (CPI). Retirement will be possible within a 'corridor' at ages between 62 and 68. Pension benefits are reduced by 4.2 per cent per annum if a person retires before the statutory retirement age of 65. The bonus for delayed retirement is calculated accordingly.

For insured persons who have already earned contribution periods, a so-called parallel calculation will be made. More specifically, the benefits will be calculated on the basis of the legal situation before and after the harmonization of the pension system. The pension is then calculated as a weighted average of the entitlements earned under both schemes.

The proposed harmonization of contribution rates failed, however. Though the contribution rates for peasants and the self-employed were increased to 15 and 17.5 per cent respectively, these rates are still lower than the general contribution rate of 22.8 per cent. Finally, the General Pension Act has also modified the '10 per cent cap' imposed by the pension reform of 2003. This cap was fixed at 5 per cent for 2004 but was then gradually to increase to 10 per cent by 2024.

The third step taken to overhaul the pension system will lead to a multi-pillar system in the long run. Even though the government did not introduce a formal 'Three-Pillar System' as originally proposed, two reforms launched by the centre-right coalition nevertheless have, *de facto*, paved the way for a move in this direction. The National Council unanimously adopted the Federal Act on Corporate Staff Provision (*Bundesgesetz über die betriebliche Mitarbeitervorsorge*) in 2002. The main idea of this bill was to adapt the traditional severance pay scheme to modern work–life circumstances and to convert severance pay into supplementary private pensions that, in the long run, should serve as a sort of second pillar. Employers pay 1.53 per cent of monthly salary to special funds in charge of programme administration. All private sector employees (including apprentices and employees with marginal jobs) are covered under this programme from the first working day onwards. The benefit is due after the termination of the employment contract. Individuals can either draw a lump-sum payment equivalent to the accumulated capital or claim a pension. The latter option, however, is more appealing since no taxes are levied in this case.[21]

The third pillar of the future pension system will consist of subsidized individual savings. This pillar is based on public subsidies paid to private forms of saving such as life insurance. Payments up to €2,165 (2008) annually are publicly subsidized at a rate ranging from 8.5 to 13.5 per cent. In 2008, the subsidy rate was 9.5 per cent so that the maximum subsidy amounted to €205 per year. Contracts must have a policy period of at least 10 years and cannot be signed by a person aged 65 and over. In a manner similar to the pensions derived from the second pillar, the accumulated capital is tax-free unless the capital is claimed before the 10-year period. The take-up of this programme is high. In 2008, almost 1.2 million contracts have been closed.

1.3.4.2 LABOUR MARKET POLICY

While the statutory pension scheme was clearly subject to a third-order transformation, the reforms implemented in the realm of unemployment compensation were less far-reaching. Nevertheless, the measures enacted included second-order changes for the first time. In its first government programme, the coalition repeatedly heralded measures to eliminate fraud and to combat the misuse of unemployment benefits (see Government Programme 2000: 19, 24, 33). Closely connected to this approach was the announcement of the intention to improve the targeting of social benefits: 'Targeting of benefits is low and has to be subject to a permanent audit' (ibid.: 17, 23).

Overall, the ÖVP–FPÖ government has further intensified retrenchment. The first law passed in late 2000 modified the previous settlement in unemployment insurance in several respects: the surcharge for families was reduced by more than one-third, the net replacement rate of unemployment compensation was lowered to 55 per cent, the qualifying period was extended, and sanctions were tightened. The adjustment of benefits offered by unemployment insurance and unemployment assistance to wages and inflation was suspended. The government expected savings of €182 million resulting from this package. Moreover, the coverage of unemployment insurance declined since recipients of a subsistence benefit (*Beihilfe zur Deckung des Lebensunterhalts*) are no longer insured and do not qualify for unemployment compensation in this case.

---

[21] The payout of the accumulated capital is subject to a tax rate of 6 per cent.

The government also increased the pressure on the unemployed to accept a job. Regulations concerning suitable job offers and a reasonable time-span to commute to and from work were tightened. The so-called job protection clause (*Berufsschutz*), a provision preventing individuals being required to accept a job falling short of his or her skills, was limited to 100 days and supplemented by a system aiming to preserve previous salary levels (*Entgeltschutz*).[22] The latter, henceforth, guarantees 80 per cent of the salary underlying the calculation of unemployment compensation for the first 120 days of unemployment and is subsequently reduced to a floor of 75 per cent. In addition, unemployed individuals have to provide evidence of active engagement in job search. At the end of its second term in office, however, the government has, in part, resiled from retrenchment in this area, as a supplementary allowance was established to top-up the unemployment benefit for low-income groups.

Moreover, recent labour market policy has been increasingly shaped by European employment policies. The goals spelled out in the Lisbon agenda, such as activation, employability, and a higher labour market participation of women and older persons, have certainly influenced the recent reform trajectory, with the Open Method of Coordination serving as major transmission mechanism. Since the labour market participation of the elderly labour force is traditionally very low, and given the fact that the ÖVP–FPÖ government has radically curtailed early retirement, the government has enacted some measures to enhance the employment opportunities for this group. The main approach has been to reduce non-wage labour costs for the elderly, with females aged 56 + and males aged 58 + henceforth exempt from unemployment insurance contributions, which are covered by general funds devoted to labour market policy. Moreover, the ÖVP–FPÖ government has also increased expenditure devoted to active labour market policies. Special emphasis has been put on measures to improve the skills of women and to combat youth unemployment. With its Job Promotion Act passed in 2005, the government has finally made an attempt to create new jobs in the low-wage sector. The coalition introduced a so-called service check to create (legal) jobs in private households and to provide minimum social security for the home help. The service check can be bought at the tobacconist or post office. The price includes accident insurance (1.4 per cent) and administrative costs (0.6 per cent). The remuneration must not exceed a maximum of €456 (earning limit of €333 plus holiday compensation payment) per month. So far, however, the take-up rate has been low. Finally, the government paved the way for in-work benefits, albeit on an experimental basis only. The programme adopted consists of wage subsidies (*Kombi-Lohn*) paid to younger and elderly long-term unemployed who may receive half of their previous unemployment assistance as a subsidy in a

---

[22] This measure is one of the few examples for corporatist policy-making in the early 2000s.

new job up to a maximum of €1,000 per month. However, this measure turned out as ineffective as the take-up rate was extremely low.

1.3.4.3 HEALTH CARE

Cost containment was once again the major impetus for the reforms that have taken place in the health-care system. Out-of-pocket payments in case of hospitalization and prescription charges were raised, while a new co-payment for outpatient treatment in hospitals was established to redirect patients from hospitals to the outpatient sector. However, this new deductible was overruled by the Constitutional Court and the federal government finally was forced to drop it. Instead, the government proposed to impose co-payments of up to 20 per cent of medical treatment costs. However, this legal provision has so far not been enforced. Finally, the ÖVP–FPÖ government replaced the sickness insurance certificate by an e-card for which patients have to pay a so-called service fee of €10 per year. As a result of the ever-increasing co-payments, the share of private health expenditure as a percentage of total health expenditure has continuously increased. Though wage earners with very low income, pensioners, and children are exempt from many co-payments, the high share of private out-of-pocket expenditures has a clearly regressive impact, which, of course, is further strengthened by the fact that low-income groups face a greater risk of illness (Ziniel 2003).

The ÖVP–FPÖ coalition also intended to harmonize the contribution rates of blue- and white-collar workers. To achieve the latter goal, however, the contribution rate for white-collar workers was raised. Moreover, and in accordance with policies previously foreshadowed by the Grand Coalition, the contribution rate for old-age pensioners was raised. Finally, a new surcharge on health insurance was imposed for all insured to cope with the rising costs resulting from non-occupational injuries.

Some funding measures imposed by the ÖVP–FPÖ government led to a path departure in health insurance. First, free co-insurance for childless couples was abolished. However, married couples without children, but not those in heterosexual or homosexual partnerships, are entitled to a special contribution rate of 3.4 per cent. Second, the government deviated from the traditional principle that health insurance contributions are paid in equal parts by employers and employees. In an effort to reduce non-wage labour costs, the contribution rate for employers related to the health insurance of blue-collar workers was reduced. The ÖVP–FPÖ coalition also tinkered with the idea of replacing compulsory health insurance by an obligation for individuals to take out some kind of health insurance. This far-reaching proposal was rejected by an expert committee and, in consequence, abandoned by the government.

The financial consolidation of the health-care system was hampered by the fact that several of the funding reforms enacted by the government were overruled by the Constitutional Court. The major reason was that the rapid speed of legislation ('speed-kills') led to a poor quality of the bills passed by parliament (Mosler 2004). One of the failed measures related to a special health insurance contribution for old-age pensioners receiving additional pensions from public institutions. The Court also repealed the taxation of pensions drawn from accident insurance on the basis that this measure was adopted without a reasonable transition period. Finally, a reform of the compensation fund of health insurance carriers was declared unconstitutional in 2004.

Hospital funding was again a major site of reform activities. The state treaty of 1997 regulating the financing of the health-care system was prolonged for an additional 4 years in 2000 and finally replaced by a new state treaty in 2004 setting the basis for a major reform of the health-care system (the so-called *Gesundheitsreformgesetz* 2005). At its centre stood an organizational reform (involving the establishment of a Health Care Agency plus a Health Care Commission at the federal level and the establishment of nine Health Care Boards plus nine Health Care Platforms at the *Länder* level), the extension of performance-oriented reimbursement to the outpatient sector (at least in the long run), the integration of all health sectors into a single system of medical planning, efforts to reallocate the supply of medical services from the hospitals to the outpatient sector, quality management, and an electronic moderniza-tion of the health system. Moreover, the federal and the *Länder* governments agreed on cost-containment measures and revenue increases equivalent to €300 million in each case.

Enhancement of benefits has remained rare throughout this period. How-ever, the ÖVP–FPÖ coalition improved the social security of caregivers (e.g. pension insurance) and increased support for preventive medicine in the wake of the 2005 Health Care Reform Act.

1.3.4.4 FAMILY POLICY

The change of government was also paralleled by a conservative turnaround in family policy (Obinger and Tálos 2006). Family policy was a major issue in the general election of 1999. As previously mentioned, Austria was and still is facing very low fertility rates like most other continental countries. Even though there is strong evidence from comparative research that generous cash transfers and long leave periods are detrimental to fertility rates (Castles 2003), the centre-right government further strengthened the classic familialist policy trajectory. The most important measure in this respect was the replace-ment of the parental leave allowance by a universal childcare benefit. Parental leave originally was an insurance-based, that is, employment-related, benefit that guaranteed a lump-sum payment for parents who have paid unemploy-ment contributions for a certain period. This scheme was fiercely defended by the Social Democrats because it provided incentives for women to enter the labour force. Compared to the parental leave allowance, entitlement to the childcare benefit is detached from labour market participation and the maximum duration of entitlement has been increased from 1 year to 30 months where only one parent draws the benefit. If both parents take care of the children, the maximum duration is 3 years. In addition, the transfer payment and the ceiling for additional earned income have been raised. The new benefit offered a lump-sum payment of €436 per month and could be combined with earnings up to €14,600 per year.

This new approach was clearly conservative in nature as it was based on generous transfer payments and long leave periods, thus providing strong incentives for women to exit the labour market. Given the extremely low number of childcare facilities for children younger than 3 years, the childcare benefit was designed to bridge the gap caused by the lack of formal provision for this age cohort. At the same time, this policy was in line with the ideological orientation of both governing parties, which are strongly inclined to the notion that children under three should be raised by the family. It therefore comes as no surprise that no major efforts have been undertaken to enhance the provision of formal childcare arrangements.

During its second term of office, however, the government did enact some reforms to reconcile work and family life with measures aimed at making workplace arrangements more flexible. In 2004, the coalition launched a bill that introduced a right of part-time work for parents up to the seventh birthday of the child. Yet the legal right to part-time work was restricted to parents with an employment record of 3 years in companies with at least twenty employees. This means that about 30 per cent of wage earners are not covered by this legislation. Part-time work for reasons of child-raising for this group is only possible on the basis of negotiations with the employer.

In 2002, a so-called family hospice leave was introduced which allows wage earners to quit their job up to 6 months in order to nurse a severely sick or dying relative. However, this leave is unpaid[23] and those in homosexual partnerships are not entitled to avail themselves of such leave. Though the opposition criticized these provisions, the bill was unanimously passed by parliament.

Overall, the early 2000s marked a period of significant welfare state restructuring. By openly advocating retrenchment and showing little hesitation about coming into conflict with the trade unions, the centre-right coalition ignored 'new politics strategies' (Pierson 1994). However, the coalition paid a heavy price, since both parties suffered a series of significant electoral defeats at the *Länder* level. This holds in particular for the right-wing populist FPÖ, which came to power on a platform of appealing to the losers of globalization and disgruntled voters of the SPÖ. This loss of political support contributed, among other things, to the split of the Freedom Party into two camps in 2005.

---

[23] In cases of financial hardship, however, caregivers can apply for a special grant.

Jörg Haider founded the 'Alliance for the Future of Austria' (*Bündnis Zukunft Österreich*, BZÖ). Moreover, the ÖVP experienced a significant defeat in the general elections held in late 2006 when the party obtained only 34.3 per cent of the vote (2002: 42.3 per cent). The FPÖ gained 11 per cent of the vote and thus remained at the level to which the party was downsized in the general election of 2002 (in 1999 the FPÖ gained 27 per cent). Even though the BZÖ won seven seats in the National Council (equivalent to 4.1 per cent of the vote) in 2006, a continuation of the centre-right coalition was no longer viable given the severe tensions between FPÖ and BZÖ. Since the Social Democrats came out as the strongest party in 2006, a new Grand Coalition under Social Democratic auspices took office in January 2007.

1.3.5 Once again: a SPÖ–ÖVP government (2007–?)

Even though the economy was booming, the coalition has been ill-fated from the outset. Once in office, Social Democrats did not stick to core campaign pledges such as the abolition of university tuition fees. Moreover and very much akin to what had occurred in the late 1990s, the coalition parties obstructed each other in many policy areas, so that it came as no real surprise when the coalition finally collapsed midway through 2008. However, the Grand Coalition again took office after the general elections held in September 2008.

In its first government agenda (see Bundeskanzleramt 2007), the SPÖ–ÖVP coalition announced major reforms in several areas of the welfare state, most particularly health-care governance (including long-term care) and poverty alleviation. The programmatic focus on fighting poverty certainly marked the most significant programmatic change in comparison with the previous centre-right government. For example, the coalition reached a consensus to introduce a sort of means-tested basic income (*bedarfsorientierte Mindestsicherung*). This measure was to be supplemented by the introduction of a minimum wage of €1,000 per month, higher cash benefits offered by unemployment assistance for low-income groups and, finally, improvements in the social protection for those in atypical occupations, notably quasi-freelancers (Bundeskanzleramt 2007: 55, 108–10). In contrast, the government proposed no major changes in the pension system, as the few modifications they planned could be achieved without significant changes in the benefit and contribution regime. However, the government did announce its intention to set up an expert commission which would deliberate an overhaul of invalidity pensions and to increase the pressure on the *Länder* and municipalities to extend pension harmonization to their civil servants (Bundeskanzleramt 2007: 107–9). In the realm of family policy, the coalition agreed upon some modifications of the childcare benefit and announced its intention to extend the number and opening hours of childcare facilities and after-school care clubs. Other plans included a further liberalization of working-time regulations and a new codification of labour law. With an eye to the Danish flexicurity model, the coalition finally announced its wish to promote active labour market policy of a kind that would 'activate, encourage, and qualify the unemployed instead of administering them' (ibid.: 53–4).

1.3.5.1 FAMILY POLICY

The coalition agreed on a somewhat modified version of the childcare benefit introduced by the centre-right government in 2007. As an alternative to the existing maximum benefit duration of 3 years (with a monthly benefit level of €436), it became possible to receive a higher benefit for a shorter period. Three such variants were initially introduced, with, for example, a benefit of €798 per month if the benefit was claimed for 18 months only.[24]

Eventually, in 2009, the Grand Coalition introduced an earnings-related childcare benefit as a fourth alternative. This variant replaces 80 per cent of the last net salary for up to 14 months (with a ceiling of €2,000 and a minimum benefit of €1,000). With these measures the coalition sought to increase the freedom of choice for families on the one hand, and to improve the reconciliation of employment and family work on the other. The government also increased the family allowance for families with three or more children and relaxed the qualifying criteria to the so-called multiple-child bonus (*Mehrkinderzuschlag*) by lifting the income limits. Based on a new fiscal equalization regime valid from 2008 until 2013, the *Länder* and the federal government pledged to provide €60 million each during the period up to 2010 to increase the number of childcare facilities and to improve the language skills of (migrant) children.

Ironically, both parties suggested further initiatives in family policy after the breakdown of the coalition in July 2008. In the run-up to the general election held in September 2008 both parties sought to outperform each other in proposing new measures in this area. While the ÖVP proposed to disburse the family allowance thirteen times per year (this proposal was adopted by parliament a few days before the election date), both parties arrived at a consensus on introducing a cost-free and compulsory kindergarten year for 5-year-old children. The latter measure was passed by the Council of Ministers in May 2009. Henceforth the federal government will provide €70 million per year for this programme which is the responsibility of the *Länder*.

1.3.5.2 PENSIONS

The area in which the government was able to realize major parts of its agenda was poverty alleviation. In 2007, the minimum pension (equalization supplement or *Ausgleichszulage*) was increased to €726 (singles) and €1,091 (couples)

---

[24] In addition, the earnings limit up to which the benefit can be combined with paid employment was further lifted.

per month. Since inflation increased to a level unknown for many years, the federal government enacted a further benefit increase in 2008 and decided to pre-draw the price adjustment of pensions scheduled for 2009. Once again, this measure was adopted on the verge of the general elections in 2008. In addition, the government decided that the insured with long-term insurance records should be exempt from deductions in case of early retirement until 2010 and improved the social protection of caregivers by covering fictitious employer's pension contributions. However, the envisaged overhaul of invalidity pensions did not take place.

1.3.5.3 LABOUR MARKET POLICY

Since the 1990s, demand for low skilled labour has declined in the wake of technological changes and increased international competition. In consequence, the unemployment rate of the less-well-educated labour force continuously increased as did the number of atypical jobholders. The Grand Coalition was much more concerned about these developments than its predecessor in office. Already in 2007, the peak associations of the social partners agreed to establish a (gross) minimum wage of €1,000 per month for full-time employees. The implementation took place through collective agreements at the industry level. The minimum wage for part-time workers is calculated in proportion to their working time.

After protracted negotiations and as a part of its anti-poverty package, the government, social partners, and the nine *Länder* reached an agreement to introduce a uniform nationwide, albeit means-tested, minimum income scheme (the so-called *bedarfsorientierte Mindestsicherung*). The net benefit level was eventually fixed at €733 per month (paid twelve times per year).[25] Eligibility for employable people was tied to willingness to work and property or income is with few exceptions taken into account. In practice, this programme, therefore, means little more than a nationwide harmonization of the territorially fragmented social assistance benefits offered by the *Länder*. Based on a state treaty according to section 15a of the Federal Constitution, this programme should become effective from September 2010 onwards.

Unemployment insurance was revised in two important ways. In contrast to the early 2000s, the social partners, who had issued two white papers on labour market policy in 2006 and 2007, were strongly involved in the decision-making process.

First, employees with earnings up to €1,100 were to be, henceforth, exempted from contribution payments, whereas unemployment contribution

[25] Initially, the benefit level was fixed at €747 to be paid fourteen times a year. Due to ÖVP resistance the coalition agreed on a cutback of both the benefit level and the number of yearly payments in summer 2009. It is now up to the *Länder* to provide a thirteenth or fourteenth payment.

rates of employees with earnings between €1,100 and €1,350 per month were lowered. The resulting significant revenue shortage for unemployment insurance is covered by the federal budget. The government's main motive was to compensate for rising price inflation by higher net wages and, in consequence, to stabilize domestic consumption. Overall, this measure is a second-order policy change as it involves a new funding mechanism as well as a departure from the traditional funding parity in unemployment insurance since employers still have to pay the full contribution rate of 3 per cent.

Second, social protection of atypical workers was improved. This happened under the slogan of flexicurity. Quasi-freelancers (*freie Dienstnehmer*) were incorporated into compulsory unemployment insurance and coverage was extended to this group in other social insurance branches as well. Moreover, the self-employed were entitled to take out voluntary unemployment insurance (opting-in). At the same time, the government promoted labour market flexibilization. Based on a compromise reached by the social partners, the coalition implemented the announced deregulation of working time. This package included the lifting of normal work time up to 10 hours a day and a set of further measures aimed at deregulation. Compensatory measures remained rare and were mainly restricted to a new overtime supplement for part-time workers.

In its second government agenda published in late 2008, the Grand Coalition has agreed upon various active labour market policy measures to improve the skill levels of problem groups and (albeit with budgetary reservations) to introduce a minimum floor in unemployment insurance by increasing the replacement rate offered by unemployment compensation and the emergency benefit for low-income earners. The issue soon was put on the agenda against the backdrop of the global financial crisis in early 2009. However, the decision-making process was still in flux at the time of writing. However, parliament unanimously passed a reform package to cope with the crisis. The measures adopted include the extension of short time work to a maximum of 24 months, the establishment of a foundation to combat youth unemployment, modifications of partial retirement (*Altersteilzeit*), the introduction of a new combined wages model (*Kombi-Lohn*) and, finally, wage subsidies for small enterprises (i.e. the non-wage labour costs of the first newly hired employee are covered by the Labour Market Service).

1.3.5.4 HEALTH CARE

Health-related reform activities concentrated on long-term care in the beginning. Since 80 per cent of the people in need of care are living at home, households had often illegally employed (cheap) nursing staff from Eastern Europe. Under the label 'care emergency' (*Pflegenotstand*), this phenomenon was a major political issue in the run-up to the 2006 general election. The Grand Coalition responded to this problem with the so-called Home Care Act

(*Hausbetreuungsgesetz*), which provided the basis for the legal employment of qualified nursing staff in order to ensure round the clock (24 hours) care of severely handicapped persons in private households. Employment of a home help is financially supported by public grants under certain circumstances. For example, the income of the person in need of care is taken into account for eligibility. Based on a state treaty, the federal government and the *Länder* provide €40 million annually for this purpose. Further financial support is offered by a special fund for handicapped people under the Long-term Care Act. As a side effect, the government expected rising (legal) employment in the care sector.

In contrast, the envisaged reform of the health-care system more or less failed. The government was only able to reach an agreement with the *Länder* governments to continue the Health Care Reform Act of 2005 (see above). Pressure to act emerged from the fact that some sickness funds had accumulated substantial deficits. A reform proposal drafted by the social partners in early 2008 that was later adopted by the federal government, involving saving measures and the establishment of a holding company in charge of medical planning and financial control, was harshly criticized by the medical profession and, in consequence, led to a strike of doctors. Hence, the major reform impetus once more was to strengthen public control over the health-care system. The ensuing negotiations did not lead to a solution so that the entire reform failed in summer 2008. This was the icing on the cake in a long list of conflicts between the coalition parties. When the Social Democrats, battered by a series of electoral defeats at the *Länder* level, announced a U-turn in European integration policy, the Christian Democrats eventually ended the coalition in July 2008.

Overall, the social policy reforms launched by the first Grand Coalition in the new millennium are remarkably consistent in three respects. First, the bulk of measures adopted in the four policy areas under scrutiny led to welfare state expansion rather than retrenchment (Obinger 2009). This policy course was certainly facilitated by rapid economic growth and declining unemployment until the advent of the credit crunch in late 2008. In contrast, the reform proposals involving elements of cost containment such as the health-care reform failed. Second, most of the measures enacted explicitly or implicitly responded to new social risks. Examples include the reforms responding to the problems and challenges of long-term care, the measures designed to cope with higher poverty risks of low-income groups, and efforts to improve the social protection of atypical workers. The changes enacted in unemployment insurance also fit into this pattern. Third and finally, the mid-2000s have witnessed the comeback of the social partners in social politics. Several of the reforms based on pre-parliamentary compromises were reached by the peak associations of labour and capital. With the Social Democrats back in office it was no longer possible to bypass the trade unions. In addition to the changed political configuration, favourable economic performance facilitated cooperation and log-rolling in the pre-parliamentary arena.

The Grand Coalition's social policy course can be best understood as an attempt to deal with the consequences of the welfare state changes implemented by the centre-right coalition. Poverty alleviation neither was a relevant topic under the ÖVP–FPÖ government nor did the centre-right government undertake any major efforts to cushion the effects for atypical workers and low-income groups that resulted from the tightened contribution–benefit nexus in the pension system. However, while the return of the Social Democrats to power is a part of the explanation of the new turn in policy, the political left made no efforts to undo the structural reforms enacted by the preceding government. Apparently, the Social Democrats have accepted the necessity of far-reaching structural reforms (e.g. pension policy) and they were perhaps even grateful that somebody else had done this unpopular job for them, especially since, as a side effect, the unpopularity of doing it helped them to regain office.

In sum, the Grand Coalition's policy trajectory is not really surprising as it mirrors exactly the configuration underpinning the rapid welfare state expansion during the post-war period: cooperation between two basically pro-welfare state parties and closely affiliated interest organizations operating against a macroeconomic backdrop that allows for the distribution of productivity gains. The global financial crisis brought this short-lived boom to a sudden end. At the time of writing, it is unclear what the consequences of the crisis for the welfare state will be in the long run. As in many other countries, the recession has led to a huge budget deficit and, in consequence, will lead to rising levels of public debt in future. Along with the mounting social needs induced by the crisis this will almost certainly increase the pressure on cost containment in the years to come.

1.4 Patterns and driving forces of welfare state change

In retrospect, social policy development since the mid-1970s can be separated into four major phases almost exactly coincident with particular governmental constellations. The first phase lasted from 1970 to 1986 and was politically moulded by a Social Democratic hegemony. The following phase was framed by European integration, a remarkably changed international political economy and, in political terms, by a Grand Coalition. The advent of the third phase coincides with the centre-right government that took office in 2000, whereas the revival of the Grand Coalition 2007 once more went along with a change in social policy and politics. These phases are characterized by remarkable differences in scope, intensity and content of social policy reform, and strongly corroborate the notion concerning the specific reform sequences typical of

(a) Number of pensioners per 1,000 pension insured, 1971–2006 (5-year intervals)

(b) Female labour force as percentage of total labour force, 1948–2006 (10-year intervals)

Figure 1.3: Socio-economic changes, 1948/1971–2006

Source: Handbuch der österreichischen Sozialversicherung, Vienna (various issues).

the transformation of Bismarckian welfare states (Palier 2006, 2010; Palier and Martin 2008).

Socio-economic problem pressure was the most important factor triggering reform activities. Despite the fact that Austria's macroeconomic performance was better than in many other advanced democracies, the period examined is characterized by increasing socio-economic problem pressures over time. This holds true for the level of unemployment and, in particular, public debt. Moreover, demographic changes together with the spread of early retirement programmes led to an increasingly unfavourable relationship between the economically active population and pensioners (see Figure 1.3*a*). The greying of society and an extremely low effective retirement age not only put the already expensive pension system under strain, but also created new social risks as the number of frail elderly significantly increased. Given the continuously rising labour market participation of women (cf. Figure 1.3*b*), which is traditionally higher than in many other continental welfare states, but without reaching the employment levels of liberal and Nordic welfare regimes, pressure for public intervention in the area of long-term care increased. Finally, the number of atypical jobholders continuously increased albeit that the erosion of standard employment contracts occurred later and to a lower degree than in other western countries.

However, the impetus resulting from these changes in economy and society was structured and mediated by political and institutional variables, notably the partisan complexion of government, a permissive constitution, and existing welfare state patterns. Moreover, socio-economic problem pressure is also itself a product of political decisions taken in the past. In the 1970s, the left (successfully) managed the crisis by relying on deficit-financing, higher social security contributions, and various short-term measures such as labour shedding via early retirement programmes and labour hoarding. However, the pronounced reliance on these means caused negative feedback effects in later periods. While societal and economic changes created new social risks and pressures to adapt the antiquated regulations and principles enshrined in Bismarckian welfare state arrangements to changing realities, the political options and fiscal capacities available to policy-makers to respond to these demands continuously narrowed.

The reason was the remarkably changed domestic and international environment. Economic denationalization and European integration reinforced these developments, but are hardly the direct causes of welfare state transformation. These factors rather played an indirect role as they undoubtedly undercut the economic policy repertoire, and increasingly framed and channelled domestic, economic, and social policy discourses towards supply-side oriented policy conceptions. Examples include an emerging consensus on the need to stabilize non-wage labour costs and to strive for tax cuts and privatizations. The concrete measures to be taken for implementing these goals, however, were politically contested. The same holds for the measures by which the fiscal requirements imposed by the Treaty of Maastricht and, later on, the Stability and Growth Pact should be addressed. Again this was an indirect effect of European integration (Leibfried 2005), since these regulations only affected countries violating the fiscal criteria and which, in any case, do not legally bind countries to impose cutbacks in social policy.

However, given the sheer size of the welfare state in advanced democracies it is, however, highly probable that the welfare state will become a site of expenditure cutbacks. For the Austrian case, EU accession was, indeed, a lash for policy-makers to rein in the public debt accumulated since the 1970s, and which exceeded the critical thresholds spelled out in the Maastricht Treaty just at the time of EU accession. Even though the policy route taken to stabilize public finances was fiercely contested and led to the breakdown of the Grand Coalition in 1995, EU accession paved the way for welfare state retrenchment. Austrian EU membership was therefore a critical juncture that significantly affected social policy outcomes. Moreover, and arguably even more important in the long run, EU accession contributed to a shift in the balance of power between labour and capital and, in consequence, to a decline of corporatism irrespective of the return of social partnership in the very recent past.

What therefore distinguishes the four phases of welfare state change from each other is the scope and intensity of the reforms implemented, the underlying mode of decision-making, and the ways in which the mounting socio-economic problems were perceived and addressed. In addition, the policy choices and the associated policy outcomes in each phase had a strong impact on policy-making in subsequent periods (Table 1.1).

Table 1.1: Phases of social policy development in Austria, 1970–2009

Stimulus	Phase	Context	Diagnosis and therapy	Politics	Content of economic and social policy	Type of policy change (Hall)	Consequences
End of the 'Golden Age'	1970–86	Social Democratic single-party government and SPÖ–FPÖ coalition, relative economic success despite oil crisis	Welfare state as a automatic stabilizer in a period of crisis	Negotiation-based	Austro-Keynesianism, expansion of the welfare state, labour shedding via early retirement, labour hoarding in state-run industry, higher social security contributions	First- and second-order changes	Low unemployment but mounting public debt, labour market problems were masked and shifted to the pension system
Consequences of phase 1	1987–99 (Two sub-periods with EU membership in 1995 as a watershed)	Grand Coalition, rising public debt and unemployment, de facto collapse of state-run industry	Modernizing and adapting the welfare state and the economy to a new (international) environment	Negotiation-based with declining role of corporatism in the 1990s	Moderate supply-side course in economic policy, benefit-contribution nexus was tightened, co-payments (health care), long-term care allowance, balanced reforms	First- and second-order changes	Mounting public debt, far-reaching structural reform failed because of conflicts within Grand Coalition and social partners
		EU membership and EMU formation	Cost containment to meet convergence criteria (since mid-1990s)		Predominance of benefit cutbacks since EU accession	Second-order changes	
Consequences of phase 2	2000–6	Centre-right government committed to neo-liberal agenda and debt	Structural reforms to make the welfare state viable in a more competitive environment: containment of	Majority rule to bypass veto power of unions, big-bang strategy ('speed-kills')	Pronounced supply-side oriented course, multi-pillarization and harmonization of pension, activation of	Third-order changes	Pronounced supply-side orientation, dualization between insiders and outsiders, recommodification,

						First- and second-order changes	
		containment, EMU and European single market, EU eastern enlargement	non-wage labour costs, better targeting of benefits needed, deregulation and flexibilization		unemployed, neo-conservative family policy		higher inequality in the long run
Consequences of phase 3	2007–9	Grand Coalition, economic boom but high inflation (until 2008), global credit crunch	Compensating the losers of previous social policy reform, compebnsation for price inflation, and labour market problems caused by the global credit crunch	Negotiation-based	Various measures to cope with poverty and new social risks, continuation of supply-side economic and labour market policies ('flexicurity'), failure of health-care reform	First- and second-order changes	Funding problems of health-care system unsolved, mounting public debt resulting from global recession

Source: adapted from Obinger and Tálos (2010); cf. Palier (2010).

The 1970s were characterized by an expansion of social benefits under a left single party government. The economic repercussions of the oil crisis were relatively successfully managed with coordinated policies and strongly buffered by the welfare state. Full employment was the prime goal of the left-wing cabinet and this goal was achieved by means of a broadly Keynesian economic strategy. Financing problems of the welfare state were mainly addressed by raising social security contributions. This strategy of muddling through, however, imposed heavy burdens on the succeeding cabinets, notably in fiscal policy. Welfare state expansion came to an end with the short-lived SPÖ–FPÖ government (1983–6), which simultaneously marked the cross over to the second phase in which welfare state retrenchment began to exert a real influence in Austria.

This second period was shaped by a renewed Grand Coalition and lasted from 1987 to 1999. Framed by mounting public debt, deep changes in the international political economy and EU accession in 1995, the room of manoeuvre in fiscal and monetary policy was significantly constrained. In consequence, the Grand Coalition bid farewell to Austro-Keynesianism and adopted a moderate supply-side-oriented course in economic policy. Nevertheless, the incumbency of the SPÖ–ÖVP government can be divided into two sub-periods with EU accession as the major watershed. Until the mid-1990s, mostly balanced reforms were legislated in social policy. Expansion measures such as the introduction of the long-term care allowance and enhanced family cash benefits actually outweighed benefit cuts, albeit at the expense of soaring public debt. The imperative of budget stabilization in the shadow of the Treaty of Maastricht led to progressively larger benefit cuts in the second half of the 1990s. Despite their restrictive impact on beneficiaries, the reforms enacted in this sub-period were highly path-dependent and can be classified as first- and second-order changes according to Peter Hall's three-staged typology of policy change (Hall 1993). Apart from the fact that ideological differences between the governing parties hampered a fundamental change of the status quo, this outcome was also a result of corporatism. Though the Austrian *Sozialpartnerschaft* showed symptoms of decline, corporatism nevertheless remained basically intact in the 1990s (Tálos 2005*b*, 2008). Since the major peak associations of labour and capital traditionally were the gatekeepers of the existing Bismarckian social welfare system, and because trade unions remained strong enough to block more radical reforms, corporatism was a key factor accounting for the path-dependent reforms legislated by the Grand Coalition.

The third period is also connected to a particular governmental constellation. The political deadlock under the previous Grand Coalition led to dramatic electoral losses for the SPÖ and the ÖVP in 1999. The business-wing and the neo-conservatives[26] within the People's Party seized the opportunity and

---

[26] Note that the architects of this coalition including Wolfgang Schüssel and Andreas Khol were pushed aside when a new Grand Coalition was established in 2007.

formed a coalition with Jörg Haider's FPÖ in 2000. In an effort to bring about a paradigm shift in economic policy towards a pronounced supply-side strategy, social policy was subordinated to labour market flexibility, structural competitiveness, and debt containment. This move was also a response to the EU eastern enlargement. Even though Austria's export economy and financial sector massively benefited from EU enlargement, it was at the same time perceived as a threat since north-eastern Austria was now surrounded by low-wage and low-tax economies. In order to achieve these goals, however, the government had to change the rules of the game. Hence, the negotiation-based adjustment path characterizing previous periods was abandoned. Instead, the ÖVP–FPÖ coalition increasingly relied on majority decisions and deviated from corporatist policy-making in order to bypass the informal veto power held by the trade unions under this setting. Based on a 'big-bang' strategy (Starke 2008) with the slogan 'speed-kills' as the basic leitmotif of policy change, the ÖVP–FPÖ government quickly launched a series of far-reaching reforms that for the first time included third-order changes in particular sectors of the welfare state. What therefore distinguishes the ÖVP–FPÖ government from its predecessors is not only the depth and scope of the reforms enacted, but also the politics of social policy-making.

The 'reform sequence hypothesis' advanced by Bruno Palier (2006) as well as the importance of the partisan complexion of government for explaining social policy outcomes is corroborated by the social policy reforms enacted by the incumbent Grand Coalition since 2007. Even though it is perhaps too early to speak of a new phase in social policy given the cabinet's short term in office, this fourth period witnessed the end of retrenchment. Policy change was motivated by attempts to cushion the consequences of the reforms adopted by the preceding centre-right government. Further stimulated by socio-economic problem pressures such as inflation and demographics, the measures adopted mainly focused on long-term care and marginalized groups of welfare recipients at high risk of poverty. A balanced distribution of power resources in government, a recurrence of corporatism and, until 2008, a booming economy paved the way for a moderate expansion of the welfare state. The supply-side turn in economic and labour market policy remained unchanged, however. While the government and social partners increasingly became committed to a flexicurity approach in labour market policy, inheritance tax as well as capital transfer tax were phased-out in July 2008 in the wake of a ruling of the Constitutional Court. Even the OECD warned that the 'abolition of the inheritance tax and other wealth-related taxes such as the gift tax should be reconsidered' (OECD 2007b: 172).

Though the four periods described so far are discernible in all policy fields examined in this volume, not all sectors of the welfare state have undergone as deep a transformation as the Austrian *pension system*. Financial considerations in the first place but also demographic changes and changed political priorities have been significant factors accounting for this transformation. Despite

73

differences in the scope of the various reform activities and their increasingly restrictive impact on benefits over time, the changes effected by both the SPÖ–FPÖ coalition and the SPÖ–ÖVP government were largely path-dependent in character and therefore failed to achieve any fundamental shift in the traditional approach taken in this field. The centre-right government also imposed a broad range of benefit cutbacks, but it succeeded in combining retrenchment with an overhaul of the pension system leading to substantial changes in structural and organizational arrangements, the spectrum of benefits, and the underlying goals enshrined in the hitherto existing system. More specifically, the traditional state-centrist pension system with public pensions accounting for more than 90 per cent of all old-age benefits was transformed into a multi-pillar system. This transformation was accompanied by a rollback of the pronounced occupational fragmentation enshrined in the previous system and a stronger accentuation of the equivalence principle, with pension credits connected to periods devoted to child-raising as major exception. Though the recent reforms will only take effect in the long run, it can already be concluded that the Austrian pension system has been subject to a third-order change in recent years.

The *health-care system*, in contrast, has not been subject to any fundamental reform over the past three decades. Cost containment was the main impetus for various reform activities, which mainly included first and, to a lesser extent, second-order changes. The political response seeking to address the cost-explosion in the health sector has been to enhance revenues by increasing contribution rates and co-payments, and to strengthen public control over the health-care system. The latter approach comprised a restructuring of hospital financing and measures to improve hospital planning in order to reduce overcapacities in this sector. Given the jurisdictional split in this sector, most reforms were based on negotiations between the federal government and *Länder* executives. Moreover, this policy-style was also prevalent during the period of Grand Coalition cabinets. The centre-right government, by contrast, announced its intention of enacting more fundamental reforms. However, some of these efforts were overruled by the Constitutional Court. Although the Austrian health-care system still contains solidaristic elements and strongly crowds-out markets, recent years have weakened these features. The prime example is the increase in private health-care financing resulting from escalating co-payments and deductibles.

Unemployment insurance was further expanded in the 1970s when unemployment was virtually non-existent in Austria. Full employment ceased to exist in the early 1980s, however. The rise in unemployment in the 1980s and changes in employment patterns fuelled a series of reforms which increasingly became more restrictive over time. More specifically, the development of unemployment insurance since the early 1980s can be separated into two phases. Once again, EU accession in the mid-1990s marked the crucial turning point. While reforms of unemployment insurance combined selective improvements with modest benefit cuts until the early 1990s, retrenchment clearly prevailed in the subsequent period. Cutbacks of social benefits were paralleled by tighter quali-fying conditions and stricter sanctions. The ÖVP–FPÖ government has further intensified this policy approach. In a manner similar to many other Western countries, and not least because of European Union stimuli, activation and active labour market policies have been strengthened, whereas passive benefits have been subject to cutbacks. Retrenchment of cash benefits came to a halt under the Grand Coalition which together with the social partners promoted 'flexicurity' as the overriding goal of labour market policy.

Family policy has been clearly expanded over the past 30 years. However, this expansion has by and large followed the traditional familialist policy trajectory with its strong emphasis on monetary transfers. A slight path departure occurred under the Social Democratic single party government, whereas the Grand Coalition cabinets could not agree on a joint course of action in this field and therefore enacted path-dependent, that is, transfer-oriented policies. The major exception refers to increased efforts in the late 1990s to enhance the extent of childcare facilities. Yet this policy was short-lived and came to a grinding halt in 2000. Since then the centre-right cabinet has further strengthened the classic male breadwinner model. With the exception of a right for part-time work for parents, the measures adopted, such as the new universal childcare benefit, are mainly based on traditional population policies encouraging women to leave the labour force. The government's frequent rhetoric of freedom of choice for families has been more window dressing than a reality, as the centre-right coalition did not make any major effort to increase the number of childcare facilities. The incumbent Grand Coalition, by contrast, agreed upon a flexibilization of the childcare benefit and increased efforts to enhance institutional childcare facilities by means of public grants.

If we compare the four phases with regard to the role of political actors, we can conclude that parties do matter in accordance with partisan theory. The most pronounced policy shifts occurred under a left single party government in the 1970s and under a centre-right coalition in the 2000s. Whereas the left single party government not only refrained from welfare state retrenchment but even enhanced the reach, and to some extent remodelled the make-up of the welfare state within just a few years, the centre-right coalition likewise rapidly imposed a series of structural reforms which included also major benefit cutbacks. However, the content of social reforms and the extent to which parties have shaped social policy is conditioned by economic circumstances, the policy legacy of the past, and partisan veto players. In the first half of the 1970s, the left benefited from a low-level of debt and a prospering economy. The welfare state was expanded and enriched with some Social Democratic elements but without undercutting its traditional Bismarckian contours. The Social Democratic single party government bequeathed not only a more generous welfare state, but also a significantly increased level of debt, higher social contribution rates, mounting structural problems in the nationalized industry sector, as well as a series of myopic policy measures that were enacted to cope with the crisis in the wake of the oil shocks. Early retirement programmes and labour hoarding created an ever-increasing fiscal pressure on the government which was further increased by the collapse of large parts of the state-run sector.

The Grand Coalition started to deal with some of these problems and took a new line in economic policy. However, due to considerable ideological differences between both party camps and their allied interest organizations, the social policy reforms adopted did not go beyond first-order changes in most cases. The compromise achieved was based on balanced reforms and included benefit cutbacks and, mainly as a response to societal changes, the introduction of new benefits. While the Grand Coalition initiated a change in course towards supply-side oriented in economic policies, it failed to cope with ballooning public debt. EU accession finally forced the Grand Coalition to adopt a tighter approach in fiscal policy. As a consequence, Social and Christian Democrats imposed two comprehensive austerity packages and paved the way for second-order social policy changes in which restrictive measures prevailed. Tensions between both parties and the social partners increased, while welfare state retrenchment undercut political support for the coalition. It was right-wing populist Jörg Haider who benefited most from this situation. The rise of the Freedom Party brought about a change in government in 2000. For the first time in the Second Republic, a centre-right coalition came to power. Given the relatively small ideological distance between Christian Democrats and the Freedom Party in economic and social policy, the coalition imposed far-reaching reforms which included third-order policy changes. Finally, the return of the Grand Coalition in 2007 once more brought a policy change as the coalition set the course for welfare state expansion against the backdrop of a booming economy and a revival of corporatism.

The strong impact of parties detected in this chapter is a corollary of a permissive constitution. At first glance, Austria's system of government seems to be veto-ridden. As shown above, however, the Constitutional Court is the only institution that holds real veto power and whose rulings exerted a considerable impact on pensions (e.g. higher retirement age for women), health care (abrogation of several funding measures such as the taxation of benefits from accident insurance), and family policy (e.g. reintroduction of dual system of income support to families). The impact of federalism is mainly restricted to family policy, social assistance, and the health-care system where the division of jurisdiction either was a source of mounting cost (health care), due to the duplication of efforts with regard to hospitals and medical equipment, or prevented coordination between cash provision and social services (family policy). The policy route taken in the health sector was therefore to increase public control over the health-care system in order to reduce oversupply in the hospital sector. Policy change was typically negotiated between the executives of different branches of government. Where family policy is concerned, the juris-dictional divide between cash benefits (federal competency) and social services (*Länder* competency) along with the incongruent political complexion of govern-ment at both levels of government is certainly a reason for the shortcomings with respect to childcare facilities for toddlers. The only way for the federal government to intervene in the field of social services is to use its spending power in order to provide subsidies to the constituent units which — with the exception of Vienna[27] — are typically controlled by the Christian Democrats.

Even though the Austrian Federal Constitution provides various instruments of direct democracy, the impact of direct democracy on social policy outcomes is negligible (Müller 1998). Binding referendums are rarely practised (e.g. EU refer-endum), whereas other types of direct democracy are blunt instruments that either are initiated by the federal government or — as it is the case for the popular initiative — can be easily overruled by parliament. Contrary to the situation in Switzerland, direct democracy does not offer real veto powers to the people.

1.5 Austria: still a Bismarckian welfare state?

Did the social policy changes enacted since the early 1970s lead to a transform-ation of the Austrian welfare state and, in consequence, a departure from the traditional Bismarckian make-up of the welfare state? If we put the evidence together, social policy development over the past four decades is characterized by Janus-faced reforms which have strengthened some aspects of the Bismarckian legacy enshrined in the Austrian welfare state but have also weakened others.

A first example of a path departure refers to the occupational fragmentation of the welfare state which has to a considerable extent been diminished. The prime example is the introduction of a unified pension system in 2005 which now includes (federal) civil servants. A similar development took place in health insurance, where differences between the blue- and white-collar workers in terms of benefits (with few exceptions) and contribution rates have been removed. Irrespective of these achievements, important differences remain with regard to contribution rates and co-payments related to health insurance as between the bulk of the insured covered by the General Social Insurance Act and farmers, civil servants, and the self-employed.

Other health-care-related reforms can be seen as more ambiguously related to the question of whether or not the Bismarckian legacy was reinforced. One example is the introduction of long-term care insurance in 1993. On the one hand, this programme is universal and financed from the general budget.

---

[27] It comes as no surprise that Vienna has the highest coverage of institutional childcare facilities in Austria.

Moreover, the benefits it provides are not income-related but rather provided as lump-sum payments contingent on the scope of care, seemingly indicative of a clear departure from the traditional welfare state set-up. On the other hand, this programme reinforces the role of the family in social provision, since its main objective is to compensate for (additional) care-related costs and to remunerate the efforts of caregivers, that is, women.[28] At the same time, it is often overlooked that this programme has also strengthened the service orientation of the welfare state, because the *Länder* have agreed to establish a nationwide supply of nursing services until 2010. A second Janus-faced example is the abolition of contribution-free co-insurance for childless couples. While this measure indicates a break with previously existing Bismarckian principles, the matrimonial principle was again privileged by the reform, since married couples (but not other forms of partnership) are entitled to a special health insurance contribution rate to insure the non-gainfully employed partner.

The shift towards a multi-pillar pension system unambiguously marks a further path departure from the traditional way of doing things. Two aspects are of particular relevance. One is a shift in the public–private mix towards private and therefore less redistributive forms of benefit provision (Castles and Obinger 2007); the other results from the *de facto* departure from the idea that public pensions should secure previously achieved standards of living. Even though the statutory pension system guarantees about 80 per cent of the average income earned over a 45-year period, a very high replacement rate in comparative perspective (OECD 2007a), it is clear that future pensions can no longer guarantee status preservation for the increasing number of people with atypical work careers. Moreover, benefit indexation has been detached from wage development as pensions are henceforth to be indexed with reference to the consumer price index.

Finally, labour market policy clearly deviated from the traditional approach of providing cash benefits. Activation of unemployed and other active measures gained importance over time, while cash benefits have been reduced and qualifying conditions tightened. Financing is another example of a path departure since older employees and low-income earners are either exempted from contribution payments or have to pay lower contribution rates. The revenue shortfall is covered by public funds with a view to reducing the non-wage labour costs of these problem groups. In addition, measures such as wage subsidies and the service check are indicative of efforts to create jobs in the low-wage sector. Finally, working-time flexibility was increased. However, these measures were counterbalanced by the inclusion of atypical workers into social insurance and extended employment rights for this group (Bock-Schappelwein and Mühlberger 2008).

---

[28] The same can be said for the family hospice leave. Given the gender asymmetry in pay, it is very likely that it will be mainly females who withdraw from the labour market to nurse close relatives.

Regardless of these examples, there is evidence that the Bismarckian roots of the Austrian welfare state have in other respects been reinforced. The most important example of path-conforming adaptation is the tightening of the contribution–benefit nexus, which has largely been achieved via the accentuation of the equivalence principle. Pensions, for example, are henceforth to be calculated on the basis of an individual's lifetime contribution record, whereas benefit calculation was based on the five 'best' contribution years in the early 1980s. Recommodification through strengthening the equivalence principle is also a major trend in unemployment insurance.

Family policy is still very much attuned to the assumptions of the classic male breadwinner model. Indeed, it is arguable that the familialist approach has been reinforced in the early 2000s, when the centre-right government strengthened the traditional modality of Austrian family policy which is based on a combination of long spells of leave periods with very generous cash benefits. The prime instance of a conservative U-turn in family policy was the new universal childcare benefit, which replaced the employment-related parental leave scheme. Only recently and only modestly has this neo-conservative approach been revoked by the new Social-Democratic-led Grand Coalition.

Despite recent attempts to establish new modes of funding welfare expenditure, the Bismarckian legacy has been preserved in terms of welfare state financing. The four phases of social policy development are also mirrored in this area. As outlined above, various governments responded to the mounting economic and labour market problems with increases in social security contributions until the mid-1990s. As a result, both the share of social security contributions as a percentage of total tax revenues and the contribution/GDP ratio reached an all-time high in 1995 (OECD 2006a). Against the backdrop of the supply-side turn in economic policy and EU accession, the stabilization of non-wage labour costs gained increasing importance in the political debate. Increased efforts to curtail social security contributions along with a series of benefit cutbacks contributed to a trend reversal in the late 1990s. Nevertheless, social security contributions continue to represent by far the most important pillar in welfare state financing.

In sum, the most pronounced structural changes have occurred in the pension system and labour market policy. In contrast, health care and family policy have mainly been subject to recalibration without any fundamental restructuring, so that the basic principles underlying traditional welfare state provision have not fundamentally changed. Taking all policy sectors together, the contemporary Austrian welfare state still manifests salient Bismarckian traits. However, the contemporary arrangement of social security should not be seen simply as a frozen landscape inherited from the past, but rather as what might properly best be described as a 'partially defrosted' Bismarckian welfare state.

2

Denmark: The Survival of a Social Democratic Welfare State

2.1 Introduction

According to the efficiency hypothesis, the high-spending, high-tax Danish welfare state should be under considerable strain in the era of globalization and socio-economic modernization. And indeed, the Danish welfare state has seen a lot of changes in the last three decades. Most of these changes, however, have not been in line with the expectations of the efficiency thesis. The universal and generous nature of the system has largely been preserved. Furthermore, Denmark has been able to overcome a major socio-economic crisis without relinquishing its commitment to the Scandinavian welfare model. The current cyclical crisis stems from a huge decline in exports. As a consequence, unemployment escalated in the first half of 2009. However, because of its previously excellent labour market performance, Denmark still has one of the lowest unemployment rates in the European Union (EU). But it has not been always like that. In earlier decades, high levels of unemployment and economic constraints subjected the Danish welfare state to very considerable strain.

In this chapter, we elaborate welfare state changes in four policy sectors in the years from 1973 onwards. That year has been chosen as the starting point because, for Denmark, it marks a watershed — in at least three important ways. First of all, like most Western welfare states, Denmark was hit hard by the first oil crisis. The economy shrank, the unemployment rate went up sharply, price inflation peaked at double-digit levels, and there was a marked balance-of-payment deficit that lasted throughout the 1980s. Secondly, in 1973, Denmark joined the European Commission (EC). From the very beginning, membership was controversial and has remained so. In total, six referenda have been held in connection with EC/EU membership (see Annex). As a consequence, Denmark remains outside of the EMU (i.e. retains its national currency, the *Krone*) and has opted out of certain aspects of EU judicial cooperation. A third event represents a break: as a result of the so-called earthquake election in December 1973, the

80

previously stable party system — centred on a dominant Social Democratic party — disintegrated. Five additional parties acquired parliamentary seats. As a result, coalition governments without a stable majority in parliament became the rule, leading to an unusual degree of political instability as these governments were no 'majority governments in disguise', relying on varying coalitions of support at different times and in relation to different policies (Strøm 1990: 198). The frequency of elections also increased markedly: between 1973 and 1993 alone, Danish voters went to the polls nine times.

During the entire period under investigation, minority governments were the rule (see Table 2.1). The big change that marked the beginning of the period was in the partisan composition of government. Until 1973, the Danish party system[1] followed the typical Scandinavian pattern with a dominant Social Democratic party (the *Socialdemokratiet* in the Danish case), a smaller Socialist or Communist party (the *Socialistisk Folkeparti* in parliament since 1960, *Kommunistiske Parti* until 1960), two bourgeois parties (*Konservative Folkeparti* and *Venstre*) representing farmers and the urban middle class, and a party that both has been in left- as well as right-wing governments, the Social Liberal Party (*Radikale Venstre*) representing urban intellectuals, teachers, etc. With the earthquake election of 1973, the populist Progress Party (*Fremskridtspartiet*), the Centre Democrats (*Centrumdemokraterne*), the Socialist People's Party (*Socialistisk Folkeparti*), the Christian People's Party (*Kristendemokraterne*), and the Communists (*Danmarks Kommunistiske Parti*) entered parliament. Despite the increasing fragmentation of the party system, the Social Democrats remained the largest parliamentary party until 2001, as it had been continuously from 1924 onwards, and held office almost continuously from 1924 to 1982 (with only one exception, from 1973 to 1975). Nonetheless, from the 1970s onwards, the significance of small (centrist) parties increased as they frequently held the key to power. In the early 1990s, for example, the Social Liberal Party (RV) deserted the centre-right government of which it had been a member in favour of a coalition with the Social Democratic Party, helping the latter into office (see Table 2.1).

---

[1] The principal Danish parties are: *Socialdemokratiet i Danmark*, Social Democrats (SD) established in 1871; *Det Konservative Folkeparti* (prior Højre), Conservative Party (KF) established in (1876) 1915; *Venstre, Danmarks liberale parti*, Liberals (V) established in 1870; *Socialistisk Folkeparti*, Socialists (SF) established in 1959; *Radikale Venstre*, Social Liberals (RV) established in 1905; *Retsforbundet*, Centrist Liberals (RF) established in 1919 (they no longer run for parliament); *Kommunistiske Parti*, Communists (DKP) established in 1920; *Venstresocialisterne*, Left-Wing Socialists (VS) established in 1967; *Kristeligt Folkeparti/Kristendemokraterne*, Christian Democrats (KrF) established in 1970; *Fremskridtspartiet*, a right-wing protest party (FrP) established in 1972; *Centrumdemokraterne*, Centre Democrats (CD) established in 1973 (defunct); *Socialistisk Arbejderparti*, trotskyist Socialist Workers Party (SAP) established in 1980; *Fælles Kurs*, left-wing party (communists) (FK) established in 1987 (defunct); *Enhedslisten*, Red–Green Alliance established in 1989 originally an alliance of DKP, SAP, and VS; *Dansk Folkeparti*, right-wing populist party (DF) established in 1995; and *Liberal Alliance* (earlier *Ny Alliance*), right-leaning Social Liberal Party (LA) established in 2007.

Table 2.1: Governments and elections in Denmark, 1973–2009

Government (name of prime minister)	Election	Term in office	Coalition[a]	Type of government
Jens Otto Krag IV	21.09.1971	11.10.1971–05.10.1972	SD	Minority
Anker Jørgensen I		05.10.1972–19.12.1973	SD	Minority
Poul Hartling	04.12.1973	19.12.1973–13.02.1975	V	Minority
Anker Jørgensen II	09.01.1975	13.02.1975–30.08.1978	SD	Minority
Anker Jørgensen III	15.02.1977	30.08.1978–26.10.1979	SD & V	Minority
Anker Jørgensen IV	23.10.1979	26.10.1979–30.12.1981	SD	Minority
Anker Jørgensen V	08.12.1981	30.12.1981–10.09.1982	SD	Minority
Poul Schlüter I	10.01.1984	10.09.1982–10.09.1987	KF, V, CD, & KrF	Minority
Poul Schlüter II	08.09.1987	10.09.1987–03.06.1988	KF, V, CD, & KrF	Minority
Poul Schlüter III	10.05.1988	03.06.1988–18.12.1990	KF, V, & RV	Minority
Poul Schlüter IV	12.12.1990	18.12.1990–25.01.1993	KF & V	Minority
Poul Nyrup Rasmussen I		25.01.1993–27.09.1994	SD, RV, CD, & KrF	Majority
Poul Nyrup Rasmussen II	21.09.1994	27.09.1994–30.12.1996	SD, RV, & CD	Minority
Poul Nyrup Rasmussen III		30.12.1996–23.03.1998	SD & RV	Minority
Poul Nyrup Rasmussen IV	11.03.1998	23.03.1998–27.11.2001	SD & RV	Minority
Anders Fogh Rasmussen I	20.11.2001	27.11.2001–18.02.2005	V & KF	Minority
Anders Fogh Rasmussen II	08.02.2005	18.02.2005–23.11.2007	V & KF	Minority
Anders Fogh Rasmussen III	13.11.2007	23.11.2007–05.04.2009	V & KF	Minority
Lars Løkke Rasmussen		05.04.2009–?	V & KF	Minority

[a] See Footnote 1.
Source: Own compilation.

At first sight, Denmark looks like a country without major institutional veto players — Denmark's parliamentary monarchy does not have an influential Constitutional Court nor does the monarch exercise executive power. However, due to the emergence of coalition governments, the number of partisan veto players has increased. Moreover, actors which are not fully fledged constitutional veto players influence Danish policy-making. In case of minority governments, the parties in opposition can shape legislative policy output to a significant extent. Not surprisingly, minority governments are seen as one reason for the consensual policy-making style in Denmark (Due et al. 1994; Jørgensen 2002; Schmidt-Hansen and Kaspersen 2004). It is also the case that Danish corporatist relationships are traditionally marked by close cooperation between state and centralized interest organizations. The main social partners (above all *Landsorganisation i Danmark*, LO, the peak organization of the Danish trade unions and *Dansk Arbejdsgiverforening*, DA, the umbrella organization of employers), for instance, regularly participate in reform commissions. Arguably, consensual policy-making has an influence on welfare state reform. Thus, rather than radical welfare state reform, the need to find a compromise suggests the likelihood of incremental change.

Moreover, because counties and municipalities are the main providers of health-care and social services for children and the elderly, much welfare policy in Denmark requires cooperation between the central government and local authorities. In order to administer these services, counties and municipalities can levy their own taxes. In addition, they receive bloc grants from the central government.[2] These are annually negotiated between the national government and local authorities, represented by two centralized interest groups: Local Government Denmark (*Kommunernes Landsforeningen*, KL) and Danish Regions (*Amtsrådsforeningen*, ARF). In 2007, a so-called Structural Reform was enacted reducing the number of municipalities from 273 to 98 and replacing the thirteen existing counties with five regions. While the counties previously had the right to raise taxes, the newly established regions do not.

In conjunction, minority governments, social partnership, and decentralization limit the government's room for manoeuvre. Despite this and due to the widespread willingness to cooperate and the small size of the political elite, political actors have been regularly able to overcome these institutional hurdles and to react swiftly to new challenges.

Before analysing the reform policies of the last 30 years, we will briefly describe the formation and subsequent development of the Danish welfare state. These formative years, as will be shown, not only shaped the institutional set-up of the Danish welfare state but also shaped attitudes towards the welfare state. The encompassing welfare state satisfies the demands not only of the needy but also of the middle classes (Rothstein 2000), underpinning their

---

[2] Subsidies from the national government are the largest source of funding of local services.

strong solidarity towards the welfare state. This legacy of cross-class support limited the range of possible reforms during the period under investigation.

2.2 The history of the Danish welfare state

In what follows, we will describe the three main phases of welfare state development in Denmark: the formative phase (1891–1924), the consolidation period in the interwar years, and the 'Golden Age' expansion between 1945 and 1970.

2.2.1 Formative phase

Denmark was a welfare state pioneer. The first legislation on social policy was passed at the end of the nineteenth century: the Poor Law and the law on old-age pensions in 1891. Everybody above the age of 60 then became entitled to a means-tested old-age benefit (*alderdomsunderstøttelse*). Eligibility criteria and benefit levels were left to the municipalities. However, the state provided funding to the municipalities. In 1892, the Health Insurance Law was implemented. The state recognized former privately organized health funds, but although the organizational set-up was largely left intact, tax-financed public grants were given to the sickness funds under certain specified conditions. Associations were only allowed to accept members from the specified occupational groups, but, at the same time, had to accept unemployed or unskilled workers. In a similar vein, the Unemployment Benefit Law of 1907 recognized prior private unemployment insurance schemes but introduced tax-financed public grants to supplement their funding. In the following years, the discretionary elements in the Danish welfare state were reduced and statutory social rights were established. In 1922, for example, the means-tested old-age benefit (*alderdomsunderstøttelse*) was transformed into a defined benefit system (*aldersrente*),[3] co-financed by state and municipal taxes. Gradually, the state took over responsibility. Thus, the voluntary insurance associations (*kasser*)[4] run by trade unions were replaced or supplemented by statutory schemes.

   The formation of the Danish welfare state must be seen against the backdrop of the evolution of the trade union movement on the one hand and of the development of an urban–rural coalition on the other. From the early beginnings, the development of social rights was linked to the labour movement. Although Denmark was a late industrializer, the institutionalization of industrial

---

[3] With the pension age raised to 65 years.
[4] The *kasser* were tied to trade unions and hence, membership was sectoral. The underlying principle was the insurance principle. Thus, the individual became a member of a voluntary collective organization which insured against the risk of becoming dependent on public relief in case of accident, sickness, or unemployment.

relations occurred relatively early. In 1899, employers' organizations and trade unions agreed on mutual recognition and a system of centralized bargaining in the so-called September Compromise. This major event was the consequence of the so-called Big Lockout. The strengthening of social rights can be seen as a direct response to labour conflicts. During the 3-month lockout, workers received help not only from workers in neighbouring countries but also from farmers (Due et al. 1994). This support enabled workers to demonstrate their power vis-à-vis the employers' organizations which, as it turned out, had over-estimated their own strength. The backing of the workers by the farmers helped to bridge the urban–rural cleavage (Rokkan 1994) and, as in other Scandinavian countries, this 'red–green alliance' remained an important factor underpinning the further development of the welfare state. Gøsta Esping-Andersen (1990) notes that during the first half of the twentieth century, all the Scandinavian welfare states owed something to this alliance which imposed universalist demands on the ruling elites. Improving social rights irrespective of labour market status was also in the interest of the small and medium peasants in Scandinavia. Petersen (1985) shows that, in the constitution of the Danish pension system, political decision-makers deliberately decided against taking over the German 'Bismarckian' system, because, amongst other things, they disliked employer contributions and the compulsory character of social insurance provision. It was in the farmers' interest — the core constituency of the Liberal Party — to benefit from the developing social insurance but to avoid paying for it (Petersen 1985).

2.2.2 Interwar consolidation — the Steincke reforms

After their 1924 electoral success, the Social Democrat-led government established social policy as a separate policy field by setting up the Ministry of Social Affairs. In 1933, the Minister of Social Affairs, K. K. Steincke, passed major reforms aimed at improving bureaucratic efficiency, establishing binding rules of financing, and further shifting social benefits from administrative discretion to statutory rights. The reform amalgamated fifty-five different laws and regulations into four laws: (*a*) the Unemployment Insurance Act, (*b*) the Accident Insurance Act, (*c*) the National Insurance Act, which included health insurance as well as disability insurance and old-age pensions, and (*d*) the Social Assistance Act which covered all remaining contingencies. This legislation made membership in a health insurance fund as well as in an old-age pension fund obligatory. State subsidies were the major revenue source for both funds. It is noteworthy that the structural settings of the health insurance funds remained virtually unchanged for almost four decades (until 1970).

Until the Second World War, the Danish welfare state was characterized by the insurance principle (Christensen 1998; Jonasen 2006). Pensions and health insurance were declared mandatory for people with incomes below a certain threshold, while unemployment insurance remained voluntary and organized on the basis of the Ghent system. Membership in the union-run unemployment scheme (*a-kasser*) was a precondition of the right to receive a benefit. Apart from members' contributions, however, tax-financed public subsidies represented an important share of funding. By 1993, about 40 per cent of unemployment benefit expenditure was derived from state subsidies (Arbejdsdirektoratet 2007).

2.2.3 The 'Golden Age'

Against the backdrop of economic modernization and Social Democratic dominance, Denmark significantly expanded its welfare state in the 'Golden Age'. As in the other OECD countries, this period from 1950 to 1973, was characterized by high rates of economic growth and increasing living standards. From 1953[5] to 1970, all eight governments were minority governments led by Social Democrats. In this period, numerous laws were passed, establishing a universal, encompassing 'Social Democratic' welfare state (Esping-Andersen 1990).[6] The rapid expansion of social protection after the Second World War is illustrated by the growth of public social expenditure from around 10 per cent of GDP in the late 1940s to 17–18 per cent of GDP by the end of the 1960s (Greve 1999: 45). Nor was it only the Social Democrats who supported the welfare state (Christensen 1998). Given the good economic situation, the Liberals advocated a universal welfare state as early as 1953 in order to serve their agrarian clientele (cf. Petersen 1985), while the Social Democrats still defended the traditional *kasser*-system until the 1960s. Nevertheless, the main trend of this period was the universalization of social protection. In both old-age pensions and in health care, the prior systems (*kasser*) were replaced by universal public schemes on the basis of citizenship rather than membership and contribution record.

In 1956, the universal *old-age pension* (*Folkepensionen*) was introduced. Prior to this major reform, pension entitlement had been conditional on health insurance membership. Now all Danes above the age of 67 years became entitled to a flat-rate basic amount independent of their previous labour market attachment. For the full benefit, 40 years of residence in Denmark was also necessary. Further reform occurred in 1964. Benefit levels were improved and an income-tested supplement as well as a supplementary labour market pension (*Arbejdsmarkedets Tillægspension*, ATP) was introduced.

---

[5] In 1953, a new constitution was enacted abolishing the former two-chamber parliament with the *Folketing* now consisting of 174 representatives elected in their constituencies and 2 representatives each for Greenland and for the Faroe Islands.

[6] Esping-Andersen classifies Denmark as an outlier of the Social Democratic welfare regime: 'Denmark is a more traditional heavily petit bourgeois society in which the social democrats have pursued a significantly more moderate political programme' (Esping-Andersen 1980: 4), see also Section 2.2.4.

The ATP is a fully funded, defined contribution scheme. Nevertheless, the Danish ATP never achieved the same importance as its Swedish counterpart. As was also the case in respect of the first-tier public old-age pension, the ATP entitlement age was 67 years.

The traditional system of *health insurance* was gradually replaced by a universal National Health Service between 1970 and 1973 and delegated to the counties. As part of a broader reform of the municipalities' and counties' task, a broad majority in the parliament acknowledged the reform proposal of the Social Democratic government. The Danish National Health Care Service was a fully tax-financed and universal scheme granting free-of-charge access to comprehensive provision to all citizens.[7] Counties were given responsibility for financing and service provision. Because hospital services were municipally run, doctors and nurses in the hospitals were public employees. Counties raised their own taxes and received annually negotiated state subsidies. General practitioners operated as gatekeepers to the system. They acted as private entrepreneurs in accordance with agreements between their professional organization and the Health Insurance Negotiating Committee, receiving fixed prices for their services as well as activity-based reimbursements.

In contrast to the developments in pensions and health care, Danish *unemployment insurance* remained voluntary and organized according to the *Ghent principle* with state-approved, union-run funds (*a-kasser*). By 1970, there were sixty-three different unemployment insurance funds — based on industry sectors — with around 800,000 members in total. The uninsured have to rely on a means-tested social assistance scheme administered by the municipalities. In 1968, the financing rules of unemployment insurance were changed. As a result, the biggest share of financing came from state subsidies (Arbejdsdirektoratet 2007). In addition, the members paid an administration contribution which varied across funds. In 1969, a public employment service was established to reduce mismatch problems in the labour market. In 1970, the rules for state approval of unemployment insurance funds were tightened, while membership criteria were loosened. Benefits accounted for 90 per cent of previous income, up to a maximum level. The Ghent system is generally assumed to be one reason for the high level of trade union density in Denmark (Due and Madsen 2007).

Another important feature of the Danish welfare state that emerged during the 'Golden Age' was an activist *family policy*. Due to the economic boom of the 1950s and 1960s, demand for labour, including female and immigrant labour,

---

[7] However, in contradistinction to universalist principles, two types of membership remained: group A and group B. For an additional fee, people in group B had direct access to specialists and hospitals as well as free choice of a GP, while group A-members were limited in their choice of a GP.

grew and unemployment decreased.[8] In order to integrate women into the labour market and to enhance education for all children, childcare was expanded early on. From 1946 onwards, the scope of public childcare services was expanded beyond children from poor families (whose mothers had to work) to all children. In 1965, the distinction between well-off and underprivileged children was abolished, making public childcare truly universal. Moreover, the 1964 Child and Youth Care Act regulated the quality of crèches and kindergartens by stipulating uniform national rules regarding the personnel–child ratio and opening hours. In 1967, paid maternity leave was introduced. In total, 14 weeks of maternity leave were granted, starting 8 weeks before birth. While public childcare was significantly expanded, the Danish paid maternal leave period remained fairly short compared to the other Scandinavian countries.

In summary, welfare state reform during the 'Golden Age' established the principle of universalism across virtually all programmes. In the major fields of social policy, schemes moved from the insurance type towards broader coverage, higher benefits, a wider range of risks covered, and more tax-financing. As a consequence, we can describe the *status quo* of the Danish welfare state at the end of the 'Golden Age' as universal and generous.

2.2.4 The Danish welfare state — a Social Democratic model

In Esping-Andersen's famous typology (1990) Denmark is classified as a country representing a Social Democratic welfare state regime. This type of welfare state is characterized by universal, tax-financed transfer payments and comprehensive, high-quality social services caring for children and elderly people, and others. As already noted, the universal welfare system helped to insure the solidarity of the middle classes (Baldwin 1990; Rothstein 2000): 'All benefit; all are dependent; and all will presumably feel obliged to pay' (Esping-Andersen 1990: 28). In order to maximize independence from the market ('decommodification') and the family ('de-familialization'), benefits were generous and based predominantly on citizenship rights (Arter 1999; Kvist 1999; Green-Pedersen et al. 2004). The state was directly responsible for the delivery of welfare either as transfer payments (e.g. old-age pensions, child allowances) or as high-quality social services (e.g. public childcare, hospitals). State intervention was seen as a means of redistributing income.

Moreover, the Scandinavian regime was 'committed to a full-employment guarantee and entirely dependent on its attainment' (Esping-Andersen 1990: 28). The welfare state took over caring responsibilities in order to advance women's labour market integration not only through services but also through

---

[8] From 1950 to 1960 unemployment decreased from 3 to 1.7 per cent and further to 0.9 per cent in 1973 (Danmarks Statistik 2001).

family transfers and leave regulation. Furthermore, the large share of public sector employment created additional demand for female labour. Overall, the Danish welfare state was praised for its women-friendly policy (Hernes 1987). Despite the dominant role of the state, cooperation between state and social partners was a key aspect of the Scandinavian model of welfare. This was true not only in respect of wage bargaining, but also of welfare state programmes, for example, the voluntary unemployment insurance scheme (Mailand 2009).

However, the institutional set-up of the Danish Welfare state differs from the ideal typical description of the Social Democratic welfare state regime,[9] because in the 1950s and 1960s the other Scandinavian countries and especially Denmark's neighbours, Sweden and Norway, expanded their basic security systems towards earnings-related provisions, whereas in Denmark old-age pensions remained a flat-rate benefit (Korpi 2002). Still, Denmark resembles the Social Democratic model, for example in the extent of its social service provision, and therefore differs from the Liberal model (e.g. United Kingdom). Moreover, in terms of generosity, Scruggs and Allan (2006) in their reanalysis of Esping-Andersen's decommodification scores show that in 1980 benefit generosity index is high in Denmark although with considerable variation between the different schemes.

As our later analysis shows, the main elements of the Social Democratic welfare state have been preserved despite some retrenchment and restructuring.

2.3 Welfare state reform since the early 1970s

2.3.1 Anker Jørgensen (1973–82) — a period of economic and political crisis

While the 1950s and 1960s were a period of welfare state expansion and economic prosperity, the 1970s were characterized by political conflict and economic crisis. In March 1970, the incumbent Social Democratic government presented a report which advised against further welfare state expansion on grounds of the overall trend of public expenditure development which was seen as problematic (Perspektivplanlægning 1970–85; Friisberg 1978). Instead, the report proposed a reduction in public expenditures as well as a halt to tax increases. This marked the end of the 'Golden Age'. However, the real turning point was the year 1973. The context of social policy-making was then affected by at least three events: the first oil price shock, the earthquake election, and Denmark's accession to the European Community.

After the first oil price shock, all Western welfare states confronted economic problems. In Denmark, a sudden terms-of-trade deterioration by about

---

[9] For example, in a publication of 1989 Gøsta Esping-Andersen himself says that Denmark approximates the 'liberal' model (Esping-Andersen 1989).

15 per cent (Johansen 1986) led to soaring unemployment and inflation, negative growth, and an increasing balance-of-payments deficit. However, the poor performance of the Danish economy was not only a consequence of recessive trends in the world economy but also of poor governance. The incumbent Social Democratic-led government attempted a classic Keynesian strategy, but failed to forge a viable compromise with the social partners. The government shied away from forcing the unions to adopt a moderate wage policy or from interfering in the pricing policy of business. A price–wage spiral was set in motion when in 1973 nominal wages increased by 20 per cent in just 1 year (Nannestad and Green-Pedersen 2008). A coordinated strategy could not be achieved since the social partners proved unable to agree on wage restraint, while the government failed to intervene directly in wage-setting.

Although the close link between the Social Democrats and trade unions would have led to expectations of successful cooperation, their relationship was strained by the failure of the Social Democratic-led government to put into practice the concept of 'Economic Democracy' (*Økonomisk Demokrati*, ØD). ØD was a kind of 'market socialism', consisting of two key ideas: (*a*) democratic management of each productive enterprise by work councils and (*b*) democratic management of capital investment by a collective fund. Neither the idea of 'Economic Democracy' nor the conflict over its introduction was specific to the Danish case as we find similar developments in Sweden around the same time. Overall, Denmark's inability to implement a viable Keynesian strategy in the face of economic crisis seems 'to contradict Katzenstein's thesis that small, open countries adapted more easily to the economic shocks of the period than did larger countries' (Nannestad and Green-Pedersen 2008: 35).

Moreover, Denmark's accession to the European Community in 1973 fuelled the political crisis. In contrast to Norway, where membership failed in a referendum, the Danish people voted with a majority of 63.3 per cent in favour of membership in 1972. Nevertheless, Euroscepticism remained strong. The day after the referendum, the Social Democratic Prime Minister Jens Otto Krag stepped down due to intra-party dissent (Mørch 2001). The strongly pro-European Krag had had a hard time in his party because almost half of the Social Democrats and almost all parties of the left had been against Denmark's accession. Anker Jørgensen took over as prime minister and Social Democratic leader.

Jørgensen's government was soon shaken by the 'earthquake election' of December 1973. The Social Democrats lost twenty-four seats and were not able to find the necessary support in parliament to stay in office (see Annex). Still, the succeeding government under the heading of the Liberal Poul Hartling was only short-lived and Anker Jørgensen was back in office with a Social Democratic minority government as early as 1975. The main problems of the Liberal government had been its limited parliamentary support (only 22 members out of 179) and its unstable support base in parliament. Although the

Liberals were able to increase their share of seats in 1975 by twenty, they were not able to form a government again. Instead, Anker Jørgensen established a Social Democratic minority government supported by the Social Liberals and the Socialist Party. But even though the Social Democrats were able to increase their share of seats in parliament from forty-six in 1973 to sixty-eight in 1979 (thereby almost reaching their pre-crisis level of seventy seats in 1971, see Annex), they were always dependent on the support of more than one opposition party. As a consequence, throughout the 1970s, we find weak governments whose ability to implement coherent economic and social policies was restricted.

The first oil shock did not immediately lead to a new economic policy because the government expected the crisis to be short term only. Only in the second half of its term did the Jørgensen government finally apply a broader range of economic policy instruments. Overall, the response had a broadly Keynesian character. From 1976 onwards, the Social Democrats finally started to intervene in wage-setting. Moreover, incremental currency devaluations and fiscal expansion were aimed at kick-starting the economy. 'Fiscal and budgetary policy increasingly aimed at replacing "import heavy" consumption by labour intensive consumption. In practice this meant curbing private consumption (which is import intensive) in favour of expanding public employment and consumption (which is labour intensive)' (Nannestad 1991: 169). On the revenue side, the VAT rate was lifted from 15 to 18 per cent and then 22.25 per cent between 1977 and 1979 and an energy tax was also introduced.

However, the economic crisis did not come to an end. The failure to improve economic performance weakened the Social Democratic government. New elections were called in 1981 in which the Social Democrats lost ten seats. After less than 9 months in government, the fifth Anker Jørgensen government stepped down and Poul Schlüter from the Conservative Party took over as head of a new centre-right coalition government without calling for new elections (see Table 2.1).

2.3.1.1 LABOUR MARKET POLICY

Despite the difficult economic situation, major welfare reforms did not take place in the 1970s. Especially at the beginning of the crisis, unemployment was seen as a temporary phenomenon. Still, numerous minor changes were implemented in labour market policy. In sum, they eased the conditions of unemployment insurance benefit receipt. The dominant policies of that time involved a cushioning of periods of unemployment through generous cash transfers as well as by measures to reduce labour supply (Cox 1998). By the end of 1978, a further new programme was introduced: the job-offer programme (*jobtilbudsordning*), which guaranteed unemployed people public employment or subsidized work. In virtue of these measures, the long-term unemployed became entitled to 9 months of work in the public or private sector. This can be regarded as a first step towards activation. 'However, the main motivation was to prevent the long-term unemployed from dropping out of the unemployment insurance system due to the rule that all benefit claimants must have had at least 26 weeks of work within the last 3 years' (Torfing 1999: 13). Some people in the welfare administration called these job offers an 'unemployment benefit generator', because, in practice, they allowed almost infinite benefit receipt (Bogedan 2009). From 1980, a job offer was offered after 1 year of unemployment instead of at the end of the 3-year benefits period as before. It was renamed *arbejdstilbudsordning* (ATB) and extended to training and retraining measures.

An early retirement scheme (*efterlønsordning*) was introduced in 1979, allowing people over 60 to leave the labour market and receive a benefit equivalent to an unemployment benefit. Benefit receipt was tied to a contribution record of at least 10 years. As early as in 1979, 41,000 persons were on early retirement benefits (Pedersen 2007).

2.3.1.2 PENSIONS

Further developments in old-age pensions were overshadowed by the dispute over 'Economic Democracy' (ØD) mentioned earlier. Due to employers' fear of 'ØD through the backdoor', Denmark — in contrast to Sweden, for instance — never adopted a major earnings-related system on a pay-as-you-go (PAYG) basis. Instead — as will be shown in Section 2.3.2 — funded schemes were developed. The Danish version of second-tier pension ATP could never secure the same sort of standard of living for the elderly as it did in Sweden. Yet, despite persisting calls for a supplementary scheme guaranteeing more equivalence to previous income, the trade unions preferred a pension based on a collective investment fund in line with the ØD philosophy, whereas the employers favoured an additional Swedish-style PAYG scheme. A reform commission (*pensionsreform-sarbejdsgruppe*) was set up which included the social partners. In 1977, the commission proposed three reform options for the second pillar: First, things should stay as they were, second, there should be a further supplementary pension based on length of contributory record or, third, there should be an earnings-related supplementary pension similar to the Swedish ATP. Thomas Nielsen, the head of the trade unions' peak body (LO), favoured the second option as it would not close the door on an eventual adoption of ØD. It came as no surprise that this provoked the opposition of the employers' organization (Dansk Arbejdsgiverforening, DA). As a result, the commission proved unable to agree on a single scheme (Due and Madsen 2003), while the government was unwilling to impose a solution against the wishes of the trade unions.

In retrospect, this non-decision had major unintended consequences for the development of pensions. 'By 1980, two-thirds of the Danish working population had access to the national pension only, which offered replacement rates of only one-third of wages for many groups' (Green-Pedersen 2007: 455). From this starting point, private occupational pension arrangements were spreading steadily. Moreover, in some sectors of the economy (initially, especially in the public sector), additional pension schemes were made subject to collective agreements. Gradually, the Danish pension system was transformed into a three-pillar system, consisting of the basic public first-pillar pension, the second-pillar labour market pensions agreed upon by social partners, and various forms of private old-age provision as the third pillar.

2.3.1.3 HEALTH CARE

The universal National Health Service had only just been implemented by the early 1970s and its subsequent development can best be described as consolidation. One aspect of that consolidation was an increased degree of decentralization. However, the national government sought to keep control over this development. Thus, among other things, the counties' annual hospital development plans had to be approved by the Ministry of Health. These plans were rather technocratic and focused on detailed proposals concerning how hospitals should go about achieving their allotted tasks. Health promotion was high on the political agenda, too, and it was debated in connection with better working conditions. To this end, a new agency, the Occupational Health Service was established in 1975. Its task was mainly to monitor occupational health and safety at the national level and to provide specific advice to firms.

From 1980 onwards, hospital services, which were run by the counties, became subject to very tight budgetary control. State grants to counties changed from the principle of covering hospitals' expenses to general grants based on negotiations between the central government and counties' representatives (ARF). Counties were to be responsible for an efficient allocation of resources. In contrast, expenditure on primary health care and pharmaceuticals was more difficult to control owing to the independence of general practitioners (GPs).

2.3.1.4 FAMILY POLICY

Cost containment was the order of the day in family policy, too, but as demand for family services grew markedly, the overall result was mixed. In 1976, cost containment for childcare institutions was agreed upon by the government and the local authorities in their annual budget negotiations (Petersen 1998). However, since the increasing participation of women in the labour market made more day-care places necessary, additional day-care places were established in 1976, based on a recommendation of the Social Reform Commission. In total, 2,000 kindergartens and 1,000 after-school care clubs and crèches were established. The state guaranteed the municipalities that they would be reimbursed for up to 50 per cent of the total costs. In order to attain both aims — cost control and better coverage — the ratio of qualified personnel to children was lowered, resulting in larger groups and poorer service quality. However, following strong protests, qualitative standards were again raised from 1978 onwards. Between 1978 and 1980, the government developed standards for day care in order to guarantee a minimum quality across the country.

Already in the 1960s, the increase in female labour force participation and changing gender roles lead to a change in family patterns: Birth rates decreased, the age of women giving birth to their first child increased as did the number of divorces. The male breadwinner model was eroded and was gradually replaced by the new dual-earner family model. Moreover, this cultural change took place despite rising unemployment in the 1970s. In consequence, the need for public childcare increased markedly.

In 1977, the Jørgensen government transformed the universal family allow-ance into an income-tested benefit with the aim of reducing spending. This option was preferred to an opposition proposal of an across-the-board cut of 10 per cent. Moreover, the Social Democrats wanted to increase redistribution with the new scheme which was part of the tax system and limited benefits for the well-off. From 1980, the universal maternity leave was extended by another 4 weeks of leave immediately after birth. The benefit level was equal to the sickness benefit and amounted to 80 per cent of previous earnings in 1980. Overall, the Danish family policy at the beginning of the 1980s had a triangular structure: (*a*) cash benefits for families with children, (*b*) comprehensive provi-sion of state-run day-care institutions for children, and (*c*) maternity and par-ental leave with generous income compensation.

Taken together, the social policy developments during Anker Jørgensen's time in office were rather contradictory. On the one hand, the economic crisis and budget constraints led to cutbacks in family and health policy. On the other hand, the crisis was widely seen as a temporary phenomenon. Thus, unemploy-ment benefits were enhanced in order to cushion the effects on wage earners. It was only by the end of the Social Democratic term in office (and after the second oil crisis) that the awareness of the magnitude of the economic prob-lems facing Denmark grew. At the same time, the Social Democratic minority government increasingly failed to find majorities in parliament. When their proposal for further economic measures failed in 1982, Anker Jørgensen resigned and was replaced by the conservative Poul Schlüter. While the Social Democrats had hoped that Schlüter would be prime minister for a short tran-sition period only, he remained in office for the next 10 years.

2.3.2 Poul Schlüter (1982–93) — from the brink of the abyss to the politics of cost containment

The conservative Poul Schlüter formed a minority government in 1982, consisting of four parties: the Conservative Party, the Liberals, the Centre

Democrats, and the small Christian Party. Moreover, the Social Liberals played a decisive role for the survival of the government. Due to their position at the centre of the political spectrum, their role has often been that of a 'kingmaker'. On occasions, they have chosen to support the Social Democrats (as in the subsequent government), at other times, they have given support to governments of the centre-right. This time, Poul Schlüter's close relationship to the Social Liberal leader Niels Helveg Petersen helped to get the necessary parliamentary majority for what became known as a 'Four-Leaf-Clover' minority government. Not only did the Social Liberals help form the Schlüter government, they also brought it to an end when they withdrew their support a decade later.

The 1980s were by no means a period of political stability: '[T]hroughout the 1980s, Denmark was governed by different coalitions of bourgeois parties and most of the time these minority governments could not rely on stable support from other parties in all policy areas' (Binderkrantz 2003: 288). This constant search for parliamentary majorities also meant that the government often made major policy concessions to opposition parties, including the Social Democrats. All in all, the Schlüter years were 'golden times' for the centrist parties, which not only participated in government but were also influential in terms of policies. The new focus of decision-making was also apparent in the relationship between the government and trade unions, who were often excluded from decision-making during this period (Due and Madsen 2003). The government moved towards a less consensual style of policy-making (Damgaard 1989) by excluding trade unions and — to a lesser degree — employers' organizations from policy formation.

The need to find support for their policies in the parliament forced them to make concessions especially in the field of welfare policies. Nevertheless, in contrast to his predecessors, Schlüter did not retreat in the cases when he was overruled by the opposition especially in defence and foreign policy (Miller 1996).

In economic terms, when Poul Schlüter came to power in 1982, it was widely believed that Denmark was standing 'on the brink of the abyss'[10] (Nannestad 1991), a picture used by several politicians of the time. Denmark was suffering from the repercussions of the second oil crisis — with inflation, unemployment, budget deficit, and the balance-of-payments deficit all running high — but as early as in the period between 1983 and 1987, the country began to enjoy something of an economic recovery. Economic growth rates increased and unemployment declined. Moreover, on this occasion, in contrast to the aftermath of the first oil

---

[10] The term was first coined by the Social Democratic Minister of Finance Knud Heinesen in 1979. Additional measures such as the car-free Sundays introduced in the aftermath of the second oil crisis produced a sense of crisis in the public. The succeeding Conservative Prime Minister Poul Schlüter used this perception of crisis to legitimate otherwise unpopular reforms.

shock, inflation was brought under control. This development was a result of both more favourable international trends and domestic economic policies. Soon after entering office, the government enacted a crisis package, which, for the first time, broke with the earlier Keynesian paradigm. Its central aim was to create a business-friendly climate in order to stimulate employment growth in the private sector. In October 1982, eleven bills were introduced in parliament which, among other things, abolished the automatic price index-ation of wages (*dyrtidsregulering*) and introduced a waiting day for sickness benefits.

Social Democrats and trade unions strongly opposed the government's economic and social policies. This culminated in the 1985 collective bargaining round ending without a result. The unions' demand for a 5 per cent wage increase was ignored by the employers' side and a general strike, one of the worst industrial disputes in Denmark since the Second World War, followed. The government eventually intervened and proposed wage increases of 2 per cent in the first year and 1.5 per cent in the second. Furthermore, mandatory pension savings for all employees with an annual income above DKK150,000 were introduced[11] in order to avoid overheating the economy. At the same time, the government proposed reducing the employers' social insurance contribution rate by 1.5 per cent while raising corporation tax rate from 40 to 50 per cent. Further economic measures followed in 1986: The Easter package (*påskepakken*) and, in October, the 'potato cure' (*kartoffel-kuren*). The first included higher luxury taxes, which led to protest from the conservative clien-tele. The second reduced tax deductions for private loans, thereby particularly affecting home buyers.

Despite the government's intervention, economic problems returned in 1987. 'The severe deterioration in the balance of payments, reaching its maximum deficit of about 5 per cent of GNP in 1986, triggered political measures that abruptly and quite literally turned a number of the previous years' economic trends upside down' (Nannestad and Green-Pedersen 2008: 45). Between 1987 and 1992, economic growth remained particularly low and unemployment once again increased.

European integration remained divisive in Danish politics. In 1992, the Danish people in a referendum rejected the Maastricht Treaty by a small margin (40.5 per cent in favour, 41.7 per cent against) creating a crisis at the European level. The issue could only be resolved by the Edinburgh Agreement of Decem-ber 1992 that granted Denmark various opt-out clauses. This agreement was ratified by the Danish people in 1993.

However, it was neither the state of the economy nor the European issue that brought down the Schlüter government but rather a scandal concerning the

---

[11] At the time, the fixed exchange rate of Danish kroner to Deutsche Mark (DKK100 equalize approximately DM26), US$1 = DKK6.44.

treatment of Sri Lankan refugees.[12] A decade of conservative rule abruptly came to an end when Poul Schlüter assumed responsibility for the scandal and resigned in January 1993.

2.3.2.1 LABOUR MARKET POLICY

The turn towards supply-side economic policies was also reflected in the Schlüter government's main labour market reforms, the character of which was coloured by the general policy of cost containment of the 1980s. With unemployment still increasing at the beginning of the Schlüter government's term in office, the problem of long-term unemployment also became more acute. Thus, in 1982, the government altered the law on job offers (*arbejdstilbudsloven, ATB-loven*), initially introduced in 1978. A 2-month training period for the long-term unemployed was created and benefits for people under the age of 25 years were cut back to encourage the take-up of job training. Thanks to the economic upswing, unemployment indeed started to fall as did the number of those participating in the job offer scheme. Between 1983 and the end of the 1980s, the number of people covered by such measures was almost halved.

Further reform continued in the following years. On the revenue side, employers' and employees' contributions to the labour market fund were raised. On the benefit side, the maximum nominal unemployment benefit level was not adjusted to rising prices between 1982 and 1986, which meant a *de facto* benefit cut. In 1985, the young unemployed had to endure even greater benefit cuts. On balance, the Schlüter government's measures on unemployment insurance amounted to substantial cutbacks (Green-Pedersen 2002). At the same time, a shift towards more active policies took place. Instead of the former 'second job offer' policy that prevented people from losing their benefit entitlements by offering them public or private sector jobs, a new 'training offer' was introduced. Those who did not get back into work after their first job offer (ATB) were now entitled to training. This move was also driven by skill shortages in the mid-1980s, since decreasing unemployment revealed the necessity for further skills formation. From 1986, the new right to take up training was further expanded by giving the unemployed a wider choice of training measures such as continuous vocational training and vocational training for the younger unemployed. However, participation in training notwithstanding, people had to stay available for labour market participation.

Even so, the reduction of labour supply was an important strategy for coping with mass unemployment. Thus, in 1992, a new scheme was unveiled entitling

---

[12] The reunion of families from Sri Lanka was put on hold at the end of the 1980s, and refugees who had been living in Denmark for no longer than 2 years were sent home. Known as 'Tamilen-Scandal', this violation of the Aliens Act by the Minister of Justice Erik Ninn-Hansen and his protection by Poul Schlüter occasioned the first impeachment proceedings in Denmark in 80 years.

long-time members of unemployment insurance between 55 and 59 years of age to a special 'transition benefit'. Furthermore, from the age of 60, they could receive an early retirement benefit (*efterløn*). These measures were a result of compromise as an earlier governmental plan to make older unemployed dependent on social assistance benefits had failed due to the resistance of the trade unions and most of the parliamentary parties.

Unemployment benefits nevertheless remained one of the biggest single items in the budget. In 1991, a commission was appointed to address this issue and presented its recommendations in a report claiming that 'the challenges and pressures to the Danish welfare model, which can be summarized under the headings of structural unemployment and structural competitiveness, force us to make a shift from the safety-net model to a trampoline model' (Torfing 1999: 15). For the commission, this implied stronger activation of the unemployed through further education and qualification. Interestingly, the commission's proposals also helped to secure the support of the trade unions for the tightening of benefit eligibility that was eventually enacted by the succeeding Social Democratic-led majority government in January 1993 (see Section 2.3.3 for details).

2.3.2.2 PENSIONS

The lack of an earnings-related pension supplement drove the debate about the future of the old-age pension system. When LO President Nielsen stepped down in 1982, the ØD project was finally buried. Still, no major restructuring of the Danish pension system could be agreed on. An important attempt to solve the pension issue had been the establishment of a joint commission of LO and Social Democrats. Among other things, it proposed universal occupational pensions. In the course of the 1984 budget debate, the Liberal Minister of Finance, Henning Christoffersen, recommended the introduction of occupational pensions to be agreed upon by the social partners. His intention was to prevent high wage increases and to encourage long-term savings (Due and Madsen 2003). Fears on the part of the employers' association (DA) of an 'ØD through the back door' had gradually faded, but the employers would still have preferred a private pension system. Again no legislative changes were achieved.

In contrast, significant developments took place at the level of collective agreements. The diffusion of occupational pension schemes on the basis of collective agreements that had already started in the previous decade gained momentum in the Schlüter years. As early as in 1985, 20 per cent of the labour force was already covered by such schemes and by the late 1980s a point of no return was passed. Especially with the 1989 agreement on occupational pensions for municipal civil servants, this new path in pension policy was deepened. The government welcomed these decentralized solutions and encouraged the social partners to continue. In 1991, two big branches, the manufacturing sector and the building industry, joined the trend (Due and Madsen 2003). In the 1993 rounds, occupational pensions were further consolidated.

Overall, these schemes, which can be regarded as pathbreaking from a long-term perspective (Andersen and Larsen 2002), mark an important turning point in the Danish pension system. They established a supplementary scheme alongside the existing universal public old-age pension. The new pillar was based on earnings-related benefits that reflected status differences. The occupational pensions were defined contribution schemes, which meant that no guarantees were made regarding levels of benefit on disbursement. They were financed by contributions two-thirds of which were paid by the employer and one-third by the employee. The level of contributions was part of the collective agreement so that an increase in contributions to the occupational pension scheme could be used as an equivalent to ordinary wage increases. Initially, contributions started at a level of 0.9 per cent of earnings and an increase to 9.0 per cent by 2004 was already agreed upon in 1991. Pension funds were based on non-profit principles and jointly administered by the social partners. Benefits would be paid out from the age of 65 and there was an element of choice as to the form of disbursement (e.g. lifelong pension, pensions in instalments, and capital pension). Additionally, parts of the contributions could be drawn on in the case of disability, critical illness, or death. However, despite the spread of occupational pensions since the 1970s, the second pillar is still not universal, since part of the workforce remains uncovered by such schemes.[13]

The Danish first-tier, public old-age pension (*Folkepensionen*) consists of two elements: a universal flat-rate basic amount and an income-tested supplement. Thus, although in general, the public old age pension is independent of previous work record, the total sum of the pension received depends on the pensioner's present income and marital status. Minor changes in 1982 and 1983 increased the income-tested component of the pension relative to the basic amount.

In sum, the overall picture of the Danish pension system at the end of Schlüter's term in office was one of a three-pillar system, even though there was still no legal basis for the second pillar. Thus, at the beginning of the 1990s, the Danish pension system already somewhat resembled the 'three-pillar scheme' advocated for by international organizations such as the OECD and the World Bank. However, this outcome was coincidental.

> It is interesting to note that the international debate on the need for pension reform fuelled by the OECD report *Reforming public pensions* (OECD 1988) and the World Bank report *Averting the old age crisis* (World Bank 1994) had no

---

[13] In 1993, such schemes mainly existed in the industrial branches (e.g. building industries, electronic industries).

influence on the debate on pension reform in Denmark. But maybe these organizations could have learned something by studying the Danish reform process already under way in the late 1980s.   (Ploug 2003: 72)

2.3.2.3 HEALTH CARE

In line with the Schlüter government's general policy of cost containment, health-care financing became the centre of policy attention in the 1980s, with dispute arising between the government and the counties on issues particularly relating to the hospital sector (Vrangbæk 1999; Vrangbæk and Christiansen 2005). Although, as previously noted, the counties are responsible for health-care financing and delivery, the national parliament retains overall legislative responsibility. It is national law that defines the framework for decentralized activities. The law regulates, for instance, who is entitled to services. In order to curb costs, new methods of management were introduced during the 1980s and there were attempts to stimulate competition. In primary care, similar measures were discussed in the annual budget negotiation rounds between the minister of health and the counties, represented by ARF, but without major consequences. The cost-containment policy of the 1980s was remarkably successful and expenditure growth came to a halt. At the same time, however, new problems emerged. Since the counties were free to set their own priorities, specialization in the hospital sector increased and differences in health provision between counties widened.

From 1991 onwards, the national government started to intervene more frequently in the counties' health policy via annual budget agreements that contained ever more detailed stipulations (Vrangbæk 2001; Hansen and Jensen 2004). Two themes can be seen as crucial: freedom of choice for patients and organizational changes along the lines of the New Public Management. The first important event in this respect was the 1992 free hospital choice initiative.

Previously, patients could choose a hospital exclusively within their home county. Only a minority of counties let patients living close to county borders choose a hospital in a neighbouring county. This option, however, affected very few patients, and hospitals' incentives to accept these patients were small. The very limited extent of hospital choice reflected a strong emphasis on controlling expenditures by rationing health care. Since the counties wanted to retain control over how the freedom of choice option would operate, they took the initiative to pre-empt national action and introduced freedom of choice throughout Denmark in October 1992 (Vrangbæk and Østergren 2004). However, this step brought with it a degree of financial uncertainty. Previously, counties could calculate their projected expenditure relatively simply on the basis of data about the county population and its social structure, but this actuarial link was now loosened.

However, the counties' political gambit failed, and on 1 January 1993 freedom of choice was introduced by national law. It allowed patients to choose among public hospitals, if the receiving hospital was willing to accept the patient. A broad majority in the Folketing supported this bill, but the different parties did so with different objectives in mind. Some MPs — belonging to the market liberal wing of Venstre — wanted to move in the direction of a marketization and, in the long run, privatization of health-care provision, while others — including the Social Democrats — were guided by the wish to strengthen patients' rights but within the existing public system.

2.3.2.4 FAMILY POLICY

Danish family policy moved — albeit at a slower pace — in a similar direction to that of health-care services: that is more freedom of choice in services and, at the same time, more central control in the use of the state subsidies. However, benefits were not cut back. On the contrary, they were actually expanded, especially at the beginning of Schlüter's period in office. In 1984, maternity leave was extended from 14 to 20 weeks and then to 24 weeks in 1985. Previously, longer absences from work due to childcare were not an option. Moreover, the 10 weeks following the 14 weeks maternity leave became available also for the fathers where both parents were working. This marks a new turn in family policies reflecting changing gender roles (Leira 2006). In 1991, the fathers' role was further strengthened as the right to paternal leave became independent of the mothers' attachment to the labour market. From 1992, an additional, more flexible 'childcare leave scheme' became available. It entitled both parents to leave of up to 52 weeks for every child aged less than 8 years. The scheme aimed both at reducing unemployment and at dealing with a shortage in the supply of day-care services.

In 1987, the centre-right majority in parliament reintroduced the universal child benefit, abolished in 1977 (by the Social Democrats). At the same time, child benefits were differentiated into four schemes: a universal child benefit, an additional child benefit, an additional payment for single parents, and an allowance for orphans. The resurrected universal child benefit was granted to all families with children below the age of 18 — regardless of income or savings. At the beginning, in 1987, it was paid as a tax allowance but later transformed into a tax-free cash benefit (usually paid to the mother). This is why the responsibility remains with the Ministry of Taxation, even though in other respects, family status has no significance in the Danish tax system and there are no special family tax deductions. Moreover, Danish taxes in general are based on the individual, which from a gender perspective makes the tax system an important part of '[t]he active use of labour market and family policies to promote a significant change in women's position' (Lewis 1995: 18). After 1990, the level of the universal child benefit was dependent on the child's age, with higher benefits for younger children. This was intended to reflect the fees parents have to pay for childcare facilities for younger children since crèches are more expensive than kindergartens.

In the late 1980s the problem of waiting lists for childcare became more pressing. By 1988, 37,000 children were waiting for a day-care place. The government set up a commission to look into the issue and in 1990, as a first response, allowed the establishment of private kindergartens. Individual municipalities were left with the choice of whether they wished to subsidize these.

The opening up of welfare services towards private initiatives under the Schlüter government was a new turn in Danish social policy. Still, the share of private providers remained remarkably low. The centre-right government did not refrain from introducing new taxes or raising existing ones in order to balance the budget: between 1982 and 1993, total tax-pressure on the individual actually grew from 47 per cent to 51 per cent of personal income. All in all, the differences between the Conservative-led government's and their Social Democratic predecessors' policy reforms turned out to be surprisingly small, with the change in rhetoric far greater than the transformation of policy. This is true not only of the marketization of social services, but also in respect of labour market policy (which became supply-oriented) and the development of benefits.

2.3.3 Poul Nyrup Rasmussen (1993–2001) — Social Democratic change or changing the Social Democrats?

The new Prime Minister, the Social Democrat Poul Nyrup Rasmussen, started his term in office in 1993 under circumstances similar to that of his predecessor: not with an election but with the resignation of the former government and the formation of a new coalition in parliament. He headed a majority coalition government together with the Social Liberals (RV), the Centre Democrats (CD), and the Christian Party (KrF). This was a rather unusual alliance in terms of policy positions which can only be explained by the sudden retreat of the Schlüter government (see Footnote 12).

The conflicts among the members of the previous centre–right coalition under the chair of Poul Schlüter had led the Social Liberals to signal in the run-up to the 1994 election that they would participate in a future Social Democratic-led coalition. This change of loyalty became possible only when Chairman Niels Helveg Pedersen, a friend of Poul Schlüter's, stepped down. His resignation paved the way for Marianne Jelved who became a strong partner of Poul Nyrup Rasmussen (Holstein 2003). In general, since the 1990s political stability has increased and elections as well as changes in government have become less frequent.

Due to the worldwide recession, 1993 was a difficult year for the incoming government. Unemployment, in particular, was high (10.7 per cent).

But compared to the crisis of the early 1980s, other indicators such as price inflation (1.3 per cent) and the budget deficit (2.9 per cent of GDP) were much more favourable (Green-Pedersen and Klitgaard 2008: 152). There was even a balance-of-payment surplus of 3.9 per cent of GDP. Moreover, only a year later, a remarkable upswing led to high growth rates and falling unemployment. The public budget started to register surpluses and inflation was kept at an acceptable level. Within a relatively short period of time, Denmark was transformed from 'the sick man of Northern Europe' into the 'Danish miracle', managing to preserve a high level of social security while at the same time reducing unemployment (Schwartz 2001).

In terms of economic policy, at first the Social Democrats favoured a classical Keynesian economic strategy. Thus, the labour market reform of 1994 was accompanied by an expansive fiscal policy and a public investment programme: 'The aim was to "kick start" the economy well ahead of an expected international economic recovery' (Nannestad and Green-Pedersen 2008: 56). However, this also produced a new budget deficit.

From 1995 onwards, Keynesian economic policy shifted in favour of fiscal consolidation, a policy stance which was also favoured by the Social Liberals. Tax reform was implemented and public spending reduced in order to balance the budget and bring down public debt. The tax reform adopted by Parliament in June 1998 lowered marginal tax rates for both capital income and income from work. In order not to lose revenue, the tax base was simultaneously broadened and green taxes increased (energy taxes on oil, natural gas, coal, etc. and a petrol tax).

As the coalition could not agree on the annual budget for 1997, the Centre Democrats left the government. The Social Democrats continued the coalition with the Social Liberals even beyond the 1998 election and tried to enhance cooperation with the Liberal Party. European integration also reappeared on the political agenda. Prime Minister Poul Nyrup Rasmussen would have liked to join the EMU and Denmark fulfilled all criteria required to implement the third stage, but in the 2000 referendum vote, the Danes rejected participation in the Euro. One of the most important reasons was the fear that the comprehensive welfare state could suffer under a common currency.

Shortly after the terrorist attack of 9/11, Poul Nyrup Rasmussen called an early election. But instead of a confirmation of the ruling coalition, the opposition took over.

Overall, the success of the Liberal party leader Anders Fogh Rasmussen in the election of 2001 came as a surprise, as the Social Democrats had been rather successful in reducing unemployment and generating economic growth. Two reasons seem to be the most likely explanations for their defeat. The first is the early retirement benefit scheme (*efterløn*). In his 1998 election campaign, Poul Nyrup Rasmussen had promised not to touch the scheme which enjoys particularly high support among union members, but also among the public at large. When the government introduced cutbacks just after the 1998 election, this was widely perceived as a broken promise. The second reason was the growing success of the right-wing Danish People's Party (DF), which was able to combine an exploitation of xenophobic attitudes (Andersen 2003) with a broadly pro-welfare position, especially in respect of benefits for the elderly. In 2001, the DF increased its share of the vote from 7.4 to 12 per cent. However, the Liberal party had been the winner of the election (up from 24 to 31.2 per cent). Together with the Conservatives, they formed a new government under the leadership of Anders Fogh Rasmussen (Liberals) supported by the Danish People's Party.

2.3.3.1 LABOUR MARKET POLICY

Although the composition of the first Poul Nyrup Rasmussen government was highly unusual and made policy-making difficult, the government still managed to introduce what became one of the most important social policy reforms of the period under review. Denmark became well known in policy-making circles across the OECD for the labour market reform of 1994, which was seen as providing a role model for successful welfare state restructuring. Reformers in other countries still refer to the Danish activation policies introduced in the mid-1990s. This was because unemployment was reduced without negatively affecting other macroeconomic measures such as inflation and interest rates, as had been the case in Denmark 10 years earlier.

The labour market reform package was based on the proposals of two commissions (the social commission, Ploug et al. 1992, and the so-called *Zeuthen-udvalg*, Udredningsudvalget Sekretariatet 1992) appointed by the previous centre-right government in 1992. The former only included experts, while the latter also included the social partners, which was of great assistance in the implementation phase. This involvement by the social partners was in the classic Danish corporatist mode, with the social partners having a major role in formulation of legislation with relation to the labour market and its administration (Due et al. 1994), although that mode had been somewhat weakened over the course of the Schlüter years (Bogedan 2009).

The initial 1994 reform was readjusted twice, in 1996 and in 1998. In 1994, a number of new instruments were introduced enshrining the principles of entitlement and obligation. On the one hand, the individual recipient had the obligation to participate in training schemes and other measures. On the other, he/she was entitled to an 'individual action plan' (IHP), a binding contractual arrangement between the unemployed person and the employment agency. The reform initiative contained training measures and subsidized employment schemes, including a new job rotation model which allowed employees to go on leave either to care for children or for further training or on a sabbatical during which they were replaced by an unemployed person.[14]

The benefit period was split into a 'passive' and an 'active' period. In addition, the idea was to set up the 'individual action plan' early on, during the period of regular benefit receipt. The maximum benefit period was limited to 7 years with activation starting at the latest after 4 years. 'The stipulation of a seven year maximum benefit period, including time spent in activation offers, was not only an incremental step and an end to a virtual infinite benefit period for a small number of people, but represented a revolutionary change in policy thinking' (Kvist 2000: 21). It marks a paradigm change in terms of the goals of unemployment policy from compensating income loss to a more demanding policy of getting people back into the labour force. In line with this change in labour market policy goals, the Social Democratic-led government coined the slogan 'rights and duties' for the reform, because the unemployed had the right to receive an activation offer, but at the same time a duty to accept it where it was reasonable in the sense of taking account of the wishes and skills of the unemployed as well as labour market demand in terms of qualification (Bogedan 2005). Offers included among other things retraining (training for those under 25), subsidized employment, and so-called *fleksjobs* for people with diminished ability to work. Furthermore, the activation offer no longer requalified for benefit receipt — 'the unemployment benefit generator' effect was ended — and the long-term unemployed who were unable to find a regular job within the 7-year period were left to the social assistance scheme.

In 1996, the maximum benefit period was further reduced to 5 years and to 4 years in 1998, of which 3 years should be spent in activation. In other words, over a period of only 5 years, the maximum benefit duration was significantly cut, from more than 8 years to 4 years. As in the 1980s, cutbacks focused particularly on the young unemployed. For those under the age of 25, eligibility criteria were further tightened, activation commenced already after 6 months, and the unemployment benefit was reduced to the level of the 'education benefit' (SU), a universal benefit given to everybody in education over the age of 18 years.

However, benefit retrenchment was compensated in terms of the range of activation measures and the degree of choice between them. In case of non-compliance with the 'individual action plan', the recipient risked benefit cuts. This increased the incentive to take up a job outside his/her previous occupation, although the favourable labour market situation of the period somewhat reduced overall pressure on the unemployed.

---

[14] The childcare leave was based on the scheme introduced in 1992 and was extended to all parents — employed or unemployed — with children under the age of 9. With the economic upswing of the second half of the 1990s the fear of labour shortages grew and only the childcare scheme was retained, being later replaced by new parental leave legislation in 2002.

Summing up, although the labour market reforms of the 1990s must be regarded as an instance of retrenchment, since benefit duration was shortened and eligibility became strongly conditional, research has demonstrated that the unemployed were largely satisfied with the new rules, with the unemployed often stating that 'individual action plans' were largely based on their own ideas (Langager 1997).

2.3.3.2 PENSIONS

With the same intention as in labour market policy, that is, of getting more people into paid work, the *early retirement scheme* (*efterløn*) was also cut back in 1998, with the Social Democratic-led government, together with the Liberal Party, seeking to make it more attractive to stay longer in the labour market. The right to early retirement benefits was cut from 7 to 5 years due to a lowering of the retirement age, incentives were provided to encourage people not to retire before the age of 62 years, the minimum contribution period was raised to 25 years, and a separate early retirement contribution was introduced.

As noted, the general retirement age for the old-age pension was *lowered* to 65. This was intended to reduce spending on considerably higher early retirement benefits. There were other changes in pension entitlements, but these were not explicitly introduced as old-age pension reforms, but were rather the result of a decision to make all social benefits taxable from the end of the 1990s. In order to render this tax reform revenue-neutral for pensioners, the pension level was raised accordingly. At the same time, however, the share of the income-tested part of the public old-age pension was raised from below 25 per cent to almost 50 per cent (Kvist 1999; Andersen 2008). This affected the universality of pension provision without affecting eligibility criteria. The calculation of benefits was changed so that more people will have a larger part of their public old-age pension reduced because of income derived from other pensions. This will mean *de facto* cuts in future old-age pension for persons receiving occupational pensions (Green-Pedersen 2007). These 'smart' changes in entitlements by the then Minister of Finance, Mogens Lykketoft, have all the classic hallmarks of blame avoidance through 'retrenchment by stealth' (Pierson 1994, 1996).

The second-tier ATP scheme was extended to the unemployed and to people on sickness benefits (1996) as well as to the recipients of rehabilitation benefits (2003) (Andersen 2008). People on early retirement benefits were allowed to pay voluntary contributions to improve their entitlements. Already in 1993, recipients of unemployment, maternity, and sickness benefits had been given access to the ATP scheme to improve their long-term financial prospects.

A new scheme, the *Special Pension Savings Scheme* (*Særlig pensionsopsparing*, SP), was introduced in 1999. SP was an individual pension saving scheme, introduced in order to curb consumption. Every wage earner was required to contribute 1 per cent of gross earnings. The scheme was administered by the

ATP and benefits were to be paid out at the age of 65, either as monthly instalments over a period of 10 years or as a lump sum. The design of SP was, in principle, somewhat redistributive as contributions were based on individual earnings, while benefits were based on length of employment.

2.3.3.3 HEALTH CARE

In health policy, the problem of hospital waiting lists became prominent in the 1990s. In 1994, patients' waiting times were limited to a maximum of 3 months. The maximum waiting time was further reduced in 1999 for life threatening illnesses and, in 2002, it was generally reduced to 2 months combined with extended free choice allowing access to private hospitals and hospitals in other countries (e.g. Germany and Sweden). Alongside these changes, the Social Democratic-led government altered hospital financing to activity-based funding with fixed rates ('money follows patient').[15] For patients receiving treatment outside their county of residence, the home county was obliged to pay at diagnosis-related group (DRG) rates, which are often higher than the fixed rates used for within-county providers. Therefore, competition between counties was increased as it became profitable for hospitals to attract patients from other counties. In a more psychological sense, hospitals increasingly felt themselves as being in a competitive situation (Vrangbæk 1999).

2.3.3.4 FAMILY POLICY

During the 1990s, family policy in Denmark was about the extension of parental leave as well as expansion of public childcare. In respect of the former, the Social Democratic-led government continued the earlier lead of the Schlüter government in re-familializing childcare (Leira 2006). The parental leave was modified several times — among other things, two extra weeks for fathers became available in 1997, but eventually abolished in 2002 under the subsequent centre-right government.

In respect of the latter, the dual-earner model remained the underlying concept of family policy. In 1996, the Rasmussen government proposed a 'childcare guarantee'. From the year 2000, every child from the age of 26 weeks to 5 years (i.e. until pre-school) was to be entitled to a day-care place. This law built on developments at sub-national level that had been in progress for some time. As early as in 1994, 152 out of the 275 municipalities had offered a childcare guarantee. The government now tried to force the remaining municipalities to offer the same guarantee. In exchange, these municipalities received extra funding which made the national childcare guarantee a costly

---

[15] By 2001, hospitals accounted for about 49 per cent of the counties' expenditure (Danish Regions 2001).

policy for the government. The introduction of this guarantee was the most important change in family policy during the period under review.

To sum up, the Social Democratic-led government in many ways continued the economic and social policies of their centre-right-wing predecessors: 'Learning from the Conservatives approach to managing the macroeconomic situation, the Social Democratic-led governments of the 1990s have pursued active labour market policies on sound economic grounds' (Kvist and Ploug 2008: 198). Thus, thanks to the economic recovery, the government was able to combine measures of debt reduction with welfare state expansion, especially in the field of childcare. Nevertheless, retrenchment policies that during the centre-right period had only been discussed were eventually enacted during the Poul Nyrup Rasmussen years. Examples include the cutbacks in unemployment and early retirement benefits (*efterløn*). Structural changes also occurred, especially in health care, where competition was enhanced, in labour market policies, where 'activation' became the key principle, and in pensions, where universalism was diluted by greater income-testing.

2.3.4 Anders Fogh Rasmussen (2001–9) — the liberal turn

With the 2001 election, the Liberal Party under Anders Fogh Rasmussen's leadership superseded the Social Democrats as the biggest group in parliament. The newly elected prime minister, in contrast to his predecessors, came into office after a major electoral success gaining fourteen seats — and not because the government had lost its majority in parliament. The ensuing centre-right government was supported by the anti-immigration Danish People's Party (DF). The DF's political style and its campaign advertisements led to an unusually high degree of polarization in Denmark and even to protests abroad.

Despite tensions caused among others by the involvement of Danish troops in Iraq from 2003, and an international crisis about cartoons in a Danish newspaper supposedly defaming Mohammed and Islam in 2006, Anders Fogh Rasmussen managed to stay in office. Although losing four seats, he won the election of 2005, but in autumn of 2007 he was forced to call early elections because of a feared loss of parliamentary support. The plan to strengthen the government did not work out and the Liberals ended up in a significantly weakened position (losing another six seats) and, missing out on a parliamentary majority by just one seat, had to rely — in addition to the Danish People's Party — on an MP from the Faeroe Islands to be able to govern. In contrast, the DF managed to further increase their total of seats from twenty-two in 2001 to twenty-five in 2007. Their continuous support for the centre-right minority government made support from other parties unnecessary. As will be shown below, these political developments were conducive to a less consensual policy style. Finally, in 2009, Anders Fogh Rasmussen stepped down to take over a post at NATO without calling for elections. His former Minister of Finance, Lars Løkke Rasmussen, then became prime minister.

Anders Fogh Rasmussen had at one time the reputation of being an ardent neo-liberal — in 1993 he had published the book 'From the Welfare State to the Minimal State' (*Fra socialstat til minimalstat*) in which he advocated extensive reform of the Danish welfare system along market-liberal lines, that is, lower taxes, less government interference in corporate and individual matters, etc. Thereafter, however, he had taken a progressively more moderate stance and, in the 2001 election campaign, he even ran on a pro-welfare state platform advocating additional state subsidies in health care in order to reduce waiting times. For example, in 2002, a government initiative was started to reduce inequality in health through prevention and health promotion measures directed towards vulnerable groups. Equally important were policies for the elderly, tax policy, and policies relating to foreigners (Bille 2001). The tightening of immigration by, for example, impeding marriages for Danes with non-Danes, led to conflicts with the EU because it disturbed the free movement of labour in the EU. The conflict became visible in 2008 in the struggle over the Lisbon treaty. During the election campaign, Rasmussen signalled his adherence to what he described as a 'contract policy' whereby politicians would state what they would do if they were to obtain office and commit themselves to establish and implement these changes if re-elected. This commitment can be seen as a response to the Social Democrats' credibility crisis following the changes to the early retirement scheme (*efterløn*, see above).

In contrast to their predecessors, the new centre-right government inherited a sound economic situation and low unemployment. In terms of economic policy, the Liberal Party largely followed their Social Democratic predecessors. Despite the new government's priority on further reducing state debt, the marginal rates of income tax were actually lowered. In order not to stifle domestic demand, the government called a 'tax moratorium', which meant that, from 2002 onwards taxes should not be increased. Rather than raising taxes, the idea was to generate revenue through higher economic growth. The tax moratorium came under heavy fire from the parties on the left on the grounds that it was 'antisocial' and 'only for the rich'. After 2004, the government went further, opting for cuts in taxation. Employees in the bottom tax bracket received a 3 per cent tax reduction and the lower limit of the middle bracket was raised in order to benefit middle-class families.[16] In 2007, the middle tax bracket was completely abolished.

---

[16] In the Danish tax system, the earned income of each spouse is taxed separately (OECD 2009*a*), and the individual taxpayer is taxed by the central government as well as being liable for local income taxes (from 2007, the counties ceased to levy taxes). Before 2007, the income tax collected by the central state was divided into three brackets: a basic tax rate (*bundskat*), a medium rate (*mellemskat*), and a top rate (*topskat*), depending on personal income (Ganghof 2004).

Political resistance was provoked by the government's plans to reallocate competencies between the national level, counties, and municipalities. From January 2007, the number of counties (now: regions) and their competencies were altered as was the financing and organization of the municipalities. This reform also exemplified the centre-right government's preferred policy-making style: instead of consensual policy-making and broad agreement on major reforms, the opposition was excluded from negotiations.[17] When the government presented its proposals in 2004, the public expected a long debate and negotiations with the Social Democratic Party. Instead, the Danish People's Party stated right away that they supported the proposal. In consequence, the government was no longer dependent on support by other parties in parliament, negotiations with the Social Democrats and other parties broke down and the reform was enacted without changes or any further negotiations.

This structural reform created bigger entities by the amalgamation of 271 municipalities into 98, as well as thirteen counties into five regions. This meant a substantial redistribution of responsibilities. Many of the responsibilities of the former counties were taken over by the enlarged municipalities (regions retain their role in health care, but most other tasks were moved to state level or to municipalities). Additionally, the structure of financing changed: regional taxation was removed and municipal co-financing of health services introduced. Special training and education were now in the hands of the local authorities which played a larger role in unified employment initiatives. Furthermore, all welfare services were touched by the territorial reform — health care, employment services, social assistance, care for the elderly, and family services. Looking at the content of the reform policies themselves, the reform looks less 'radical'. Rather the reform was along lines established earlier, such as the gradual increase of national-level steering in health care and public childcare. Nevertheless, these seemingly incremental steps will have far-reaching impact. This is best illustrated by the move towards more decentralized employment policies for both insured and non-insured unemployment. This provoked resistance by the trade unions which feared that their influence in the Ghent-type unemployment insurance system would diminish as a consequence. Moreover, workers may well become less organized in the future because the tie between trade unions and employment policies is likely to be loosened by related administrative changes.

A second reform package affecting the welfare state was prepared by the so-called welfare commission — again without participation of the social partners — and was passed in 2005 with a broad consensus in parliament (government plus DF and the votes of the Social Democrats and Social Liberals). The overall aim was to adapt the Danish welfare state to globalization

---

[17] Moreover, in contrast to major reforms in the past, the social partners were not included in the commission preparing the reform.

and demographic changes (Velfærdskommissionen 2005). In contrast to the long list of proposals in the final report of the Commission, the *de facto* reforms implemented in parliament were limited (Andersen 2008). The most important reform concerned early retirement and old-age pensions (see below). However, the agreement encompassed a wide array of policies from education to immigration (Bille 2007).

During Anders Fogh Rasmussen's term in office, Denmark witnessed fundamental public debates concerned with foreign policy as well as policy concerning foreigners (Bille 2007). Denmark took part in the war against Iraq and Afghanistan. In 2006, the so-called Mohammed-crisis took place, when a cartoon in a Danish newspaper linking the prophet Mohammed to terrorism provoked widespread international criticism. 'The cartoon crisis and the presence of Danish military forces in Iraq and Afghanistan meant that Denmark was no longer just a cute little country playing by itself in the corner. Denmark had been thrust directly into the centre of one of the global dimensions of conflict' (Bille 2007: 940).

However, as will be shown in what follows, welfare state benefits were not subject to major programmatic retrenchment during this period of Liberal government, although 'one could argue that the incremental steps constitute qualitative changes over time' (Kvist and Ploug 2008: 198).

2.3.4.1 LABOUR MARKET POLICY

In labour market policy the government continued the overall activation course. Already in spring 2002, it introduced a new 'service job scheme' incorporating the existing 'job-offer programme' (ATB). Against the backdrop of decreasing unemployment, the government sought to improve the match of supply and demand in the labour market. For the first time, employment offices became responsible for both insured and uninsured unemployed.

At the same time, the Rasmussen government reduced spending on active labour market policy. Instead, work obligations and the removal of disincentives to work became the main instruments of labour market policy. This move towards a workfare strategy suggested not only a change in the instruments used but also a paradigm change (Linke-Sonderegger 2009), although it was never labelled as such by the government (see discussion and conclusion below). In contrast, as part of the 2003 action plan 'More People in Work' (Beskæftigelsesministeriet 2002), the government declared its commitment to improve reintegration of the unemployed in the labour market by measures to harmonize and simplify the rules governing municipal action. Moreover, a new right to an activation offer in the first 100 days of unemployment was introduced. Other moves were less welfare-oriented. In order to ensure that social assistance was always less attractive than paid employment or unemployment benefits, the government defined a maximum level of social assistance.

In addition, the reform reduced the generosity of social assistance for young people under the age of 25 and tightened the monitoring of the unemployed (Green-Pedersen and Klitgaard 2008).

In a manner similar to the thrust of other welfare state reform, competition was extended to unemployment insurance. Interbranch insurances were permitted, a possibility most funds made use of in short order. Competition also fuelled the trend to a decreasing number of *a-kasser* (from fifty-four in 1973 to thirty-three in 2006).[18] In 2005, the government enhanced competition even further by allowing the unemployed and people on early retirement to change funds and by fully abolishing the sectoral organization of unemployment insurance. Insurance bodies were now able to compete for members via variable contribution levels. So far the consequences of enhanced competition in unemployment insurance are hard to judge. Still, two things can be seen: First, new unemployment insurance schemes have arisen which are not linked to the trade unions. Second, traditional unemployment insurance schemes have lost members because levels of compensation for people with middle and higher incomes are relatively low (Due and Madsen 2007). Some insurers, as well as the trade unions, therefore started to offer additional insurance schemes guaranteeing compensation up to 90 per cent of former income for those on higher incomes.

In 2004, so-called job centres were introduced, merging the former national employment service (AF) and the municipal administration of social assistance for the uninsured unemployed to create a 'one-stop shop' for job seekers. Already in 2001 the centre-right government had transferred social assistance to the auspices of the Ministry of Employment, thereby emphasizing the obligation to work. The one-stop shop policy was enacted against major resistance from trade unions who feared a loss of their former influence in the governance of the employment agencies.

The *early retirement scheme* (*efterløn*) remained a point of dissent. In 2003, a welfare commission was established in order to deal with the issue. Having regard to the Social Democrats' previous experience, the centre-right government feared losing public support by cutting back benefits. A broad agreement, encompassing the Liberals, the Conservative Party, the Social Democrats, the Danish People's Party (DF), and the Social Liberals, was reached in June 2006. The reform will not be fully implemented before 2022, when the pension age for early retirement will be fixed at 62 years. The Danish People's Party, which is strongly in favour of the scheme, prevented further cuts.

---

[18] Membership in trade union run unemployment insurance funds was formerly limited to the branches the unions were representing. Interbranch funds, due to their wider membership, are meant to open up the possibility of changing funds for the insured and thereby promoting competition.

2.3.4.2 PENSIONS

There was less continuity in old-age pensions. Only 2 years after its introduction, the individual savings scheme (SP) was abolished in 2001, immediately after Anders Fogh Rasmussen's assumption of office, phasing out over the period up to 2007 (Andersen 2007). Introduced with the aim to curb consumption, the individual savings scheme played only a marginal role in the Danish system of old-age protection.[19] In addition, the centre-right government in 2003 introduced a small[20] supplementary pension benefit.

As part of the proposals of the welfare commission, the pension age will once again rise to 67 years between 2024 and 2027. The early retirement age was changed to 62 years. This will generate significant savings as the early retirement scheme is now less generous and less easily accessible, in contrast to the situation of the late 1990s. As another example of the changed policy-making style of the Rasmussen era, the social partners were excluded from decision-making. Admittedly, the government agreed the 'welfare reform package' with the opposition. More significantly, however, it was decided that any future increase in life expectancy of 60-year-olds should be added to these age brackets (62 years for early retirement and 67 for old-age pensions). As life expectancy in Denmark developed extraordinarily badly from the late 1970s through until 1995,

> [T]his means that if Denmark catches up with the *current* life expectancy in countries like France, Switzerland, Sweden or Iceland within the next couple of decades, age brackets of early retirement will be raised to around 65 years and pension age to 70 years in a foreseeable future — and even more in the longer run. Unless the parties decide not to follow their own decision, this is in fact a very radical reform. But it is significant that it only concerns age brackets. The other aspects of the pension system — and services for the elderly — were not questioned at all.   (Andersen 2008: 17)

2.3.4.3 HEALTH CARE

Wide-ranging structural changes took place in health care. Health-care services, especially in the hospital sector, remained controversial. The waiting list problem, in particular, was high on the agenda. In 2003, the government offered the counties additional money (DKK1.5 billion accounting for between 1 and 2 per cent of the annual budget) if they could prove that waiting times had been reduced or at least measures to this end had been taken. In a similar vein, 'free

---

[19] Interestingly, following the financial crisis of 2008, parliament decided that, in the period from 1 June 2009 until 31 December 2009, SP would become payable prematurely in order to stimulate consumption.

[20] The initial small benefit was increased in the subsequent budget negotiations and recently as part of a crisis package. This increase was the brainchild of the DF, the populist right-wing party, whose intention is the improvement of old-age pensions.

choice' was extended: Patients who had been waiting for an operation for more than 2 months were given the right to seek treatment abroad or in a private hospital (with full reimbursement). The extension of free choice led to the introduction of quasi-markets in the hospital sector. It is still the case, however, that only a minority of patients[21] exercise the right to 'free choice'. From 2003 patients were permitted to change their GP whenever they wanted (previously only once every 6 months).

A new phenomenon has been the emergence of private health insurances schemes offering 'fast track' operations in private hospitals. Although the number of patients treated in private hospitals in total numbers is still low, it has risen threefold since 2002. Private provision is a relatively new phenomenon and its (relative) spread is a challenge to the traditional state-dominated system.

The overall picture is not one of a real 'marketization' of the Danish hospital sector. The introduction of free choice of hospitals can only be assessed as a type of quasi-market within the public system (Vrangbæk 1999). In the future, these changes could lead to far more private initiatives and might therefore have the potential to undermine the universal and publicly funded character of the Danish health-care system. But from today's point of view, this is guesswork. Until the present, the Danish health sector has preserved its overall characteristics as a decentralized, tax-financed, and universal scheme with only minor co-payments.[22]

2.3.4.4 FAMILY POLICY

The idea of 'free choice' has also played a role in family policy. While the Schlüter government had, in 1990, already allowed the establishment of private kindergartens, the centre-right government under Anders Fogh Rasmussen reached an agreement with the municipalities to grant an extra 'at-home' benefit to parents of children under the age of 5 years. This conservative policy goes against the spirit of the dual-earner model since the parent who receives the benefit (usually the mother) is not allowed any income from work. Interestingly, this measure was introduced under the heading of 'free choice'.

At the same time, the Social Democratic policy of a childcare guarantee was also maintained. As a result, Danish childcare is still exceptionally encompassing and of high quality. About 90 per cent of all children aged 3 to 5 years attended publicly provided childcare in 2003/4. These coverage rates are among the highest in the OECD world (OECD 2009b). In the age group of 0 to 2 years,

---

[21] In 2002, 11 per cent of non-acute patients were treated in a hospital outside their home county (Lassen and Kjellberg 2004).

[22] In contrast to the other countries studied in this volume, there has been no change in terms of co-payments for pharmaceuticals and medical aids.

about 62 per cent of all children are in childcare, which is even more clearly above the OECD average. Furthermore, the Danish system is also characterized by high-quality care measured, for example, in terms of the ratio of qualified staff per child (OECD 2002).

In 2004, the centre-right government established a Ministry for Family and Consumer Affairs, thus giving family policy a distinguished status. All family policies were now finally concentrated in one Ministry. Previously, responsibility for child and family policies was spread among a number of ministries, including the Ministry of Taxation and the Ministry of Social Affairs. Yet the change was short-lived: as early as 2007, the Ministry was disestablished and family policies again divided among a new Ministry of Welfare, the Ministry of Justice, and the Employment Ministry.

The centre-right government left maternity leave untouched but amalgamated the various leave schemes (maternity, paternity, and parental leave) into a so-called flexible child leave in 2002 (for details, see Pylkkänen and Smith 2003; Ray 2008). While the mother remained entitled to 18 weeks of maternity leave — 4 weeks to be taken prenatal and 14 weeks after the birth of the child — the father now had only the right to 2 weeks of paternity leave to be taken during post-natal maternity leave. Before, fathers had been entitled to 4 weeks, 2 during post-natal maternity leave and 2 to be taken during or immediately after parental leave. Once the child is 14-weeks old, *parental leave* applies which is to be 'shared freely' between fathers and mothers and was extended from 10 to 32 weeks (up to 46 weeks with no additional benefits) in 2002. Thus, the non-transferable 2 'father-weeks' were abolished, albeit that this earmarking had been extremely successful in increasing the take-up rate of paternity leave from 1998 to 2001 from 7 per cent to 24 per cent (Borchorst 2006).

Compensation during maternity, paternity, and paternal leave depends on the sector of employment concerned. In the public sector, there is full-wage compensation. For the privately employed, the compensation depends on collective agreements between employers and trade unions. Some have agreed on full pay during maternity/paternity and parental leave. While compensation for the remaining recipients of maternity and paternity leave remained unchanged, the compensation rate for parental leave was lowered from 100 to 60 per cent of maternity/paternity leave in 2002. Generally, since men tend to have higher earnings than women and since more than 50 per cent of mothers are entitled to full pay during parental leave — because they are employed in the public sector — most households have a strong economic incentive to let the mother use the parental leave period, although it can be shared between the parents. The former childcare leave scheme which had been created in 1992 and had entitled both parents, whether employed or unemployed, to leave of up to 52 weeks for every child aged less than 9 years, was scrapped for children born after 2001 by the 2002 reform.

Since 2004, the family allowance has been automatically adjusted to prices. Denmark now has the most generous system of family allowances in the Scandinavian countries (OECD 2007c: 18). In contrast to the overall policy of cost containment, family allowances have been dramatically increased during the period under investigation (ibid.).

Although family policy traditionally has had a 'women-friendly' orientation in Denmark, it has been subject to 're-familialization', for instance through the new 'at-home' benefit for the parents of children under the age of 5 years and the prolonging of paternity leave.

In contrast to Anders Fogh Rasmussen's earlier views expressed in the 1993 book in which he advocated an extensive reform of the welfare system along market-liberal lines, under his government, the Danish welfare state was transformed in a relatively incremental manner. However, although the reforms undertaken in this period cannot be classified as radical, the changes may well have a more far-reaching impact in the future. During this period, a further dose of free choice and competition was applied to social services and the welfare 'market' was opened to private providers. These changes may alter the role of the state not only as a provider of social services but also as an employer. However,

> [s]ome change might be interpreted as 'systemic retrenchment', and from the outset, it was an explicit aim of the Liberal-Conservative government in 2001 to reform the welfare state in slow motion by introducing institutional changes that could have a normative impact. However, this was gradually given up in favour of a more 'Social Democratic' course simply in order to stay in office.
>
> (Andersen 2007: 8)

Thus, despite the centre-right government's intention of reducing public spending and several measures designed to prevent further increases, public spending has continued to rise by approximately 1 per cent more than inflation per year.

Moreover, the financial crisis of 2008–9 made enhanced public spending absolutely necessary. Denmark — like other Western economies — implemented economic stimulus packages to cushion the dramatic decreases in exports. However, due to its open economy and dependence on world markets, Denmark has been among the countries hit hardest by the crisis. Among other initiatives, there have been efforts to stimulate demand by investing in infrastructure, the 'green' economy, and health industries as well as an initiative to increase quality in public welfare services. Furthermore, Denmark has introduced measures to improve the design and capacity of its employment policies to respond to the new and pressing needs resulting from the economic crisis. Conspicuous among them has been an investment in modernizing and improving the administrative capacity of the Public Employment Services with a view to coping with expected problems of labour market transition.

2.4 Discussion and conclusions

When looking back over 30 years of Danish welfare state reforms, the first impression is that reform activity has been considerable. Across our four policy areas — labour market policy, pensions, health care, and family policy — there have been numerous changes in parameters of coverage, benefit levels, eligibility criteria, and organizational structure. First-, second-, and third-order changes all took place (see also Table 2.2 below) in the period covered by this analysis. The most important third-order or paradigm change concerns — as in other countries — the shift from passive, demand-oriented, labour market policies designed to provide income replacement and some make-work schemes towards wholesale supply-oriented activation. The 1994 reform, in particular, with its emphasis on 'rights and obligations' and on employability, marks this shift. Moreover, instruments and institutional settings were quite frequently changed, with the introduction of quasi-markets in the hospital sector and of free choice in welfare services just two instances. Moreover, '[m]ore recently, the trend has been towards selectivism, e.g., the "special treatment" for youth, and income-tested benefits' (Kvist and Ploug 2008: 198). Thus, while the changes may not have weakened the solidarity of the middle classes, they have increasingly differentiated between those who depend on

Table 2.2: Welfare state change in Denmark since 1973

Policy area	Direction of change	Extent of change
Labour market	Benefit *retrenchment*, special rules for the young unemployed, rights and obligations in activation (*expansion* of spending on active labour market policies), administrative changes	*Third-order change:* new paradigm = 'From limiting labour supply to "more people in work"'
Pensions	*Retrenchment*: cuts in the early retirement scheme, future cutbacks due to structural changes, 'restructuring without legislation' *Expansion*: extra benefits for poor pensioners, voluntary occupational pensions based on collective agreements	*Unclear* whether three-pillar pension scheme represents third-order change
Health care	*Cost containment* in the 1980s *Expansion* of health expenditure on hospitals in the 1990s	No paradigm shift but *new instruments and settings*: decentralization, limited 'free choice', and quasi-markets
Family policy	*Expansion*: parental leave, family allowances, childcare	No paradigm shift but *new instruments and settings*: 'free choice', more 'user' rights, support for parents caring for their child at home

Source: Own compilation.

the flat-rate universal public schemes (as in pensions and unemployment benefit) and those who are entitled to additional (collectively bargained) schemes. These developments could possibly lead to a fundamental change in the nature of the Danish welfare state (Kvist and Ploug 2008). What started out as minor adaptations of instruments (e.g. cuts in benefit duration of unemployment benefits, greater income-testing of old-age pensions) could lead to (intended or non-intended) paradigmatic change. A similar line of argument might well suggest that the opening of public welfare services to private providers and introduction of market-type instruments could in the long run lead to a new paradigm which deposes the state from its current role as Denmark's main welfare producer.

However, to date, no overall regime shift away from the established Social Democratic model can be observed. The Danish welfare state is still universal, tax-financed, generous, and based on comprehensive social services. The universal child allowance, maternity and sickness benefits, the universal flat-rate public old-age pension, and encompassing public welfare services in child and elderly care which are, in principle, free of charge all illustrate the Social Democratic or 'Scandinavian' character of the system. Labour market policy is now even more in accordance with the full-employment guarantee which is inherent in the model. This guarantee implicitly guided policy-making in the 1990s, which was mainly about enhancing labour market attachment and securing the long-term sustainability of the system. The overall picture notwithstanding, some cutbacks were enacted, particularly in transfer schemes such as unemployment and early retirement benefits (*efterløn*). Nevertheless, not only decommodification but also what has been termed de-familialization remain at high levels. However, some developments are ambiguous. On the one hand, de-familialization has been promoted as in other countries by expanding social services generally. On the other hand, the expansion of parental leave leads to a degree of re-familialization. The same ambiguity applies in respect of decommodification. While in the first half of the period under review, benefit levels and eligibility were at the centre of reforms, but, since that time, the structural make-up of the welfare state has increasingly attracted reform attention. In international comparison, benefits still remain generous and therefore decommodifying. At the same time, tightened conditionality signifies some degree of re-commodification.

The incremental pattern of restructuring described here reflects a dialectic of continuity and change. Although a number of typically liberal principles have gained some purchase in recent years, it would be misleading — as already pointed out — to speak of a transformation of the Danish welfare state into a liberal welfare state as expected by the efficiency hypothesis. Rather than being an exemplar of social expenditure retrenchment, Denmark seems to confirm the 'growth to the limits' thesis (Kittel and Obinger 2003), with expenditure stagnating at a high level at and around just under 30 per cent of GDP.

In *labour market policy*, a change to supply-side policies can be observed. In line with changes in other Western European welfare states, particularly the United Kingdom, we find activation policies and workfare strategies in Denmark, too. However, policy changes did not amount to an overall shift towards the liberal model. High employment is a precondition for the functioning of the Social Democratic model and has therefore always been central to Danish labour market policy. The expansion of welfare services has itself been a very important source of jobs growth. This helped Denmark to establish a service economy without having to resort to the low-wage strategy observed in many other countries and thereby to find a solution to the 'trilemma of the service economy' (Iversen and Wren 1998). The trilemma arises as countries increasingly fail simultaneously to achieve the three goals of fiscal discipline, employment growth, and income equality. The Danish example shows that employment growth is possible without relinquishing the other two goals (Bogedan 2008). Even though at the beginning of the new century Denmark has reduced state debt and created jobs growth, this smooth development was hardly the norm in the earlier periods under investigation here. Rising unemployment, skyrocketing in the early 1980s to over 11 per cent, made labour market policy quite crucial. The problem was increasingly seen as a structural rather than a cyclical one. That being so, the measures adopted emphasized social investment, for example through education and training of the young unemployed.[23] Overall, labour market policy followed the Social Democratic education concept by focusing on lifelong learning. Moreover, the idea of lifelong learning was closely connected to the aim of increasing competitiveness by increasing productivity. At the same time, benefit levels were lowered, duration shortened, and conditions of access tightened. The centre-right government further tightened conditionality. Recent studies also show that — albeit to a minor degree — inequality has increased since 2001 (Arbejderbevægelsens Erhvervsråd 2006).

Danish labour market policy is frequently seen as exemplifying principles of 'Flexicurity', combining flexible labour market regulations (dismissal rules, etc.) with one of the most generous social security systems of the world. This strategy received international attention and was associated with the Danish employment 'miracle' of the late 1990s and early 2000s (Torfing 1999; Kvist 2003). Many of these ideas were later taken up by the European Employment Strategy (EES). Together with comprehensive active labour market policies, the Danish

---

[23] Benefits for immigrants, by contrast, came close to workfare strategies known from liberal welfare states (Andersen 2007).

approach is sometimes described as the 'golden triangle' (Arbejdsministeriet 1999; Madsen 2006). Active labour market policy is where we find the clearest example of a paradigm change in the sense of Hall's threefold classification of policy change (Hall 1993). This is true not just at the micro level (the relationship between the individual unemployed and the social welfare administration), but also at the macro level. It was no longer the fight against unemployment that guided reform, but the wish to achieve sustainable economic and labour market development through better training and higher productivity.

One can also find major structural change in *pension policy*, particularly the move towards a multi-pillar model. Over time, the Danish pension system has come close to the ideal advocated by the World Bank (1994). However it is unclear whether this development can be properly described as a paradigm shift since the Danish pension system has never been deliberately designed in this way (Green-Pedersen 2007). Instead, the development of old-age pensions was marked by a long period of deadlock. Non-decisions led to the emergence of funded, occupational pensions agreed upon and administered by the social partners. By the early 1990s, a point of no return had been reached when a majority of the labour force was covered by an occupational pension scheme. Until the present, there has been no legislation regarding the second pillar. Consequently, people with weak labour market attachment who are not covered by collective agreements do not have access to second-pillar pension benefits. When looking at the whole period under scrutiny, the Danish pension system has undergone a major transformation from the residual public old-age pension in 1973 to an elaborated three-pillar system consisting of the basic public first-pillar pension, the second-pillar occupational pensions jointly established by the social partners, and various forms of private old-age provision. In the future, the system as a whole will become less universal because of the decreasing role of the public old-age basic pension. The new supplement targeted at poor pensioners further highlights the increasing division between old-age pensioners with insufficient additional coverage, such as the long-term unemployed, and the well-protected core workers. However, this is closely linked to the liberal traits of the Danish welfare state described above. The public basic security is still universal and paid regardless of labour market integration. The recent changes, as yet not fully implemented might, however, lead to more far-reaching change at some future time when fewer pensioners will benefit from the public old-age pension.

The Danish early retirement benefit (*efterløn*) was part of unemployment insurance. The scheme experienced a strengthening of conditionality over the past decade, starting with the 1998 reform, through the lengthening the minimum contribution period, the introduction of a separate early retirement contribution, and the provision of incentives to delay early retirement to the age of 62 or later. These cutbacks were in line with the shift in labour market policy from reducing labour supply to lifting employment rates (Cox 1998).

Waiting time problems in the late 1980s and early 1990s attracted a lot of negative publicity in *health care*. Due to rising media attention, the different governments from the mid-1990s provided additional and more targeted funding in order to reduce waiting lists. Nonetheless, the problem is, as yet, unsolved.

In general, the modernization of welfare services in Denmark has been theoretically embedded in the New Public Management approach. Thus, a market perspective and principles of private sector management have been introduced in many programmes. In the 1980s, efforts focused on cost containment (e.g. through new methods of management). From the mid-1990s, and pushed, in particular, by the centre-right government, increased freedom of choice has been introduced both to promote competition and to improve quality. To some extent, these reforms built upon the Scandinavian tradition of user influence and co-management (Andersen 2007). Marketization does not, however, represent a paradigm shift, since it was integrated as an element in a predominantly public system in terms of funding and provision. The primary health-care sector, in particular, has remained almost untouched by these developments.[24] User fees did not play a major role in reform debates. Even free choice, the centrepiece of the reforms, remained limited. In general, visiting a hospital or specialist without a referral from a general practitioner is still not possible (Vrangbæk 1999). Free choice only applies to the patients' right to choose a hospital in a different county, introduced in 1992. However, this right is restricted by the counties' right to reject a patient from another county under certain circumstances. Moreover, despite the waiting time problem, Danes remain very reluctant to use private hospitals or hospitals abroad. A possible reason may lie in the lack of supporting measures (e.g. patients must pay for transport themselves). Proximity to the hospital is important for most patients, too, because they want to be close to family and friends. However, the introduction of free choice and the expansion of private insurance and private hospitals undermine one of the founding principles of the Danish welfare state — equality — by establishing a 'fast track' to hospital treatment for some.

In a manner similar to that in health care, freedom of choice, increased user rights, and competition were also introduced in *family policy*, notably in the childcare sector. However, private providers play even less of a role than in health care (Andersen 2007). The introduction of a childcare guarantee is the most important change in family policy, rendering provision even more generous than at the beginning of the period under investigation. The strong service orientation of the Danish welfare state is more supportive of the dual-earner model than in the other Scandinavian welfare states (Ellingsæter

---

[24] The only change is that patients can now change their family doctor whenever they want and not just at the beginning of a new year.

1998). In general, spending on family policy has increased continuously despite economic pressure.[25] Other fields of expansion have been family cash benefits and leave arrangements.

The question is how these changes can be assessed in a systematic fashion. Regarding level and direction of change, there has been much discussion among welfare state researchers as to how to conceptualize welfare state change. As we can see from the Danish example, there has been no uniform liberalization of the welfare state (see also Streeck and Thelen 2005*b*) and the majority of changes have taken place in an incremental fashion. Following the classification of Peter Hall (1993), it is possible to discern changes at all levels of magnitude: in settings (first-order change), changes in instruments (second-order change), and changes of paradigms (third-order change). As we have noted at several points in our presentation, the most fundamental change in the Danish welfare state in the period studied here is the introduction of the 'activation-paradigm', marking an important change in both labour market policies and in provision for old age (see Table 2.2). It is important to stress, however, that this paradigmatic change did not change instruments and settings likewise. For example, the basic security old-age pension is still paid regardless of labour market participation and the duration of unemployment benefits is in international comparison still long. Thus, in contrast to Hall (1993), we speak of a third-order change without there necessarily being any first- or second-order change. A paradigmatic change is given, when the overarching aims of a scheme is altered. Moreover, the social services in health and childcare continued their public provision path. In these fields, changes took place at the organizational level but without any fundamental change in the character of the provision.

However, even the paradigm shifts in labour market policy and arguably in pensions did not steer the Danish welfare state away from the Social Democratic model. Incremental changes and consensual policy style characterize the Danish pattern of welfare state change.[26] Nevertheless, these incremental changes have transformative capacity (Streeck and Thelen 2005*a*) by adding new schemes to existing ones or by conversion of old institutions to new purposes. This applies when one looks across the different sub-areas of the welfare state. Financing, benefits, benefit delivery, and regulation were modified (see Table 2.3), but the core characteristics of the 1970s were maintained. Clearly, the Social Democratic Danish welfare state has survived. But, as in

[25] Not all parents benefited from this expansive course, because public spending became more 'selective' (Ploug and Kvist 2008). Extraordinary measures for small groups indicate this development.

[26] Although consensualism has changed over time and the incumbent government has deliberately departed from the traditional path of corporatist policy-making, the existence of minority government still imprints the need for a cooperation and compromise which is lacking in a majoritarian system.

Table 2.3: The welfare mix in Denmark in the 'silver age'

Financing	Benefits	Delivery	Regulation
Tax-financed	Universal + generous social rights based on citizenship	State monopoly in social policy provision High-quality services	Wide-ranging state intervention
Additional contribution-based schemes	*Tightened conditions for benefit receipt*	*Private providers*	*Less statutory governance Introduction of quasi-markets More 'freedom of choice'*

Source: Own compilation.

other countries, paradigm change is much less ambivalent in economic policy.

With regard to the *financing* of the Danish welfare state, and despite the growth of contribution-based schemes, tax-funding remained dominant. Conditions for benefit receipt were tightened and the share of *benefits* conditional on either need or contributions has grown. But, on the whole, the Danish welfare state is largely characterized by the universality and generosity of its benefits, especially in the service sector, which is extremely large compared with other OECD welfare states and even large by Scandinavian standards (only Sweden is in the same league). This may, however, change in the future since non-decision in old-age pensions could have set off a political dynamic towards lesser universalism (Green-Pedersen and Klitgaard 2008). As universalism has been a key to widespread support of the expensive tax-funded welfare state (Rothstein 2000), conflicts are likely to grow if an increasing number of people does not benefit from the public old-age pension. Hence, the important issue is whether the observed changes will further diminish universality. Social services were to some extent opened up to private providers, but the state still disposes of an almost unchallenged monopoly in the *delivery* of benefits. As already pointed out, despite some experimentation with free choice and markets, state-based hierarchical steering is still the most important mode of *regulation*. This overall pattern of continuity despite manifold socio-economic challenges clearly needs to be explained.

2.4.1 Explaining the reform pattern

The determinants of Danish welfare state change are both external pressures and political institutions. The primarily negotiation-based politics of reform explain the observed incremental reform pattern. Moreover, the fact that most governments in the period under investigation were minority governments made compromises with other parties in parliament essential (Bogedan 2009). Table 2.4 summarizes these factors driving welfare state change in Denmark.

Danish welfare state reforms were triggered by rising *socio-economic problem pressure* — most clearly visible in the 1970s and early 1980s when the country stood 'at the brink of the abyss'. The economy shrank for 2 years (1980 and 1981), unemployment rates were among the highest in the OECD (about 10 per cent in the early 1980s), price inflation reached two-digit levels, and the balance of payment was in deficit for the whole of the 1980s. The economic difficulties had negative consequences for public finance, too. While the Danish government stimulated demand with a traditional Keynesian approach, it proved unable to prevent a price–wage spiral. In a similar vein, benefits such as unemployment and early retirement benefits (*efterløn*) were at first *expanded*. Only later on were benefits cut back in explicit response to socio-economic challenges.

Hence, in contrast to Austria in the mid-1990s, EU accession (1973) was not the main critical juncture in Denmark. Arguably, *Europeanization* furthered the diffusion of supply-side policy instruments in Denmark as well. In other aspects, it is more difficult to assess the European influence on Danish policy-making. As in the other countries of our sample, unemployment came increasingly to be seen as a structural problem. In Denmark this prompted the paradigm change in labour market policy in the 1990s. However, the aim of the EC to improve labour market performance in the member states by the use of the EU's employment strategy (EES) has — in the case of Denmark — been like 'reforming the best pupil in the class' (Jacobsson 2003). Rather, Danish policy actors feel that Danish policy has been exported to the EU and that Denmark is well ahead of other countries in this policy area (Mailand 2009).

Although demographic pressure has been building up with sub-replacement fertility rates and an ever growing share of people above the age of 65, the structure of the contemporary Danish welfare state is such that *demographic changes* are less of a critical issue than in most other Western welfare states. First, the public old-age pension scheme has become increasingly based on income-testing. Thus, when in future more pensioners become entitled to occupational benefits, they will automatically lose entitlement to the income-tested supplement and public spending per pensioner will thereby be reduced. Secondly, the funded, defined contribution pillar has expanded. Hence, if life expectancy continues to rise, benefits will drop. Thirdly, services for the elderly such as municipal home help and day-care act as functional equivalents to cash transfers. As a result, the future costs of demographic change are shared more

Table 2.4: Phases of social policy development in Denmark, 1973–2009

Stimulus	Phase	Context	Diagnosis	Politics	Content of economic and social policy	Consequences
End of Golden Age	1973–82	(Predominantly) Social Democratic single-party minority governments, unstable governments	Temporary crisis, higher social benefits to curb income losses, traditional Keynesian policies to stimulate demand	Negotiation-based	Compensation of income losses (increase in unemployment benefits), introduction of early retirement scheme, expansion of welfare services (especially childcare)	Economic policies could not stop price–wage spiral, increasing female employment, skyrocketing unemployment, mounting public debt
Consequences of phase 1: 'at the brink of the abyss'	1983–93	(Predominantly) 'four-leaf clover' minority governments (KF, V, CD, KRF)	Change in economic policies to overcome the crisis, cost containment to control public expenditures, fixed exchange rate policy	Negotiation-based due to the need to find ad hoc majorities, but major labour conflict (1985, 1989)	Trade unions forced to accept wage restraints, in the beginning cutbacks in benefits, fixed exchange rate policy (towards D-Mark)	Smooth reduction of public debt, decline in unemployment, peak level in 1992, structural reform failed because of lacking majorities
Consequences of phase 2: 'towards the job miracle'	1993–2001	Social Democratic-led minority governments (1993–4 majority)	Unemployment as a threat to the welfare state, diminish mismatch problems by further education and lifelong learning	Negotiation-based, common effort of trade unions and employers, decentralization of industrial relations	Mix of demand- and supply-side-oriented economic policy, benefit cutback in transfers, subtle move towards free choice and marketization in welfare services	Budget surpluses and reduction of public debt, unemployment halved, activation of the unemployed, unchanged high level of public spending, less universalism in old-age pensions
Consequences of phase 3: 'liberalizing the Scandinavian welfare state'	2001–9	Centre-right governments (supported by right-wing populists)	Structural reforms to modernize and adapt the welfare state to a new (international) environment and demographic changes, enhanced flexibility	Exclusion of social partners, instead cooperation with 'experts', fixed supporting party in parliament	Workfare (supply-side orientation), free choice initiatives, New Public Management	Expansion of private provision and competition in welfare services, dualization of benefits between Danes and immigrants, slight increase in inequality

Source: Own compilation based on Table 1.1.

equally between different levels of government than elsewhere. Fourthly, early retirement benefits, after being used as a labour market instrument, were scaled down from the late 1990s onwards.

As in Austria, welfare state transformation in Denmark was triggered by socio-economic developments. Still, political parties and institutions mattered both for the extent and content of reforms. Although the differences in policies between governments of different *partisan complexion* were not large, the devil is in the detail. The supply-side orientation emerged in the 1980s and spread across the partisan spectrum, even to the Social Democrats. They increasingly incorporated some neo-liberal elements in their economic and social policies. While they did not relinquish universalism, they adopted the idea of rights and obligations tied to benefit receipt (Frenzel 2002: 126). However, the different political parties still preferred different policy instruments (Klitgaard 2004). The Social Democrats preferred active labour market policies and a social investment strategy of increasing qualifications to meet the productivity requirements of high wages. The parties of the right favoured the adoption of minimum wages combined with a lowering of unemployment benefits. Partisan differences were not restricted to labour market policy but also showed up in family policy. Although an expansionary field across the board, the centre-right government left a specific imprint in this latter policy area. The at-home benefit, for example, diverged clearly from the dual-earner policy promoted by most Danish governments since the 1970s.

Despite some conflict, the overall picture of social policy-making has been one of broad compromises. Most reforms were accepted by the opposition, so that, when changes in the partisan complexion of government occurred, different emphases but no major U-turns can be observed. Due to the widespread willingness to cooperate and the small size of the political elite, political actors were also able to react swiftly to new challenges.

> Ironically, the Danish welfare state's capacity to adjust was enabled by some of the very structural features that rational choice theory argues contribute to the collapse of the welfare state. The multi-leveled corporatist structure of Danish politics and governance along with the widespread popular support of the welfare state have prevented major distributional changes like those in the U.S., Britain, New Zealand, and lately, parts of Canada. (Albæk et al. 2008: 17)

Social partnership, the close cooperation between the trade unions and employers' organizations, one of the cornerstones of the Social Democratic welfare state, was important throughout the period under review — albeit not without conflicts. In consequence, the social partners helped to reform the unemployment benefit as well as old-age pensions. In the latter case, the social partners themselves organized a new scheme (second pillar). In the first case, they were part of a tripartite cooperation with the government. This style of policy-making integrates corporatist actors through the creation of pre-parliamentary commissions as a forum of interest intermediation (Jørgensen 2002; Schmidt-Hansen and Kaspersen 2004).[27] These commissions were appointed in order to prepare policy reforms and to accommodate conflicting interests. For example, the acclaimed labour market reforms of the early 1990s were agreed upon in a tripartite commission. A consensual style of policy-making is still important today. Nevertheless, the involvement of social partners has decreased (Bogedan 2009). For example: The two big welfare commissions under the Anders Fogh Rasmussen government were set up without the involvement of the social partners. Admittedly, in other cases they have instrumentally taken on board the social partners in commissions and in tripartite agreements (e.g. sickness absenteeism) in order to bypass the Social Democrats in parliament. Moreover, the bond between the trade union peak body (LO) and the Social Democratic Party was loosened in 1995 when they ceased to be mutually represented on each others' boards.

The Danish veto player structure, marked by a lack of important institutional veto players (with the partial exception of the counties) on the one hand, and frequent minority governments and a tradition of social partnership on the other, should lead us to expect neither policy stalemate nor radical policy change. This is confirmed by the empirical evidence: as we have seen, there were adaptations in such central Danish welfare policies as the public old-age pension scheme and labour market policy, but reforms remained moderate in scope. Although the guiding principle changed from a more passive approach to activation, other principles remain unchanged, such as low stratification and a strong emphasis on equality as well as generosity.[28] Thus, labour market policies did not lead to a larger low-wage sector and Denmark actually expanded public employment in welfare services. In this latter, area, what we see is a new balance between central and regional governments. During annual budget negotiations between municipalities and counties on one side and the national government on the other, more and more structural issues were debated. By such means, the government pursued its policy of a more centralized steering of the welfare sector (e.g. introducing free choice in hospital sector by law, promising a childcare guarantee) by decentralizing provision in order to offer citizen-friendly welfare services. Similarly, the employment service was decentralized.

---

[27] By contrast, Denmark was not among the welfare states where governments and social partners agreed on social pacts (combining wage moderation and social policy reform in one bargain) during the 1990s.

[28] Data from the OECD Employment Outlook (2006*b*) shows that Denmark has high net replacement rates and the longest unemployment benefit duration among twenty-six OECD countries in 2004. Moreover, the average net replacement rate over 5 years of unemployment is highest. The findings of Scruggs and Allan (2008) reinforce the liberal traits of Danish welfare state, though Denmark scores high on benefit equality and universalism over time.

With regard to welfare state structures, the power resource school has traditionally argued that universal welfare states are immune to large-scale cutbacks because they also include the middle class (Korpi 1983; Esping-Andersen 1990: 33). This theoretical assumption seems to be confirmed by the pattern of reform described here. It seems that the encompassing character of the Danish welfare state has shaped the values and expectations of the Danish electorate and hindered major retrenchment (Klitgaard 2004).

Overall, the Danish trajectory is an example of major policy stability under circumstances of domestic crisis. Even today, Denmark combines economic openness with a generous and encompassing welfare state. Moreover, Denmark is widely envied for its combination of excellent labour market performance and low levels of poverty and inequality.

2.5 Annex

Table 2A.1: Election results, 1971–2007

Election	Turnout	Seats												
		SD	V	KF	RV	SF	CD	KrF	FrP	VS	EL	DKP	FK	DF
21.09.1971	87.2	70	30	31	27	0	0	—	—	—	—	0	—	—
04.12.1973	88.7	46	22	16	20	11	14	7	28	0	—	6	—	—
09.01.1975	88.2	53	42	10	13	9	4	9	24	4	—	7	—	—
15.02.1977	88.7	65	21	15	6	7	11	6	26	5	—	7	—	—
23.10.1979	85.6	68	22	22	10	11	6	5	20	6	—	0	—	—
08.12.1981	83.2	59	20	26	9	21	15	4	16	5	—	0	—	—
10.01.1984	88.4	56	22	42	10	21	8	5	6	5	—	0	4	—
08.09.1987	86.7	54	19	38	11		9	4	9	0	—	0	0	—
10.05.1988	85.7	55	22	35	10	24	9	4	16	0	—	0	0	—
12.12.1990	82.8	69	29	30	7	15	9	4	12	—	0	—	0	—
21.09.1994	84.3	62	42	27	8	13	5	0	11	—	6	—	—	—
11.03.1998	86	63	42	16	7	13	8	4	4	—	5	—	—	13
20.11.2001	87.1	52	56	16	9	12	0	4	0	—	4	—	—	22
08.02.2005	84.5	47	52	18	17	11	0	0	—	—	6	—	—	24
13.11.2007	86.6	45	46	18	9	23	0	0	—	—	4	—	—	25

Notes: SD, *Socialdemokratiet* (Social Democrats)/SF, *Socialistisk Folkeparti* (Socialist People's Party)/DKP, *Danmarks Kommunistiske Parti* (Communists)/VS, *Venstresocialisterne* (Left-Socialists)/FK, *Fælles Kurs* (Common Course)/EL, *Enhedslisten* (Unity List)/CD, *Centrumdemokraterne* (Centre Democrats)/KrF, *Krist. Folkeparti/Kristendemokraterne* (Christian People's Party)/RV, *Radikale Venstre* (Social Liberals)/V, *Venstre* (Liberals)/KF, *Konservative Folkeparti* (Conservatives)/DF, *Dansk Folkeparti* (Danish People's Party)/FrP, *Fremskridtspartiet* (Progress Party).

Table 2A.2: Referenda associated with EU membership, 1972–2007

Date	Subject of the referendum	Result (total number of persons entitled to vote, %)		Outcome
		Yes	No	
2.10.1972	Denmark's accession to the EEC	56.7	32.9	Accession on 1 January 1973
27.02.1986	European Single Act (consultative referendum)	42.0	32.7	Denmark accessed the EC package
02.06.1992	Maastricht Treaty	40.5	41.7	Denmark did not accede to the Treaty
18.05.1993	Edinburgh Agreement	48.6	37.0	Denmark acceded to the Maastricht Treaty supplemented by the Edinburgh Agreement
28.05.1998	Amsterdam Treaty	41.3	33.6	Accession to the Amsterdam Treaty
28.09.2000	Single currency	40.5	46.1	Denmark did not adopt the single currency

Source: Own compilation.

3

New Zealand: Retrenchment and Reconstruction

3.1 Introduction

In our sample of four small open economies, New Zealand is the country in which the most radical changes took place. No programme was left unscathed by various governments' attempts at retrenchment and reform, and there have been fundamental transformations in some areas. A number of large-scale changes, however, were reversed or significantly watered down by subsequent governments. Indeed, one of the most interesting developments in New Zealand has been the lack of the kind of slow-moving, incremental transformation expected by the 'new politics' literature. Instead, policy change was often abrupt, surprising to voters, inconsistent, and, in many cases, short-lived.

Many analysts attribute this typical pattern of policy change to New Zealand's 'village-like polity' (James 2005: 20). At least up to the 1993 electoral reform, New Zealand was indeed an extreme case on a number of dimensions central to comparative politics. The country's political system — with a unicameral legislature, single-party majority governments, combined with strong party discipline and a government unchecked by strong courts, a rigid constitution, or institutions of federalism — was an almost pure example of a Westminster democracy (Lijphart 1987), in some ways, 'more British than Britain'. The number of 'institutional veto players' (Tsebelis 1995, 2002) was zero, leading us to expect the kind of rapid and radical pattern of policy change that we do, in fact, observe. Furthermore, the Westminster polity fostered an adversarial policy style between the two major parties. In 1993, the electoral system was changed from a single-member plurality system (or 'first past the post') to the mixed-member proportional (MMP) formula (a variant of proportional representation (PR)). This had repercussions in terms of, among other things, the number of parties in parliament and the type of cabinets formed. Whereas New Zealand traditionally was a country of almost constant single-member majority governments, coalitions and/or minority governments are now the norm.

Yet, as we will see, an explanation that centres only on political institutions, fails to capture the importance of socio-economic problems that emerged after the traditional New Zealand political economy passed its peak in the 1960s and 1970s. It also neglects the role played by partisan ideology — especially the anti-welfare ideology of some of the key conservative politicians of the 1990s. It is important to note, however, that social policy in New Zealand since the mid-1970s has not been just about retrenchment. We will show that the country experienced a turbulent journey, leading from expansion in the 1970s, through moderate, then radical retrenchment in the 1980s and 1990s, to renewed expansion at the beginning of the new millennium.

3.2 Innovation and development: the first 70 years in the history of the New Zealand welfare state

At least twice during its history, namely, at the end of the nineteenth century and in the 1930s, New Zealand was regarded a pioneer of social protection. The first major social reform, the Old-Age Pensions Act of 1898, made New Zealand the world's second country — preceded only by Denmark (Overbye 1997) — to introduce a comprehensive public pension. In principle, all long-term residents over the age of 65 years could apply for a pension, but benefits were small, means-tested, and subject to strict conditions, including 'moral' as well as ethnic criteria (McClure 1998: 14–23; Thomson 1998). Overall, the pension already contained many of the basic design features of the New Zealand welfare state: It was tax-funded, pay-as-you-go-financed, centrally administered by the state, and the benefits were flat-rate, means-tested, and not tied to a previous contributory record. A number of small programmes, including a work accident insurance (1900), rudimentary housing programmes (1905, 1906), widows' (1911) and miners' (1915) pensions and a small family benefit scheme (the world's first in 1926) were added in the early decades of the twentieth century, but it was not until 1938 that the government set up a comprehensive social security scheme.

The second period of innovation in social policy took place under the first Labour government between 1935 and 1949. Labour's election platform in 1935 included the blueprint for a universal citizenship-based system of social security. At the core of the plan were a generous universal public pension from age 60 and a universal health system. The implementation of these sweeping plans, however, failed. Eventually, the Labour government settled for a system which still entailed a wide range of different benefits — covering not only old age but also sickness, unemployment, and so on — of which most, however, were means-tested and not universal, as initially planned. The only exception was the so-called Superannuation benefit, a small payment for every New Zealander older than 65.[1] All other main cash transfers of the 1938 Social Security Act were means-tested, including the Age Benefit that was available from age 60, existing family allowances, and invalids' pensions, as well as new transfers such as the sickness and unemployment benefits. The family benefit became universal only in 1945.

The introduction of a universal national health service could also only partly be realized. In secondary care, the government more or less achieved what it had set out to do, namely, to establish a fully universal and comprehensive system of 'free' hospital care. However, a compromise between the government and the medical profession was implemented in respect of primary care: Doctors remained private practitioners, almost exclusively paid on a fee-for-service basis. The government subsidized part of the doctors' fees via the General Medical Services (GMS) benefit. While at the outset, in 1941, the GMS still covered two-thirds of the full doctor's fee, that share had diminished to about one-third by the 1970s, due to non-adaptation to fee inflation (Gauld 2001: 18). The health system could, therefore, be described as a 'dual system', in which hospital care was predominantly public[2] and primary care was private, yet subsidized.

Although the 1938 Social Security Act was, to some extent, less generous than promised, it must still be seen as one of the pioneer reforms of modern welfare state development, even by international standards. New Zealand was the first country in the world to enact a *comprehensive social security system* to cover all major income risks by updating existing schemes and setting up new benefits. This was also acknowledged by an ILO report in 1949 which stated that the 1938 Act 'more than any other law, determined the practical meaning of social security, and so has deeply influenced the course of legislation in other countries' (1949: III).

However, during the 1950s and 1960s, while most other OECD countries underwent dramatic changes and set up large, often universal social security programmes, there had been little change in New Zealand. In contrast to welfare states such as those of Sweden or Denmark, New Zealand, sharing a number of features in the first half of the twentieth century was never transformed into a 'Social Democratic' welfare state but, at first sight, maintained its essentially 'liberal' shape. Not only were there no major reforms, but the financial expansion of the welfare state seemed to slow down significantly. While social expenditure as a percentage of GDP rose markedly in almost all OECD countries during those years, in New Zealand, the level actually *declined*

---

[1] The level of superannuation was set to rise constantly and was eventually intended to match the means-tested age benefit. This was achieved by April 1960.

[2] By the 1970s, about 20 per cent of hospital beds were private and funded through private insurance (Gauld 2001: 19).

for several years in the 1960s (Castles 1996: 78). In other words, New Zealand was losing its status of a pioneer and was gradually falling behind other countries. How was this possible?

According to Francis G. Castles (1985, 1996), we can answer this puzzle only by looking at New Zealand's wider political economy. In reality, New Zealand — and Australia, also — was not a 'liberal' welfare state, but rather what Castles calls a *wage earners' welfare state*. Material hardship and inequality were never addressed exclusively through traditional tax-and-spend policies, but through a more diverse range of 'social protection by other means' (Castles 1989), labour market regulation in particular. The most important element was the state-dominated system of wage arbitration dating back to the 1894 Industrial Conciliation and Arbitration Act. Effectively, it led to high wage compression and a wage level which, at the beginning of the twentieth century, was explicitly defined as a 'family wage', in principle, sufficient to support a dependent wife and two or three children. By providing social protection through the primary distribution of income from employment, the state, therefore, moderated the need for direct income transfers and services. Favourable socio-economic performance — at least up until the 1960s — full employment, trade protectionism, a favourable demographic profile, a strong male breadwinner family model, and high home ownership rates also helped sustain the wage earners' model. The formal welfare state had a much more residual role than in other OECD countries since it catered primarily for those outside the labour market. As we will see, however, due to mass unemployment from the 1970s onwards and as a result of policy reforms in the 1980s and 1990s, the wage earners' model has now ceased to function and New Zealand today clearly resembles a liberal welfare state stripped bare of its functionally equivalent policies (Castles 1996; see also Starke 2008).

Before examining welfare state reforms during the period of analysis, we need to take a look at the *status quo ante* of the early 1970s. The broad contours of the New Zealand welfare state were still the ones that had been established in the 1930s. But in 1972 and 1973, two new schemes were introduced. The *first* was ACC,[3] a comprehensive accident compensation programme replacing the small and inefficient Workers' Compensation scheme for occupational accidents. In addition, the new scheme was to cover a wide range of contingencies, including road accidents and medical malpractice, and apply to New Zealanders as well as visitors to the country. The benefits included earnings-related weekly payments (as high as 100 per cent of previous earnings during the first week and 80 per cent thereafter), medical and rehabilitation benefits, and lump sum payments. ACC became the only social insurance-type scheme in New Zealand. The *second* new benefit introduced in the early 1970s was the Domestic Purposes Benefit (DPB), a means-tested payment primarily for lone parents. Previously, lone

---

[3] ACC stands for Accident Compensation Commission, the scheme's governing body.

parents could receive an emergency benefit in case of need, but the 1973 reform made the benefit statutory and extended it to new categories of beneficiaries (McClure 1998: 179; see also Goodger 1998).

If we now try to sketch out the overall shape of the New Zealand welfare state at the beginning of the 1970s, we can still find the remarkably simple structure inherited from the 1938 foundation. The benefits were still overwhelmingly cash transfers rather than in kind. Most working-age benefits, such as unemployment and sickness benefits, were means-tested. Universal provision could be found only in secondary health care and pensions. The benefits were almost exclusively flat-rate and designed to provide a basic income for all New Zealanders. The lack of earnings-related provision — the only exception being accident insurance — is perhaps the most striking feature for a modern OECD welfare state. This meant, for example, that there was neither an unemployment insurance scheme for core workers with earnings-related benefits based on contributions, nor a second-tier earnings-related pension, two elements that, by that time, had been introduced in almost all OECD countries, and certainly, in all European countries. In 1974, a Labour government tried to break this pattern by introducing an earnings-related pension, but the new scheme was short-lived and soon replaced by a more gener-ous version of the old pension (see below). Accident compensation was also exceptional with respect to the mode of financing. While all other benefits were funded out of general revenue, ACC was in part financed from special employers' premiums and levies from motor vehicle owners. Private welfare provision did not play a large role outside of primary care, where private out-of-pocket payments had become an important source of funding. There is very little historical data on private pensions, but traditionally, the issue of private provision for retirement has not been an important factor in New Zealand politics (OECD 1993), in contrast to the other English-speaking welfare states (Hacker 2002; OECD 2009c).

As will be shown in the following sections, none of these elements has been left untouched during the period from the mid-1970s onwards. However, des-pite large-scale changes, New Zealand has remained a welfare state largely built upon the principle of needs-based assistance and dominated by flat-rate, tax-financed transfers.

3.3 Expansion, retrenchment, reconstruction: New Zealand's welfare state since the 1970s

3.3.1 Welfare conservatism, crisis, and confusion: The Muldoon era, 1975–84

3.3.1.1 THE ECONOMIC CHALLENGE OF THE 1970S

The 1975 general election saw a change in government from a Labour to a National government. During one 3-year term in office, the Labour government had introduced new social policy programmes, perhaps hoping to repeat the earlier electoral success of the reformist 1930s government. Not only did Labour fully implement accident insurance, set up the lone parent benefit DPB, and raise benefit rates, but, in 1974, it also introduced New Zealand Superannuation, a contributory second-tier pension with earnings-related benefits. Labour's scheme was, in fact, a compulsory savings model. Employers and employees would pay equal contributions into a central fund, from which, eventually, actuarially fair pensions could be drawn upon entering retirement (see Collins 1977 for details). Yet, the full phase-in period of the new pension would be about 40 years, a fact which allowed the conservative opposition to launch a counterproposal for an immediate expansion of the universal pension that eventually succeeded after their coming into office in 1975 (see below).

The 1970s were difficult times, economically. Although with respect to some basic short-term indicators, New Zealand was still doing relatively well — real economic growth in 1975 was 4 per cent and the official unemployment rate stood at 1.2 per cent — it was already showing signs of crisis with respect to other dimensions. Price inflation, for example, was already reaching double-digit levels, with 12.7 per cent annual consumer price inflation in 1975 (all figures taken from Dalziel and Lattimore 2004) and the twin impact of rising oil prices and a massive fall of agricultural prices had important consequences for New Zealand's balance of payments. The most notable event was a 30 per cent fall in New Zealand's terms of trade in 1974/5, leading to a balance-of-payments current account deficit of 14 per cent of the GDP.

Apart from short-term problems, the development in the early 1970s also demonstrated a number of vulnerabilities that were specific to New Zealand's political economy. A key problem was that economic development was, to a large extent, based on the agricultural sector's international competitiveness. Export revenue from this sector could be used to finance the manufacturing sector which had developed behind protective barriers and which lacked competitiveness (Jones 1999). The result can be likened to the 'import substitution industrialization' (ISI) strategy of many developing countries in the twentieth century (Schwartz 2000). This strategy, however, brought specific risks due to the high dependence on a relatively narrow range of products and markets. In the case of New Zealand, the movement of wool, meat, and dairy prices became one of the key crisis indicators. This was demonstrated as early as in 1966, when a slump in wool prices led to the first, albeit marginal, rise in unemployment in years. In terms of agricultural markets, Britain remained important, despite some diversification. By 1965, more than half of all exports were still going to Britain (Easton 1997a: 142). When, in 1973, the United Kingdom joined the European Economic Community (as it was then called) this came as a shock to many New Zealanders as the country lost its privileged access to the British market for agricultural products. At the same time, however, the British accession was more a sign than the real cause of the new trade relationships.

Even before 1973, access to the British market was already more difficult and other export destinations had been increasing in importance. Nevertheless, the wool price slump in 1966 and the events of 1973 mark the 'end of the golden weather' (Gould 1982) in the economic history of New Zealand. This sense of a watershed provided the backdrop for many of the fundamental economic reforms of the 1980s.

The 1975 election result was, once again, a two-party affair. The conservative National Party won fifty-five of the eighty-seven seats against Labour's thirty-two seats and Robert Muldoon became prime minister. The 'Muldoon era' began, lasting almost 9 years. Muldoon had a dominant position in government because, in addition to being prime minster, he also held the finance portfolio. Historians usually emphasize his attitude of social and cultural conservatism and his wariness with respect to economic and social reforms, particularly compared to successive governments. He was decidedly *not* a member of the 'New Right' conservatism that was emerging in America and Britain, but saw himself rather as an advocate of the lower middle class — the 'ordinary bloke', in New Zealand parlance. This also meant defending the existing welfare state against criticism from economic advisers and New Right politicians, including those within his own party. To some extent, this defence has been related to Muldoon's undeniable populist leanings which, often enough, clashed with more technocratic policy proposals from his advisers. The development of social policy between 1975 and 1984 demonstrates that he was willing and able to override both expert opinion and more radical voices within the National Party on the basis of electoral considerations. Moreover, up until the early 1984, Muldoon could usually count on the support of the National caucus, the parliamentary party. Electoral success helped to delay New Right dominance in the National Party. Only after the lost election of 1984 and the ensuing leadership change was there generational change from 'old' to 'new' conservatives within the National Party (James 1992: 259–63). This is one of the reasons why the welfare state was not radically cut back during the first sub-period from 1975 to 1984. The preferences of the party leadership mattered. Nonetheless, some reforms — particularly in the field of pensions — did take place and will be described in more detail.

3.3.1.2 LABOUR MARKET POLICIES: SEARCHING FOR A RESPONSE TO MASS UNEMPLOYMENT

Unemployment emerged as a major problem in New Zealand only from about 1978 onwards, that is, a few years later than in most other OECD countries. Since the days of the 1930s Depression, New Zealand had a remarkable employment record. During the post-war decades, unemployment rates were usually around 0.1 per cent or lower! This also explains the marginal role of the unemployment benefit and employment policies more generally in the

New Zealand welfare state: 'In effect the most important unemployment benefit in New Zealand was full employment' (Easton 1979: 57). Yet, the country did
not remain unaffected by world economic troubles: Between 1975 and 1984,
the unemployment rate increased from 1.2 to 4.4 per cent and the issue of
mass unemployment entered the political debate. Rising rates prompted two
policy changes in the late 1970s: First, in 1979, an indirect cut in the unemployment benefit for childless beneficiaries — realized through a new tax on their
benefits — and, secondly, at around the same time, a significant expansion of
active labour market measures.

Active labour market schemes in the 1970s were usually based on wage
subsidies paid to local bodies and community organizations who took on
unemployed people for a limited period of time (Higgins 1999: 262; see Gill
1989 for an overview of labour market schemes). In 1979, the Muldoon government significantly expanded these programmes by allocating NZ$55 mil-
lion to active labour market policies (McClure 1998: 208). From the early 1980s
onwards, however, the use of wage subsidies came under attack from Treasury
experts for their alleged displacement effects and, as a consequence, some
programmes were abandoned (Koopman-Boyden and Scott 1984: 141). Overall,
despite rising unemployment figures under Muldoon, it was pension policy, not
labour market policy that attracted most attention between 1975 and 1984.

3.3.1.3 PENSIONS: THE LAST BIG EXPANSION OF THE WELFARE STATE

The year 1975 was an extraordinary one for New Zealand pension policy. It saw
the change in government after a campaign that was largely based on two
different projects for the future of the old-age pension: Labour's earnings-
related New Zealand Superannuation scheme, legislated in 1974, and National's
competing universal flat-rate National Superannuation proposal which ultimately prevailed. With hindsight, it comes as no surprise that National's scheme
proved to be more popular with voters. One of the main problems of Labour's
plan was that it was an extremely long-term project that did not generate any
immediate effects visible to voters — apart from a new contribution of 4 per
cent of wages from employees and employers. The pension would reach ma-
turity only around 2015, a fact which inspired National's campaign slogan 'New
scheme starts half century sooner' (Booth 1977: 104).

Moreover, the central fund, to which all contributions would go in the
meantime — and which, according to the Labour Minister of Finance Bill
Rowling, 'would provide a considerable financial resource directly available to
the Government to pursue a growth policy' (cited in Collins 1977: 29–30) —
was vigorously attacked by conservative politicians. National famously released
an advertisement during the election campaign, highlighting the alleged danger of such a big government-controlled fund. The cartoon spot featured 'three
Cossacks dancing across the television screen to the words, "Indeed one day the

Government could wind up owning literally everything. And you know what that's called don't you?"' (Booth 1977: 131).[4] But there were other, perhaps more realistic problems. Women were likely to lose from a contributory, strictly earnings-related pension, due to low female labour market participation and wage inequality between women and men (McClure 1998: 190–6). Older workers close to retirement were likely to receive only a very small additional pension. In general, the exact benefit level was impossible to determine in advance since it depended largely on the development of wages and the returns from the central fund. On the whole, the pension was difficult for many New Zealanders to understand.

National's proposal, introduced in 1975, did not have any of these apparent 'flaws'. It was simple, based on the existing welfare state architecture — as it can be seen as an enhanced version of the existing universal component of the public pension — and generous. It was paid from age 60 to all New Zealanders at a level of 80 per cent of gross average ordinary weekly wages for a married couple (combined benefit) and 48 per cent for a single person.

By international comparison, it was in terms of the *minimum* pension, and not the standard pension, that New Zealand was generous in 1980 (Scruggs 2004). Due to the absence of an earnings-related second tier, New Zealand's standard pension was rather meagre. However, one has to bear in mind that most of the elderly owned a mortgage-free home which should significantly reduce the need for cash transfers in old age. And indeed, even before the introduction of the new benefit, there was little evidence that many elderly people were facing hardship. An official survey of living standards in the 1970s showed that only a small minority of the elderly were poor and concluded that 'a selective approach, aimed directly at those in hardship, was the most appropriate way of dealing with the situation' (cited in Booth 1977: 118). In a similar vein, a — generally pro-welfare state — Royal Commission report of 1972 had recommended leaving the pension system as it was (Royal Commission of Inquiry into Social Security 1972: 215). All this suggests that the reasons for the introduction of National Superannuation were primarily based on electoral considerations. Labour's poorly publicized new scheme had given Muldoon a unique opportunity to counter with a much more popular proposal just before the general election and he seized that opportunity without much hesitation. Historian Keith Sinclair later famously described National Superannuation as 'the biggest election bribe in the country's history' (Sinclair 1991: 316; cf. McClure 1998: 191).

However, the enormous cost of National Superannuation soon became a problem. Officials had warned Muldoon early on about the fiscal consequences of the policy but he took no heed of that advice. The hike in pension expenditure after 1977 was not so much the result of the higher pension level but

---

[4] The spot can be viewed at http://www.filmarchive.org.nz/offsite/elections/C1555NatSuperannuation.html (accessed 19 December 2008).

rather fuelled by the lower eligibility age of 60 years instead of 65 years as before. Between 1975 and 1984, the number of pensioners rose by over 55 per cent and within the first 4 years of the National government, net expenditure on the aged increased from 3.6 per cent to 5.7 per cent of GDP (New Zealand Planning Council 1979: 78). Moreover, the overall fiscal situation worsened at the end of the 1970s. By 1979, the budget deficit stood at 8.4 per cent of GDP. In addition to the cut in the unemployment benefit (see above), the government, therefore, decided to reduce the pension level in 1979. This was done by changing the calculation base from gross to net wages (for details, see Preston 2004).

Other cost-containment measures had been discussed but ultimately dismissed, including a retirement age of 62 years (New Zealand Planning Council 1979: 195) and a clawback tax similar to the controversial 'superannuation tax surcharge' introduced by the Labour government 6 years later. What was appealing about the change eventually implemented was its low visibility. Technical changes of the calculation mechanism are, by their very nature, usually a matter for pension experts. Moreover, the retrenchment decision did not show up in the form of a decreasing nominal benefit rate. High wage growth at the end of the 1970s made it unnecessary to lower the pension level in order to reach the 80 per cent target (Preston 2004: 16). The wider public, therefore, barely took notice of this first pension cut.

3.3.1.4 HEALTH POLICY: FROM BOLD IDEAS TO CAUTIOUS CHANGE

In health care, pressure for reform began to build up in the 1970s (Gauld 2001: 31–8). The need for cost containment, for better access to services, and for a better coordination of different areas of health care all entered the debate. In 1975, the predecessor Labour government issued a White Paper which, based on a review of different aspects of the health system, proposed a number of organizational changes including the establishment of fourteen partly elected 'regional health authorities' (RHAs), replacing the existing hospital boards. The RHAs would have greater responsibilities than hospital boards — for instance, in the coordination of primary, secondary, and tertiary care. A significant new idea mentioned in the White Paper was the 'purchaser–provider split' that later became the hallmark — and the bone of contention — of health reform in New Zealand (Gauld 2001: 33). Yet, Labour did not implement these plans. They failed for several reasons including the opposition of the medical profession who feared that many of the profitable opportunities for additional private practice would have become impossible after the reform.

Ironically, many of the ideas contained in the White Paper were eventually legislated by the successive Muldoon government. In contrast to Labour, however, the conservative National government tried to involve interest groups and health care experts in the formulation of the policy and tested the new structure by means of two pilot schemes before its nationwide implementation (Gauld 2001: 35). Because of this cautious and pragmatic approach, final legislation was enacted only in 1983 and implemented largely under Labour after Muldoon's election defeat of 1984. The result was a system of fourteen Area Health Boards (AHBs), responsible for the planning and management of service delivery in their areas. Secondary and tertiary health care as well as public health were to be the responsibility of the AHBs, while the system of primary care remained largely unchanged. About two-thirds of government health expenditure were eventually allocated to AHBs from 1983 by using a population-based formula (Blank 1994: 124; European Observatory on Health Care Systems 2001: 26; Gauld 2001: 36–7). The move to such a funding formula marked a new emphasis on cost containment. Perhaps most importantly, the health reforms under Muldoon were the slow and rather pragmatic beginning of a long-term decentralization process which, in the 1990s, was to result in a number of much more radical and — at least partly — ideologically driven reforms (European Observatory on Health Care Systems 2001: 25).

Accident insurance saw only a few small changes between 1975 and 1984. The ACC system, set up in 1973, had come under criticism from employers and some right-wing politicians in the late 1970s. Employers complained about what they saw as excessive insurance levies for work-related accidents. While a government-sponsored review called for wide-ranging cutbacks, these plans met with fierce protests by interest groups. The 1982 Accident Compensation Act eventually included both retrenchment elements — for example, reduction in the level of compensation from 100 to 80 per cent of earnings during the first week — as well as a number of expansionary ones — such as higher lump sum compensation for some types of accident (Campbell 1996).

3.3.1.5 FAMILY POLICY: AN EXPERIMENT IN TARGETING ASSISTANCE

Family policy did not play a very prominent role in the post-war New Zealand welfare state. There are even scholars who claim that New Zealand 'has never had an explicit family policy' (Koopman-Boyden and Scott 1984: 170). One — rather unorthodox, but certainly important — instrument of family policy in the wider sense was the 'family wage' as part of the wage earners' welfare state described earlier in this chapter (see also Shirley et al. 1997). The other, formal, instrument was the universal Family Benefit. Introduced after the Second World War, the Family Benefit had been neglected by politicians. Since it was not indexed but rather adjusted in an ad hoc fashion, the benefit's real value eroded over the years, from about 8 per cent of average wages in 1946 to around 3 per cent by 1983 (St John 2001: 3). Social security spending on children as a percentage of GDP declined by more than 60 per cent between 1950 and 1979 (New Zealand Planning Council 1979: 78). However, the pension cut of 1979 released resources that were then used to double the Family

Benefit to NZ$6 weekly, which was to be the last ever increase before the abolition of the benefit in 1991. High inflation in the 1980s soon devalued the universal benefit but the government rejected calls for a further increase (McClure 1998: 200).

In the 1970s, the conservative government also tried to target family transfers more effectively, initially by turning the existing tax exemptions — dating back to 1914 — into tax *rebates* (Koopman-Boyden and Scott 1984: 144–50). By their very nature, tax exemptions tend to be regressive because of the positive effect of a progressive tax rate on the size of the concession for higher income groups. Rebates, by contrast, grant a fixed dollar amount to all income categories. Yet, they were insensitive to the number of children in the household and did not reach families without significant taxable income. In short, they were a rather blunt instrument for targeting assistance to the needy (Koopman-Boyden and Scott 1984). There were attempts to fix these problems: New rebates were introduced and others terminated (Nolan 2002: 2–3). Overall, family policy under Muldoon was marked by frequent changes — or 'experimentation' — and a turn towards needs-based assistance.

Other measures of the Muldoon years included a reduction in the value of the main benefit for lone parents, the DPB in 1977 as a response to concerns about rising beneficiary numbers, the growing fiscal burden of the DPB as well as the moral effects of granting a benefit to lone mothers. Conservative politicians claimed that this had led to irresponsible behaviour and family instability (McClure 1998: 179–89). A DPB review committee argued for benefit cuts and tighter eligibility, but also for more social workers (Easton 1981: 91–4; Hughes 2005: 3–4). While the government chose not to implement most of the committee's recommendations, it did introduce a significant benefit cutback for the first 6 months of receipt in 1977. The idea was to make the benefit less attractive during the period just after a marriage breakdown and thus to discourage family break-up. Despite the cutback, however, the number of lone parents receiving the DPB rose further.

Family policy in New Zealand traditionally put an emphasis on cash transfers. In-kind benefits, especially childcare services, received much less attention. Childcare was largely left to voluntary community action and, predominantly, to mothers. This was evidence of the strong institutionalization of the male breadwinner model up until the 1980s. But attitudes started to change from the mid-1970s, with participation rates in childcare facilities increasing by a factor of seven between 1976 and 1987 (Shirley et al. 1997: 271). One of the innovations emerging in the early 1980s was Te Kohanga Reo ('language nest'), early childhood education in Maori language. This 'childcare revolution' was, however, almost entirely user-driven and not particularly encouraged by the state. It was not before the late 1980s that the government gradually gave up its non-interventionist position (Meade and Podmore 2002).

In parental leave legislation, New Zealand is also clearly a laggard country. The Maternity Leave and Employment Protection Act of 1980 for the first time protected pregnant women from dismissal and provided for up to 26 weeks of unpaid leave during pregnancy or after the birth of a child. Yet, the National government narrowly focused on issues of job protection and refused to grant any new benefits to women on leave or introduce a gender-neutral parental leave scheme (Callister and Galtry 2006).

3.3.1.6 SOCIAL POLICY DURING THE LONG 'DECADE OF CONFUSION'

The 1970s have been described as a 'decade of confusion' in relation to welfare state change (McClure 2003). This statement even applies up to the end of the Muldoon era in 1984. The 'confusion' stemmed from the government's lack of a coherent policy about the welfare state. The most important decision was, without a doubt, the introduction of a generous universal pension at the beginning of the period. On the whole, instead of drastic cutbacks as a response to the economic crisis, the period between 1975 and 1984 was marked, at first, by a dramatic expansion of state involvement and then — in part precisely because of this expansion — by stagnation as well as some moderate retrenchment from 1979 onwards. But it is important to note that, despite being a conservative government, the National government of the 1970s and early 1980s was a far cry from what emerged at around the same time as the New Right movement in Britain and the United States. Especially in economic policy, but also in social policy, the Muldoon government was traditionalist, and deregulation and retrenchment remained very limited and largely driven by problem pressure, not market-liberal ideas.

Overall, more money was being spent, especially with regard to elderly people, family policy became more (but rather poorly) targeted, health was decentralized, and working-age benefits became slightly less generous. But apparently none of this was the outcome of any set of overarching principles but was rather the consequence of short-term exigencies and the pressures the government was facing. A similar verdict, however, could be made about the succeeding government, the so-called Fourth Labour Government. Yet, while both governments had a short-term policy focus and were reform-shy in the field of social policy, they diverged sharply in economic policy matters. Here, the Fourth Labour Government introduced sweeping changes that fundamentally restructured the New Zealand economy.

3.3.2 Rogernomics and the welfare state: Labour, 1984–90

3.3.2.1 CONTEXT, CONTENT, AND OUTCOMES OF THE ROGERNOMICS REVOLUTION

Labour came to power in turbulent times. The economic measures introduced by the preceding National government in the early 1980s were an uneasy mix of liberalization and heavy state intervention — among other things, there was a wage and price freeze between 1982 and early 1984 — and they proved insufficient in easing the pressure on the economy and the budget. To make things worse, the country was hit by an acute currency crisis in 1984. Pressure on the New Zealand Dollar had been building up for some time and both the Reserve Bank and Treasury advocated a devaluation of at least 15 per cent. But Muldoon was not willing to devalue (Gustafson 2000: 384–5). He called an early election for July 1984, hoping to bolster his mandate. By the mid-1980s, however, his policies and leadership style had become very unpopular. Most observers, including financial market actors, expected a Labour victory and devaluation just after the election in much the same manner as had occurred in Australia the year before. Eventually, the Reserve Bank ran out of foreign currency reserves and suspended all foreign exchange dealings until further notice. The incoming government had to act and, even before having been sworn into office, devalued the dollar by 20 per cent.

This devaluation was but the first step in a series of measures that were aimed at liberalizing and deregulating an economy that was seen as inefficient and that was famously likened to a 'Polish shipyard' by the new Prime Minister David Lange (cited in Kelsey 1997: 38). Although the election campaign had been relatively vague with respect to economic policies and although there were even grounds for expecting a broadly Keynesian adjustment from the new Labour government (Mulgan 1990: 15–16), a strong faction in cabinet tried to push through radical economic changes once in office. The so-called troika, made up of Roger Douglas, the new Minister of Finance, and his two associate ministers David Caygill and Richard Prebble was the driver of change. However, they were not the only politicians to support what was to become known as 'Rogernomics'. Prime Minister Lange also stood behind Rogernomics together with a majority of cabinet members. Only the Labour caucus (the parliamentary party) and the Labour rank-and-file in particular tended to be much more sceptical, if not hostile, to the radicalism of the economic reforms. But in the centralized political system of pre-1993 New Zealand, their influence on legislation was usually small.

Rogernomics entailed important changes in virtually all areas of economic policy (on Rogernomics, see also Bollard 1994; Boston 1987; Easton 1989*b*, 1997*b*; Hawke 2004; Kelsey 1997; Quiggin 1998; Silverstone et al. 1996). The financial sector was the first target of reform, which started off with the floating of the exchange rate and financial deregulation, including the abolition of exchange controls (dating back to the 1930s), a new liberal regulation for portfolio investment and repatriation of profits, and the deregulation of the banking sector (e.g. abolition of interest rate controls and of foreign ownership restrictions of domestic banks). The financial reforms paved the way towards more foreign ownership of New Zealand businesses, a development that became highly controversial in the following years. It also fuelled financial speculation — temporarily halted by the 1987 stock market crash — and riskier lending practices (Quiggin 1998: 83). Price stability was to be the principle objective in monetary policy. A target of 0–2 per cent inflation was set. In 1989, the Reserve Bank Act made the central bank independent from government and fully institutionalized this target-based regime.

Although the process of opening up New Zealand's economy to the world had begun under the previous government, it was speeded up under Labour. Unilateral trade liberalization involved the removal of highly protectionist quotas and the lowering of import tariffs according to the so-called Swiss formula. This meant that high tariffs (e.g. in the footwear, clothing, and automobile industry) were cut further than low tariffs, with the final aim of harmonizing the tariff structure at a low level. Export subsidies were also terminated. Closely connected to the decision to expose the domestic economy to foreign competition was product market liberalization. Among other things, the government abolished price regulations, tax concessions for agriculture, ended the wage-price freeze imposed by the Muldoon government, removed other, more specific price controls, ended state-monopoly rights, for instance, in telecommunications and electricity, liberalized shop trading hours, and changed the regulation of mergers.

Already in its first electoral term (1984–87), the government introduced a comprehensive programme of corporatization of the state sector (Bollard and Mayes 1993). The so-called state-owned enterprises (SOEs) were supposed to adopt private-sector management structures and practices. Ports, airports, utilities, and other state enterprises were restructured along business lines. Corporatization was introduced as a means to enhance efficiency in the state sector. One of the principles was that commercial and non-commercial goals were to be strictly separated. The managers in charge were accountable to Ministers for the achievement of performance targets but otherwise were to be relatively independent from direct interference. The explicit aim of corporatization was to enhance efficiency in the state sector. Yet, in many cases, these changes were undertaken with a view to facilitating the eventual privatization of state assets — at least, this is what Treasury officials had in mind; most Labour politicians at the time publicly denied wishing to privatize (Easton 1989a: 124). Yet, from 1987 onwards, Labour radically changed its position and started to sell off state assets on a massive scale. Some of the more important SOEs that were fully or partly privatized included Air New Zealand, New Zealand Telecom, and the Bank of New Zealand. The funds thus raised by the early 1990s amounted to NZ$9 billion, equivalent to approximately 12 per cent of GDP (Bollard and Mayes 1993: 327). This makes it one of the largest privatization programmes in the OECD. In many cases, the companies went to foreign investors — a fact that became a politically contentious issue in the 1990 election.

The state sector also became the testing ground for 'New Public Management' theories, with government departments completely restructured by separating policy strategy units (the ministries) from the operating functions of funding and providing services (State Sector Act 1988). The relationship between the two tiers was to be contract-based. Moreover, the Public Finance Act of 1988 required government departments to move to business-like accounting practices and output-oriented budgeting, which proved difficult in areas in which 'output' is hard to define. In the 1990s, many of these ideas spilled over into other policy areas, such as health care and housing.

Another example of far-reaching change was tax policy (Stephens 1993). On the one hand, the top personal income tax rate was lowered twice, in 1985, from 66 to 48 per cent and, in 1988, to 33 per cent. Corporate rates were brought in line with personal rates. The tax base was simultaneously broadened. On the other hand, the tax mix changed significantly. This was due to the introduction of a Goods and Services Tax (GST), a value-added tax at a uniform rate of 10 per cent (later 12.5 per cent) in 1986. The GST was very unpopular, not least because the government was committed to a uniform rate. That is, food, clothes, and similar items were taxed at the full rate, in order to avoid distortions. The two elements of the tax reforms, cutting income tax rates for high-income earners and increasing consumption taxes, had a regressive distributional impact, despite the fact that compensation measures were introduced, especially for low-income families (see below). Moreover, the tax mix, and hence, the financing base of the welfare state, shifted from direct, particularly personal income, to indirect, above all, general consumption, taxes. Table 3.1 shows that the 1986 introduction of the GST boosted this type of revenue from GSTs, while other types of taxes, in particular personal income and property taxes, contributed much less to total state revenue than before. Note also that, in stark contrast to the vast majority of other OECD countries, social contributions play no role at all in New Zealand's tax structure.

One sector that was spared from big changes during the 1980s were industrial relations (Deeks 1990). The 1987 Labour Relations Act allowed for a decentralization of wage bargaining but at the same time introduced incentives for small unions to merge and increase their organizational power (see Barry and Walsh 2007 for the effect on trade union structures). Also, in the context of

Table 3.1: Sources of tax revenue in New Zealand, 1975–2005, in percentage of total taxation

Source of tax revenue	1975	1980	1985	1990	1995	2000	2005
Taxes on income and profits	66.5	69.8	69.4	59.6	61.3	60.0	63.0
Personal income	54.3	61.6	60.5	48.0	45.0	43.1	41.1
Corporate income	11.8	7.8	8.3	6.5	11.9	12.4	16.8
Taxes on property	9.2	7.9	7.4	6.8	5.4	5.3	4.9
Taxes on goods and services	24.2	22.3	23.1	33.6	33.4	34.7	32.1
Total taxation	100.0	100.0	100.0	100.0	100.0	100.0	100.0

Source: OECD (2007*d*).

corporatization, wage bargaining practices in the public sector became more like those in the private sector (State Sector Act 1988). But, on the whole, industrial relations under the Fourth Labour government were clearly marked by continuity.

The bulk of the Rogernomics package was prepared, legislated, and implemented very quickly, with the government using the opportunities provided by New Zealand's Westminster polity. A coherent and ideologically committed group in cabinet was able to push through the changes at great speed under conditions of collective cabinet responsibility, strong party discipline — 'backbench rebellions' are almost non-existent — and the absence of formal veto players such as a second chamber of parliament, a constitutional court, or federal institutions. The philosophical justification for 'Rogernomics' as well as technical advice mostly came from economists in the Treasury, who also prepared two influential post-election briefing papers for the government: *Economic Management* (New Zealand Treasury 1984) and *Government Management* (New Zealand Treasury 1987). These documents laid out a comprehensive market-liberal vision of minimal state intervention in the economy and widespread use of market mechanisms in the state sector (Boston 1991; Easton 1994) and are still regarded as the blueprint of Rogernomics (Jesson 1989; Kelsey 1997; Goldfinch 2000).

However, as the example of social policy demonstrates, there were important limits to Treasury influence and they mostly refer to political preferences. Many members of the Fourth Labour government, including Prime Minister Lange, were much more cautious in the welfare state field than in overall economic policy reform. They effectively blocked the full-scale extension of Rogernomics to social policy, for example, by establishing a largely pro-welfare Royal Commission on Social Policy in 1986, which was supposed to bolster the case against radical welfare state retrenchment. The success of this move was limited but it indicates that there was no consensus within the cabinet and the Labour Party as a whole on which way to go in social policy.

The overall success of Rogernomics in terms of macroeconomic outcomes is still subject to debate (see e.g. Dalziel 2002; Evans et al. 1996; Hazeldine and Quiggin 2006), but in the short term the reforms did not help much. On the contrary, the restructuring of the manufacturing sector due to regulatory changes, the end of trade protectionism, and privatization were followed by rising unemployment in the late 1980s and low economic growth. Comparing New Zealand's macroeconomic development in the 1980s and early 1990s with Australia's is particularly instructive: Although both countries were facing relatively similar problems at the beginning of the period and, as a response, started to liberalize around the same time, Australia's overall performance has been markedly superior to New Zealand's, a fact that many authors attribute to the much more moderate and less disruptive reform process in Australia (Quiggin 1998; Dalziel 2002). Somewhat surprisingly, Labour was re-elected in 1987 — a first since 1946 — albeit for reasons that had little to do with economic policy but more with foreign policy and reforms in other non-economic fields (Mcallister and Vowles 1994).

The fragile balance between the radical advocates of Rogernomics and more moderate reformers in the Labour cabinet, however, was seriously tested after the election (see Clark 2005). When Roger Douglas unilaterally presented plans to introduce a 'flat tax' and a benefit reform in late 1987, Prime Minister David Lange — who thought it was 'time for a cup of tea' in economic restructuring — was forced to publicly contradict his own Minister. The tensions continued and, in 1988, Douglas resigned only to be reinstated by the parliamentary Labour Party a few months later. He did not return to his post as Minister of Finance, however, but was given only portfolios (Police and Immigration) in which he was no longer able to pursue his economic programme.[5] This whole episode was an evidence that Prime Minister Lange had lost the support of Labour MPs. He resigned. In the time between Lange's resignation and the 1990 general election, Labour was unable to regain voters' confidence. Geoffrey Palmer, Lange's successor, lasted just over 1 year in office and was followed by Mike Moore who led the government for 2 months before the scheduled election of 1990. The result was disastrous for Labour. The party lost twenty-eight seats (in the ninety-seven-seat parliament) and its share of the popular vote dropped from 48 to 35.1 per cent as compared to the 1987 election. A National government took over again.

The welfare state reforms introduced by Labour between 1984 and 1990 were limited compared to what happened in the field of economic policy in the same period as well as compared to what happened in the field of social policy after 1990. Just as much as the Labour government of the 1980s is correctly associated with radical economic reforms, the post-1990 National government is remembered for what were probably the most radical welfare state retrenchment initiatives in any OECD welfare state (Starke 2008). But before describing National's attack on the welfare state, we will first look at the changes Labour brought to the welfare state between 1984 and 1990.

3.3.2.2 LABOUR MARKET POLICIES: FROM DEMAND TO SUPPLY

Despite increasing unemployment — the national unemployment rate rose from 4.4 per cent to 7.8 per cent between 1984 and 1990 — labour market policies were not at the centre of Labour's policy programme. There was, however, a cutback in the unemployment benefit. In 1987, the government decided to raise the eligibility age for the standard unemployment benefit from 16 to 18 years. This meant a benefit reduction of 26 per cent for this group, since school leavers were from then on only eligible for the lower youth

---

[5] In 1993, Roger Douglas founded a radical market-liberal party, the Association of Consumers and Taxpayers (ACT).

rate until they reached the age of 18. Moreover, the government refrained from reversing their predecessors' decision to cut the benefit for childless beneficiaries.

In active labour market policy, the emphasis shifted from wage subsidies and direct intervention to employability and supply-side measures. Most subsidy-based labour market schemes were ended and replaced with Access, a training scheme, in 1987 (Gill 1989; Higgins 1999: 262).

3.3.2.3 PENSIONS: CUTTING BACK THE UNIVERSAL SCHEME

As often, the political debate about the reform of the New Zealand welfare state centred on the field of old-age pensions. By 1984, pension expenditure in New Zealand had risen to 7 per cent of GDP which was, at the time, an above-average level by OECD standards. Around the same time, Austria spent 11 per cent of GDP on pensions (1985), Denmark 6.9 per cent, and Switzerland only 6 per cent (OECD 2006c). According to the same OECD data, pension expenditure in New Zealand accounted for over 40 per cent of total public social expenditure (including health). Meanwhile, the budget deficit had again grown to 8.7 per cent of GDP by 1984. Upon gaining office, the Labour government immediately started to look for ways to cut costs.

A few months after the election, the government announced a new 'super-annuation tax surcharge', a tax clawback on high-income pensioners. The decision in favour of the surcharge and against other options — for example, an across-the-board pension cut or, as in 1979, less generous indexation rules — was legitimized on grounds of equity considerations. The budget statement claimed that there 'was an inescapable conclusion...that there were other priorities for welfare expenditure than assisting those superannuitants who already had enough income on which to live comfortably, particularly the pressing need for assistance for low income families' (cited in Periodic Report Group 1997: 58). Technically, the surcharge was an additional tax of 25 per cent on top of the regular income tax pensioners had to pay. There was a threshold, set at a relatively high level in order to make sure that it would exclude the rich rather than target only to the very poor. The level of income at which the pension was fully clawed back was (by 1990) equivalent to 2.5 times the average wage (OECD 1993: 64). Nonetheless, the surcharge affected up to around a third of pensioners, at least to some extent (Periodic Report Group 1997: 59; Starke 2008: 84).

What made the surcharge so controversial was that its effect was very similar to a means test and, since Labour had pledged in the 1984 election campaign *not* to means-test superannuation, the surcharge was seen as a broken promise by many Labour voters. The frequent changes of parameters such as the rate of the surcharge and the exemption threshold (see Periodic Report Group 1997: 59 for an overview) certainly did not help to restore confidence, either. In 1984, the National Superannuitants Federation, later renamed Grey Power, was founded and started to lobby against Labour's pension policies. Grey Power very soon attracted thousands of pensioners as members and obtained considerable media attention — and, arguably, some influence on pension policy — during the 1980s and early 1990s.

At the end of Labour's second term in office, pension policy appeared back on the agenda. This time, it was not only high-income pensioners who were affected by retrenchment but all pensioners. In the 1989 budget, the government announced a new indexation formula and a higher eligibility age. The latter, however, was not implemented before the change of government in 1990. But the new indexation rules had a lasting effect on the level of superannuation which, however, went largely unnoticed by the wider public. The government decided to bring the pension level gradually in line with other benefits by linking it to the lesser movement of either the wage index or consumer prices. The level for a married couple thus decreased from 80.5 per cent of average wages in 1988 to 72.2 per cent in April 1991 — when the additional pension cuts of the National government kicked in (Preston 2004: 41).

A number of changes concerned private pensions. Traditionally, private provision did not play a very big role in New Zealand. By the late 1980s, only about 15 per cent of those above the age of 60 received a private pension, in most cases a small occupational pension (St John 1992: 13). Between 1988 and 1990, the government abolished all kinds of special tax treatment of private pensions. It followed the Treasury's view that these tax concessions were likely to distort savings and investment patterns and were poorly targeted (New Zealand Treasury 1987: 299–300). Until the recent introduction of the KiwiSaver scheme (see below), the reforms in the late 1980s made New Zealand *the only OECD country* to regard private pension savings as just another type of savings, with no tax incentives or public subsidies available (Yoo and Serres 2004).[6]

3.3.2.4 HEALTH POLICY: MUCH TALK, LITTLE CHANGE

Although the Labour government resisted major new changes to the health sector — apart from implementing the system of AHBs started under the predecessor government — it commissioned two important reviews that set the scene for some of the wide-ranging health reforms of the 1990s (Gauld 2001: 55–67). The first of these reviews, the Health Benefits Review (Scott et al. 1986), provided a comprehensive analysis of the New Zealand health system and recommended increased competition among providers (Gauld 2001: 57–8). Yet, the authors also sounded a note of caution about the benefits of competition and emphasized, for example, the need for better information about the costs and effects of services in order for competition to function properly.

---

[6] Investment in housing is an important exception to this rule.

The second review under Labour — the Hospital and Related Services Taskforce, known as the 'Gibbs Report' after its chairman, Alan Gibbs, a businessman — was more radical. The title of the report, 'Unshackling the Hospitals' (Hospital and Related Services Taskforce 1988), already indicated a much more optimistic view about structural health-care reform. Based on a — highly controversial — estimate of potential efficiency gains as high as 30 per cent, the report recommended a new structure for New Zealand's hospital sector based on the 'purchaser–provider split' combined with an internal market between providers (Hospital and Related Services Taskforce 1988: 26–37).

The government largely ignored the recommendations of both the Health Benefits Review and the Gibbs Report. There were some changes with regard to hospital management structures and, in the process of setting up the Area Hospital Boards (AHB) system (enacted under the previous government), the government put an emphasis on performance-oriented accountability agreements between the AHBs and the Minister of Health and tried to infuse a dose of professionalism by putting government-appointed AHB members alongside the elected members in the late 1980s (Blank 1994: 126; Scott 1994: 28). But overall, Labour shied away from any fundamental reforms.

At the same time, there is no unequivocal evidence that the health system was in 'deep crisis' in the 1980s (Gauld 2001: 67–77). On the whole, it appeared to work relatively well at an affordable level of cost. This is not to deny that there were problems in some areas: The 1980s were, for example, a time of lengthening surgical waiting lists, rising out-of-pocket expenditure, and, in consequence, increasing numbers of people buying private insurance (Hopkins and Cumming 2001).

The lack of reforms under Labour does not mean, however, that the various reports and recommendations issued in the 1980s were without any consequences. On the contrary, it is likely that they helped to shift the climate towards more competition-oriented policies in the longer term. And indeed, many of the ideas that featured in the Health Benefits Review and the Gibbs Report were taken up by the conservative government of the 1990s and put into action.

In accident insurance, the Labour government planned to remove inequities between the regular health system and ACC benefits. The idea was to extend the coverage of ACC benefits to all forms of incapacity — not just incapacity caused by accidents (Campbell 1996; Stephens 2005). At the same time, Labour would have lowered the level of compensation by introducing a waiting period and a flat-rate benefit during the first weeks of benefit receipt. The plans were never enacted because of the change in government of 1990. The only real change to ACC was a significant increase in the level of contributions in the mid-1980s (St John 1999: 159).

3.3.2.5 FAMILY POLICY: MOVING FURTHER TOWARDS A TARGETED SYSTEM

In family policy, Labour tried a novel approach and departed even further from the traditional universal design than the previous National government. Starting off with Family Care, a tax rebate of NZ$10 available on a per-child basis in addition to the Family Benefit and other tax benefits, the government attempted to target assistance more effectively than existing tax rebates had done (Shirley et al. 1997: 256). Only 'working families' with paid work of at least 30 hours weekly per household were eligible. Moreover, Family Care would go directly to the principal caregiver, not the principal earner.

As already mentioned, the government introduced the GST in 1986. In order to alleviate the burden for families, a family transfer package was introduced simultaneously. At the centre of the package was Family Support, a refundable tax credit to working as well as non-working low-income families which replaced a number of tax benefits and which was to become the main family transfer over the years. In addition, a new Guaranteed Minimum Family Income (GMFI) was added, a tax credit available to working families only (Nolan 2002: 6–7). However, there is anecdotal evidence that take-up rates of Family Care and the GMFI were very low, possibly due to the stigma associated with means-tested assistance and the complicated application procedures (McClure 1998: 216). Nonetheless, the deliberate distinction between 'working families' and 'non-working families' became more pronounced with Family Care and the GMFI. This distinction was also visible in the delivery of benefits (McClure 1998: 218). While working families received their payments, including Family Support, through a tax adjustment by the Inland Revenue Department, beneficiaries received it as a welfare benefit from the Department of Social Welfare.

Family policy under Labour was thus marked by a shift in emphasis towards means-tested benefits. This shift was further intensified by the non-adjustment of the universal Family Benefit during times of high-consumer price inflation. By 1991, it was worth less than 1 per cent of average wages (St John 2001: 3). However, the newly introduced Family Support was not inflation-proof, either. Consequently, its real value also declined markedly during the late 1980s and up to the mid-1990s (St John 2004: 7).

A number of further changes affecting families were made in the mid-1980s. First, in 1986, the lone parent benefit cut of 1977 was repealed, that is, the full amount of DPB during the first 6 months of receipt was restored. Second, in 1987, the government extended parental leave. It was still to be unpaid leave but it now also applied to fathers. The combined period of leave for both parents could be up to 52 weeks and the eligibility criteria were relaxed (Callister and Galtry 2006). Third, things started to move with respect to family services, particularly childcare. Although the Muldoon government had started to review funding and regulation at the beginning of the 1980s, it was only under Labour that policy changes were introduced (Meade and Podmore 2002; Mitchell 2005). In 1985, regulations were revised in order to make sure that each centre had at least one trained supervisor. The government also wished to strengthen the educational aspect of pre-school centres and, in the following year, shifted the entire responsibility for childcare from the Department of Social Welfare to the Department of Education. Further, more fundamental reforms followed the 1988 *Before Five* White Paper. The government aimed at widening access to services, improving the quality of care, while at the same time maintaining the diversity of services, which were usually provided not by the state but by parents or the third sector. Moreover, the cultural aspect had to be addressed since Maori childcare and education providers were becoming very popular in the 1980s. As a result of the *Before Five* review, early childhood services received considerably higher levels of funding and a new funding mechanism was set up, based on direct payments to providers according to a per-child, per-hour formula and a targeted childcare subsidy for parents on low income.

3.3.2.6 STAGNATION AMIDST A REVOLUTION: THE FATE OF SOCIAL POLICY UNDER LABOUR

In sum, the second sub-period under review, the Labour government of 1984 to 1990, was marked by a number of welfare state cutbacks, but not by the wholesale attack on the welfare state that some had perhaps feared — and others had hoped for. An early academic assessment of the period was even entitled 'Social Policy: Has There Been One?' (Koopman-Boyden 1990). The contrast with the radicalism of Rogernomics in the area of economic policy can hardly be overstated. Most areas of social security remained safe from the reforming zeal of Roger Douglas and his associates. Only in pensions were some significant reforms introduced. The superannuation surcharge, one of the most unpopular of Labour's policies, as well as the new indexation rules made the pension less generous and even excluded some high-income earners altogether. In family policy, Labour also shifted towards needs-based policies.

In the 1980s, we can see Labour moving gradually away from its traditional universalist welfare state philosophy which, at least as a long-term goal if not real policy, had been a core principle from the 1930s onwards. Under the difficult economic conditions of the 1980s, Labour politicians still saw a crucial role for the welfare state, but wanted to target resources more clearly at the needy. According to some authors, this may have paved the way for the more radical retrenchment policies of their successors. In this view, the Labour government should be seen 'not so much as the executioner of New Zealand's welfare state, but rather as its gravedigger' (Castles and Shirley 1996: 89). Without the ensuing 1990s cuts, Castles and Shirley's verdict would probably have been less pessimistic. However, with respect to the wage earners' welfare state, Labour can indeed be seen as a 'gravedigger'. Some of the Rogernomics reforms undermined central pillars of the wage earners' model such as trade protectionism.

3.3.3 The welfare state under attack: 1990–9

3.3.3.1 ANTI-STATE IDEOLOGY, FISCAL CRISIS, AND POLITICAL TURBULENCE IN THE 1990S

In 1990, the National Party ran an electoral campaign with the slogan: 'Creating A Decent Society'. As the Labour Party had done 6 years earlier, National chose to issue an election platform that was relatively vague on issues of welfare state reform. Voters, therefore, had reason to expect a great deal of continuity in this area. Once in office, however, National revealed a set of policies that amounted to a radical attack on the welfare state, perhaps the most radical attack ever seen in an OECD country. What had happened?

Senior members of the government of Prime Minister Jim Bolger, including his Minister of Finance Ruth Richardson, later claimed that, upon coming into office in November 1990, they discovered a fiscal situation that was much worse than expected (Richardson 1995: 79). The previous government's fiscal outlook, as presented in the 1990 budget documents, had projected a falling deficit for 1991 and 1992 (Dalziel 1992: 24). But following the general election, a Treasury briefing paper presented revised figures. After taking into account new projections of the state of the economy, the fiscal outlook appeared much worse, with a financial deficit rising to 4.8 per cent of GDP in 1991 before reaching 5.7 per cent of GDP by 1992 and 6.3 per cent in the following year. What is more, the country's largest bank, the Bank of New Zealand, in which the state was still the majority shareholder, was in deep trouble and needed a bailout of NZ$620 million — already the second massive cash-injection in little more than a year. And, in early 1991, as if to stress the urgency of the situation, the rating agency Standard & Poor's announced a downgrade of New Zealand's long-term credit rating, citing the high level of overseas debt as the main reason.[7]

The economy was indeed in a bad shape. In the early 1990s, New Zealand slipped into a serious recession. The bottom was reached in 1992, when the economy diminished by 1.2 per cent in real terms and the unemployment rate hit 10.4 per cent. And some groups were affected much more than others. The unemployment rate for Maori and Pacific Islanders was more than three times that for Pakeha (Europeans). It was only from 1993 onwards that the economy started to recover and unemployment began to fall. The fallout from the 1997 Asian financial crisis brought a brief downturn, with almost zero growth in 1999. However, with hindsight, we can see that the economic crisis

---

[7] In 1990, the balance of payment current account deficit was 4.1 per cent of GDP and public overseas debt stood at 28.6 per cent of GDP (Dalziel and Lattimore 2004).

of the 1980s and early 1990s was over in 1993, which, as we shall see, also took some pressure off the welfare state.

National's attack on the welfare state was announced just 53 days after election night. The government unveiled a so-called Economic and Social Initiative (Bolger et al. 1990), a 'mini budget' which laid out the plan for the welfare state. Several task forces were established early on to finalize the details (Boston 1994*a*; Jacobs and Barnett 2000). Further reforms were announced together with the 1991 budget, the 'mother of all budgets' as it was called by Ruth Richardson (see below for details).

Although the government was certainly trying to respond to the urgency of the economic and fiscal situation in 1990/1, it became clear in many statements by Prime Minister Jim Bolger, Minister of Finance Ruth Richardson, and Minister of Social Welfare Jenny Shipley that the government saw the radical restructuring and downsizing of the welfare state as a preferred goal, not just as a way to cut costs (see e.g. Bolger 1990; Richardson 1995: 84, 207–8). 'Benefit dependency' became one of the buzzwords, the size of the state was consistently portrayed as 'excessive' by leading National politicians, and the new goal of the welfare state was articulated as being merely to provide a 'safety net' (Shipley 1991: 13). The Bolger government was clearly an anti-welfare government and rather pro-welfare voices in cabinet and the parliamentary party, such as former Prime Minister Muldoon or Minister of Maori Affairs Winston Peters, had no significant influence on policy. Peters, the most outspoken critic within the government, was dismissed from cabinet in 1991. He went on to found a new party, New Zealand First, and again became influential when New Zealand First went into coalition with the National Party in 1996.

National's retrenchment measures of 1991, however, were extremely unpopular with the electorate. Not only is retrenchment an unpopular type of policy *per se* but many voters felt, once again, betrayed by a government that had announced moderation and consensus before the election and turned to policy radicalism thereafter. The 1993 general election saw National re-elected but with a seriously diminished majority — National merely held a one-seat majority in the House of Representatives. In a referendum held in parallel to the general election, voters also decided in favour of a new electoral system, based on the German model of proportional representation. The new, MMP system was seen by many as a way to make radical unilateral government decision-making of the kind occurring in the 1980s and 1990s less likely (see Mulgan 1995; cf. Castles 1994) and, after 1993, New Zealand did indeed enter a period of transition which saw National governing in coalition with new minor parties and as a minority government. The first MMP election in 1996 then marks the 'official' start of multiparty politics in New Zealand. After lengthy post-election negotiations, National entered into a coalition with Winston Peter's populist New Zealand First Party. The result of those negotiations was also a new, more generous position in welfare matters. That coalition broke apart as early as

1998, less than 2 years after the election. National continued as a minority government under Jenny Shipley, the first female prime minister in the history of the country, until the 1999 general election.

In economic policy, National continued the liberalization process started under Labour in the 1980s. Privatization of state assets continued, as did the process of trade liberalization. In 1994, the National government introduced the Fiscal Responsibility Act which continued to change the fiscal policy framework along the lines of earlier legislation such as the State Sector Act and the Public Finance Act (Janssen 2001). Although the Fiscal Responsibility Act did not provide a basis for mandatory fiscal targets (e.g. deficit ceilings), it introduced increased reporting requirements on the fiscal situation and short- and long-term strategy. It was also based on 'principles of responsible fiscal management' which focused on reducing the public debt. Overall, in economic policy there were few revolutionary reform acts, but this is probably also due to the fact that most of the liberalization work had already been done by Labour. By the early 1990s, New Zealand was already simply one of the most liberal economies of the OECD world. But there was one area where National clearly went beyond Rogernomics: industrial relations. In 1991, the Employment Contracts Act (ECA) effectively dismantled the traditional arbitration system which, under Labour, had seen only minor reforms.

The ECA was one of the most controversial pieces of legislation of the 1990s. It replaced the existing system of 'industry awards' and collective bargaining with a system primarily based on individual contracts. A number of traditional trade unions rights were abolished. For example, unions lost their privilege as bargaining partners. Other forms of employee representation were allowed, including in-house staff associations or the use of lawyers. In fact, there was not a single reference to the term 'trade union' in the Act. As expected, the ECA dealt a serious blow to the trade union movement in New Zealand (Harbridge and Walsh 2002). The importance of unions in terms of their number, membership, and density dwindled in the 1990s,[8] collective bargaining coverage declined and wage differentials widened. The ECA also had important consequences for the wage earners' welfare state model (see discussion below).

The second area in which the new government went much further than the Labour government of the 1980s was, of course, social policy. In the 1990s, National (and National-led) governments in New Zealand introduced wide-ranging changes to all areas of the welfare state. Not only did they decrease the *generosity* of benefits but they also changed the welfare state's *organizational structure of provision*, mainly in the area of health and accident compensation.

---

[8] Membership was almost halved between 1989 and 1999 and density fell from 42 per cent in 1991 to 17 per cent in 1999 (Barry and Walsh 2007: 64).

Workfare emerged as a new theme in the mid-1990s. We will now look at the reforms in the four sub-areas in more detail.

3.3.3.2 LABOUR MARKET POLICIES: ACTIVATING THE UNEMPLOYED

All tax-financed benefits, including the unemployment benefit, were seriously affected by the 1991 benefit cuts. Announced in the 'mini budget' of November 1990, they were effective from 1 April 1991. The nominal unemployment benefit rate for single adults was reduced by 9.6 per cent and by 10.7 per cent for single parents with one child. Young adults (20–24 years) had to bear the deepest cutback of 24.7 per cent. The real extent of retrenchment was even higher, due to price inflation and because the government also decided to cancel the price adjustment of all working-age benefits for 1 year. At the same time, waiting periods — for instance, in cases of 'voluntary unemployment' — were extended to a maximum of 26 weeks. The eligibility age for a number of benefits was also lifted, shifting more responsibility towards families. An early study of the likely distributive effects of the benefit cutbacks, including the effects of a reform of housing assistance, showed that, despite the government's assurance that the changes were designed to target resources to the genuinely needy, the outcome was almost the opposite: The largest reductions in disposable income, both in absolute and in relative terms, fell on low-income families (Waldegrave and Frater 1991).

Workfare, that is, a stronger emphasis on beneficiaries' availability for work, was announced in December 1991 alongside the benefit cuts. Although the unemployed had been legally required to actively look for work since 1938, historians of economic policy usually emphasize that this requirement was not enforced very strictly. The new work test would have applied not only to the unemployed but also to lone parents whose child was at least 7 years old. However, due to resistance within the National Party — not least from Prime Minister Bolger — the plan was shelved for the time being. But from the mid-1990s onwards, the issue appeared back on the agenda. Work testing was applied somewhat more rigorously in relation to the unemployment and sickness benefit, but also, for example, in the field of accident compensation. Community work schemes were set up — on a small scale at first — in order to provide work for those who could not find private sector employment. Case management and specialized schemes for transition into work were also set up (Mackay 2003: 106–7).

When National formed a coalition with New Zealand First in 1996, activation and welfare-to-work policies were introduced on an even larger scale (Higgins 1999). The coalition agreement included the Community Wage, a workfare scheme which replaced the unemployment training and sickness benefit. Beneficiaries were expected to participate in community work or training in return for their benefit. Yet, there were problems with the scheme from the beginning;

most particularly, difficulties in finding enough work in the community sector. The Community Wage reform also included an element of benefit retrenchment. The merger of unemployment and sickness benefit in 1998, in effect, reduced the nominal sickness benefit rate for new applicants by between 4 and 17 per cent, depending on family status and age (Starke 2008: 122).

In the mid- to late 1990s, welfare-to-work policies went beyond people on the unemployment benefit. 'Benefit dependency', not just unemployment, was seen as a problem. While the number of people receiving the unemployment or training benefit decreased from 1993 onwards, the number of working-age people on other benefits continued to rise (Mackay 2003: 102–3). That is why work testing was gradually extended to other categories, including the sick, widows, lone parents, and the partners and spouses of beneficiaries. To some extent, this policy was reversed after 1999 (see below).[9]

3.3.3.3 PENSIONS: AN UNPLEASANT SURPRISE

The National government provoked a huge public outcry when it revealed its plans for old-age pensions in 1991. After multiparty talks had failed earlier that year, the government had to act unilaterally and presented its wide-ranging plans together with the 1991 budget. The idea was to transform the pension into a highly targeted social assistance-type benefit. As we have seen, the surcharge, which had introduced an element of income-testing, did not exclude as many potential beneficiaries as the other means-tested benefits. Labour's surcharge was rather designed primarily to exclude the rich. Knowing that the surcharge was highly unpopular, National promised its abolition in the 1990 election campaign. Once in office, however, the exact opposite plan was revealed. Suddenly, National wanted to tighten means-testing significantly (for details, see St John 1992). The eligibility age would rise from 60 to 65 over a phase-in period of 10 years. In addition to the means-tested pension, there would be a universal element, but only from age 70.

Pensioner groups, the opposition, and also many National Party politicians vigorously criticized the plans. Grey Power and other interest groups organized nationwide pensioner protests. Only months after their announcement, the pension reforms were withdrawn. The changes that were eventually implemented, however, still involved retrenchment, including a higher surcharge rate (from 20 to 25 per cent), a lower exemption threshold, a rising pension age, the suspension of the annual indexation for two consecutive years, and a change to adjustments to prices thereafter.

---

[9] Another related reform merged the Income Support service — responsible for assessing benefit eligibility and paying out benefits — and the New Zealand Employment Service into a new Department of Work and Income. The merger was intended to facilitate the transition to work — and thereby meet the work test obligations — through a better integration of services into a 'one-stop shop' for beneficiaries (Mackay 2003: 108).

In addition to these short-term cutbacks, the government was struggling for a long-term reform of the pension. First, it set up a task force to examine the interplay of private and public provision. The task force did not come up with any major reform recommendations but argued largely in favour of the existing 'hands-off' approach, that is, voluntary, non-subsidized private pensions. Secondly, with respect to public provision, the government tried to revive the idea of multiparty talks. The goal was to agree on a pension scheme across party lines and keep the issue out of the 1993 election campaign. The political dynamic that led to the 1975 'election bribe' — when National introduced a costly universal scheme to counter Labour's pension plans — should be avoided at all cost. The resulting 'MultiParty Accord on Superannuation', signed by National, Labour, the left-wing Alliance, and the United Party, largely secured the status quo, that is, a pension at age 65 (from 2001), with a surcharge and indexed in line with prices but within a 'wage band' of at least 65 per cent and not more than 72.5 per cent of average wages.

The Accord had one serious flaw in that it was not signed by New Zealand First. Winston Peter's populist party, which had an important constituency among wealthy pensioners, made the abolition of the surcharge one of its main campaign planks. As the 1996 election drew closer, all other parties except National, also distanced themselves from the Accord and the surcharge in particular. Under pressure from intense party competition, even National saw itself forced to soften the surcharge parameters in 1996, thereby cutting the number of pensioners affected by the clawback by more than half (Periodic Report Group 1997: 59). Finally, during the coalition negotiations with New Zealand First in 1996, National grudgingly agreed to a full abolition of the surcharge. Another point in the coalition agreement was a new second-tier compulsory savings scheme that would be subject to a referendum. A scheme was worked out but, since it was difficult to understand and would have made many New Zealanders worse off, the proposal was rejected in a referendum in 1997 by an overwhelming margin of 91.8 per cent (Preston 1997).

There was a noticeable shift to the right in social policy with the leadership change in the National Party that brought Jenny Shipley to power in 1997 and the end of the coalition with New Zealand First in 1998. Among other things, the Shipley minority government, with support from the market-liberal Association of Consumers and Taxpayers (ACT) and some former New Zealand First MPs, changed the pension formula. The 'wage floor' which ensured that the pension would be tied to the average wage, at least in the long term, was lowered from 65 to 60 per cent of average wages (married couple rate), a change which was estimated to generate savings of NZ$2.6 billion over 10 years (Weaver 2002: 27). Although it did not directly reduce the level of the pension but rather slowed down future increases, it was widely regarded as a 'pension cut' and provoked angry reactions by pensioner groups such as Grey Power.

The government, however, explicitly legitimized the change by pointing to the effects of the recession following the Asian financial crisis.

3.3.3.4 HEALTH POLICY: THE TRIALS (AND ERRORS) OF MARKET-BASED PROVISION

Health policy was subject to some of the most radical policy changes of the 1990s. Reforms entailed attempts to target benefits on the one hand and, even more importantly, large-scale organizational restructuring on the other. Many of the changes introduced in the first half of the decade were highly controversial and some were later partly or fully reversed. Especially after the 1996 election, there was a partial U-turn in health policy away from the market, competition, and efficiency considerations and towards more state control and increased funding.

With respect to targeting, the government unveiled plans to introduce new co-payments in hospital care and a revised subsidy regime in primary care in 1991. Subsidies for general practitioner (GP) visits became more clearly means-tested, by increasing subsidies for low-income households, beneficiaries, and families receiving partial income support and, at the same time, reducing subsidy rates for children of higher-income earners (Davis et al.1994: 115). Pharmaceutical co-payments were designed in a similar manner.[10] Hospital co-payments proved to be one of the most controversial elements of the reform. They were introduced for outpatient and inpatient services in hospitals from early 1992 but, after a huge public outcry, were abolished only 13 months later (Gauld 2001: 95–6).[11]

The most important changes, however, were made in relation to the overall structure of the system. The policy was outlined in the so-called Green and White Paper published together with the 1991 budget (Upton 1991; see Gauld 2001: 84–6). Yet, many of the ideas can be traced back to the 1988 Gibbs Report (see above). Other, more direct, channels of influence were different advocacy groups, ministerial bureaucrats (especially from the Treasury), and overseas consultants reporting about the reform experiences of other countries, including the United Kingdom and the United States (Jacobs and Barnett 2000).

In a manner similar to the British reform, the restructuring was centred around the purchaser–provider split: On the funding side, four RHAs replaced the fourteen elected AHBs and were to act as the main purchasing organizations, each with a single budget to buy primary and secondary health-care services as well as disability support — three service areas that had been separately financed until then — on behalf of the population in their area. In terms of provision, the change was just as radical: The government regrouped public hospitals and community services into twenty-three profit-oriented Crown

---

[10] From 1 July 1996, the subsidy regime was made more generous (Ashton 1999: 138).
[11] Only outpatient charges for high-income patients were continued.

Health Enterprises (CHEs) and made them to compete with private hospitals, GPs, and voluntary organizations in an internal market for contracts with the RHAs (Ashton 1999).[12] The CHE boards were in many cases appointed with members coming from the business community rather than health professionals in order to emphasize the commercial orientation of the new bodies. More than half of the twenty-three chief executives did not have prior experience in health management (Gauld 2001: 89). This was perhaps one of the main reasons for the extremely high turnover rate of CHE executives during the first years. In general, the restructuring created new actors and dramatically transformed the relationships between actors in the health field (Fougere 2001). Contracts, which had been used from the 1980s onwards in a limited way, now became the key instrument in the public health system. However, the large-scale introduction of contracting was highly problematic because of a lack of appropriate information about service costs and quality and because of the high transaction costs of contracting itself (Ashton et al. 2004).

In studying the health reforms in New Zealand, it is easy to overlook what did *not* change: Most importantly, New Zealand retained its predominantly public health system. The role of the state as the dominant source of funding was not questioned by the government and at no time was a full privatization of health care, such as advocated for by the Business Roundtable, a neo-liberal think tank, on the agenda (Jacobs and Barnett 2000). Furthermore, the practice of subsidized fee-for-service in the primary sector did not change despite the formal integration of primary care into the RHA system. This also meant that the budget for general practice remained uncapped. Purchasing for accident victims under the accident compensation (ACC) scheme was not integrated into the RHA system of funding, except for a small number of services (Ashton 1999: 138).[13] Nor did the health reforms directly affect the benefit catalogue. A National Advisory Committee on Core Health Services was established to help define a list of essential services to which 'everyone should have access, on affordable terms and without unreasonable waiting time' (cited in Gauld 2001: 97; see also Blank 1994: 98–109). Yet, the process of creating a base for identifying priorities in service provision proved to be too controversial because it clashed with the traditional notion of 'universal' hospital services in New Zealand. The core services project was, therefore, shelved in 1993.

[12] Initially, the government had also planned to introduce competition between purchasers. The idea was to give consumers an option to choose between the RHA and privately run health plans that would purchase services on their behalf. This proposal, however, proved too complex to implement and was therefore abandoned (Ashton 1999: 137).

[13] The government also tried to find ways how to restructure purchasing and provision of (population-based) public health. A Public Health Commission (PHC) was set up at arm's length from the Ministry of Health as a key advisory body. However, due to problems of accountability and frequent tensions between the Ministry and the PHC, the latter was disestablished in 1994 (Gauld 2001: 122–5).

It is hard to say to what extent the 1993 health reforms led to changes in performance (Ashton 1999: 140–50). Health sector performance is difficult to measure, and when measurable, there is still plenty of room for debate if and to what extent the reforms should be seen as the cause of a particular development. The least we can say is that the high expectations of some of the reform advocates did not materialize: health costs did not decrease — they even tended to increase, and RHA and hospitals were running large deficits in the mid- to late 1990s — and waiting lists grew even longer which led to a significant expansion of the private insurance market. On balance, the verdict of different authors seems to be that, when measured against their own objectives, the health reforms of 1993 failed (Ashton 1999; Gauld 2001).[14] This was also increasingly recognized by the government.

The wind started to turn in the mid-1990s and a number of reforms were reversed. The general thrust was one of 'less market' and more centralized control. This change was partly a response to the protests by providers and those who worked in the sector. But discontent had spread to the public at large. Most reversals came after the 1996 election. During the election campaign, health policy and the widespread view that the reforms had failed (for survey evidence, see Laugesen 2005) had played a very prominent role. The re-reform of the health system structure was mainly driven by New Zealand First, the new junior coalition partner, but it was clear by then that even National politicians were dissatisfied with the new structures. In 1997, the four RHA were merged into a single purchasing organization, the Health Funding Authority (HFA). Apart from centralization, the functions of the purchasing body did not change much. On the provider side, profitability as *the* key goal was removed from the statute of CHEs. Instead, the notion of a 'public service' was explicitly mentioned. However, even public providers were still to act in a 'business-like' manner. The real implications of this change in rhetoric are, therefore, unclear. In terms of service rationing, points-based 'booking systems' for the management of surgical waiting lists were set up in order to make waiting lists more transparent and easier to manage. However, many problems and inconsistencies remained with the system (Gauld 2001: 168–73). With a view to widening access to health services, from July 1997, children under 6 years of age received free GP visits and pharmaceuticals. The user charges that were still in place, that is, part-charges for hospital outpatient and day-stay services were also removed (Ashton 1999: 140).

It is obvious that the post-1996 coalition government tried to dilute the market element in the health system to some degree and, at the same time,

---

[14] To be fair, it should also be noted that most experts acknowledge that the reforms brought a number of improvements, for example, greater cost transparency and cost awareness in the health sector, innovation in service provision (including Maori health providers), and the successful establishment of Pharmac, an organization which regulates pharmaceuticals and negotiates bulk deals with pharmaceutical companies on behalf of the RHAs.

concentrate resources at the centre. The government also introduced more explicit rationing methods such as the booking system for waiting lists. However, many crucial design elements of the 1993 reforms, especially the purchaser–provider split, were not questioned.

Other areas connected with the health policy field that underwent changes in the 1990s were the sickness benefit and accident insurance. The sickness benefit was seriously affected by the 1991 benefit cuts. The nominal benefit reductions were of up to 20 per cent, with less severe reductions of below 10 per cent for married beneficiaries and lone parents with two or more children. When the Community Wage was implemented as part of a movement towards activation in 1998, the sickness benefit was again cut back (see above).

The reforms of ACC, the accident insurance scheme, were wide-ranging in the 1990s. Faced with rising costs of compensation during the 1980s, the Bolger government planned to introduce elements of privatization and competition into the scheme. The reforms were implemented in two steps. First, in 1992, ACC benefits were cut back. Several lump sum benefits were abolished, survivor's benefits reduced, and eligibility criteria tightened (Campbell 1996; St John 1999). The funding structure was also changed in order to relieve employers from the burden of financing some of the non-work-related injuries. The latter were now to be funded from the earners' account and a new petrol tax (in the case of motor vehicle accidents). The 1992 Act also introduced a modicum of experience-rated bonuses and risk-based premiums and, thus, reduced cross-subsidization between different employers (Duncan 2002). Work capacity testing for beneficiaries was also announced but implemented only from 1997 onwards. Secondly, in 1998, a fundamental structural reform was introduced in the area of work accidents very much in the spirit of the 'more market' reforms in health care, housing (Murphy 2003), and other policy areas. For employers, work-injury insurance on behalf of their employees remained compulsory but the state monopoly of insurance provision was abolished. Instead, employers were now able to choose between a state-run scheme and various commercially provided schemes. The change was reversed by the incoming Labour-led government in 2000.

To sum up, in the 1990s, health care in New Zealand was marked by an unprecedented degree of experimentation: 'Big bang' changes were followed by reversals and adjustments in the face of administrative problems and outright hostility from doctors, nurses, and the general public. Many of the changes introduced in 1993, however, most importantly, the purchaser–provider split, survived the 're-reform' (Gauld 2001).

3.3.3.5 FAMILY POLICY: THE END OF UNIVERSALISM

Family transfers had already been far from generous in New Zealand, and were made even less generous. Research based on model families had demonstrated that, by 1992, New Zealand had one of the least generous family assistance packages in the OECD (Stephens and Bradshaw 1995). The National Party largely continued Labour's policy of targeting towards needy families as well as towards 'working families'. The first important policy decision occurred together with the 1991 benefit cuts when the universal Family Benefit was abolished. Yet, the cut did not affect all families. For low-income families, the Family Benefit was amalgamated with Family Support, the main means-tested transfer. Although the abolition of the Family Benefit made considerable extra resources available to the government, it was perhaps one of the least controversial of the measures introduced in that year (McClure 1998: 238). This was due to the fact that the value of the benefit had been allowed to erode since its last increase (to NZ$6 per week, per child) in 1979, still under the Muldoon government. By 1991, its value was less than 1 per cent of average wages (St John 2001: 3).

In terms of income-tested assistance, National introduced a new benefit called the Independent Families Tax Credit (IFTC) in 1996. The IFTC — later renamed Child Tax Credit (CTC) — was important in that it provided significantly higher assistance than Family Support (the benefit available to all needy families). Similar to the old universal Family Benefit, Family Support had lost in real value due to non-indexation since its introduction in 1986. The IFTC/CTC effectively restored the real value of family assistance by 1998 to its initial 1986 level but *only* for working families (St John 2004: 7). Thus, the dual structure of family assistance, originating under Labour during the 1980s, but with little real significance due to low take-up rates, was strengthened with this reform. The resulting architecture was complex (Nolan 2002), but the overall thrust remained the same: basic assistance for low-income families topped up with more generous tax credits made available for working families only.

Childcare and early childhood education had been made subject to new regulations in the late 1980s. Now, various types of early childhood centres (childcare centres, kindergartens, parent-run play centres, Maori language centres, etc.) received equal funding on a per-child basis. Means-tested subsidies to help low-income families with paying for childcare were available from the Department of Welfare (Meade and Podmore 2002). The sector grew further throughout the 1990s and enrolment rates were quite high by 1999: 14 per cent of under-2-year-olds, 82 per cent of 2- to 4-year-olds, and 95 per cent of 4- and 5-year-olds were enrolled (Mitchell 2005: 184). The number of services increased significantly, too: from 2,572 in 1990 to 3,340 in 1999 (ibid.). However, to a large extent, this must be seen as a demand-driven rather than a policy-induced development. In fact, at the beginning of the 1990s, there was even a phase in which the government tried to reduce its own responsibility in favour of a more market-based approach (Mitchell 2005). Among other things, funding was frozen, regulations eased, and some state-provided services were privatized. Yet, as in many other policy fields, the mid-1990s saw a slow turn away from the pure market model and towards more state involvement, partly because higher enrolment rates had been accompanied by decreasing quality of services. Funding was improved and, in

1996, the government introduced a bicultural national curriculum — called Te Whariki or 'the woven mat' — for early childhood education (May 2002).

3.3.3.6 CUTBACKS AND RESTRUCTURING: SOCIAL POLICY UNDER NATIONAL

To sum up, the period from 1990 to 1999 under conservative-led governments saw the most turbulent struggle around New Zealand's welfare state since the 1930s. The first 3 years of the decade, in particular, were ones of deep benefit retrenchment in virtually all areas of the welfare state.[15] The 1991 benefit cuts were among the most radical retrenchment decisions in the OECD. The economic and fiscal situation after the change in government played a big role, but so too did the government's general scepticism — to put it mildly — with regard to the welfare state. Moreover, driven by ideas about the superiority of the market mechanism for benefit provision and service delivery, the health, housing, and accident compensation sectors were extensively remodelled. To a varying extent, the separation of purchaser and provider roles, contracting, competition, and privatization were introduced into policy areas that, until recently, had been firmly under state control and governed by hierarchical structures. The hoped-for efficiency gains from this restructuring were not, however, forthcoming. Therefore, from about the mid-1990s onwards, and particularly once National had entered a coalition with New Zealand First, we witness some partial reversals, namely, in pensions and health care. Further reversals came after 1999, when a Labour-led coalition entered office. They will be described in the next section together with a number of new policy initiatives that led to renewed welfare state expansion rather than retrenchment.

3.3.4 Rebuilding and reshaping the welfare state: 1999–2008

3.3.4.1 MMP POLITICS IN FULL SWING: THE POLITICAL AND ECONOMIC BACKGROUND

The 1999 general election — the second MMP election in New Zealand — ended 9 years of conservative rule. National gained only 30.5 per cent of the vote in the 1999 election, the lowest share in the party's history.[16] It was not just the party

---

[15] The social consequences of retrenchment — although they cannot be described in great detail here — were considerable. Early reports of an increasing use of charity-run 'foodbanks' in New Zealand cities and growing demand for discretionary 'special benefits' were already evidence of rising hardship among beneficiaries (Mackay 1995). During the late 1980s and early 1990s, absolute poverty rates rose significantly — although, due to a decreasing median income level, relative poverty fell for a brief period (Stephens 2000) — and income inequality scaled up (Podder and Chatterjee 2002). Of course, part of this development had also to do with the consequences of Rogernomics.

[16] The record was again broken only 3 years later, when National got a mere 20.9 per cent of the vote.

system that had changed since the electoral reform. Via the influx of small parties, the basis for government formation had become less secure compared to the dominant single-party majority pattern prior to 1996. Moreover, in the period since 1999, governing by minority coalition has become the rule rather than an exception. First, a coalition of Labour and the Alliance — a grouping of several small left-wing parties — formed a minority government supported by the Green Party. The Labour Prime Minister Helen Clark was re-elected in 2002 and 2005 and, even after the Alliance's split in 2002, she found allies among the smaller centre and left-wing parties to keep her in office and to cooperate with the government in getting legislation through parliament (Bale and Bergman 2006). Contrary to the common prejudice, this period of minority and coalition government has been quite stable in political terms. This might also have had to do with the benign economic situation. In 2008, there was a change in government following a general election. A National-led government was sworn in, supported by three small parties: the Maori Party, ACT, and United Future. As under the previous governments, the small parties hold ministerial posts outside cabinet. Given the rules of collective cabinet responsibility, this allows them to disagree with government positions that lie outside their portfolio.

Economic conditions in New Zealand were very good between 1999 and the beginning of the global financial crisis in 2008 when New Zealand slipped into a recession and unemployment started to rise again. Nonetheless, up until then, unemployment had fallen continuously, down to a 22-year low of only 3.5 per cent in late 2007. High economic growth rates helped to consolidate the budget and, with regard to the fiscal situation, New Zealand had a continuous positive operating balance between 1994 and 2008, before the financial crisis pushed the budget into the red again. The Clark government's economic policy was much less dogmatically market-liberal compared to their — National *and* Labour — predecessors. For example, the government has bought back stakes in privatized enterprises — the government purchased a 82 per cent ownership stake of Air New Zealand in 2002 and, in 2008, renationalized the railway services. The top income tax rate was lifted from 33 to 39 per cent. However, a return to post-war interventionism was clearly not intended.

Some re-regulating changes important to Labour's core constituencies were introduced, for instance, the repeal of National's ECA of 1991. The government replaced it with the Employment Relations Act (ERA) in 2000. The new legislation was an attempt to rebuild some of the structures by supporting unionization and collective bargaining. Both had sharply lost ground during the 1990s. In 2000, trade unions regained legal protections as preferred bargaining partners and access rights to workplaces. Importantly, though, it was *not* a full return to the pre-ECA arbitration regime. The Labour-led government was keen to appear fiscally conservative and economically liberal and, overall, its economic policies were praised by international bodies such as the OECD and the World Bank (OECD 2005; World Bank 2006).

The good economic climate probably helped to ease pressure on the welfare state. In any case, and in stark contrast to much of the 1990s, retrenchment was not on the agenda. (Moreover, it has not reappeared on the agenda after the change in government in late 2008.) During their time in opposition, the Labour leadership had moved the party's position in economic and social policy clearly away from Rogernomics and back to a position where state intervention was less sceptically regarded. But there were also a number of new themes.

The overall catchphrase in many initiatives was 'social development' (Michalski and Cheyne 2008; Lunt 2009). The Ministry of Social Policy was even renamed Ministry of Social Development to highlight the new approach to policy. The aim was to foster better coordination between different policy sectors — including social services, education, even justice — in order to achieve better outcomes (see e.g. Ministry of Social Development 2001, 2005). Outcomes, in turn, were here understood to go beyond income, employment, or other social indicators to comprise a more comprehensive notion of 'well-being'. The main way to achieve better social outcomes was through 'investment'. Obviously, some of this echoes the Third Way debate in the United Kingdom (Dalziel 2001; but see also Esping-Andersen et al. 2002). Crucially, the new rhetoric did *not* consider social policy a threat to economic competitiveness, as earlier governments tended to see it. As the 2005 Briefing to the Incoming Minister put it: 'To compete globally, New Zealand has to succeed socially' (Ministry of Social Development 2005: 3). Even the Treasury, once the hotbed of neo-liberal economic and social reform ideas, significantly tamed its rhetoric. The goal was to build an 'inclusive economy' (New Zealand Treasury 2001).

While Helen Clark's Labour-led government was certainly much less welfare-sceptic than the conservative governments of the 1990s, it also became clear that no simple return to pre-1991 social policy was on the agenda. Means-tested cash benefits for working-age beneficiaries such as the unemployment and sickness benefit were acknowledged as an important instrument in the short term, but, nonetheless, much more emphasis was given to changing long-term patterns of exclusion and the 'need to tilt spending towards social investments' (Ministry of Social Development 2005: 4). Pre-1991 benefit levels were *not* restored. Instead, the government tried to restructure the welfare state by expanding a number of selected benefits, especially tax credits for working families. Another related theme of the Labour-led governments was the continuing emphasis on activation and welfare-to-work policies (see below).

3.3.4.2 LABOUR MARKET POLICIES: FROM 'HARD' TO 'SOFT' ACTIVATION

In principle, the Labour-led government of Prime Minister Helen Clark continued on the lines of activation begun in the mid-1990s. In 2001, some work obligations — those for sickness beneficiaries and for lone mothers on the DPB — were abolished. The work test for beneficiaries with children was softened. The Community Wage — the workfare scheme introduced by National — was ended and there were again separate benefits for the unemployed and the sick. Furthermore, the government tried to move beneficiaries into work through case management combining tight monitoring and a wider range of employment and training opportunities. One new instrument was a formal Job Seeker Agreement which is 'negotiated' between the unemployed person and the employment service and fixes work obligations and other responsibilities as well as a plan for achieving the goal of getting ready for employment.

Enhanced case management was extended to other groups of beneficiaries. For instance, beneficiaries receiving the widow's benefit or the lone parents benefit (DPB), are expected to work out a so-called Personal Development and Employment Plan (PDEP) with their case manager. This plan may, but does not necessarily, include paid work. Other types of activity include training and employment-focused seminars. Failure to meet the requirements will result in sanctions, namely, a benefit reduction of between 20 and 50 per cent. And the use of sanctions under the Labour-led governments indicates that the 'soft' approach to activation was not always as soft as it sometimes appeared. The number of beneficiaries facing sanctions for failing to meet the requirements tripled between 2002 and 2005 (*New Zealand Herald*, 15 May 2005).

In 2003, a new package called 'Jobs Jolt' was unveiled, consisting of ten initiatives aimed at activating the unemployed. The most controversial elements of the package were the extension of the work test to the — formerly exempt — group of unemployed people aged 55–59 and new mobility restrictions for beneficiaries. In order to prevent unemployed people from moving to rural areas with little employment opportunities, the government designated 259 so-called Limited Employment Localities — more commonly known as 'no-go areas' — to which unemployed persons were not allowed to move while on a benefit. The package also set up new employment coaching services and job partnerships with industries.

On the whole, there has been some continuity between the conservative and Labour activation strategies of the 1990s and 2000s. However, the mix of 'carrot' and 'stick' measures was tilted towards the former and more assistance was provided on a voluntary basis. Beneficiaries other than the unemployed usually did *not* become subject to a 'hard' work test regime anymore. Instead, the emphasis was on support and monitoring.

3.3.4.3 PENSIONS: TOWARDS A MULTI-PILLAR SYSTEM

There was a policy reversal with respect to New Zealand Superannuation, the universal public pension. The government of Helen Clark restored the 'wage floor' of 65 per cent of average wages in 2000, after the short-lived National minority government had lowered it to 60 per cent in 1998.[17] Overall, the political climate around pension policy has calmed down considerably. Most reforms introduced under the Labour-led government were in principle supported by the main opposition party (and many of the minor parties). The universal public pension seems well protected, at least in the medium term. It is possible that the issue of a higher retirement age may appear back on the agenda at some point but any attempt to tightly target the pension — similar to the National government's proposals in the early 1990s — has become a political non-starter. However, there has been change, both in terms of financing the public pension and in terms of the 'second pillar' of occupational pensions.

Although New Zealand has traditionally had a relatively young demographic profile, the country is not immune to population ageing. Yet, the 'greying' of the population is projected to be less dramatic than in other OECD countries, most notably in Continental Europe. In New Zealand, the share of the population over 65 years is projected to rise from 12 per cent in 2005 to over one-quarter from the late 2030s (Bryant 2003; Statistics New Zealand 2006*a*: 8), which is still a rather moderate rise by international standards. New Zealand's ethnic composition also matters in this respect. While the group of New Zealanders with European ancestry ('Pakeha') has a higher median age and share of people over the age of 65, so far, population ageing has been much less pronounced for New Zealand's other major ethnic groups, that is, particularly for Maori and Pacific Islanders. To some extent, this is due to significantly higher fertility rates among Maori and Pacific Island New Zealanders (Ministry of Social Development 2004: 24). Despite better demographic conditions, New Zealand will not escape rising levels of age-related expenditure. Expenditure on Superannuation is projected to rise to just over 8 per cent of GDP (New Zealand Treasury 2003), which would still be lower than *current* pension spending in Germany and France.

In 2001, and in order to respond to the demographic changes, the government established the New Zealand Superannuation Fund to pre-fund part of the expenditure burden expected once the baby boom cohorts start to retire. The Fund is a 'tax-smoothing' device in the sense that — without affecting individual pension entitlements — the government pays a contribution in order to fund a part of the future costs of the pension. Initially, the government contribution was projected to amount to about NZ$2 billion a year on average for about 20 years. Contributions were set to decrease to zero in the 2020s, when the Fund will start to pay out (New Zealand Superannuation Fund 2006) and was supposed to directly provide up to 14 per cent of the total cost of Superannuation — or even up to 30 per cent, once the tax receipts from investments are factored in (Periodic Report Group 2003: 41). However, the current financial crisis has

---

[17] From 2006, the wage floor was lifted to 66 per cent.

changed the picture dramatically. With the 2009 budget, and the reappearance of budget deficits, the conservative Minister of Finance suspended regular contributions until 2021. To what extent this suspension can be counterbalanced by larger contributions in the future to meet the target of co-financing future superannuation spending is currently unclear.

Despite the current uncertainties, New Zealand has moved away from the purely pay-as-you-go pension system it had previously had. Again, as with the ill-fated introduction of a compulsory savings model in the 1970s, a Labour government was the driving force. But, in contrast to the earlier reform, the establishment of the so-called Super Fund did not change the parameters at the level of entitlements. The battles of the 1990s had probably taught the government the lesson that touching Superannuation is extremely risky in electoral terms.

The Labour-led government also initiated a new campaign to boost workplace savings, based on the — controversial — conviction that New Zealanders were not saving enough for retirement. Among other things, the coverage of occupational pensions had decreased throughout the 1990s. A working group was set up in 2004 to look into the different options, but it was made clear by the government that there would not be a return to the tax incentives that had been in place before 1988 (St John 2005b). What finally emerged was KiwiSaver, a wholly new scheme open to all employees. The original model was announced in the 2005 budget and extended twice by the Labour-led government, in 2006 and 2007. In essence, KiwiSaver is a voluntary savings scheme with employee contributions of 4 per cent of gross salary matched by equivalent employer contributions. Yet, in order to boost participation in the scheme, the government is using the 'soft paternalist' instrument of automatic enrolment (see Sunstein and Thaler 2003). All new employees will be automatically enrolled *unless* they choose to opt out. Existing employees can join the scheme as well.

Interestingly, given the government's initial dislike of tax incentives, the government eventually decided to supplement KiwiSaver with various financial 'sweeteners', including a NZ$1,000 'kick-start' payment, a small annual fee subsidy, and tax credits to both savers and employers of up to NZ$1,040 per account and year. The money is invested in a single KiwiSaver account selected by the saver. The financial industry provides a range of KiwiSaver products which have to fulfil a number of requirements (e.g. low fees, portability). To what extent the new instrument will affect the typical income mix in old age depends on the level of participation in the long term. Although KiwiSaver is formally a voluntary scheme, automatic enrolment is expected to significantly increase the take-up. The government estimates that '50% of New Zealanders aged 18–65 will be actively contributing to KiwiSaver or a complying superannuation fund' (New Zealand Treasury 2007: 27). So far, participation has exceeded initial expectations. By May 2008, the number of KiwiSaver accounts had grown to over 600,000, but since enrolment started only in mid-2007 it is too early to tell at present how the scheme will develop in the future and whether or not it will become a significant 'second-pillar' pension.[18] The new conservative government, shortly after having been sworn into office in late 2008, announced a number of changes to the scheme. The most important were a cap on the level of employer contributions and the abolition of some of the tax benefits attached.

In sum, pension policy has seen new developments since the Labour-led government of Helen Clark took office in 1999. After reversing the last pension cutback of the conservative retrenchment period, two new elements were added: the Superannuation Fund and KiwiSaver. Both have moved New Zealand away from the traditional pure pay-as-you-go single-tier approach towards a partly pre-funded, multi-tier system.

3.3.4.4 HEALTH POLICY: BACK TO THE STATE

In the 1999 general election campaign, health policy was, again, a prominent issue. Labour vigorously criticized the National government 'for its narrow focus on the production of services rather than the improvement of health, for having fragmented a public service, for fostering inappropriate commercial behaviour, for increasing transaction costs, and for lacking local democratic input' (Devlin et al. 2001: 1171). Between 1999 and 2008, the Clark government concentrated on two big projects in health policy: *first*, a 're-reform' of public health sector organization and, *second*, a fundamental reform of the funding and organization of primary care.

The central legislation in terms of the first reform project was the New Zealand Public Health and Disability Act of 2000. It established twenty-one District Health Boards (DHBs) responsible for both funding and provision of services in their districts, thus abandoning the purchaser–provider split of 1993. Consequently, the HFA, the central purchasing body, was disestablished and funding was devolved to the DHBs. Public hospitals were brought under the ownership of the health boards, marking one of the clearest breaks with the purchaser–provider split philosophy. Interestingly, with the new system, New Zealand seems to have come full circle, as it very much resembles the AHB system legislated by the Muldoon government and implemented during the 1980s before being scrapped by National in the 1990s.

The focus of the DHB reforms still lay on the devolution of funding and responsibility but within a more community-oriented system instead of the market model of 1993. The main difference to the older system set up in the

---

[18] Some economists are already highly sceptical when it comes to the expected positive effects on national savings levels (Gibson and Le 2008). It may well be that a lot of public expenditure is being spent on achieving an insignificant rise in the saving rate, due to (potentially inefficient) shifts between different types of saving rather than real additional saving.

1980s was that the 2000 Act also included primary care amongst the DHB responsibilities.

Although DHBs were intended to have a great deal of autonomy and responsibility in providing and coordinating health services, the management of funds, and contracting with providers, the Ministry of Health tried to steer the system in a number of ways, for instance, by defining policy targets and long-term aims in national 'strategies' for various groups and services. On occasion, the Ministry also intervened in more direct ways in decisions taken by individual DHBs (Ashton 2005).

Probably the most important of these strategies was the 'Primary Health Care Strategy', launched in 2001. Most of the reforms in the primary health sector were consciously legislated by the government on the basis of the overall strategy, but recent policies also built on earlier proposals and some (unintended) consequences of earlier reforms. The reorganization of primary care provision, for example, had its roots in the market-based reforms of the 1990s. The 1993 health reforms sparked the growth of so-called Independent Practitioner Associations (IPAs). GPs and other health providers worked together in IPAs of various sizes and organizational forms, in part inspired by similar developments in the US health system. One of the main motivations for providers to join was the fact that IPAs were in a better position to negotiate contracts with the purchasing bodies in the quasi-market system (Ashton 1999: 143). IPAs spread very fast in the 1990s and by 1999, over 80 per cent of GPs belonged to an IPA (Barnett and Barnett 2004: 56).

The Clark government tried to capitalize on the growth of primary care organizations in order to achieve some of the aims set out in the 'Primary Health Care Strategy', above all, the twin objectives of a better coordination of care providers and a reduction in inequalities in the access to services. Health inequality had been an issue for a long time. Inequalities in New Zealand usually reflect socio-economic status as well as ethnic and geographic factors. To a large extent, these inequalities in access were simply rooted in the persistence of important financial barriers to primary care access.[19] Recall that while, in the area of secondary care, maternity, and mental health services, the Labour government of the 1940s had established a universal national health service, primary care was left to operate as a private, fee-for-service system, only supported by state subsidies. The level of co-payments was still high in most cases. Earlier initiatives aimed at improving equity in access to services had proved largely ineffective in the 1980s and 1990s (see Barnett and Barnett 2004 for an overview).

---

[19] This has been confirmed by survey data. In a five-country study, the share of New Zealanders claiming to have had problems of access to services because of cost was 34 per cent, almost as high as in the United States (Schoen et al. 2004).

The new organizational model promoted by the government from 2002 onwards was the Primary Health Organization (PHO). PHOs are networks of primary health-care providers (GPs, nurses, and other providers). Although the PHO itself must operate on a non-profit basis, it can enter into contracts with both non-profit and commercial providers. There is a large variety in the size and composition of PHOs but the main difference from the earlier IPAs is the focus on service coordination and on improving access. By July 2007, there were eighty-one PHOs around the country, covering 95 per cent of the population.[20] Capitation was introduced as a new funding mechanism and extra funding was provided to insure a reduction of out-of-pocket expenditure for the most vulnerable groups.[21] With the long-term aim of significantly reducing or abolishing co-payments for all New Zealanders, the government started to roll out the new mechanism in an incremental fashion from 2002 onwards, with particularly vulnerable groups — in terms of geographic location, age, ethnicity, and chronic health conditions — receiving the higher funding rate first. That rate was then extended to other groups. Early evaluations showed that, as intended, the use of primary health services increased. Most New Zealanders also benefited from lower fees but in some cases, for example for children, the expected fee reductions via higher government funding could not be achieved (Cumming and Gribben 2007).

With respect to coordination of service providers and the integration of services, PHOs can be seen as a way to introduce 'managed care' practices in New Zealand (Howell 2005). Contracting does not take place directly between the purchasing agency and the service provider but between the agency and a PHO, that is, an association of service providers. However, there is relatively little direct competition between PHOs for funding and patients. Instead, competition appears to be stronger at the level of service providers (GPs, specialists, physiotherapists, etc.) for contracts with PHOs.

The one crucial policy change with respect to the accident compensation scheme ACC since 1999 was the reversal of the decision to open up work accident to competition with private providers. In 2000, the Labour-led government restored the state monopoly. All private contracts were terminated and the ACC took over responsibility for entitlements. In 2001, the government also reintroduced lump sum payments for permanent impairment that had been replaced by regular benefits in 1992 (Duncan 2002). The legislation also put a greater focus on injury prevention and rehabilitation, alongside traditional issues of compensation.

---

[20] These figures are according to the Ministry of Health's web site http://www.moh.govt.nz/moh.nsf/indexmh/phcs-faq (accessed 16 October 2007).

[21] Capitation means that PHOs receive a fixed amount of money per patient and not for each time a patient sees the doctor.

To sum up, the Clark government shifted the New Zealand health system towards a more universal model, especially in the area of primary care.[22] Widening access to services and lowering co-payments were the prime objectives in this respect. More money is going into the health system in order to finance the costly transition towards a universal primary care system. More generally, and not just in the area of primary care, there was an emphasis on community-based governance — within the limits of sometimes strong national guidelines and strategies — at the expense of market mechanisms that had been the focal point of the 1990s. To be sure, private providers still play an important role and contracting is still a prime tool in the governance of the sector, but health policy appears more pragmatic today than during the times of global policy blueprints and the purchaser–provider split.

3.3.4.5 A FAMILY POLICY PARADOX?

A comparative study of eighteen core OECD countries demonstrated that, by 2001, and despite much activity around family assistance since the 1970s, New Zealand was still a laggard in terms of the value of the child benefit package typically given to both middle- and low-income families (Stephens 2003). It is, thus, perhaps not very surprising to see that family policy became one of the major reform fields of the post-1999 Labour-led government. The economy was back on track but there was a widespread feeling that many low-income families were being left behind. According to a widely cited international study of child poverty, New Zealand had the fourth highest level of child poverty among twenty-six OECD countries, behind Italy, the United States and Mexico (UNICEF 2005). The government's response was a massive expansion of work-focused family assistance.

In principle, the government's main policy did not differ from that of its predecessors', but it was significantly more generous. The dual structure of basic safety-net-type benefits on the one hand — notably Family Support, now called the Family Tax Credit — and additional in-work tax credits on the other, was preserved. The government of Helen Clark did *not* restore the universal Family Benefit that had been abolished in 1991. Instead, in May 2004, it announced the massive, NZ$1.6 billion 'Working for Families' (WFF) benefit package. The package, which was phased in over a period of 3 years, affected both Family Support as well as the tax credits for working families. On the first count, the level of the former Family Support payment was significantly increased and automatic indexation to prices was introduced (from 2008 onwards). However, in real terms, the increase merely restored the 1991 benefit level, because the Family Support had lost in purchasing power throughout the 1990s, due to infrequent and insufficient *ad hoc* adjustments (St John 2005a: 11). A number of supplementary

---

[22] Another example of this trend is the gradual reduction of asset testing in long-term residential care from 2005 onwards (Ashton and St John 2005).

means-tested benefits, including the accommodation supplement and childcare subsidies, were also increased. These changes were relatively straightforward and created little controversy.

In contrast, the second major element of WFF, the so-called In-Work Tax Credit (IWTC) was subject to more intense debate. Neither its aims nor its design were fundamentally different from existing tax credits. Its predecessors, however, suffered from low take-up rates. Labour's IWTC (also called In-Work Payment) represented an important expansion of these earlier benefits in the sense that more families, including many middle-income families, became eligible. The aim was to 'make work pay' by reducing effective marginal tax rates and thereby attenuating disincentives to work. The abatement zone of the means test was lifted to higher incomes. From 1 April 2007, a family with two children earning up to NZ$86,740 became eligible for the IWTC. However, the parents must work at least 30 hours per week on a regular basis (20 hours in the case of lone parents). Otherwise, they could only claim the Family Tax Credit — that is, the benefit formerly called Family Support.[23]

WFF was probably the biggest expansion of the welfare states since National Superannuation was introduced in 1975, although this expansion must be seen against the backdrop of a significant erosion of the real value of family assistance during the 1990s (Johnson 2005: 15). According to government estimates, when using the 60 per cent of median household income poverty line, child poverty is expected to fall by 30 per cent, while the reduction is estimated to be even as high as 70 per cent when using the 50 per cent of median income benchmark (Perry 2004). And this is despite the fact that, in terms of the distribution of extra resources, it was not the poorest families but rather those just *above the poverty line* who benefited most from the changes in family assistance (Johnson 2005). Take-up was high, in contrast to earlier benefits: 371,300 families received a tax credit in the tax year ending in March 2007 (Inland Revenue and Ministry of Social Development 2007). In 2000, the number of families receiving a comparable credit was only 120,000 (Nolan 2002: 26).

Apart from 'WFF', there is one other important reform by the Labour-led government that should be mentioned. In 2002, paid parental leave was introduced, bringing New Zealand finally closer to the majority of OECD countries (Henderson and White 2004). Recall that previously there was only unpaid parental leave, introduced in the early 1980s. The left-wing Alliance, Labour's coalition partner from 1999, had made paid parental leave a central plank of its campaign. The scheme introduced in 2002 was enhanced further in 2004 to

---

[23] To confuse readers (and citizens) even further, there are two additional tax credits, the Minimum Family Tax Credit (ex-Family Tax Credit, ex-Guaranteed Minimum Family Income) and the Parental Tax Credit, which are usually not available for recipients of other main state benefits.

bring the country in line with current ILO standards in terms of the duration (as laid down in the Maternity Protection Convention of 2000).[24] Paid parental leave of 14 weeks (initially 12 weeks) became available to employees and many self-employed persons and could be taken by either parent. The entitlement represented the gross weekly pay up to a maximum amount of currently NZ$391.28 per week (in June 2007). There was no means test which remained an unusual feature for New Zealand social policy. In addition, many employees became entitled to extended unpaid leave of up to 52 weeks as well as to maternity leave during pregnancy. Overall, despite the reforms, New Zealand's parental leave policy remains one of the least generous in the OECD in terms of duration, benefit level, flexibility, and employment criteria (Families Commission 2007).

Childcare also received increasing attention. In 2004, funding was substantially increased and several qualification initiatives were introduced. One of the problems is the high fee level, despite government subsidies (OECD 2004*a*: chapter 4). The government, therefore, raised the subsidy rates and income thresholds in 2004 and, in 2007, introduced 20 hours per week of free childcare for all 3 and 4-year-olds (Mitchell 2005: 190).

Expanding family policy on several fronts was one of the focal points of the Labour-led government's agenda. The sector saw much restructuring, in terms of both cash transfers and services, and funding was significantly increased. On the one hand, when looking at the 'WFF' package, one might argue that the government merely enhanced the existing targeted system of family assistance by providing more resources. On the other hand, by extending family cash transfers to many middle-income households, the government could be seen as diverging from the course of strict targeting to the neediest. There may be many reasons for this seemingly paradoxical development, including electoral reasons, but the reforms in paid parental leave and childcare corroborate the impression that the government turned towards more universal policies for families. However, this does *not* mean that targeting is dead. Indeed, while income-testing may have been relaxed through various reforms, the prioritization of working families has become stronger rather than weaker. Arguably, if the new paid parental leave — which is not available to those outside or at the margins of the labour market — is added, the various reforms have deepened the divide between working and non-working families.

3.3.4.6 A NEW MOOD IN WELFARE POLITICS

Despite the programmatic talk about 'social development' and 'investment', the Labour-led government's social policy reforms seem more pragmatic than ideological as compared to those implemented in the 1990s. To be fair, conservative-led

---

[24] The New Zealand parental leave scheme is, however, still below the ILO benchmarks in terms of eligibility criteria and the level of payment (Families Commission 2007: 18).

governments had already returned to pragmatism from the mid-1990s onwards, given that many of the earlier reforms that had followed the blueprint of benefit cuts and market-based provision had failed to deliver; but Helen Clark's government avoided applying such a 'one-size-fits-all solution' from the beginning. A number of dominant themes can nonetheless be detected. *First*, there was an increase in funding in most fields, particularly in family policy and health. This boost can almost certainly be attributed to a large extent to the clement economic and fiscal situation after 1999. The establishment of the Superannuation Fund was also possible thanks to constant budget surpluses. *Second*, structural reforms were reversed in many areas, particularly when it comes to internal markets and commercialized provision of services. The government strengthened the community and non-profit element. *Third*, and despite this, the market remained a central element in two respects. On the one hand, the 'work first' or 'activation' approach to the unemployment benefit and a number of other working-age benefits was stressed. On the other hand, private provision for old age received more attention and, with the introduction of KiwiSaver, the government effectively ended the 'hands-off' approach to retirement savings. *Finally*, universalism returned to the New Zealand welfare state, in the form of a universal approach to primary care, non-means-tested paid parental leave, and free childcare. The extension of family tax credits beyond low-income families can also be seen in this light.

3.4 New Zealand: from expansion to retrenchment and back

3.4.1 Summing up the changes

When reviewing the historical narrative, we can easily see that the New Zealand welfare state has undergone massive changes in all of its constituent parts since the 1970s. At the same time, there was still much continuity. This is because, despite their radicalism, reformers in New Zealand have usually changed the parameters of extant institutions or have, at times, introduced new elements to those structures. Genuine 'path departures', however, have been surprisingly rare, at least with respect to the formal welfare state. Let us look at the broad policy trends in the four policy sectors over the whole period under review, summed up in Table 3.2.

In the area of *labour market policy*, there has been a significant shift from demand-side active labour market programmes to more individualized 'activation' and 'workfare' approaches, especially with the introduction of the 'Community Wage' in the 1990s. This trend was paralleled by retrenchment, culminating in the 1991 benefit cuts, which, it should be noted, have not been restored by subsequent governments ever since.

Pension policy has been the politically most controversial area. The universal pension scheme that was introduced by a conservative government in 1975 still

Table 3.2: Policy change in New Zealand since 1975 in four social policy areas

Policy area	Expansion or retrenchment?	Structural reforms
Labour market	Benefit retrenchment, namely, for young unemployed and those without children	From demand-side to supply-side measures; activation
Pensions	First expansion, then retrenchment (temporarily targeted, lower replacement rate, higher eligibility age)	Strict one-tier policy at the beginning, later introduction of voluntary, subsidized occupational pension; pre-funding of public pension
Health care	Expansion of health expenditure; temporary targeting; reduction of co-payments in primary care	Decentralization; introduction of market mechanisms; later return to more state-led provision structures
Family policy	Abolition of universal benefits; expansion of targeted in-work transfers; paid parental leave; expansion of childcare	Targeting; work focus

Source: Own compilation.

is in place today (albeit under a different name). Yet, this masks the numerous reforms and re-reforms that took place in the 30-odd years in between. Most reforms have made the public pension less generous or have targeted it towards low- and middle-income pensioners by introducing the 'surcharge'. The targeting was ended in the 1990s but, as compared to the late 1970s, the pension is now less generous for all. While, in the late 1980s, all state subsidies for private provision were abolished, recently, an element of individual, state-subsidized provision has re-entered the scene in the form of the occupational KiwiSaver scheme. KiwiSaver also represents a step away from the traditional pay-as-you-go system and so does the Superannuation Fund.

The most far-reaching structural reforms can be found in the field of *health policy*, however. Here, subsequent governments have experimented with new structures of funding, provision, and regulation. The organization of the health system was decentralized from the 1980s onwards. Furthermore, in the 1990s, governments tried to introduce market mechanisms at different levels. A general 'purchaser–provider split' was intended to increase competition and transparency and thereby generate large efficiency gains. When these gains did not materialize, the radical market-oriented structure was watered down and, from 1999, largely abolished. Breaking up monopolistic state provision was initially also a goal of the reform of accident compensation but this reform did not withstand a change in government, either. In terms of the services provided and the funding structures, we can find stronger targeting (via means-tested subsidies and limited co-payments) in the 1990s. Yet, more recently, there has been clear shift towards a more universal health system again, especially in the area of primary care.

Finally, *family policy* has been an area of almost constant experimentation. Since the 1970s, targeted family cash transfers and tax benefits have been completely redesigned. The universal Family Benefit, by contrast, was first neglected and finally abolished. Family transfers became more differentiated and fragmented in an attempt to target towards low-income families and, increasingly, towards so-called working families. In recent years, means testing has become somewhat less strict and benefits now reach large parts of the middle class, while the goal of 'making work pay' has been retained, if not strengthened. Meanwhile, the DPB, the benefit mostly claimed by lone mothers, has experienced various cutbacks and has also been supplemented with 'activating' conditions. Paid parental leave is a relatively new phenomenon but unpaid leave dates back to the early 1980s. The importance of services for families, childcare in particular, has grown immensely since the 1970s. While this was, to a large extent, a demand-driven development, the government gave up its hands-off approach in the 1980s and both regulation and public funding have increased in the area of early childhood services.

3.4.2 The fate of the wage earners' welfare state

As already mentioned earlier in this chapter, the so-called wage earners' welfare state, Australasia's specific way of dealing with income risks and inequality, has vanished. True, some elements of the model are still in place, namely, the high level of home ownership and low unemployment. Yet, the two main pillars of trade protectionism and strong labour market regulation are things of the past. The Rogernomics reforms of the 1980s opened up New Zealand's economy to foreign competition by lowering tariffs and by abolishing the still existing quantitative restrictions on trade (Lattimore and Wooding 1996). The deregulation of the labour market took longer. It was only under the National successor government that the traditional arbitration system was scrapped with the 1991 ECA. Trade union influence declined markedly and has not recovered ever since. The ECA, thus, removed the central pillar or the wage earners' welfare system. The traditional strategy of 'social security by other means' — especially by means of a 'family wage' — became impossible.

It is, however, difficult to analyse to what extent the demise of 'social security by other means' had repercussions for the formal welfare state. Recall that historically, labour market regulation and other policies can be seen as functional equivalents for direct cash transfers and a more universal welfare state (Castles 1985). Strictly speaking, one might, therefore, expect an expansion of the formal welfare state once its 'outer line of defence' has been demolished. But such a straightforward functionalist account is probably misleading. When looking at the policy pattern, we can see that both the formal *and* the informal pillars of the welfare state were attacked at the same time. In other words, the functional trade-off, if it still exists, did not guide political decision-makers in the 1980s and 1990s. In the new millennium, a thoroughly liberalized and 'globalized' New Zealand has again been turning towards somewhat more interventionist social policies but they differ markedly from the old ways of the wage earners' model. Rather they are much more in line with developments in other 'liberal welfare regimes', such as found in Britain.

3.4.3 How much change?

Table 3.3 is an attempt to sum up social policy change during the period since 1975. The first period coincides broadly with the conservative Muldoon period (1975–84). In many ways, it was a time of transition. While the welfare state was still on a course of expansion — particularly for 'deserving groups' such as the elderly — in the mid-1970s, this changed from about 1979 onwards, when the economic and fiscal crisis forced the government to introduce the first, if minor, cutbacks. Overall, however, this was a period of state interventionism and the kind of economic liberalization that took centre stage from 1984 was not yet on the agenda. The social policy changes that did take place were mostly *first-order changes*, in the terminology of Peter Hall. National Superannuation, for example, was, in effect, a more generous version of the existing universal part of the public pension.

By 1984, what had been economic problems were now regarded as an economic 'crisis' and there was an overwhelming consensus that 'something had to be done'. This 'something' turned out to be the Rogernomics programme of structural economic reform — a dramatic third-order change in economic policy — to a large extent pushed through during Labour's time in office. Labour's social policy record between 1984 and 1990 largely consisted of trimming costly programmes. In particular, it was pension generosity that was reduced, but other areas, such as health care, were largely left untouched. The general trend during the 1980s was one of stricter *targeting*. Targeting the universal pension, and, to some extent, family benefits to low- and middle-income New Zealanders can be seen as a *second-order change*, because the overall welfare paradigm, the ideas about the aims of social security were unchanged.

The speed and scope of welfare state reforms were radicalized after the change in government of 1990. The conservative National Party pushed through radical retrenchment measures in virtually all programmes and tried to introduce market mechanisms in the provision of social services. In this vein, the health sector was reformed in a fundamental way. To be fair, the economic and fiscal situation was still difficult. The structural reforms of the 1980s had, if anything, exacerbated the labour market situation, at least in the short term and the recession affected the government's fiscal situation. However, the important difference between the conservative government of the early 1990s and its predecessors was the explicitly anti-welfare state ideology that, for several

Table 3.3: Social policy change in New Zealand, 1975–2008

Phase	Context	Diagnosis	Politics	Content of economic and social policy	Type of policy change	Consequences
1975–84	Conservative government led by defender of traditional welfare state	There is no welfare state crisis	Adversary Westminster politics; strong party competition	Heavy state intervention in economy, some export diversification; expansion of welfare state to 'deserving groups' (elderly, needy families)	First-order changes	Inflation, fiscal problems, low growth rates
1984–90	Centre-left government faced with immediate currency crisis and economic problems	Radical economic reform necessary for growth; economic competitiveness through opening up	'Crash through or crash' in economic policy; more cautious in social policy; popular foreign policy	Structural reforms of the economy ('Rogernomics'), corporatization and privatization, trade liberalization; pension cutbacks, no change in most other social welfare programmes	First- and second-order changes	High unemployment; continuing fiscal problems; decline of the wage earners' welfare state
Early 1990s	Conservative government, some ministers vigorously anti-welfare state	Excessive state expenditure and intervention leads to perverse incentives and crowding out of more effective private sector activities	Radical 'big bang' reforms (no blame avoidance tactics)	Continuing privatization, state sector reform and new fiscal framework; radical welfare state retrenchment, market mechanisms in health and social service provision	Third-order changes	High unemployment, income inequality, political discontent; electoral reform; end of the wage earners' welfare state
Mid-1990s–today	Conservative coalition government, later minority governments, Labour-led governments from 1999, economic recovery	Part of the structural reforms and retrenchment measures of the early-1990s were not successful or unpopular among voters	Coalition politics; more consensual	Reversals of past decisions in pensions, health, accident compensation; activation; expansion of needs-based family policy	Second- and third-order changes	Decreasing poverty rate; higher social expenditure

years, dominated social policy. Retrenchment was not just seen in terms of fiscal savings but in terms of restoring the balance between state and society. Moreover, the government did not hide its intentions or try to conceal painful measures through 'blame avoidance' strategies.

Many of the changes introduced between 1990 and 1993 can be seen as genuine *third-order changes*. Although, technically, the 1991 benefit cutbacks involved only a lower benefit level, they can still be regarded as third-order changes. The reason is to be found in the new ideas and goals associated with the welfare state. The welfare state as a 'safety net' only for the 'genuinely needy', advocated by the conservative National Party, was different from the welfare state aimed at providing a basis for participation in the community. Even though the means-tested structure of benefits was not changed — with the exception of family benefits — the underlying philosophy was new and this is sufficient to classify the benefit changes as third-order changes.

The third period in social policy begins in the mid-1990s and continues up until today, hence, does *not* coincide with the periods according to the partisan orientation of government. We can see that the first reversals in pension policy came in the run up to the 1996 election, which was also the first MMP election in New Zealand. What is more, from the mid-1990s, the economy started to recover. Under more recent centre-left governments, there have even been a number of significant expansionary reforms in social policy. The reversals were mostly *second-order changes*, as they involved changing the structures of provision in health-care and accident compensation. There were also *third-order changes*, however, especially in terms of activation policies and the recent initiatives in family policy. Here, a paradigm shift in social policy is most evident since both were introduced as part of Labour's 'social investment' strategy. Although the focus on working families can be traced back to the early 1980s, it was only recently that it has become the dominant theme in family policy.

3.4.4 Reasons and explanations

3.4.4.1 GLOBALIZATION AND DOMESTIC PROBLEMS

Before examining the role globalization played in welfare state transformation, we have to note that, among the small OECD countries, New Zealand is one of the least globalized. This is true in terms of both trade as a percentage of GDP as well as in terms of outward FDI (Foreign Direct Investment) (but not inward FDI, see Figure 1 in the Introduction). To some extent, this status of New Zealand as a 'wary globalizer' is due to its specific industry structure, geographical distance to the other industrialized countries, and a long history of trade protectionism.

With respect to globalization as a driving force for policy change, the most obvious development is the demise of the wage earners' welfare state. After all, trade protectionism was, at least implicitly, part of that strategy. Moreover, it appears that, in general, strategies based on forms of 'social protection by other means' have not survived the latest wave of globalization or have been significantly altered. This holds true not only for the wage earners' welfare states of New Zealand and Australia but also for countries such as Japan and the former socialist countries of Central and Eastern Europe. Instead, there has been a *'structural convergence* ... towards what might be described as the mainstream Western welfare patterns' (Mishra 2004: 69). As explained earlier, however, the exact repercussions of the end of New Zealand's traditional political economy for the welfare state more narrowly understood (which is the main subject of this book) are somewhat unclear.

In any case, we can see that arguments about globalization did *not* figure prominently in the welfare state debate in New Zealand, compared to, for example, arguments about work incentives, efficiency of provision, or poverty. There were episodes, however, when the global economy entered the picture. The most important example is the downgrade of New Zealand's credit rating by Standard & Poor's in 1991. Conservative politicians at the time took this downgrade very seriously and highlighted it in order to stress the urgency of the situation at the beginning of the 1990s. Most of the harsh 1991 benefit cuts, however, had already been announced at the time of the downgrade, so it would be difficult to construct a direct causal link between this financial sector intervention and welfare state retrenchment. In 1998, Jenny Shipley, the conservative prime minister, announced a pension cutback and linked it directly to the repercussions from the Asian financial crisis. Again, this shows how New Zealand's — real or perceived — vulnerability to world market movements has been an element in the debate. Still, globalization as a threat to the welfare state has never been as dominant a theme as it was in many continental European countries.

In a manner similar to that of other small countries, for instance Switzerland (see Chapter 4), problem pressure, namely, pressure stemming from *domestic economic problems*, has been one of the main forces driving social policy change in New Zealand. This does not mean that policy has been entirely determined by functional necessities. Problem pressure (*a*) motivated policy initiatives by triggering a search for policy solutions, (*b*) gave political entrepreneurs the opportunity to present their — often ready-made — 'solutions', and (*c*) facilitated the justification of painful measures, especially regarding benefit retrenchment. These (interrelated) reasons underpin the relatively clear empirical pattern we observe in New Zealand. The change from expansion (up to the mid-1970s) to retrenchment (from the late 1970s to the mid-1990s) and back to expansion (since 1999) is in line with this interpretation. To be sure, economic problems did not suddenly start in the late 1970s. There had been some economic troubles in the 1960s. But it was not before about 1978 that virtually all important indicators — including fiscal indicators — deteriorated markedly. New Zealand entered a long period of crisis and, arguably, did not fully recover before the mid-1990s.

The crisis period was, thus, almost exactly the period of benefit retrenchment (Starke 2008). There were important differences between governments (see the discussion below) but the main direction was restrictive. Rounds of retrenchment were often preceded by steep increases in unemployment, for example, in the early 1980s and again during the period from 1987 to 1992, when the unemployment rate shot up from around 4 to over 10 per cent. Not surprisingly, a similar pattern can be demonstrated with respect to economic growth rates and fiscal indicators such as the size of the deficit and net debt. Figures 3.1 and 3.2 show the development of the budget surplus and net public debt as a percentage of GDP from 1975 to 2007. We can see that very large deficits in the late 1970s to early 1990s contributed to the growing debt level, peaking at 52.2 per cent of GDP in 1992. Expenditure cutbacks and economic recovery, however, allowed debt to fall over a remarkably long period from 1993 onwards. The two periods, before and after the early 1990s, coincide broadly with the period of welfare state cutbacks and the period of reconstruction.

Low economic growth presented a particular problem, however, since New Zealand's growth performance had been relatively poor throughout the postwar decades. New Zealand slipped slowly but steadily from being, in terms of

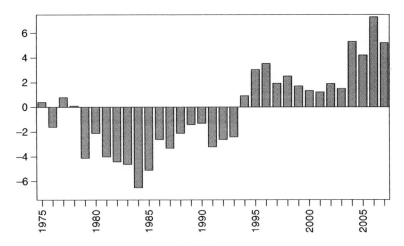

Figure 3.1: Budget surplus in percentage of GDP, 1975–2007

Note: 1975–93: Financial Surplus (table 2), 1994–2007: Operating Surplus.

Source: 1975–93: long-term data series (Statistics New Zealand 2006*b*); 1994–2007: Crown Financial Statements (New Zealand Treasury, various years); 2002–7: Budget Economic and Fiscal Updates (New Zealand Treasury, various years).

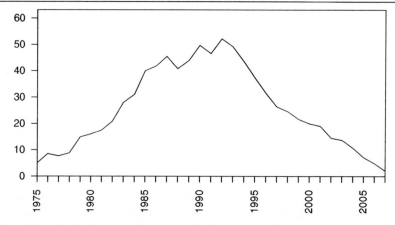

Figure 3.2: Net public debt in percentage of GDP, 1975–2007

Note: 1975–95: Net public debt; 1996–2007: Net core crown debt (without Superannuation Fund assets).

Source: 1975–95: Dalziel and Lattimore (2004: 157); 1996–2007: Budget Economic and Fiscal Updates (New Zealand Treasury, various years).

GDP per capita, the third-richest OECD country in 1950 to the sixteenth rank by 1980 (Starke 2006: 63). That is, the worldwide economic troubles of the 1970s and 1980s took on a particular meaning in New Zealand: In contrast to many European countries, the repercussions from the oil shocks did not appear as a temporary crisis after decades of outstanding economic development but rather as a significant worsening of an already lacklustre performance, when seen from a comparative perspective (see also Castles 1993).

In addition to the economic problems that were unfolding during the period under review, there were a number of specific events which magnified the country's economic problems and which, in the eyes of most New Zealanders, highlighted the need for determined policy reform. The currency crisis at the time of the 1984 snap election, the fiscal crisis discovered after the 1990 change in office, and, to some extent, the 1997 Asian financial crisis should be men-tioned. All three events preceded benefit cutbacks and politicians such as Ministers of Finance Roger Douglas and Ruth Richardson as well as Minister of Social Welfare and later Prime Minister Jenny Shipley justified retrenchment measures with reference to the dire economic and fiscal situation.

What happened during good times? In macroeconomic terms, the recovery took place from 1993 and continued — with a brief pause due to the 1997 Asian crisis — until the end of the period of analysis. Yet, on the basis of the reform narrative, we cannot simply say that, just as economic problems triggered retrenchment, good economic performance invariably led to expansion. It is fair to say that the somewhat 'softer' policies in the mid-1990s owe much to the better economic outlook at that time. Similarly, the sustained economic boom since the late 1990s can be seen as a precondition of the renewed expansionist policies of the Labour-led government. However, the 1970s demonstrate that political motives in some cases trump economic reasoning, since Muldoon's costly expansion of the public pension regime was implemented at the time economic strain was beginning to be obviously apparent.

During the retrenchment period another issue entered the field of social policy: the reorganization of provision, especially in the field of social services and health care but also with respect to the administration of cash benefits and the structure of public administration more generally (Boston et al. 1996). To some extent, this may have had to do with problem pressure also — after all, reorganization was supposed to increase the efficiency of provision and thereby ease the pressure for cost containment — but this is certainly not the whole story. Although many of the initiatives to introduce market mechanisms in the provision of social services coincide with the economic difficulties of the early 1990s, in terms of more sector-specific indicators of problem pressure, the association is relatively loose. According to policy experts, the central subjects of reform zeal, including the health system or the accident compensation scheme, were *not* 'in deep crisis' prior to their fundamental restructuring. There were certainly problems, but these problems were often quite specific and the reform blueprints did little to address those specific problems but focused much more on the overall efficiency goals. Moreover, there is evidence that the radicalism of reform may have created more problems than it solved. We can, therefore, speculate that pro-market ideology played a role in policy change. Some of the health-care reports, for example, had more to do with a 'solution looking for a problem' than with genuine problem-solving.

3.4.4.2 THE ROLE OF POLITICAL PARTIES

Did parties matter? Again, the role of *partisan ideology* mattered most clearly with respect to benefit cutbacks and, perhaps to a lesser extent, with respect to the introduction of market-inspired mechanisms in benefit provision. The difference between the Labour government of the 1980s (which legislated only limited cutbacks and was cautious regarding the organization of provision) and their conservative successors — who drove a systematic attack on virtually all cash-transfer schemes and attempted to introduce market structures across the board — is most obvious. Despite being quite radical with respect to economic policy — witness the 'Rogernomics' revolution — Labour refrained from comparable radicalism in social policy. Prime Minister David Lange, in particular, was careful not to alienate Labour's core electoral constituencies by slashing working-age benefits during times of profound structural reform in the labour market. Some of the more important reforms in pensions, for instance the surcharge, were even couched in terms of social justice. Although the Labour government was no unconditional defender of the traditional system of social security, neither can it be regarded as an anti-welfare government, unlike the ensuing National government.

At the beginning of the 1990s, a number of key National politicians seized the opportunity given by a deep economic and fiscal crisis in order to implement wide-ranging cutbacks. The ideological position of Minister of Finance Ruth Richardson and Minister of Social Welfare Jenny Shipley — and, to a lesser extent, Prime Minister Jim Bolger — regarding the welfare state was clear: They saw the welfare state as a burden on the economy and as a source of various disincentives in terms of labour supply and 'moral' behaviour. By cutting benefits, the government intended 'to arrest New Zealand's drift from work to welfare' (Bolger 1990: 9). It is important to note that social policy reform was not only seen in the light of short-term fiscal imperatives but was also in line with a more long-term philosophy, however crude and internally inconsistent it may have been (Boston 1992). The welfare state the National government wanted was much smaller, a mere 'safety net' (Shipley 1991: 13) heavily targeted towards the 'genuinely needy'. In order to promote this vision, the retrenchment advocates within the National Party and the New Zealand Treasury thereby deliberately ignored empirical evidence showing that cash transfers were already strongly targeted towards low-income households (New Zealand Planning Council 1990: 28–34). One important new element in National's approach was the orientation towards an *absolute standard of living* when it comes to determining the benefit level — in stark contrast to the relative standard that had been one of the key social policy principles in New Zealand.

The introduction of market-like elements in benefit provision was also vigorously promoted by the Bolger government. As we have seen, the implementation of that vision encountered many obstacles and unforeseen consequences — and had to be delayed or reversed — but nonetheless, the National government left its specific ideological imprint on many policy initiatives especially in health policy and accident compensation. Certainly, partisan ideology was not the only cause of policy change. Yet, the economic and fiscal situation at the beginning of the 1990s on the one hand, and the peculiar openness of the political system on the other, provided a perfect opportunity for the National government to implement a vision of a trimmed down welfare state.

What do the two other governments that were part of this country case study — the (National) Muldoon government from 1975 to 1984 and the Labour-led government from 1999 to 2008 — tell us about the impact of partisan ideology on welfare state change? Certainly, here the case is much less clear-cut compared to the governments of the 1980s and 1990s but a number of important observations can be made nonetheless. On the surface, we might theoretically expect to find more wide-ranging retrenchment policies under Muldoon given that this was a conservative government operating under difficult economic and fiscal circumstances, just like the Bolger government of the 1990s. Yet, this is a somewhat short-sighted expectation since the Muldoon government was obviously *not* a government of neo-liberal retrenchment advocates. Not that market-liberal politicians did not exist at the time, but Prime Minister Muldoon effectively contained their influence on policy. As a self-styled advocate of the 'ordinary bloke', he was committed to the welfare state and, in particular, its traditional wage earners' aspects, and he used his dominant position as Prime Minister and Minister of Finance to secure the *status quo*. One of his main arguments in favour of more traditional policies was, without a doubt, his continuing electoral success as a party leader. It was only when, in 1984, the party suffered a devastating election defeat that the neo-liberal faction was able to change the party's policy profile. Certainly, Labour's move to neo-liberal policy positions in the 1980s (at least in economic policy) also contributed to National's shift to the right.

The case of the post-1999 centre-left governments is also more complex. At first sight, the pattern is clear: We find a Labour-led government 'rebuilding' the welfare state after a decade of retrenchment and privatization. Yet, we cannot be sure to what extent this is really due to partisan ideology since there is no empirical contrast case against which we can judge Labour's recent policy record. After all, the government was lucky in that it operated under very favourable economic and fiscal conditions. The pressure to contain costs by cutting benefits, raising taxes, or reorganizing the welfare state was much lower. Perhaps any other government would also have expanded welfare programmes, given their popularity among voters. The case is also difficult to make since some of Labour's policies have not been about a return to the traditional policies of the wage earners' welfare state but, in contrast, were designed in order to complement a highly flexible labour market — allowing for a high degree of wage inequality — within an open economy. They have generally stayed within the bounds of the 'liberal welfare regime'. However, some policies can be attributed somewhat more clearly to government parties. Paid parental leave, for example, was pushed by the left-wing Alliance upon entering office in 1999. In a similar vein, some of the recent 'universal' initiatives in health- and childcare are in line with more traditional Social Democratic approaches. Perhaps one could say that, although the post-1999 record may not be a very strong corroboration of the 'parties matter' thesis, at least it does not contradict it.

Overall, the New Zealand case exhibits a pattern of policy change that is surprisingly clearly in line with the expectations of the partisan hypothesis, according to which welfare state change can be traced back not only to economic necessities but also to party preferences. While, for example, economic problems acted as a trigger for welfare state change, the extent of change and the specific policy solutions chosen can largely be attributed to political factors, in particular the partisan complexion of government.

3.4.4.3 POLITICAL INSTITUTIONS

Institutional variables — especially those to do with *political institutions* — figure prominently in virtually all political science accounts of recent public policy change in New Zealand. To some extent, this may have to do with the fact that the high tide of neo-institutionalism in political science coincided with the wave of far-reaching reforms in New Zealand which, by and large, nicely supported those theories. Characterizations of the New Zealand political system as one of 'unbridled power' producing 'the fastest law in the west' (Palmer 1987) have been used to explain the swiftness and radical nature of policy change in the 1980s and 1990s (see e.g. Castles et al. 1996; Nagel 1998; Schwartz 2000; Huber and Stephens 2001). New Zealand's 'old' political system with a unicameral parliament, single-party majority governments, and a lack of restricting institutions such as judicial review, a rigid constitution, federalism, or a president, are highlighted to explain this radicalism, for instance, compared to Australia.

To what extent did the electoral reform of 1993 change the theoretical expectations regarding policy change in New Zealand? Recall that the 1993 reforms abolished the traditional British-style single-member plurality system in favour of a MMP representation system, largely based on the German model. As a result of the new rules, the number of parliamentary parties has markedly increased to between six and eight parties (Vowles et al. 2006). Although most of them are very small, their presence effectively prevents single-party majority governments. Since the first MMP election in 1996, coalition and/or minority governments have been the norm rather than the exception. The exact consequences of the 'new politics' under MMP for social policy are still unclear, not least because we do not yet have very strong theoretical expectations regarding the impact of the electoral system on public policy (Boston 1994*b*; Castles 1994). The most straightforward consequence is probably the higher number of partisan veto players under the conditions of multiparty politics. *Ceteris paribus*, this should make policy change more difficult. Moreover, under the old plurality system it may have been easier for government parties with relatively 'extreme' policies — that is, policy positions located far from the median voter — to implement change. This is because the electoral system regularly produced 'manufactured majorities' based merely on a plurality of the popular vote (Nagel 2000). In 1993, the government's share was as low as 35.1 per cent of the vote! Indeed, the (relatively limited) data on policy positions of parties and voters in New Zealand confirm the expectation that MMP has decreased the distance between the government and the median voter significantly (Vowles et al. 2006: 277).

To sum up the theoretical expectations, we should find more wide-ranging policy change before 1996 — the first MMP election — than afterwards, due to the lower number of partisan veto players and the possibility that the government's parliamentary majority is based on a mere plurality of the electorate. In general, the empirical pattern of change is largely supportive of these expectations. However, this institutional hypothesis neither sufficiently explains why the most radical social policy changes took place in the 1990s (and not earlier) nor does it fully capture the more recent expansionary reforms which, at least in some areas such as health and childcare, have also been quite wide-ranging. It is important to note that most other features of the political system have *not* changed with the 1993 electoral reform. There is still no second chamber of parliament, no constitutional court, etc. Once the government has secured a legislative majority for a reform measure, it can be decided and implemented very quickly.

More generally, the typical policy-making pattern in the field of social policy is still highly centralized. Although MMP and, in particular, the practice of governing by minority government has shifted the centre of decision-making slightly back into the parliamentary arena — since bargaining with non-governmental parties is necessary to secure a legislative majority — outside actors such as trade unions and other interest groups still play a relatively minor role. If they influence policy, it is through lobbying channels. Neo-corporatism, one of the major policy-making modes in other welfare states, has never been a feature of New Zealand politics. Trade unions, in particular, have usually taken little interest in welfare state reform, apart from the issue of employment-related programmes such as accident compensation and occupational pensions.[25] While in some European countries, extensive benefit reforms have been the subject of tripartite talks between the government, employers, and unions, nothing similar has taken place in New Zealand. At times, beneficiary groups such as the pensioner association Grey Power received a great deal of attention from the public and the government, especially at the beginning of the 1990s, when the National government tried to radically cut back pensions. Although it is impossible to prove, Grey Power's organized protests and effective media campaign may have influenced the government's decision to significantly water down its pension proposals.

It has been claimed that neo-liberal groups such as the New Zealand Business Roundtable (NZBR) heavily influenced policy-making in New Zealand in the 1980s and 1990s (Jesson 1989; Goldfinch 1998) and there is indeed a partial overlap between economic and social reforms and the proposals advanced by the NZBR. But at all times, lobbying groups such as the NZBR were dependent on individual powerful allies in the government, including Labour Minister of Finance Roger Douglas and the National Ministers Ruth Richardson and Jenny Shipley. And even with such ties, the Roundtable's proposals for a radical

---

[25] This is not to say that trade unions are to blame for their lack of influence. It could well be — and it appears quite plausible — that their lack of interest stems from a long-term experience of only marginal influence on the course of policy.

dismantling and privatization of the welfare state (e.g. Green 1996) were never implemented. Their ideas may have contributed to a pervading anti-welfare atmosphere among political elites but they are clearly insufficient for *explaining* policy change. To sum up, apart from pensions, interest groups have not played a crucial role in welfare state reform in New Zealand over the last 30 years.

Although small countries are generally praised for their ability to adapt to new circumstances, the speed and extent of change witnessed in New Zealand was still remarkable. Some of the change had certainly to do with the end of the post-war economic model in the 1970s and the deep economic and fiscal crisis that hit New Zealand in the early 1990s. Yet, especially in the field of social policy, this was no simple 'adaptation' to new necessities. Instead, reforms were often driven by partisan preferences rather than mere problem-solving — more than in many other OECD countries, the struggle around the future of the New Zealand welfare state became, in fact, a highly politicized matter.

4

Switzerland: From Liberal to Conservative Welfare State — a Pattern of Late Maturation?

4.1 Introduction

Welfare state change in Switzerland during the last 30 years has clearly not been as radical as in New Zealand. Nevertheless, the Swiss system of social protection has been substantially modified since the early 1970s. All major programmes have been altered, some even fundamentally, resulting in a shift from a 'liberal' welfare state regime to one that has the closest affinities to the conservative model. Furthermore, the Swiss welfare state went from being one of the lowest spending welfare states in the OECD to one of the highest. The extent of change is particularly remarkable given the dense political structure and the high number of veto players within the Swiss political system.

Switzerland is characterized by a strong vertical and horizontal fragmentation of power so that all major political parties and interest groups are incorporated into the political decision-making process (for an overview of the typical Swiss decision-making process, see Table 4.1). This makes decision-making complicated and allegedly creates a bias towards policy solutions adhering closely to the status quo (see e.g. Abromeit 1992: 176; Lehner 1992: 294). As a consequence — and despite the small size of its elite — policy-making in Switzerland is slow and often incremental as well as incoherent.

The Swiss federal government (Federal Council) is a collegial body. Its seven members have equal power and decisions are made by majority rule. Between 1959 and 2003, the seven governmental seats were allotted by the informal 'magic formula' to the four major political parties: Liberals, Christian Democrats, and Social Democrats each held two seats and the conservative Swiss People's Party held one seat. In 2003, the Christian Democrats lost one seat to the Conservatives. In 2007, the Swiss People's Party finally opted for the opposition, thereby ending the long period of oversized cabinets in Switzerland.

Table 4.1: The typical Swiss decision-making process: phases and key actors

Phase	Key actors
Initiation and preparation	Federal government and administration, parliament (parliamentary initiatives), the people (people's initiatives)
The pre-parliamentary phase 1. Extra-parliamentary expert committee 2. Pre-parliamentary hearing	Interest groups, cantonal governments, political parties
The parliamentary phase 1. Treatment by the first chamber of parliament 2. Treatment by the second chamber of parliament	Political parties, cantons
The direct democracy phase	The people, interest groups, cantons, political parties

Interest groups and constituent units (cantons) are incorporated into the pre-parliamentary decision-making process in two important ways. First, extra-parliamentary expert committees composed of representatives of all relevant interest groups, experts, representatives of cantonal governments, the political parties, and high-rank civil servants elaborate most constitutional or legal drafts. Second, the committees' drafts are generally made subject to a pre-parliamentary hearing. Usually, cantonal governments, political parties, social partners, and other interest groups are asked for a statement.

Federalism is strong in Switzerland. In addition to their extensive autonomous legislative competencies, the twenty-six cantons[1] have an important say in decisions made at the federal level. Cantonal influence on federal policy-making is exerted through three main channels: (*a*) the upper chamber of parliament (the so-called Council of States) which has equal rights and competencies to the lower house (the so-called National Council), (*b*) the constitutional right to be heard in the pre-parliamentary consultation process, and (*c*) the fact that any constitutional amendment is tied to a 'mandatory referendum' which requires the majority of popular votes in a majority of cantons as well as a majority of votes in the whole country.

In addition to the mandatory referendum, there are several distinctive instruments of direct democracy that enable citizens to overrule decisions at the federal level. By collecting 50,000 signatures within 100 days, the people can challenge any bill or decree that has passed parliament by an optional referendum (alternatively, eight cantons can initiate an optional referendum). The referendum is decided by a single majority of the popular vote. The optional referendum

---

[1] To be precise, Switzerland consists of twenty cantons and six half-cantons, resulting from splits of former cantons.

was a major driving force behind the shift of the Swiss political system from a rather majoritarian democracy in the nineteenth century to the consociational model today. Since it provides discontented minorities with a means of overthrowing decisions of the majority, it contributed to the gradual inclusion of minority groups into the political decision-making process (Neidhart 1970). A frequent use of optional referenda is therefore indicative of a (temporary) failure of the Swiss political system to develop compromise solutions through the inclusion of a large number of political actors. Moreover, 100,000 citizens may launch a constitutional initiative in order to amend the federal constitution, provided that sufficient signatures have been collected within 18 months. As for the mandatory referendum, a double majority of votes — an overall majority plus majority of cantons — is required.

These characteristics of the political system obviously have important consequences in terms of politics and policy patterns. In addition to the institutions of direct democracy and federalism, the distribution of power resources is crucial for understanding policy outcomes. Parties of the right are dominant in government and parliament, whereas the employers' strength is superior to that of trade unions. The typical policy solutions we can therefore observe in Switzerland are based on a compromise that usually favours employers' as well as right parties' interests (Kriesi 1980: 111, 693; Busch and Merkel 1992: 208–9; Schmidt 1992: 249; Jegher 1999: 202–3).

4.2 The Swiss welfare state at the end of the 'Golden Age': a 'laggard' with strong affinities to the liberal welfare regime

While Switzerland was a European pioneer in the field of workers' protection — limiting working days in industry to 11 hours and banning child labour as early as in 1877 — it was a laggard in the field of social insurance.

When the Swiss federal state was founded in 1848, the people accepted a constitution which granted only limited competencies to the Federation. Until the 1870s, social policy was an exclusive domain of cantonal and municipal legislation. Compared to other policies, the cantons were especially reluctant to cede legislative powers in economic and social policy. Before a federal welfare state could be created, several constitutional amendments were therefore necessary which are subject to mandatory referendum. It was not until 1947 that the federal parliament finally obtained legislative competencies for all major social insurance programmes. Additionally, the corresponding implementing legislation was often subject to an optional referendum which anti-welfare-groups — mainly right parties as well as business organizations — repeatedly used to block welfare state expansion (see e.g. Obinger 1998b, 2000). Therefore, it usually took not one but two attempts for social insurance bills to be put into legislation. Taken together, both federalism and direct democracy were crucial for Switzerland's status as a welfare state laggard (for the role of trade unions, see Trampusch 2008).

The federal welfare state take-off occurred only after the Second World War. The main cornerstones were the introduction of old-age and survivors' insurance in 1948, a federal unemployment insurance scheme (1952), child benefits for small farmers and agricultural workers (1953), disability insurance (1960), and means-tested supplementary pension and disability benefits (1966). In contrast to the preceding period, welfare state expansion was rarely attacked by optional referenda. The exceptional economic background after the Second World War helped to mitigate distributive conflicts. Nevertheless, Swiss welfare state expansion remained moderate.

Hence, at the end of the 'Golden Age', Switzerland, together with Australia, Canada, Japan, New Zealand, and the United States, belonged to an 'exclusive club' of rich democracies with lean welfare states, especially when as compared to the pioneers of continental Europe and Scandinavia (for details, see Obinger and Wagschal 2000). Benefit levels were comparatively low. The private sector played an important role in health insurance, as did co-payments. Social control was important, particularly in unemployment insurance as well as in unemployment and social assistance. The ideology underlying the Swiss welfare state was rather non-interventionist (see also Armingeon 1996: 81). Because of its laggard status and its underlying ideology of small government — and despite the fact that it was mainly based on social insurance — the Swiss welfare state has usually been assigned to the liberal or residual world of welfare (Esping-Andersen 1990; Armingeon 1996: 83). With regard to its structural make-up, the cantons maintained important legislative powers in many fields, including means-tested social benefits (unemployment and social assistance), health care, family policy, and personal social services.

At the beginning of the 1970s, only two social insurance schemes were universal, that is, covering the entire resident population: public pensions (*Alters- und Hinterlassenenversicherung*, AHV) and disability insurance (*Invalidenversicherung*, IV). Pensions were based on a pay-as-you-go (PAYG) system financed by equal contributions from employees and employers as well as by state subsidies. The retirement age was 62 years for women and 65 years for men. Benefits and contributions were earnings-related. While there was no ceiling for contributions, benefits varied between a floor and a ceiling. Within these limits, benefit levels depended on the contribution record. The combination of no contribution ceiling and minimum as well as maximum benefits made old-age pensions highly redistributive (Bonoli 1997: 113) — more redistributive than, for example, the German pension. In a way, the AHV was 'a compromise between the Bismarckian tradition of earnings-related contributory pensions and the Beveridgean flat-rate approach' (Bonoli and Kato 2004: 215).

Since the 1960s, a system of means-tested supplementary benefits (*Ergänzungsleistungen*, EL) has been used to provide additional support to pensioners on low income in both old-age and disability insurance. Financing was entirely tax-based, making supplementary benefits highly redistributive in favour of those on low incomes (Gärtner 2006: 77).

With regard to health care, Switzerland had neither a public health insurance scheme nor a national health service (see also Bonoli and Kato 2004: 218). Swiss health insurance (*Krankenversicherung*, KV) was voluntary and regulated only by a liberal framework law stating minimum benefits and specifying minimum requirements to be met by mutual health funds in order to receive global public grants for premium reductions. However, a number of cantons had declared health insurance mandatory and, due to the high costs of the Swiss health system, participation rates were high despite its voluntary character (Armingeon 2001: 147). Insurance was based on a PAYG system with individual flat-rate premiums depending on age at entry and gender. In addition, there were public subsidies to the (mostly private) health funds. Employers did not participate in financing and there was no non-contributory coverage of dependent family members as in many social insurance systems (Gerlinger 2003: 8). From 1964 onwards, significant co-payments were levied. In sum, the Swiss health system was primarily private, making the country, together with the United States, an exception in the OECD world.[2]

Mandatory accident insurance (*Unfallversicherung*, UV) covered only industrial workers, employees in dangerous business enterprises, and agricultural employees. Financing was via employers' contributions (for industrial accidents) and employees' contributions (for non-occupational accidents).

The design of the Swiss unemployment insurance resembled that of health insurance: It was also voluntary, although cantons had the right to make it mandatory. Funding was based on federal subsidies to unemployment funds (private, public, or run by the social partners) and employees' — but not employers' — contributions. The replacement rate was set at 65 per cent of insured income. By virtue of voluntary insurance and favourable economic conditions — especially spectacularly low levels of unemployment — affiliation remained modest. It seemed that there was simply no real need to be insured against this particular risk. The state contributed to low unemployment by regulating labour supply in a unique way: In times of decreasing demand for labour, restrictive work and residency permit regulations were used to make foreigners leave the labour market (Schmidt 1992, 1995; Wicki 2001). At the same time, women were discouraged from entering the labour market, for example, by the lack of childcare infrastructure.

---

[2] Australia's system was primarily private and voluntary before 1974.

In addition to voluntary unemployment insurance, means-tested cantonal unemployment assistance benefits were granted to those who either had exhausted their federal unemployment insurance entitlements or who were not entitled to federal insurance (such as the self-employed). The goal was to make it unnecessary for the unemployed to have to rely on the — highly stigmatizing — social assistance system (OECD 1999: 39). The majority of cantons provided an unemployment assistance scheme, but benefit levels as well as the kinds of benefits granted varied considerably.

Cantonal social assistance, which was also tax-financed and means-tested, assured a minimum income to all those who lacked sufficient income from their family or had exhausted social insurance benefits. In contrast to unemployment assistance, all cantons provided some form of social assistance. But owing to cantonal responsibility, social assistance systems varied considerably with regard to eligibility conditions, benefit levels, and procedures (Wolffers 1993). A certain degree of harmonization was achieved by the (non-binding) guidelines of the Swiss Conference for Social Assistance (*Schweizerische Konferenz für Sozialhilfe*, SKOS), an advisory body composed of experts, representatives of private social assistance associations, municipalities, cantons, and the federal government.

Finally, family policy can be considered as the 'stepchild' of the Swiss welfare state. According to the Swiss constitution, the federal government is only entitled to legislate on child benefits and paid maternity leave; all other domains of family policy are the preserve of cantonal legislation. Yet, even in the federal domains of child benefits and maternity leave, legislation was scarce. In terms of child benefits, apart from federal benefits for small farmers and agricultural workers, various cantonal allowances existed, differing in type, level, financing, and eligibility conditions. Social protection relating to maternity was regulated by various (uncoordinated) federal laws. An unpaid maternity leave period of 8 weeks following the birth of a child was laid down by labour law, while the continuous payment of wages was not guaranteed. Instead, it depended on the employer. Maternity benefits in kind were covered by health insurance.

Overall, the Swiss welfare state of the early 1970s exhibited strong liberal traits. However, given the prevalence of social insurance, a case could be mounted that it was, in reality, a conservative system of social protection in embryo. We will now analyse to what extent it has changed since that time and whether a fundamental transformation has taken place. Since, due to the 'magic formula', the partisan composition of the Swiss federal government has largely remained unchanged during the period under review, the following analysis of welfare state changes will be subdivided into decades rather than government periods, starting with the 1970s.

4.3 Welfare state reform since the 1970s

4.3.1 The 1970s: the end of a period of unrestricted economic growth

In 1974/5, the repercussions of the first oil shock hit Switzerland. The decline in the GDP growth rate in 1975 and 1976 was the greatest in the OECD. Yet the federal authorities reacted slowly to the crisis: there were a few public investment programmes but the intervention came too late, namely, at a time when the economy was already recovering (Mach 1999: 30). Despite some stabilization measures, Swiss federal fiscal policy remained pro-cyclical. Unemployment peaked in 1976 with a rate of 0.7 per cent of the labour force (OECD 1994) which was still very low by international standards.[3] Nevertheless, 'the experience . . . made clear to the public, that full employment which existed since the late 1930s, cannot be taken for granted in the future' (Armingeon 1999: 179). Since the economic recession resulted in a strongly growing deficit in the federal budget, the federal authorities enacted several measures of saving, some of them in social insurance. However, the attempt to increase federal revenue by introducing a value-added tax failed in a mandatory referendum in 1977.

The economic slump remained relatively brief and already by 1977 growth rates were on the way up again (Mach 1999: 30). Real full employment was soon restored, mainly by sending foreign workers back to their countries of origin (Obinger 1998a: 83).

4.3.1.1 LABOUR MARKET POLICIES OR 'IN CASE OF CRISIS, THE SWISS IS MOST WILLING TO ACT'[4]

With Switzerland experiencing unemployment for the first time since the 1930s, the reform of labour market policies became a clear priority.

For a start, the Swiss parliament amended the constitution in order to replace voluntary unemployment insurance by mandatory insurance for all employees. For the first time, insurance provision was to be financed not only through employees' contributions (as was hitherto the case), but also through employers' contributions. Mandatory insurance was supposed to solve the main problem of the existing system, that is, its low coverage (Bundesrat 1975: 1564). Although the number of insured persons had increased strongly in 1974, as of 1975, unemployment insurance still covered only about 32 per cent of wage

---

[3] A consequence of voluntary unemployment insurance was that a significant number of the unemployed did not register with employment offices and therefore did not appear in the official statistics (Fluckinger 1998: 371). Hence, Swiss unemployment figures prior to 1977 are likely to underestimate the real extent of the phenomenon (ibid.).

[4] This is a quotation from a speech by Konrad Graf (BGB), a member of the Council of States, on the occasion of a parliamentary debate on unemployment insurance (Bundesversammlung 1975–6: 14).

earners (APS 1975: 127–8). Moreover, the constitutional reform enlarged the role of unemployment insurance: because an increase in structural and technological unemployment was considered likely in the future, active labour market measures were now to be permitted where they enhanced the mobility and employability of beneficiaries (Bundesrat 1975: 1565; Kriesi 1980: 209).

Due to the economic situation and the unequivocal support by the social partners (Häusermann et al. 2001: 9–10), the constitutional amendment obtained the support of the majority of political actors and interest groups. It was accepted by the people in the mandatory popular vote by a large margin in 1976. Through the creation of mandatory unemployment insurance, the coverage of the Swiss welfare state was significantly extended. This reform, moreover, significantly shifted the Swiss welfare state in the direction of a conservative regime, since mandatory unemployment insurance was based on a primacy of status maintenance, with the level of benefits provided closely related to prior earnings.

The reform proceeded in several steps. First, the constitutional change resulted in an interim arrangement, which allowed a rapid reaction to rising unemployment and introduced mandatory insurance for all employees as well as new employers' contributions. It also specified that for a job to be deemed 'adequate', its wage had to correspond with the level of insurance benefits. In addition, the interim arrangement extended benefit duration for the elderly as well as for the disabled unemployed, that is, the more 'deserving' categories of the unemployed.

In 1982, the interim arrangement was eventually transformed into ordinary legislation. This time, the decision-making was slightly more controversial. The pre-parliamentary compromise, which amongst other things consisted of measures fighting benefit fraud, did not meet with the perfect satisfaction of both social partners. Potential benefit fraud also was the main reason for controversy in parliament. The main sticking point was the gradual reduction of benefits after a certain period of time ('degression').[5] Degression was only supposed to apply in periods when there was a balanced labour market and some recipients such as the elderly or the disabled unemployed were generally excluded from benefit reduction. A compromise — to cut the degression rate by half — was only finally arrived at through Christian Democratic mediation. In contrast, other parts of the reform package obtained widespread parliamentary support from the outset (see also Bundesrat 1980: 575). These measures included a new compensation benefit in case of employers' insolvency and a higher replacement rate of 70 per cent for singles and 80 per cent for married persons and for carers. New 'active' measures for enhanced mobility and employability (e.g. the new 'Zwischenverdienst', i.e. the possibility of combining income from work with benefits) did not provoke much controversy either, even though the Social

[5] For the controversial topic of reduced hours compensation where benefit fraud by employers was feared, see Bundesversammlung (1981–2: 138–41, 828–37).

Democrats would have preferred more encompassing active labour market measures (Bundesversammlung 1981–2: 126, 608). Finally, the reform measures included tight controls and sanctions as well as new pension insurance contributions levied on unemployment insurance benefits. In sum, the various elements of the 1982 reform package increased the scope of social protection. This regulation turned out to be effective throughout the 1980s, that is, as long as full employment prevailed.

At the sub-national level, some cantons including Basel-Town, Geneva, Lucerne, Solothurn, Zug, and Zurich reacted to the recession either by expanding existing unemployment assistance schemes through benefit increases and/or longer benefit duration or by introducing new cantonal aid systems for the needy unemployed.

Cantonal social assistance was also modified in the 1970s. Appenzell Inner Rhoden, Nidwalden, and Uri modernized their social assistance system by expanding social services, a general trend which had already started at the end of the 1960s. At the same time, cantonal social assistance gradually became more professionalized. The number of social assistance recipients remained at a higher level than before the economic crisis even when unemployment figures were again falling (Fluder and Stremlow 1999: 163).

4.3.1.2 THE LIMITS OF FISCAL STABILIZATION: PUBLIC PENSIONS AND HEALTH INSURANCE IN THE 1970s

Both public pensions and health insurance were subject to very similar demands and pressures in the 1970s. The growing federal budget deficit led to a reduction of federal subsidies. While the political decision-making process was more turbulent in pensions, cutbacks were more severe in health insurance.

In old-age pensions, parliament accepted a governmental decree which reduced the federal budget's share in total AHV expenses from 15 to 9 per cent. Furthermore, it temporarily transferred the authority to determine pension levels from parliament to government on condition that the government would increase benefits in 1976 and 1977. The reduction of federal grants to the universal pension system created a deficit in the compensation fund for the first time in its history (APS 1976: 132).

Reforming the voluntary health insurance scheme had been on the agenda for quite a long time. Change was considered necessary, mainly because of ever increasing health costs, health fund deficits, and the fact 'that solidarity in health insurance had been gradually on the wane' (Maarse and Paulus 2003: 603). This decline in solidarity resulted from adverse selection since premiums were related to risk (gender and age at entry) in the enrolment procedure, medical underwriting was not forbidden, and insurance companies were even permitted to reject applicants (see also Armingeon 2003: 175). Hence, health funds only competed for good health risks, while poor risks were not able to switch insurers. The substantial role of private payments in the system further reduced 'risk redistribution' in Swiss health insurance (Maarse and Paulus 2003: 603). Nor did public grants compensate for these effects as they were not targeted to those disadvantaged by the system (ibid.: 604). Since health insurance was financed by means of flat-rate premiums, 'bad risks' and low-income earners were heavily burdened with rising health costs and premiums.

Although there was clearly a need for reform with regard to the redistributive aspects of the system, the federal government's initial response to the economic recession and its repercussions involved a massive reduction in federal subsidies to health funds. Between 1975 and 1984, subsidies were cut by about 50 per cent in real terms (APS 1983: 141). Since cantonal health insurance grants were, in many cases, tied to federal ones, funds lost even more in revenue (APS 1989: 208). Meanwhile, health costs continued to grow, and health funds passed them on to the insured via significantly higher premiums. Even though the federal government had raised the franchise payment (the fixed amount the insured have to pay before health fund reimbursement kicks in) from 20 to 30 francs in 1975 (ibid.; see also Sommer 1978: 534), health funds continued their 'hunt for good risks'. As a result of these developments, existing redistribution problems were further aggravated.

While federal subsidies had been reduced in both health insurance and public pensions, pension reform returned to the agenda at the end of the 1970s. This time around, however, benefit expansion outweighed cutbacks.

In 1976, the government presented draft legislation. Reform had become necessary since the preceding decree was limited to 2 years. The so-called 9th AHV-review (as reforms of the primary law are consecutively numbered in Switzerland) had two objectives: first, financial stabilization and, secondly, the maintenance of benefit value. However, as is typically the case in Switzerland, the final reform package contained a whole range of different policy measures. The first reform objective was achieved by increasing certain types of revenue (e.g. a gradual return of federal grants to their former level) and by reducing some outlays — especially through some minor cutbacks at the expense of women. On the second count, a new indexation mechanism was set up based on a mixed index of price and wage developments. At the same time, ad hoc indexation was replaced by automatic indexation every 2 years and parliamentary indexation was replaced by governmental indexation. Consequently, benefits rose for those who were already receiving old-age pensions. Higher federal grants contributed, together with higher premiums, to the financial recovery of the social insurance system (APS 1981: 135).

Why were old-age pensions and federal subsidies expanded at all? After all, this was a time of fiscal conservatism. The answer can be found in the huge popularity of the Swiss public pension scheme. Politicians like the Christian Democratic member of cabinet in charge, Hans Hürlimann (Bundesversammlung 1976–7: 26), considered it the 'corner stone of Swiss social security' and its introduction could be seen as 'the most important event of the twentieth century' in a representative study conducted by the University of Zurich's department of sociology in 1980 (APS 1980: 129).

Despite the widespread popularity of the pensions system, a referendum was launched by a group of right-wing politicians and employers and it challenged nearly every aspect of the package, apart from the cutbacks. This was, in fact, the first optional referendum which contested a reform of public pensions. It failed, however, and, in 1978, the reform was approved by a margin of two to one in the popular vote.

In contrast, a simultaneous people's initiative for a lower retirement age of 60 launched by the extreme left was rejected — which is the usual fate of people's initiatives. The same happened a few years later to a very similar left-wing initiative. In both cases, the high cost of the proposals was crucial for their failure (VOX 1978: 8, 17, 1988: 11).

4.3.1.3 DEALING WITH THE END OF A PERIOD OF UNRESTRICTED ECONOMIC GROWTH: SAVINGS AND A FIRST MOVE TOWARDS THE CONTINENTAL MODEL OF WELFARE

For the most part, changes to the Swiss welfare state in the 1970s were strongly influenced by the economic crisis. On the one hand, even though it was only short, its repercussions on the federal budget contributed to a massive reduction of federal subsidies in social insurance, especially in health insurance where the cuts further aggravated existing redistributional problems. Due to the highly symbolic role of public pensions, federal grants to old-age pensions were gradually restored after having been cut in 1975 and benefits were even consolidated at a higher level. Because of higher contributions and higher state subsidies, the public pension scheme entered the 1980s in a good financial shape. On the other hand, the economic crisis created a 'window of opportunity' for the introduction of (generous) mandatory unemployment insurance because it demonstrated the weaknesses of voluntary insurance (see Armingeon 2001: 158). Consequently, Switzerland moved closer to a conservative model of welfare. Cantonal unemployment and social assistance were also expanded in the immediate aftermath of the crisis and social assistance was modernized. Family policy was of such marginal importance in the 1970s that it can easily be neglected. In terms of the politics of reform, the economic crisis had polarized partisan relationships as well as those between the social partners. Yet, overall, the consensual pattern of decision-making typical of Swiss politics was maintained.

4.3.2 Welfare state reforms in the 1980s: fair weather politics

While unemployment figures had been falling since 1976, they temporarily rose again in the wake of the second oil crisis. The impact of this new crisis on the Swiss labour market, however, remained limited. As in the 1970s, Swiss unemployment figures in the 1980s were among the lowest in the OECD world (Armingeon 1999: 179). Overall, Switzerland experienced a period of economic growth, reflected in an increasing tightness of the labour market, an upturn in inflation, budget surpluses at all three levels of government, and, as a result, decreasing levels of public debt (Flückiger 1998: 369; Bonoli and Mach 2000: 143–4; Bundesrat 2000: 4657–8). Yet, despite the economic boom, social assistance grew in importance during the 1980s both in terms of expenditure and recipients (Höpflinger and Wyss 1994: 133; Fluder and Stremlow 1999: 163).

In contrast to some other European and OECD countries, which experienced a profound market-liberal reorientation in economic (and social) policy, Switzerland was spared a radical 'liberal turn' (Jobert 1994; cited from Mach 1999: 31). Arguably, the low level of unemployment as well as Switzerland's continuing reluctance to become member of the European Community explains the absence of important economic reforms in the 1980s (ibid.: 31–2). Moreover, it can be argued that much of the adjustment undertaken by other countries in that period was not required in Switzerland as that country 'was already an exemplar of a flexible labor market, a decentralized system of wage bargaining, a lean (welfare) state, and a low tax economy' (Bonoli and Mach 2000: 143). Consequently, and in stark contrast to New Zealand, supply-side-oriented policy revolutionaries had little to rebel against. Still 'despite the high degree of openness in the Swiss economy, domestic-oriented producers [had] managed to obtain some measures that protected them from strong international competition' (ibid.: 138). These mainly took the form of heavy subsidies for agriculture, soft anti-cartel legislation, and an immigration policy providing cheap labour for domestic producers. These protective arrangements became increasingly visible as the international environment evolved and as, in the final years of the decade, pressure for change increased.

4.3.2.1 LABOUR MARKET POLICIES IN TIMES OF HIGH DEMAND FOR LABOUR

During the 1980s, unemployment insurance was repeatedly modified. Yet, due to the good labour market performance, the changes were relatively small. They were mostly about filling small gaps in the 1982 reform. Changes included reducing employers' cost sharing in case of reduced hours and adverse weather conditions (measures supposed to prevent dismissals in hard times) and harmonizing benefits for married persons and singles by increasing the replacement rate of the latter to 80 per cent.

Some cantons extended unemployment assistance benefit duration and/or reduced waiting days; others broadened the purpose of unemployment assistance with the introduction of activation measures (e.g. subsidies for professional training or retraining).

Nine out of twenty-six cantonal social assistance laws were revised during the 1980s. As in the 1970s, personal services, including counselling and mentoring, became increasingly important (Wolffers 1993: 45–6). At the same time, some of the more coercive aspects, such as the refund of benefits in case of economic recovery, were reduced. Middle-sized and large municipalities expanded their professional social services (Fluder and Stremlow 1999: 45). Smaller municipalities enhanced their cooperation and organized regional social services (ibid.).

4.3.2.2 THE SLOW RISE OF STATUS PRESERVATION IN PENSION POLICY

Voluntary occupational benefits as an informal second pillar of old-age protection — with public pensions (*Alters- und Hinterlassenenversicherung*, AHV) being the first, private provision the third pillar — had played an important role in the Swiss pension scheme for a considerable time.[6] This was mainly a repercussion of the late creation of a public pension scheme (1948) and the fact that, even then, public old-age benefits were very low (Bonoli and Kato 2004: 215; Degen 2006: 51, 54; for the role of business see Leimgruber 2008).

In 1972, a constitutional amendment formally institutionalized the organically emergent multi-pillar structure of the pension scheme. What was more important, however, was that the amendment was coupled with the binding mandate to declare occupational benefits mandatory and to design them in such a way that ensured that pensioners would continue to enjoy their accustomed standard of living when receiving public and occupational pensions.

This implementing legislation had a long prehistory, dating back to a compromise between the federal government, the social partners, and the already existing pension funds early in the 1970s. This compromise was not a long-lasting one. When economic conditions worsened in the second half of the 1970s, the majority of employers and pension funds cancelled the pre-parliamentary compromise with trade unions. Employers pointed out that its financial consequences were unbearable under the current worsened economic conditions, while the pension funds voiced their concern that the bill would interfere too much with their existing structures and would mostly benefit those companies which had hitherto not provided occupational benefits for their

---

[6] Non-compulsory private provision encouraged by tax concessions (the third pillar) has experienced no major modifications during the period under scrutiny here. It is mainly of interest to employees with high incomes 'since it enables them to avoid high marginal taxes' (Armingeon 2003: 174).

employees (Bundesversammlung 1977–82: 1007). Against this background, the right-wing majorities in both chambers of parliament chose the more moderate option of a defined contribution (DC) rather than a defined benefit (DB) scheme, as initially promised.

However, although, in theory, the law of 1982 required only defined contribution schemes, in practice, 'the Swiss government impose[d] a schedule of minimum contributions, a minimum rate of return and a factor for converting accumulated capital into an annuity, thereby targeting a defined level of benefit' (Queisser and Whitehouse 2003: 8). In consequence, status preservation could be realized, although only in a gradual fashion. Finally, parliament reduced the bill's redistributive component and restricted the obligation to adjust for prices to the smaller group of disabled and survivors, while the price indexation of old-age benefits was made dependent on the individual pensions funds' financial situation. Although Social Democrats and trade unions would have preferred a more generous scheme, they did not want the plan of mandatory occupational benefits to fail and grudgingly accepted the bill (Bundesversammlung 1977–82: 327, 1022, 1125–6, 1264; APS 1982: 132–3).

All in all, the law of 1982 can be seen as a first step from minimum protection to status preservation in Swiss pensions and as a further move towards the conservative welfare model. Coverage was increased by declaring occupational pensions compulsory for employees earning above an income threshold equal to the maximum public pension. 'Since people on lower earning will reach a replacement rate of at least 60% through the public pension ... participation in an occupational scheme [was] not deemed necessary' (Queisser and Whitehouse 2003: 10–11). Switzerland now had an earnings-related and fully funded occupational scheme, provided by private and public funds, and solely financed through contributions by employers and employees. As a framework law, the legislation of 1982 preserved existing structures: as in the former voluntary insurance system, employers and pensions funds maintained ample leeway for the exact design of mandatory occupational benefits.

The introduction of mandatory occupational benefits was certainly the most important event in Swiss pension policy during the 1980s. However, changes in supplementary benefits for low-income pensioners must be mentioned as well. In summary, the 1985 reform mainly resulted in increased coverage as well as in higher income limits, especially for recipients living in nursing homes, those having to pay high rents or medical treatment costs and for those cared for at home. In effect, the main result of the reform was to adjust benefits to general price inflation and rises in the cost of hospital and long-term care as well as for rents and medical care. But since there was no long-term care insurance in Switzerland either then or now, the increased consideration of nursing home costs also made supplementary benefits into a kind of (means-tested) 'nursing home long-term care insurance' (Carigiet and Opielka 2006: 34; Gärtner 2006: 75). Supplementary benefits are partly funded by the cantons, and their resistance to the initial draft legislation, persuaded the federal government to reduce costs. The reform was unanimously passed in parliament. The Liberals in particular hoped that by a selective enhancement of supplementary benefits, general increases in public pension benefit levels could be averted — at least temporarily (Bundesversammlung 1985: 285–7, 289, 1386–7, 1389–90, 1392).

4.3.2.3 BETTER MINOR CHANGES THAN NO CHANGE AT ALL? SWISS HEALTH INSURANCE IN THE 1980s AND THE INTRODUCTION OF MANDATORY ACCIDENT INSURANCE

In 1981, Swiss accident insurance was separated from health insurance and declared mandatory for all employees. Before this time, only industrial workers, employees in dangerous business enterprises and in agriculture had been compulsorily covered. However, the increase in coverage was negligible since, one way or another, 95 per cent of all employees were already insured (Wagner 1985: 187; cited from Obinger 1998b: 80). Nevertheless, mandatory insurance once again made the Swiss welfare state more structurally akin to the conservative model. The reform also granted private insurance companies access to mandatory accident insurance.

Swiss accident insurance now covered industrial accidents as well as non-occupational accidents, as long as the insured person worked at least 12 hours a week. It guaranteed temporary coverage of treatment costs, income compensation, necessary medical devices, and financial compensation for some material damages. Where an accident resulted in lasting damage, in disability, or in death, disability, survivors' benefits and a variety of other benefits were provided. Since 1981, the accident insurance set-up has seen only minor modifications.

In contrast to the accident insurance reform, an encompassing health insurance reform bill failed in an optional referendum in 1987. It had been launched by two different groups, one consisting of employers and the other predominantly of physicians and persons in charge of private hospitals. Although the reform included many different regulations, some of them highly controversial, it was the introduction of paid maternity leave, that is, a family policy measure, that was crucial for the referendum attack by employers. It was also the reason for the reform's failure in the popular vote (VOX 1987: 19). In turn, the introduction of paid maternity leave via health insurance had been an indirect counter-proposal to a proposed scheme for paid maternity leave initiated in the 1970s by left parties, trade unions, and women's organizations, which had failed in a popular vote in 1984.

After the 1987 reform proposal's rejection, parliament temporarily increased federal subsidies to health funds by about 300 million francs per year and targeted them towards women and the elderly, that is, towards 'bad risks'.[7]

---

[7] Additionally, federal government repeatedly increased co-payments by the way of ordinances (see APS 1986: 165–6, 1990: 226).

Again, the draft was an indirect counter-proposal to an analogous people's initiative launched by the Swiss Concordat of Health Funds which was (unsurprisingly) rejected by the people in 1992.

4.3.2.4 STILL OFF THE BEATEN TRACK: SWISS FAMILY POLICY IN THE 1980s

As in the 1970s, family policy was of minor importance in the 1980s. Both decades witnessed only a minor reform of federal child benefits in agriculture. In 1985, the responsibility for future benefit adjustment was transferred from parliament to the federal government (for details, see APS 1985: 151).

In contrast, an attempt to harmonize cantonal child benefits failed in the 1980s. Since the idea encountered strong resistance from most cantons as well as from Liberals, Conservatives (SVP), and employers, and since Social Democrats and trade unions gave priority to other social policy issues, both chambers eventually dismissed the idea of harmonizing cantonal benefits (see also APS 1986: 167).

4.3.2.5 THE SWISS WELFARE STATE IN THE 1980s: MODERATE CHANGES IN A GOOD SOCIO-ECONOMIC ENVIRONMENT

On the whole, Swiss welfare state development in the 1980s reflected the country's rather good economic performance. What reforms there were involved moderate first- and second-order policy changes and policy-making was largely consensual. While the creation of mandatory occupational pensions constituted by and large the most important change of the 1980s, the scheme's moderate benefit levels were a repercussion of the 1970s' economic crisis. However, the creation of mandatory occupational benefits (as well as of mandatory accident insurance) with its strong emphasis on status maintenance was another step towards the institutionalization of a conservative welfare state model. Parliament also took some tentative steps in health insurance by temporarily increasing federal subsidies to health funds and by targeting them to 'bad risk' groups, thereby increasing the redistributiveness of the system. However, a proposed encompassing reform of health insurance failed in an optional referendum. Once again, family policy was of marginal importance.

Only in the 1990s would welfare state change in Switzerland reach an unprecedented pace and extent.

4.3.3 Welfare state reforms in the 1990s: major change in conflict-ridden times

In 1991, Switzerland was again hit by recession, but unlike the crises of the 1970s and 1980s, this new recession was of long duration and had a far greater impact. Economic development stagnated at an average growth rate of 1.1 per cent per year over the entire decade. Throughout the 1990s, Swiss economic growth rates remained below the OECD average. This development was followed by budgetary crisis at all political levels. Federal debt increased dramatically: within a period of only 2 years — from 1992 to 1993 — the debt reduction achieved in the 1980s was undone (Bundesrat 2000: 4658). Although, by international comparison, the Swiss federal budget situation was in above average shape, the federal government feared that the country might lose its good reputation as an 'island of economic stability' (Bundesrat 1993b: 294, 296, 1998: 9). As a consequence, fiscal policy became a political priority of the 1990s and resulted in a variety of savings measures as well as constitutional amendments aiming at balancing the federal budget. In 1993, a fourth attempt to introduce a value-added tax was finally accepted by the people. Other changes to the Swiss fiscal system included a reduction in stamp duties on financial and capital transactions as well as tax cuts for business — even though corporate tax rates were already among the lowest in the OECD (for details, see Bonoli and Mach 2000: 163–4).

Unemployment rose and, at 4.1 per cent in 1997, reached a record high for the post-war period (OECD 2004b).[8] To some extent, this was due to the worldwide economic recession. Yet, in addition, the traditional way of regulating labour supply had become less effective, mainly because of the introduction of mandatory unemployment insurance, the increasing number of foreigners with permanent work permits, and modified employment patterns of women (Schmidt 1995; Flückiger 1998). In addition, the expansion of unemployment insurance created a further incentive for dismissals during the recession (Obinger 1998c: 86). Increasing outlays and revenue shortages soon created large deficits in the unemployment insurance compensation fund. As a result, 'the scheme was unable to meet its liabilities and had to borrow funds from the general government budget' (Bonoli 1997: 122). These insurance deficits, in turn, put a strain on federal finances (Mach 1999: 45).

While the parliaments of the European Free Trade Area (EFTA) countries Austria, Finland, Iceland, Norway, and Sweden (as well as the people of Liechtenstein) ratified membership in the European Economic Area (EEA) in 1992, the Swiss people rejected accession in the same year in an optional referendum vote. The referendum was provoked by the conservative Swiss People's Party. The no vote stemmed from opposition to an opening of product markets and increasing migration (Wagschal et al. 2002: 8). However, despite widespread Eurosceptic attitudes among the Swiss, in 1999, the government concluded a bilateral agreement with the European Union (EU) on the free movement of labour, research, public procurement, technical trade barriers, transports, and agriculture. This can be interpreted as a sort of 'EEA-lite' since it realized between 60 and

---

[8] Nevertheless, unemployment levels remained low by international standards (Flückiger 1998: 370).

80 per cent of the free domestic market that would have been created had Switzerland joined the EEA (ibid.: 34). The treaty was accepted in a popular vote in 2000. In a manner similar to that of Germany after the eastern enlargement of the EU, Switzerland accepted the introduction of the free movement of labour only with some protectionist control and sanctions regulations ('flanking measures') in order to prevent so-called wage dumping. Nevertheless, from the 1990s onwards, Swiss policy became increasingly 'Europeanized'. In addition to the bilateral agreement, Switzerland not only introduced a 'euro-compatibility check' for every new part of legislation, but also began a process of unilateral harmonization of legislation in many areas in anticipation of EU directives and regulations ('autonomous adjustment').

In conjunction, European integration, economic recession, and economic internationalization imposed strong new pressure on Swiss economic policies (Bonoli and Mach 2000: 144). In the face of developments in other OECD countries, there was a widespread feeling that Switzerland was progressively losing its attractiveness as a business location. Changes were no longer limited to those sectors which had already been exposed to international competition but also spilled over to the domestic market (Mach 1998; Mach et al. 2003: 301).

Change took place in agriculture, public procurement, the labour market, public monopolies, competition policy, and the regulation of foreign labour (for details, see Armingeon and Emmenegger 2007; OECD 2000). Swiss immigration policy was partially deregulated in 1992, especially for highly skilled workers (Flückiger 1998: 388). In addition, the (gradual) introduction of the free movement of labour with the EU largely reduced Swiss room to manoeuvre in the domain of immigration policy (Nikolai 2005: 194). The reform of the Cartel Law in 1995 was clearly inspired by EU regulations (Mach 1998: 46). Although it did not outlaw cartels altogether, it gave the newly created Competition Commission (ComCom) a strong mandate and provided a much clearer and stricter application of anti-competitive practices, thereby ending the prevalent tradition of tolerance and laxity towards cartels (Mach et al. 2003: 305). Interestingly, a number of barriers to trade still existed at the sub-national level. Therefore, a new law on the internal market was legislated in order to facilitate the free movement of goods, services, and persons between the Swiss cantons. Parliament also removed the legal basis for technical trade barriers, thereby opening up Swiss markets to greater competition (Bonoli and Mach 2000: 165).

In telecommunications, Switzerland followed a liberalization rhythm parallel to that of the EU and enacted changes in two steps. In 1991, 'value-added network services' and the market for terminal equipment were liberalized, while market regulation and service provision were split. In 1997, the post and telecom services of the public telecom company (PTT) were separated into two distinct companies (Swisscom and Die Post). The telecommunication sector was completely liberalized through the removal of public monopoly and the creation of the independent ComCom which was supposed to guarantee free access to the telecom market (Mach et al. 2003: 305–6). By contrast, liberalization of postal services was less pronounced and lagged behind the level achieved in the EU or in the other EFTA countries (Wagschal et al. 2002: 113–18). The Swiss national railways were converted into a private enterprise in 1999, though the state remains the sole proprietor. Public procurement was liberalized at the federal as well as the cantonal level after Switzerland had signed the GATT Agreement on public procurement in 1994 (for details, see Mach et al. 2003: 306). In agriculture, where Switzerland provided some of the most generous subsidies in the OECD, a first reform created the basis for direct payments independent of production, while a second one abolished all public price and purchase guarantees, reduced funds for market support, and disestablished existing parastatal protectionist organizations such as the 'cheese union' (Armingeon and Emmenegger 2007: 180).

Overall, however, Switzerland lagged behind the EU liberalization dynamic, especially with regard to the domestic market (Wagschal et al. 2002: 32, 151). However, it should also be noted that, in comparison to most other European countries, certain areas of the Swiss economy required only minor adjustments, for example, the labour market, the system of wage bargaining and the tax system (Bonoli and Mach 2000: 143, 168).

The political climate worsened significantly during the 1990s. Apart from the negative economic context, this was largely due to the fact that the most internationalized sections of the business community started to question the traditional Swiss post-war compromise (for details, see Bonoli and Mach 2000; Burkhalter et al. 1999). This compromise had meant, on the one hand, that employers benefited from peaceful industrial relations with a small number of strikes in exchange for high wages and a rather generous level of income compensation. On the other hand, export-oriented employers profited from economic openness, while at the same time accepting some non-competitive arrangements within the domestic market (Bonoli and Mach 2000). In the 1990s, however, these regulations were increasingly seen as a burden on the competitiveness of the Swiss export sector. Therefore, tensions between the export-oriented and the domestic sectors increased (ibid.: 157). Similarly, the cooperation between trade unions and employers became more difficult. As will be shown in the following sections, this development affected politics and policies.

4.3.3.1 LABOUR MARKET POLICIES: DEALING WITH 'REAL' UNEMPLOYMENT

In the 1990s, federal unemployment insurance was subject to several reforms which all resulted in a higher level of contributions. Conceived in a period of extremely low unemployment, contributions rates proved to be inappropriate in the economic slump of the 1990s (Mach 1999: 45). In 1993, the contribution rate was raised from 0.4 to 2 per cent of wages, and, only 2 years later, to 3 per cent.

In addition, a special 'solidarity surcharge' has been levied on higher incomes since 1995.

A first and temporarily limited decree was the reaction to the fact that, for the first time since the end of the Second World War, long-term unemployment had become a mass phenomenon in Switzerland. It entitled the federal government to prolong maximum benefit duration by 100 days. Yet, due to the large deficits in the unemployment insurance compensation fund, compensatory savings became necessary. The federal government, therefore, proposed to reduce the replacement rate from 80 to 70 per cent of former income for about one-fourth of the unemployed. The more 'deserving' categories of the unemployed, that is, people with dependent children, those on very low incomes, and disabled persons were spared from the cutback. Despite opposition from both sides of the political spectrum, parliament passed the decree and also decided to declare jobs with wages below the level of insurance benefits as 'adequate'.

The federal decree survived an optional referendum, launched by the small communist Party of Labour in 1993. Despite this, the optional referendum was of major *political* importance because it resulted in a stalemate between the social partners. While trade unions and, albeit only informally, also employers supported the referendum, their underlying motives differed fundamentally. Unions openly backed the Party of Labour in its opposition to benefit cutbacks. Employers, in contrast, not only wanted even deeper cutbacks but also feared that a referendum victory by the trade unions might strengthen the position of the left in a much more comprehensive unemployment insurance reform already underway. In the run-up to the 1993 referendum, the social partners proved unable to negotiate on the more encompassing reform. Whereas the temporary limitation of the first decree was supposed to give the authorities time to prepare a more comprehensive reform, the tensions between the social partners hindered the usual negotiation-based policy-making. Instead of a major review, parliament chose to issue a second temporarily limited decree. Amongst other things, it provided a new 5-day waiting period (with some exceptions) for the receipt of insurance benefits.

Eventually, unemployment insurance reform was achieved by bringing the social partners back to the negotiation table. A parliamentary committee in the National Council gave the reform process a new turn by helping to find a new compromise.

On the one hand, employers and parties of the right accepted higher contributions as well as an important accentuation of active labour market measures as demanded by unions and Social Democrats for decades. The main idea was a two-tier system with reduced entitlement to general allowances (except for the elderly), while 'special allowances' should only be granted to unemployed persons on activation measures such as training courses, employment programmes, or those who were about to start up their own business (for details, see Werner 2002: 5). Active labour market employment was to be a cantonal responsibility and regional employment agencies should replace municipal ones. On the other hand, trade unions and left parties accepted some retrenchment of passive unemployment insurance. More specifically, the formerly unlimited entitlement was restricted to 2 years. The new draft was approved by both chambers of parliament in 1995. Parliament retained some elements of the federal decrees, including the lower replacement rate (for mainly high-income and childless unemployed), the 5-day waiting period, and the right of the government to prolong the maximum period of benefit receipt. As proposed by the federal government, periods of care were to be taken into account for benefit calculation.

After accommodating the interests of the social partners, the parliamentary debate focused on cantonal issues. In 1995, 'cantons accepted that they were to provide a large number of jobs in the context of the active policy, in return for reduced contributions to the unemployment insurance fund and for more flexibility with regard to the absolute number of jobs' (Armingeon 2003: 182). Overall, the 1995 reform fundamentally altered federal unemployment insurance, particularly through the accentuation of active labour market policies. A cantonal trade union section and several unemployment pressure groups tried to attack the reform by optional referendum but were not able to collect enough signatures to enforce a popular vote.

While higher contributions allowed the federal unemployment insurance fund to balance its books, this success was short-lived: The expenditure increase provoked by the expansion of active labour market policies again put the budget in the red as early as 1996 (Bonoli 1999: 68). At the same time, the situation of the federal budget remained tense. Consequently, measures for the reorganization of the federal budget were high on the federal agenda. Within the scope of such measures, parliament already in 1996 had passed a temporary limited decree on unemployment insurance which attempted to bring about relatively small expenditure cuts (benefit reductions of between 1 and 3 per cent, depending on the benefit level and on childcare responsibilities; and a stricter definition of adequate work).[9] An optional referendum was launched by a local unemployment pressure group. The result of the popular vote in 1997 was very narrow, with 50.8 per cent of voters rejecting the decree.

Alternative ways of easing the burden on the federal budget and of reducing the insurance deficit were negotiated in informal round-table talks between the government, social partners, and cantons in 1998. They resulted in several umbrella acts by which dozens of federal acts were amended. Participants in the talks decided amongst other things to continue the debt reduction strategy based on higher contributions until 2003. They also agreed on a second

[9] Further benefit cuts were envisaged from 2007 onwards. They were designed so as to insure recipients of unemployment insurance benefits against risks of death and disability through mandatory occupational pension arrangements.

'solidarity surcharge' for the better-off and to lift the contribution ceiling. On the expenditure side, several, but, in each case, minor, benefit cutbacks were adopted, amounting to savings of 250 million francs (for details, see APS 1998: 272). However, higher unemployment contributions played a greater role than cutbacks in terms of budgetary stabilization (Bundesversammlung 1998a: 2380, 2429). Parliament passed the resolutions of the informal round-table talks as a temporarily limited decree.

An earlier attempt by the federal government to replace cantonal with federal unemployment assistance had failed in 1992 (Bundesrat 1993a: 685). Despite this failed reform, cantonal unemployment and social assistance were nonetheless significantly modified during the 1990s. As in federal unemployment insurance, activation was the major trend. Several cantons established professional and/or social reintegration measures either at the level of unemployment assistance and social assistance or as a completely new social benefit (for details see Moser 2003: 46; Wyss 1997; Wyss and Ruder 1999: 240). At the same time, the number of cantons providing 'passive' unemployment assistance only declined significantly. In general, the cantons of Latin-Switzerland, which were more seriously hit by rising unemployment and poverty in the 1990s than their German-speaking counterparts, placed a much greater emphasis on active labour market policies (see Hotz et al. 1995: 220; Wyss and Ruder 1999: 239–45). The focus was also different: In the German-speaking cantons, the main aim of such measures was professional reintegration and economic independence (e.g. through further education offers, employment programmes, training courses, placements or activities in public institutions and non-profit organizations), while in French-speaking Switzerland and Ticino, the main objective was to prevent social exclusion (e.g. with measures that foster the social networks of the benefit recipients) (Bertozzi and Bonvin 2001: 39; Strohmeier and Knöpfel 2005). Overall, important cantonal differences remained with regard to the target group, the coverage of active labour market measures, the calculation base of benefits, benefit levels, the period of benefit receipt, and the reintegration measures offered. At the same time, higher levels of demand for social assistance put the issue of cost containment on cantonal political agendas. More restrictive assessment of social assistance benefits as well as a more frequent enforcement of familial obligations to support needy family members became the order of the day (Hotz et al. 1995: 224; Ditch and Oldfield 1999: 68; Fluder and Stremlow 1999: 150).

4.3.3.2 WOMEN'S RIGHTS AND WOMEN'S DUTIES: OLD-AGE PENSIONS IN THE 1990S

In the 1990s, the public pension scheme was subject to the most important reform of the period under review, the so-called 10th AHV-review. As usual with such reviews, it contained a whole package of different measures. The main reform objectives were the equal treatment of men and women in old-age pensions and a flexible retirement age. The question how to realize equal treatment was particularly controversial. The first government draft on this issue, in 1990, was still cautious. It refrained from the introduction of a splitting of pension entitlements — which was opposed by employers on financial grounds — and retained the lower female retirement age (3 years below that of men). Instead, the federal government only proposed minor changes such as the separate payment of the couple's pension as well as a new widowers' pension. The draft also included a new pension formula which would favour low-wage earners as well as new early retirement provisions cutting benefits on an actuarially fair basis. The main ways of financing the proposed measures were raising contributions for the self-employed, federal subsidies, and the abolition of the special supplementary benefits for spouses.

However, the bill did not get through parliament. Women's organizations and (female) politicians — Social Democrats and Liberals, in particular — were strongly dissatisfied with the government's cautious approach to the abolition of gender discrimination. The bill was heavily modified by the National Council. Couples' pension entitlements were split and special (gender-neutral) contribution credits for informal care were introduced. Parliament also stipulated a gradual rise in women's retirement age from 62 to 64 over a period of 8 years. The female retirement age was the critical issue in both chambers of parliament. While the right-of centre supporters of such an increase pointed to the constitutional principle of equal treatment and the need to finance the future costs of structural and demographic developments, their 'red–green' opponents emphasized women's double burden as well as ongoing wage discrimination (Bundesversammlung 1991–4: 5, 24–39; APS 1993: 217).

In 1994, a parliamentary compromise was eventually reached on the basis of the National Council's draft. The final law also adopted many governmental propositions such as the new pension formula, higher federal grants, the new widowers' pension, and the new early retirement scheme. To prevent high-income earners being the only ones in a position to take early retirement, it was made possible to pre-draw means-tested supplementary benefits. Women's higher retirement age was supposed to be at least partly compensated for by a temporarily lower deduction for women in case of early retirement. On the whole, the 10th AHV-review abolished major gender discriminations within the Swiss pension scheme and thereby reduced the Swiss welfare state's adherence to a male breadwinner family model. The reform also increased benefits for pensioners with low incomes. Although early retirement was included in the package, in contrast to other European countries such as France or Germany, it was only available with an actuarial benefit reduction.

The major trade unions decided to launch an optional referendum against the reform. The rise in women's retirement age went completely against their call for a general lowering of retirement ages (Bonoli 1999: 66). However, since Swiss voters can only choose between yes or no in a referendum, trade unions, left parties, and women's organizations were faced with a strategic dilemma. On the one hand, they clearly opposed a higher retirement age for women. On the other, they had been fighting for more gender equality in public pensions for quite a long time. To make their point, trade unions supplemented their optional referendum with a people's initiative 'for the reform without an increase in the retirement age' which was also supported by Social Democrats. However, this attempt failed. In 1995, the reform was accepted by about 60 per cent of voters, a stronger level of approval than had been expected (APS 1995: 245). Correspondingly, and to nobody's surprise, the people's initiative of the left was rejected on grounds of high cost in 1998. An earlier people's initiative launched by the left and calling for a lower retirement age and a financial boost for public pensions had suffered a similar fate in 1995.

The 10th AHV-review realized a number of important goals in terms of gender equality but it also added about 800 million francs to the federal budget deficit (Obinger 1998b: 78). Therefore, the issue of pension finance soon made its reappearance on the policy agenda. As early as 1995 — that is, 1 year after the passage of the 10th AHV-review — parliament significantly reduced federal subsidies for the year 1996. Further governmental proposals, including index-ing pensions to prices but not wages, were turned down as all major parties agreed that social insurance for the old was much too sensitive a domain for ad hoc changes (APS 1995: 245). Although benefit cutbacks in old-age pensions were also a subject of the informal round-table talks of 1998 between the social partners, cantons, governmental parties, and governmental representatives, parliament decided against further action (for details, see APS 1998: 155–8; Bundesversammlung 1998a: 2380, 2393, 2396, 2408).

In the same year, parliament increased public pension revenues by deciding to earmark an additional percentage of value-added tax (worth about 2 billion francs) for public pensions. This was the first time since its creation in 1948 that a new source of revenue was created for old-age pensions. It was done largely in order to prepare for the effects of demographic ageing. Parliament also passed a law on gambling taxes and had these new taxes flow into the AHV compen-sation fund.

Changes in occupational pensions in the 1990s included an expanded degree of portability and a decision that parts of accumulated pension capital could be pre-drawn in order to amortize mortgages. As a result of changes in unemploy-ment insurance, recipients of unemployment insurance benefits became insured against risks of death and disability through mandatory occupational pension arrangements, which meant that an important gap in the Swiss social insurance system had been filled (Obinger 1998b: 91). However, in order to finance the increased coverage of occupational benefits, parliament accepted a general reduction of unemployment insurance benefits. This was voted down in the (optional) referendum vote of 1997.

Finally, the 1990s saw another minor reform of means-tested supplementary benefits for low-income recipients of public pensions (and disability insurance). It essentially aimed at ameliorating the situation of pensioners living at home, mainly through higher compensations for housing costs. Such measures seemed necessary because recipients living in nursing homes made up only one-third of total beneficiaries, but took up two-thirds of total costs. A further goal was to increase take-up through enhanced information, with studies showing that about 30 per cent of those entitled to supplementary benefits did not claim them, either from a sense of shame or a lack of information (Bundesversammlung 1997: 617). Even though it was clear that the reform would result in additional costs, all governmental parties agreed on its necessity (ibid.: 448–55).

4.3.3.3 A BREAKTHROUGH IN HEALTH CARE

When at the beginning of 1991 health funds threatened to raise premiums by 15 to 20 per cent on average, the Swiss federal government decided that it was time to act. For years, the main themes of the policy debate had been the continuous increase in health costs on the one hand and the permanent erosion of redistribution in health insurance on the other. Since substantial reforms are typically a lengthy process in Switzerland, the government decided to act initially through temporarily limited urgency measures — as in unemployment insurance in the first half of the 1990s. While the proposals for enhanced redistribution (e.g. targeted premium reductions for low incomes) were relatively uncontroversial, cost containment was the main debating point (for details, see Moser 2008). The new general co-payment for hospital treatments of 10 francs per day[10] — aimed to redirect patients from the (expensive) hospital to the (less expensive) outpatient domain — even provoked an optional referendum, launched by the small communist Party of Labour. Since the referendum obtained only the further support of one small right-wing party, the decree's acceptance by more than 80 per cent of voters came as no surprise.

In 1994, that is, more than 80 years after its introduction, Swiss health insurance was subject to its first comprehensive reform. Over these years, all reform attempts had either been blocked by conflicts between physicians and health funds or between left and right parties (Obinger et al. 2005: 267). This time, however, the bill even succeeded in overcoming the referendum hurdle.

Due to the large number of interests involved in the policy-making process and the long period of non-decisions, the reform included many different

---

[10] Not applying to children, chronically ill persons, and women in childbirth.

policy-measures and was intended to fulfil several goals at once. More precisely, it was supposed to enhance the redistribution between good and bad risks as well as between high and low incomes, contain health cost and premium increases, and fill gaps in the benefit catalogue. A first draft had been presented by the federal government in 1991. It was based largely on the proposals of an expert committee with representatives of health funds and physicians. The most important change was the establishment of mandatory insurance — including benefits in kind but *not* sick pay — for the entire resident population. Although 99 per cent of the population were already covered by some form of voluntary insurance (European Observatory on Health Care Systems 2000: 77), the 'former option for the well-to-do to opt out [could be] abolished by making health insurance mandatory to each Swiss citizen' (Maarse and Paulus 2003: 606). Other key aspects were full mobility in basic insurance (without restriction, waiting time, or financial loss), coupled with the health funds' obligation to contract and risk equalization between funds. The idea was to set up a 'virtuous' form of competition among funds: since risk picking was restricted, health insurance funds wishing to offer a better deal were supposed to contain their administrative expenses or to negotiate lower treatment prices with providers (Bonoli and Kato 2004: 219). In addition, the government suggested equal premiums for basic insurance — thereby abolishing all premium differences based on gender or age at entry — and higher public subsidies to be used for premium reductions for low incomes. The draft also harmonized and expanded benefits in basic insurance, primarily with regard to eldercare (at home and in nursing homes), hospital stays, and preventative medicine (Gerlinger 2003: 17). In an effort to curb spending, federal global budgeting, alternative insurance models (e.g. health maintenance organizations, gate-keeping), and hospital planning schemes were put forward. Overall, the governmental draft was extremely far-reaching, especially when taking Swiss legislative standards into account. It would affect financing, provision, and regulation in the health sector and it would have transformed the Swiss health system from a primarily private to a social insurance system.

Parliamentary decision-making took 3 years. After three rounds of debate in both chambers of parliament, important differences remained. Therefore, a so-called conference of conciliation, composed of members of the responsible committees from both chambers, had to be set up. In contrast, to the cost-containment measures, the creation of mandatory insurance with full mobility, the expansion of the benefit catalogue, as well as the premium reductions for low incomes were largely undisputed in parliament. Overall, the 1994 reform closed important gaps in the benefit catalogue, prevented the (before rather common) withholding of benefits to the chronically ill, and strengthened redistribution within the Swiss health insurance system (Gerlinger 2003). The reform also enhanced competition within health insurance.

It came as no surprise that, following the reform, an optional referendum was launched. Four referendum committees — consisting of health funds and physicians — collected enough signatures for a popular vote to take place. Opponents argued, among other things, that the law regulated too much, was too strongly oriented towards orthodox medicine, was insufficiently competitive, and too expensive for the public purse as well as for the insured (APS 1994: 224). Nonetheless, the reform was accepted by a small majority of about 52 per cent of votes in 1994. In contrast, a people's initiative sponsored by the Social Democrats and trade unions in favour of proportional funding of health care was, once again, rejected on the same day (for details, see Delgrande and Linder 1994).[11]

In 2000, parliament increased federal grants to health insurance by 1.5 per cent for the coming 4 years and passed some minor adjustments in favour of the insured (mainly facilitating the change of health funds). Again, the issue of cost containment provoked vigorous debates.[12] Since the number of physicians was already high and, as a consequence of bilateral agreements with the EU, was expected to increase even further, parliament finally authorized the federal government to temporarily restrict access for service providers (physicians and other non-medical health-care providers) in outpatient care.[13]

4.3.3.4 THE THIRD ATTEMPT TO CREATE PAID MATERNITY LEAVE

In 1999, the Swiss people rejected a bill on the introduction of paid maternity leave for the third time after earlier failures in 1984 and 1987. As a consequence, Switzerland remained the only European country not providing statutory benefits in case of motherhood. After the failure of paid maternity leave as part of health insurance in 1987, the topic was again put on the federal agenda by a cantonal initiative. The initiative was unanimously accepted by parliament. However, the corresponding bill was hotly debated. Superficially, financing was the most controversial issue. The value-added tax was set to rise in order to finance the new social insurance. Yet this made a constitutional amendment — and hence a mandatory referendum — necessary. The question, therefore, was whether the tax referendum should take place before or after the introduction of paid maternity leave. Given that the introduction of paid maternity leave would be less likely if the votes were taken simultaneously, some adversaries of the bill used the financing argument to cover their more general opposition. In particular, the idea of granting benefits to non-working mothers had encountered much resistance, mainly among (male) Liberals as well as Conservatives

---

[11] In fact, the federal government and parliament had considered the premium reductions for low incomes within the 1994 reform as an indirect counter-proposal to the initiative.

[12] Already in 1997, the federal government had again increased co-payments (for details, see APS 1997: 270).

[13] Swiss accident insurance was also modified during the 1990s, albeit only moderately. In 1999, parliament enhanced the social protection of part-time workers in non-occupational accident insurance by reducing the numbers of hours a week needed for coverage from 12 to 8.

from the SVP (Bundesversammlung 1998*b*: 744–6; 748, 2075). In the end, the bill provided paid leave for all mothers. Employed mothers were to receive 80 per cent of former income during a leave period of 14 weeks; non-employed mothers were granted a single means-tested benefit (of maximum 4,020 francs). Parliament also decided to postpone the referendum on value-added tax until 2000/1.

As already announced during the parliamentary debate, the Swiss People's Party's youth organization launched an optional referendum against the new law on maternity leave. The referendum was supported by right-wing MPs and employers. Since the people were not able to vote on the higher value-added tax before the insurance's creation, it was attacked as a social insurance 'on tick' (APS 1999: 278). Popular rejection was overwhelming.

After the failure of paid maternity leave at the federal level, the canton of Geneva was the first to create such scheme at the cantonal level (for details see Duc 2001).

4.3.3.5 THE SWISS WELFARE STATE IN THE 1990s: FROM INCREMENTAL TO PARADIGMATIC CHANGE?

The 1990s witnessed numerous reform activities in nearly every branch of the Swiss welfare state — with family policy as the only exception. Pension reform made old-age benefits more 'gender-neutral' and expanded benefits for those on low incomes. The granting of (gender-neutral) pension credits for informal care qualifies as a second-order policy change, as does the creation of new sources of revenue for the AHV which reinforced the tax-financing of the Swiss welfare state. The 1994 health reform enhanced redistribution in health insurance, between men and women, between young and old, and between high- and low-income earners and filled gaps in the benefit catalogue. It transformed the Swiss health insurance system from a predominantly private into a largely social insurance-based system — a clear third-order change. By contrast, although cost containment was a major aim of health insurance reform, it was not achieved. Health costs and premiums kept on rising after the major 1994 reform. To date, plans to set up a competitive market in health insurance have been seriously undermined by the efforts of health funds and 'consumer inertia'. Third-order policy changes also occurred in federal unemployment insurance as well as in cantonal unemployment and social assistance, where active labour market policies were significantly expanded. At the same time, employment services were centralized at the regional level in federal unemployment insurance. Despite the long economic crisis, its repercussions on the public and social insurance budgets, and calls for a deregulation of economic and social policy, benefit cutbacks without compensatory measures were restricted to labour market policies and remained modest in international comparison.

The economic crisis was an important factor in the increasing difficulties of the social partners in developing policy solutions in the pre-parliamentary phase of the decision-making process. Overall, the social partners lost influence during the 1990s; instead, parliament emerged as the key player. The fact that Swiss decision-making was less consensual than in the preceding decades is also corroborated by the high number of optional referenda.

4.3.4 Welfare state reforms in the first years of the 2000s: financial stabilization and the final emergence of a federal family policy

In the last years of the period under review, Switzerland's economy was doing rather well. Between 1997 and 2001, the unemployment rate declined from 5.2 to 1.7 per cent due to economic recovery, the rather flexible Swiss labour market, and the establishment of regional employment agencies in the mid-1990s (Bundesrat 2001: 2249; OECD 2004). After a temporary increase to 3.9 per cent in 2004, unemployment rates declined again, reaching a level of 2.8 per cent in 2007. The fiscal position also benefited from the recovery: Together with a variety of savings measures (in particular, two programmes for the federal budget's recovery and amendments to dozens of federal bills, with savings amounting to nearly 5 billion francs when taken together), increasing tax revenue due to economic recovery, and windfall revenue from the sale of Swisscom-shares, this development was also reflected in a recovery of federal finances. Between 2004 and 2007, total public debt fell from 245.8 to 235 billion francs and federal debt from 132.7 to 123.9 billion francs (BFS 2007b: 22). More savings measures were, and still are, on the political agenda. In 2001 an overwhelming majority of the Swiss people accepted a constitutional 'debt brake' which aims to balance the federal budget over the course of the business cycle (for details, see Kirchgässner 2005: 38–9).

The supply-side-oriented economic policy agenda of the 1990s was continued during the first years of the 2000s. The most important reforms were those in agriculture (2003 and 2007), competition policy (2003), and telecommunication policy (2005). The agricultural sector saw a reduction of public subsidies and a move from price support to direct payments independent of production as well as the abolition of the milk quota. In competition policy, the Swiss parliament followed the EU and United States examples by enacting direct (financial) sanctions for illegitimate uncompetitive behaviour. Finally, in 2005, parliament paved the way for a further liberalization in the telecommunication sector. In contrast, however, in 2002 the Swiss people rejected a bill on the liberalization of the energy market. It had envisaged a controlled market opening and was supposed to render Switzerland 'Europe-compatible' in this domain (Wagschal et al. 2002: 30). Overall, economic policy reforms were again strongly influenced by developments in the EU (for details, see Armingeon and Emmenegger 2007). Some economic policies, such as the liberalization of the telecom market, 'can [even] be seen as moves towards preparing for EU membership' (Bonoli and Mach 2000: 155).

But instead of EU membership, the 2000s have so far seen only a second bilateral agreement with the EU, this time on the Swiss integration into the Schengen and Dublin treaties. At present, further issues are being negotiated between Switzerland and the EU, for example, on enhanced cooperation in energy and health policy (mainly consumer protection, the fight against transmittable diseases, and general health issues), a free trade agreement in the agrarian and food domain (including, amongst other things, a gradual reduction of tariffs, quotas, and export subsidies at all levels), and the issue of company taxation.

The new millennium also saw major changes take place in Swiss politics. In 2003, and for the first time since 1959, a change occurred in the partisan composition of the Swiss federal government. When the conservative SVP gained a much larger share of the vote in the 2003 election than they had previously, the Christian Democrats lost one cabinet seat to the SVP. The second important change occurred in 2007/8. The Swiss tradition of over-sized cabinets came to an end when the Swiss People's Party left the federal government and joined the opposition. The reason was that parliament refused to re-elect the highly controversial Minister, Christoph Blocher, into the government but voted for Eveline Widmer-Schlumpf — also an SVP member — instead. This was widely regarded by the SVP leadership as a humiliation. Efforts to exclude Widmer-Schlumpf and the other SVP Federal Councillor, Samuel Schmid, from the party, as well as internal dissent over the opposition role led to the emergence of a new party in 2008 — the Bourgeois-Democratic Party (*Bürgerlich-Demokratische Partei Schweiz*, BDP). Both Widmer-Schlumpf and Schmid became members of the new BDP. However, soon the SVP became dissatisfied with its role as an opposition party and, when the former SVP and now BDP Federal Councillor, Samuel Schmid, decided to step down at the end of 2008, the governmental seat returned to the SVP only 1 year after the traditional oversized coalition government had ended. The Swiss government now consists of five parties — the liberal FDP, the Social Democrats, the Christian Democrats, the conservative SVP, as well as its spin-off, the BDP. It seems rather likely that the Swiss People's Party will soon regain its second governmental seat and that its status as an opposition party will remain no more than a temporary episode. Nonetheless, even the temporary existence of a strong opposition party must be considered a real disruption of Swiss political routines.

4.3.4.1 LABOUR MARKET POLICIES AND THE PREDOMINANCE OF BENEFIT CUTBACKS

At the end of 2003, the temporary measures to reduce the debt of the unemployment insurance scheme were scheduled to expire. They included higher contributions and additional 'solidarity surcharges' for those on higher incomes. Another reform of federal unemployment insurance was on the agenda.[14] The governmental draft of 2001 aimed at securing funding in the long run and making the insurance scheme less dependent on the business cycle (Bundesrat 2001). It contained lower general contributions but, at the same time, maintained one of the two 'solidarity surcharges' on higher incomes. The federal government insisted on maintaining grants from general revenue; indeed, it even wished to slightly *increase* them. In order to secure long-term funding, cutbacks were also proposed. With regard to benefits, the minimum contribution period was to be doubled from 6 to 12 months — partly because of the parallel bilateral agreements with the EU on the free movement of labour — while the maximum entitlement period was to be reduced by half a year from 520 to 400 days, except for elderly employees and recipients of disability and accident insurance pensions.

Most elements of that package were relatively uncontroversial, but the proposals on the 'solidarity surcharge' and the shorter entitlement period incited vehement attacks from social partners as well as from left and right parties. In 2002, the two chambers of parliament reached a compromise. With regard to the 'solidarity surcharge', a decision was made to abolish it for the time being by obliging the federal government to levy it only under circumstances when the unemployment insurance fund is facing a debt of more than 5 billion francs (APS 2002: 227). To accommodate left party and trade union opposition to the proposed reduction of the entitlement period — they were already threatening with an optional referendum — the federal government was allowed to temporarily extend the period for cantons with high unemployment. Overall, the 2002 reform can be seen as a significant benefit cut for the 'less deserving' categories of the unemployed, that is, the young and healthy unemployed. At the same time, redistribution within unemployment insurance was diminished through the general abolition of the 'solidarity surcharge' on high incomes.

As widely expected, an optional referendum was launched. It was initiated by the small Federation for the Protection of the Unemployed which had already initiated a successful referendum in 1997, and was supported by trade unions, the Social Democrats, and the Greens. This time, however, the reform was accepted by 56.1 per cent of the voters despite its rather restrictive content. It seems that, in contrast to 1997, the much more positive socio-economic background of the 2002 vote was crucial (see also Moser 2008).

---

[14] For an uncontroversial technical 'mini reform' of federal unemployment insurance, see APS (2000: 233).

More changes are currently under way. In 2008, the federal government presented a new reform draft with measures on the revenue (e.g. slightly higher contributions) as well as on the expenditure side (e.g. benefit cuts and a strengthening of the insurance principle) of unemployment insurance.

Four different tendencies characterize cantonal labour market policies in the first years of the new millennium. Firstly of all, activation continued in cantonal unemployment and social assistance. With regard to social assistance, this also complied with recommendations of the SKOS, published in 2005. Secondly, cost containment remained an important priority, with several cantons reducing their social assistance benefits, sometimes even below the SKOS-recommendations (for details, see *St. Galler Tagblatt*, 23 January 2002). Thirdly, in order to increase efficiency and lower costs, efforts have been made to enhance the coordination between different social programmes, especially between unemployment insurance, disability insurance, and social assistance, all of them focusing on professional (re-)integration (for details, see Kehrli and Knöpfel 2006: 175–9). As can be observed in Denmark and New Zealand, the idea is to create a 'one-stop shop'. Fourthly and finally, the abolition of cantonal unemployment assistance schemes — introduced in the 1990s — was reversed in a number of cantons. In 2006, eight cantons provided some sort of means-tested unemployment assistance scheme (BFS 2007a: 20).

4.3.4.2 PENSION REFORM OR 'WE DEMAND SACRIFICES ...'[15]

In May 2004, for the first time in Swiss history, a pension reform — the so-called 11th AHV-review — was rejected by the people. Compared to earlier bills, the parliamentary compromise of 2003 was clearly restrictive, especially for women who had to bear the main burden of the envisaged financial stabilization of public pensions. A lower widows' benefit and a higher retirement age (65 years, as for men) were estimated to generate savings of about 700 million francs per year. All pensioners were to contribute to the financial stabilization through a general delay of benefit indexation by 1 year. As might be expected, the parliamentary debates were highly emotional and fierce. After the bill was passed, the Social Democrats together with several trade unions decided to launch an optional referendum. Although they mainly argued that the proposed cutbacks disadvantaged women, the most important reason for the referendum was that the centre-right parliamentary majority had dropped regulations favouring low incomes in early retirement (APS 2003: 228).

Opinion polls had indicated a likely failure of the reform in the popular vote, but still the extent (68 per cent) and the homogeneity of rejection (disapproval across various socio-demographic categories) were impressive (APS 2004: 186).

---

[15] As stated by SVP National Councillor, Jean Fattebert, during the parliamentary debate on the so-called 11th reform of public pensions (Bundesversammlung 2001–3b: 12).

Even if motives for rejection were not uniform, they largely articulated concerns about losing the Swiss welfare state's achievements (Engeli 2004: 12). On the same day, an increase in value-added tax on behalf of old-age pensions (and disability insurance) was also defeated at the polls.

After the attempted stabilization of public pensions via a general reform had failed, the scheme was subject to some smaller cutbacks in 2003, owing to general saving measures on behalf of the federal budget. Despite mounting retrenchment pressures in old-age pensions, cutbacks targeted only public subsidies, *not* benefits. Yet, as pointed out by left-wing parties, these cuts actually aggravated the insurance's financial situation and, consequently, rendered future benefit retrenchment more likely.

Finally, the public pension scheme was also altered as a result of a Social Democratic people's initiative for the use of National Bank gold reserves — no longer needed for monetary policy — for the AHV. In 2005, as a counter-proposal to the initiative, parliament passed a one-time transfer of 7 billion francs from the sale of the National Bank's surplus gold reserves to the old-age pension scheme's compensation fund. In contrast (and hardly surprising), the Social Democratic initiative was rejected in 2006.[16] The same happened to two initiatives (launched by employees' associations and by the Greens) which aimed at a lower, uniform, and more flexible retirement age.

While in public pensions, adaptations in the 2000s have so far consisted of first-order change only, occupational pensions saw second-order change as well. A first reform of mandatory occupational benefits had already been scheduled for 1995, but, mainly because of the difficult economic situation of the 1990s, a legal reform was delayed (Bundesversammlung 2002–3: 163). Not until 1998 did the federal government present an encompassing reform package. The major reform objective was to adapt occupational pensions to higher life expectancies (Bonoli and Gay-des-Combes 2002: 18), mainly through a successive reduction of the minimum conversion rate used to convert individual savings into annual pensions. A further aim was coordination with the parallel eleventh revision of public pensions in respect of equal retirement ages for men and women,[17] a more flexible retirement age (with corresponding benefit decreases or increases), and the creation of a widowers' benefit. In the face of the adverse economic environment of the 1990s and negative reactions during the pre-parliamentary consultation procedure, the federal government had refrained from its initial plan of proposing increased coverage for part-time and low-income workers. It had also given up on the idea of enforcing an

[16] An analogous people's initiative launched by the conservative Swiss People's Party had already failed in 2002, as had its direct parliamentary counter-proposal. However, it was much more a preventive optional referendum than a genuine people's initiative.

[17] After the failure of the proposed equalization of male and female public pension retirement ages in the popular vote of 2004, eligibility for women's occupational benefits was set at 64 years.

automatic link between increases in old-age benefits and price increases. Price indexation of old-age benefits was to remain dependent on the individual pension funds' financial situation.

Unlike the federal government, parliament opted for more far-reaching changes by reviving the idea of increased coverage for both part-time and low-income workers. Eventually, a new compromise was reached in 2003, expected to result in the coverage of about 100,000 additional persons, most of them women (Bundesversammlung 2002–3: 926). Social and Christian Democrats had been the main advocates of increased coverage.[18]

Since the reform of 2003, occupational pensions have been subject to several governmental ordinance modifications. One change concerned the minimum interest rate in mandatory occupational benefits. Set at a level of 4 per cent in 1985, it has repeatedly been lowered, first to 3.25 per cent in 2003, and then to 2.25 per cent in the following year. This was a response to the deep (national and international) stock market slump at the beginning of the new millennium. When financial markets recovered, the interest rate was modestly raised to 2.5 for the period 2005 to 2007 and to 2.75 for 2008. Finally, the federal government in 2005 reacted to demographic changes by increasing the minimum early retirement age in occupational benefits from 55 to 58 over a period of 5 years.

In contrast to public and occupational pensions, where financial stabilization was at the centre of reforms, means-tested supplementary benefits for pensioners on low incomes are still expanding. In 2007, parliament abolished the yearly maximum benefit level for needy pensioners living in nursing homes in order to reduce the burden of health insurance in financing long-term care to some degree. A new repartition of financing between cantons and the Federation which made supplementary benefits first and foremost a federal responsibility and, as a result, increased the federal share in their financing, was also introduced.

Since 2005, preparations have been made for another reform of public pensions. The governmental draft took up important elements of the ill-fated 11th AHV-review and supplemented it with a new indexation mechanism as well as a new tax-financed and means-tested early retirement benefit. The early retirement benefit is an indirect counter-proposal to a recent people's initiative by trade unions for a flexible retirement age of 62. Parliament has not yet decided on this controversial draft and the people still have to take the vote. However, the huge popularity of the Swiss public pension scheme makes it rather unlikely that such a restrictive bill can survive an optional referendum. By contrast, the initiative has already failed in the popular vote. In occupational benefits, another revision is also on its way. Its focus lies on the creation of a new mechanism allowing a more rapid and stronger adaptation of the minimum

---

[18] Another — rather technical — reform was voted on by parliament in 2004. To tackle the serious problem of insurers' underfunding, it expanded the scope of action for insurers and extended the catalogue of possible measures to end underfunding (for details, see APS 2004: 190).

conversion rate (BSV 2005). At the same time, the federal government intends to lower the conversion rate.

4.3.4.3 REFORMING HEALTH-CARE INSURANCE BY SMALL STEPS

Health costs and premiums had kept on rising since the major 1994 reform. As a consequence, popular dissatisfaction was high. Nonetheless, in 2003, a bill which focused on cost containment and on premium reductions failed in parliament. The failure was rather unfortunate. The rejection by left-wing and green parties in the lower chamber was an important factor but not a sufficient explanation. The fact that the bill lapsed was also due to the absence of many right-wing parliamentarians from the final vote as well as to the complete abstention of the Christian Democratic faction. The Christian Democrats action was a response to the final parliamentary decision not to introduce general premium rebates for children as proposed by Christian Democratic MPs (Bundesversammlung 2001–3a: 2052–3). The only measure that was enacted was higher federal grants for premium reductions.

Only a few days after the vote in the National Council, the federal government attributed the failure of the bill to several parliamentary amendments to the initial draft (Bundesrat 2004: 4270). Consequently, the Federal Council decided to depart from the traditional path of Swiss (social) policy-making, which, as by now will be apparent, is based on carefully balanced package deals. Instead, it opted for incremental modifications in health insurance (ibid.: 4264–5). To date, parliament has already passed several bills along these lines.

Since a structural reform in 2004, reimbursement rates for outpatient medical care rest on a uniform single product catalogue ('*Tarmed*') for the whole of Switzerland. Akin to the '*Einheitliche Bewertungsmaßstab*' in Germany, every medical treatment is assigned a specific score, and consequently a specific price, which is negotiated between health insurance companies, physicians, hospitals, and public authorities. In 2005, the umbrella organizations of physicians, hospitals, health insurance companies, and insurers in accident, disability, and military insurance as well as the cantons also decided on the introduction of a diagnosis-related groups system for inpatient care, based on the German model. From 2008 onwards, this system of reimbursement will be used in Swiss hospitals and for all compulsory social insurance schemes.

Parliament also modified premium reductions. According to the new model, cantons have to reduce premiums for children and adolescents in training by at least 50 per cent for families with low and medium income. Although the jurisdiction to set the corresponding income limits was left to the cantons, it was expected that about 80 per cent of Swiss children and about 70 per cent of young adults would benefit from this new regulation. In contrast, cantons successfully vetoed the governmental proposal for a premium cap based on household income. As a consequence of the 2005 reform, cantons are now obliged to reduce premiums for those on low incomes *and* for families. However, since (increased) federal subsidies will hardly be in accordance with both types of premium reductions, much will depend on the cantonal willingness to substantially increase their own grants rather than simply shifting expenditures away from those with low incomes to families.

In a manner similar to public pensions, Swiss health insurance has seen a number of unsuccessful people's initiatives in the 2000s. Among other things, these initiatives proposed cutting health costs by restricting mandatory insurance to cover hospital costs, reducing drug prices by allowing health funds only to reimburse the cheapest drugs, and creating a single health fund.

At the moment, drafts on co-payments, the obligation to contract, modifications to the risk equalization system, preventive medicine, the development of managed care, and new financing systems for hospitals as well as for long-term care are either being prepared by the federal government or already being debated in parliament. Furthermore, the benefit catalogue and drug prices are under review.[19] Given that cost containment and financing have so far proved very controversial, a major breakthrough seems unlikely.

Since 2005, preparations have also been under way for a reform of accident insurance. Its focal points have been the supervision, the organization, and new business areas of the public Swiss Accident Insurance Agency (SUVA). As several administrative reports have now concluded that the Swiss accident insurance system can be regarded as quite efficient, plans for a complete liberalization of accident insurance and a privatization of the SUVA have been shelved.

4.3.4.4 FINALLY MOVING: SWISS FAMILY POLICY

Surprisingly, family policy was that welfare state domain which experienced the most important change in the final years under scrutiny. Apart from the new health insurance premium reductions for families with low and medium incomes, which could be interpreted as a family policy measure as well, Swiss family policy was subject to a series of transformations, ranging from first-, second-, to even third-order policy changes. They were the result of parliamentary initiatives, an instrument which enables members of parliament to propose amendments to the constitution, laws, or decrees.

The only third-order policy change was the introduction of paid maternity leave. The federal government reacted to the rejection of the paid maternity leave in the plebiscite of 1999 by proposing a reform of labour law providing maternity pay funded by the employers for a period of 8 to 14 weeks. In addition, members of all four governmental parties launched a parliamentary initiative for paid maternity leave for employed mothers only, with a replacement rate

---

[19] The federal government has already increased co-payments for original drugs from 10 to 20 per cent where a cheaper generic exists.

of 80 per cent of previous income during a leave period of 14 weeks. In order to finance this new benefit, the Income Compensation scheme for military service was to be expanded. In practice, this meant that maternity benefits would be jointly funded by employers and employees (via contributions). In the initiative's explanatory statement, there was reference to a large consensus among the political elite that the existing regulations were inadequate: on the one hand, all women were prohibited from working during the 8 weeks following the birth of a child; on the other hand, continuous payment of wages was not guaranteed but depended on the regulations of the particular labour contract (Bundesversammlung 2001–3b: 2). The parliamentary initiative found strong approval inside and outside parliament, and even among former opponents of paid maternity leave such as employers. As a consequence, the federal government dropped its own proposal in order to let the parliamentary initiative go ahead.

In 2003, the law on paid maternity leave was passed by both chambers of parliament. It was supported by Social and Christian Democrats as well as by a majority of Liberals, but largely opposed by the SVP. Several proposals for an expansion of paid maternity leave to non-working mothers were put forward but were rejected by both chambers of parliament as the most fervent supporters of paid maternity leave agreed that the failure of the 1999 reform was caused by the inclusion of non-working mothers (Bundesversammlung 2001–3b: 5–12, 25). Even the Christian Democrats — who spearheaded the idea of a so-called basic benefit for non-working mothers — now refrained from supporting such measures in order to prevent another failure in a popular vote (ibid.: 10, 18–19).

As it could have been expected, a cross-party group headed by the Swiss People's Party launched an optional referendum. Nonetheless, the bill (which included moderate benefit increases for servicemen) was accepted by a narrow majority of voters in 2004, and Switzerland became the last European country to provide women with statutory benefits in case of motherhood. With regard to the duration of maternity leave as well as with regard to replacement rates, the Swiss model of paid maternity leave remains modest in European comparison (but, with 14 weeks, is now on par with New Zealand as regards benefit duration) (see Hendersen and White 2004: 503; Tanaka 2005: 17–18). In contrast to countries like Sweden or France, paternity leave, parental leave, or educational holidays are lacking in Switzerland (Wecker 2006: 233–4).

Further adaptations, albeit only first- and second-order changes, occurred in the domain of child benefits. Since 1945, the federal government has been entitled to legislate on child benefits, an authority it made use of only for the benefit of agricultural and federal employees. As a consequence, a fragmented system of cantonal allowances had emerged, with important differences in terms of the type and level of benefit as well as eligibility age (for details, see

BSV 2006; Moser 2003). However, based on a Social Democratic parliamentary initiative, a certain degree of harmonization took place in the 2000s.

A parliamentary draft of a framework law had already been proposed in the 1990s. Although it set some minimum standards, cantonal responsibilities were largely left untouched (Jaggi 2000: 211). Still, coverage was extended from employees (covered in all cantons) to the children of self-employed and non-employed parents (covered in few cantons only) and benefit levels were to be harmonized at a comparatively generous level. However, the bill was not implemented. At the 'round-table talks' for the reorganization of the federal budget in 1998, parliament decided to freeze the draft until 2001 (ibid.: 212).

When the trade union Travail.Suisse launched a people's initiative for universal and very generous federal child benefits in the early 2000s, the parliamentary bill was revived as an indirect counter-proposal. It included universal child allowances of at least 200 francs as well as an educational allowance of at least 250 francs per child per month, independent of whether parents were employed, self-employed, or non-employed. Income limits for the non-employed and financing details were left to cantons.

Parliamentary deliberations followed a clear pattern: on the one side, Social Democrats, Greens, and a large majority of Christian Democrats argued in favour of a material harmonization of cantonal child benefits and, on the other, a majority of Liberals as well as the SVP were against. While the bill's advocates considered it an adequate way to fight the growing problem of child poverty, its opponents would have preferred a targeted approach to this end (for details, see Bundesversammlung 2005–6; Sager et al. 2003: 135, 169). In the end, parliament agreed on the harmonization of cantonal child benefits. To accommodate right-wing opposition, the self-employed were finally not included and cantons were entitled to tie non-employed parents' eligibility not only to cantonal income limits, but also to exclude them where their children were already entitled to other social insurance benefits. Overall, the harmonization of child benefits meant that employees in sixteen cantons received both higher child and educational benefits. Six cantons only increased educational allowances, while the remaining four already disposed of sufficiently high levels (Jaggi 2006: 150). Moreover, non-employed parents became generally entitled to child benefits (ibid.). Hence, the reform represented an increase in the coverage provided by the Swiss federal welfare state and indicated an increasing willingness to compensate the costs of child-raising.

As already announced before the final parliamentary vote, employers launched an optional referendum. It was supported by parliamentarians of FDP, SVP, and other liberal or right-wing parties. In contrast, the trade union Travail.Suisse withdrew its more generous people's initiative and supported the parliamentary solution. In 2006, the people accepted the new legislation (68 per cent voting in favour). Since the harmonization of child benefits obtained larger popular majorities than the creation of paid maternity leave, it can be argued that bills broadly in tune with the traditional family model have a better chance of success in Switzerland than those aiming at facilitating the reconciliation of work and family life for working women.

Another, but only minor, adaptation of Swiss family policy was the introduction of temporary federal subsidies for new daycare facilities in 2002. This measure can also be traced back to a Social Democratic parliamentary initiative. Already in the 1990s, data on childcare facilities had shown that in Switzerland demand far exceeded supply (Eidgenössische Kommission für Frauenfragen 1992*a*, 1992*b*). However, since pre-school and elementary school facilities are regulated at the cantonal and municipal level, federal involvement was problematic. Consequently, the parliamentary initiative only proposed to subsidize childcare institutions. Although the idea was generally supported by a majority of Social Democrats, Christian Democrats, and even Liberals, parliament considerably watered down the bill against the background of the federal budget deficit. It decided that grants should be lower (50 million instead of 100 million francs per year) and provided for a shorter period (8 instead of 10 years) than proposed by the initiative.

Family policy still features high on the federal agenda. In 2001, the National Council passed two parliamentary initiatives proposing the introduction of tax-financed supplementary benefits for low-income families. Such benefits already exist in the canton of Ticino. Parliament has yet to decide. In 2007, the federal government began financial support for cantonal and municipal pilot schemes involving childcare vouchers. In contrast, a tax reform which, inter alia, aimed at helping families — via higher deductions for children and new daycare deductions for working parents — failed in an optional referendum in 2004. The referendum had been launched by left and green parties as well as by eleven cantons with the so-called cantonal referendum. Still, there were aspects of the encompassing reform package other than the family measures that were at least as contentious.

Overall, the growing commitment to a better reconciliation of work and family life through enhanced childcare facilities should not be exaggerated: in Switzerland, childcare is still predominantly considered a private rather than a public matter. Public services in this domain remain of subordinate importance (Aebersold et al. 2005: 3; Pfau-Effinger 2006: 246).

4.3.4.5 CONTINUITY AND CHANGE: SWISS WELFARE STATE DEVELOPMENT BETWEEN 2000 AND 2007

Even though Switzerland's macroeconomic performance has recently improved, one major trend in social policy legislation in the last sub-period under scrutiny was the continuation of the financial stabilization path started during the second half of the 1990s. This mainly applies to unemployment insurance, where retrenchment measures such as shorter benefit duration and a longer minimum contribution period were enacted in order to secure long-term financial sustainability. Cost containment remained a crucial issue in cantonal labour market policies also. In public pensions, parliament lowered federal subsidies, but benefit retrenchment (particularly cutbacks affecting women) failed in an optional referendum. In order to cope with increasing life expectation, some cutbacks were also made in occupational pensions. At the same time, however, coverage was extended to 'new social risks'. Overall, retrenchment remained limited by international comparison. In contrast, major changes took place in family policy, although this is partly due to the fact that, until the 2000s, federal family policy was nearly non-existent. However, with the creation of paid maternity leave, this sector became subject to third-order change. Some equally important modifications were enacted at the structural level. For the purpose of activation, Switzerland (like New Zealand) enhanced coordination of employment services and related administrative structures. In health policy, the outpatient domain of Swiss health insurance saw the introduction of a uniform, single service catalogue, while in the inpatient domain there was a move to a diagnosis-related groups system.

As regards politics, the same picture of both continuity and change emerges. As in the second half of the 1990s, the political climate remained tense as illustrated by the significant number of optional referenda. However, with regard to optional referenda, two differentiations have to be made. First, their success against welfare state retrenchment seems to be crucially dependent on the socio-economic background at the time of the vote. This becomes evident, for example, if we compare the successful unemployment insurance referendum of 1997 with the unsuccessful attempt of 2002. Second, public pensions generally seem to be better protected against welfare state retrenchment than unemployment insurance, almost certainly because they enjoy more popular support.

4.4 Towards a conservative welfare state? Patterns and explanations

When we compare the Swiss welfare state in 2008 to the status quo ante in the early 1970s, five general trends stand out (see also Table 4.2).

First, the federal government and parliament have significantly increased welfare state coverage during the period under review. The most striking example is unemployment insurance, a field where prior to the creation of mandatory insurance only about one-third of all employees were covered. Today, all employees are part of the scheme. Other examples include occupational benefits, where coverage was increased threefold and child benefits, where the children of non-employed parents are now generally entitled. Although the creation of mandatory health insurance did not have a big impact

Table 4.2: Main changes to the Swiss welfare state since the early 1970s

Policy area	Increased coverage	Benefit catalogue expansion	Gender-discrimination abolition	Examples of organizational restructuring	Moves towards the continental welfare regime
Labour market	Mandatory unemployment insurance	Active labour market policies Insolvency benefits		Regionalization of employment services 'One-stop shops'	Mandatory unemployment insurance with generous, earnings-related benefits Generous cantonal benefits
Pensions	Mandatory occupational pensions Occupational pensions for unemployed, low incomes, and part-time workers	Contribution credits for informal care Widowers' benefits	Benefits independent of civil status Nearly equal retirement age Widowers' benefits		Mandatory occupational pensions with generous earnings-related benefits
Health care	Mandatory health-care insurance Mandatory industrial accident insurance Inclusion of part-time workers in non-occupational accident insurance	Premium reductions for low incomes and families Increased coverage of prevention, home care, and nursing care	Equal premiums in health and accident insurance	Enhanced competition in health and accident insurance New health insurance models	Mandatory accident insurance
Family policy	Extension of child benefits to non-employed parents	Paid maternity leave Higher child benefits	Maternity acknowledged as legitimate reason for a temporary absence from work		Contribution-funded mandatory paid maternity leave

on its coverage, it laid the basis for enhanced redistribution. Overall, these developments represent a significant expansion of the federal state's role in Swiss social policy.

Second, the benefit catalogue has been significantly modified and expanded. For example, active labour market measures were enhanced at the federal (unemployment insurance) as well as at the cantonal level (unemployment and social assistance). In unemployment insurance, a new scheme covering an employers' insolvency was also introduced. In health insurance, parliament enacted premium reductions benefiting about one-third of the Swiss population and expanded the basic benefit catalogue, mainly with regard to preventive medicine, home care, and residential care. In old-age pensions, parliament introduced contribution credits for informal care as well as a widowers' benefit which also now applies in occupational pensions. The most impressive domain of change is family policy, although this largely owes to the fact that — at least at the federal level — family policy was nearly non-existent at the end of the 'Golden Age'. Nevertheless, the creation of paid maternity leave for all working mothers was important, as were also the expansion of child benefits in a majority of cantons and the premium reductions for families with low and medium incomes.

Third, many gender-discriminations were removed. This is most obvious in public pensions where old-age benefits were made independent of civil status and gender-neutral credits for informal care were introduced, while women's retirement age was partly brought into line with that of men (64 versus 65). Widowers were finally entitled to a benefit. The increased coverage of low-incomes and part-time workers in occupational benefits (and of part-time workers in accident insurance) mainly affects women. Moreover, health and accident insurance premiums are now the same for men and women. Despite all these changes, the Swiss welfare state remains oriented towards a male breadwinner family model as exemplified by family policy.

Taken together, these developments demonstrate that, although some specific benefit cutbacks have occurred, on the whole the Swiss welfare state was expanded during the period under review. As a consequence, one could speak of a 'late maturation' of the Swiss welfare state. Furthermore, the Swiss welfare state went from being one of the lowest spending welfare states in the OECD to one of the highest. However, this is, arguably, more the result of increasing demand for social benefits and low levels of economic growth than of welfare state 'maturation'. Despite welfare state expansion, some important gaps remain, for example with regard to childcare facilities, paternal leave schemes, sick pay insurance, long-term care insurance, and the coverage of dental treatments.

Fourth, Swiss welfare state change since the early 1970s was also about organizational restructuring. This mainly applies to health insurance where the major 1994 reform restricted unfair competition between insurers through the restriction of risk picking. New insurance models (health maintenance organizations and general practitioner models) were introduced. In addition, Switzerland created a uniform single product catalogue for the outpatient domain and a diagnosis-related groups system for inpatient care. However, so far cost containment has not been successful because, among other things, the plans to set up a competitive market in health insurance have been seriously undermined by the efforts of the majority of funds (e.g. a massive wave of mergers) and 'consumer inertia' (Bonoli and Kato 2004: 219). In accident insurance, competition was also intensified when private insurance companies gained access to mandatory insurance in 1984. Municipal employment services were moved to the regional level and at the interface of disability insurance, unemployment insurance, and social assistance, the creation of 'one-stop shops' gained momentum as a way to increase efficiency and to contain costs.

Fifth and finally, Switzerland has moved much closer towards the conservative welfare model of its neighbours (see also Armingeon 2001: 150). First of all this applies to social expenditure where Switzerland, starting with levels comparable to the English-speaking OECD countries, has caught up with other continental welfare states. Social expenditure as a percentage of GDP increased from 13.6 per cent in 1973 to 27.8 per cent of GDP in 2007.[20] The state now devotes more than 50 per cent of expenditure to income replacement and around 40 per cent to poverty alleviation and health, 'ending up with a clearly continental European spending profile on all counts' (Castles 2004: 39, 104). Even if tax-financing was reinforced during the period under review, overall Swiss welfare state financing remains largely contribution-based. The emphasis on mandatory social insurance was strengthened as well as the commitment to status maintenance. In particular, this is true for occupational pensions, paid maternity leave, and accident and unemployment insurance. Benefits are generous by international comparison (Eardly et al. 1996: 130–3; Obinger 1998b: 225; OECD 1999; Wagschal et al. 2002: 58; Bonoli and Kato 2004: 212). Major examples of the generosity of the Swiss welfare state are unemployment insurance benefits, pensions (especially occupational pensions), unemployment assistance, accident insurance, and disability insurance (cf. Scruggs 2004; Korpi and Palme 2003). As already noted, the major welfare state schemes remain oriented to the male breadwinner family (Armingeon 2001: 150), and this is also exemplified by the introduction of paid parental leave for mothers only, although gender discriminations were undeniably reduced during the period under review. The role of social services is still subordinate to transfers, especially with regard to childcare, and families (read: mothers) are left with the primary responsibility for caring. A typical feature of the conservative regime is corporatism. Indeed, Swiss trade unions and employers did and still do participate in legislation and in the management of insurance schemes. Taken together, the overall regime shift is

233

mainly the result of a strengthening of the conservative elements already existing in the early 1970s. One could therefore speak of a 'late maturation' of an already inherently conservative welfare state.

However, strong liberal traits remain, especially in health care. Examples include flat-rate premiums independent of income, important co-payments, and the exclusion of dental treatments as well as sick pay. The extent of private health-care financing is only matched by the United States (Gerlinger 2003: 31). With the single exception of 1995, Switzerland consistently ranks second in terms of private expenditure devoted to health care.[21] Furthermore, the private sector continues to play an important role in the delivery of health care and the provision of occupational pensions. Overall, it is fair to describe the contemporary Swiss welfare state as a mixed type which has the strongest affinities to the conservative model of welfare capitalism.

Welfare state change in Switzerland has been 'extensive, but [often] gradual and incremental' (Armingeon 2001: 146). In the terms used by Peter Hall (1993), policy change was more one of incremental and continuous first- and second-order change than of a radical third-order paradigm shift. Most reforms altered the specific setting of already existing social policy parameters (e.g. benefit levels or contribution periods) (first-order change). Others created selective new instruments (second-order change) such as public pension credits for informal care or premium reductions for low incomes and families. The repeated widening of eligibility and access to already existing welfare state schemes for former outsiders equally qualified as second-order change. The only third-order policy changes were the major enhancement of active labour market policies, the creation of paid maternity leave, and the health reform of 1994, which moved the Swiss health insurance system from a predominantly private to a largely social insurance-based system.

Four different periods of welfare state change can be distinguished (see Table 4.3): the 1970s, the 1980s, the first half of the 1990s, and, finally, the period from the mid-1990s onwards. The overall *pattern of Swiss welfare state reform* can be best understood when the state of the economy is taken into account. Although Switzerland's macroeconomic performance during the period under review was relatively good by international standards, it worsened significantly compared to the 'Golden Age'. However, no paradigm change took place in Swiss macroeconomic policy which could have impacted on welfare state reform. During the whole period under review, Swiss economic policy was supply-side in its orientation (Armingeon and Emmenegger 2007: 182). What has changed, however, was the extent to which the market liberal ideas were translated into action. For example, many of the protectionist regulations in the domestic market were finally rolled back in the 1990s and 2000s.

Economic globalization, although sometimes mentioned in reform debates, had only a limited impact on welfare state reform during the period under

[21] See OECD Health Data 2009, June 2009, Paris.

Table 4.3: Four different periods of welfare state change

Period of welfare state reform	Socio-economic background	Major reform pattern	Key actors of welfare state reform
1970s	Short economic crisis	Financial stabilization and initial moves towards the conservative model of welfare	Pre-parliamentary actors (interest groups, cantons, political parties)
1980s	Predominantly favourable	Further movement towards the conservative model	Pre-parliamentary actors (interest groups, cantons political parties)
First half of the 1990s	Major economic crisis, low economic growth	Financial stabilization and shift in emphasis from old to new social risks	Political parties
Since the mid-1990s	Mixed, with low economic growth	Financial stabilization (with family policy as the major exception)	Political parties

scrutiny. Still, it is likely that increasing economic denationalization had an indirect effect as an important factor behind some kinds of endogenous problem pressure (e.g. public deficits, rising unemployment). Deepened European integration was also less important than might have been expected. Even though Switzerland concluded two bilateral agreements with the EU, their impact on the welfare state remained limited, perhaps with one exception: the settlement on the free movement of labour is at the root of the temporary access restriction for new service providers in health insurance and contributed to the longer minimum contribution period in unemployment insurance. Overall, increased economic globalization and deepened European integration had major consequences for Swiss economic policy (especially with regard to the Swiss domestic market), but not for social policy. However, growing economic denationalization led to tensions between (and within) the social partners.

Let us now return to the four periods of welfare state reform, largely distinguished by their socio-economic backgrounds, their patterns of welfare state reform, and — as will be seen subsequently — their key actors.

The *first period*, the 1970s, was marked by the repercussions of the first oil shock — low economic growth, rising unemployment, and a strongly growing deficit in the federal budget. However, the crisis was relatively short-lived and, by international comparison, not very deep. As a reaction to the federal budget deficit, government and parliament reduced public grants. In contrast, rising unemployment resulted in the creation of mandatory unemployment insurance. With its primacy of status maintenance and its generous benefits, most

clearly related to prior employment (and family situation), mandatory unemployment insurance stood for an important rapprochement to the conservative model of welfare. Additionally, the example of unemployment insurance
demonstrates that socio-economic problem pressure can, in some cases, trigger
welfare state *expansion*, even after the end of the 'Golden Age'. The reason for
this functionalist development can be found in Switzerland's 'welfare laggard'
status: Due to this 'laggard' position, rising unemployment in Switzerland
resulted in an expansion of unemployment insurance as it demonstrated the
deficiencies of voluntary insurance.

The *second phase* of welfare state reform largely coincided with the 1980s.
It was marked by a favourable socio-economic situation with rather sound
economic growth, low unemployment rates, and decreasing public debt.
Against this background, the Swiss welfare state was expanded through moderate first- and second-order policy changes which, as could be expected with
regard to Switzerland's status as a welfare state 'laggard', mainly benefited the
traditional welfare state clientele, for example, the elderly or the disabled. Once
again, the Swiss welfare state moved a bit closer towards the conservative
model. The creation of mandatory occupational benefits and of mandatory
accident insurance clearly falls into this pattern.

Clearly, the most important period of welfare state reform was the *third period*
in the first half of the 1990s, where Switzerland witnessed a successive deterioration of key macroeconomic indicators, with economic stagnation, budgetary
crisis at all three political levels, and unemployment sharply rising. This was at a
time when the reform intensity was highest and changes were most extensive. A
new reform pattern of balanced reforms evolved — expansive measures were
often tied to selective cutbacks (see also Moser and Obinger 2007: 339, 343).

Here, several developments coincided. To begin with, the economic crisis of
the 1990s provoked expansionary reforms such as the longer benefit entitlement in unemployment insurance. Again, rising unemployment — notably
long-term unemployment — laid bare the deficiencies of an insurance scheme
tailored to low unemployment rates and short durations of benefit receipt.
A similar development can be witnessed with regard to health care: Due to
massively rising health costs — to some extent exacerbated by the state's own
funding cutbacks in the second half of the 1970s — and their impact on
premiums and redistribution within voluntary health insurance, the inherent
weaknesses of voluntary insurance became obvious. This finally triggered a
major transformation in health care: the introduction of mandatory health
insurance with full mobility, equal premiums, and premium reductions for
low incomes. As in the second half of the 1970s, the combination of increased
endogenous problem pressure with an 'immature' welfare state contributed to a
rather functionalist welfare state expansion.

Moreover, expansion was the order of the day in many areas due to a new
set of developments: the emergence of new social risks related to changes in

the labour market and in family structures. These developments resulted in increasing activity in the domain of family policy (although the corresponding legislation was generally enacted in the first few years of the 2000s) as well as in an adaptation of pension and unemployment insurance to changed societal realities. Family poverty and the reconciliation of work and family life were at the centre of family policy reform. Several studies have demonstrated that a majority of families in Switzerland belong to the lower end of the middle class or even to the lowest social class (see, among others, Bauer 1998; Leu et al. 1997). These studies received widespread public attention in the 1990s and significantly contributed to the political priority family policy now enjoys (Sager et al. 2003: 108). At the same time, demand for childcare far exceeded the supply, and many women worked part-time instead of full-time because childcare facilities were either lacking or too expensive. In pensions, political actors focused on equal treatment of men and women as well as on a better old-age protection for low-income and part-time workers (i.e. in many cases, also women). It has to be noted that in pensions new social risks contributed to welfare state expansion *as well as* to retrenchment. Liberals, in particular, also successfully promoted a more gender-neutral pension system through an abolition of former privileges, namely the lower retirement age of women. In unemployment insurance, low-skilled workers (active labour market measures) were the main target group of welfare state change. In health, the problem was that the benefit catalogue had not been adapted to the changing needs for quite a long time. Change was therefore considered necessary especially with regard to new social risks (e.g. long-term care, maternity, and preventive medicine). Yet, a range of social needs which already were traditionally covered by the welfare state in other rich democracies (e.g. the needs of people suffering from chronic illness) have only recently been addressed by Swiss health policy.

Two factors are probably crucial for the increasing accommodation of new social risks within Swiss welfare state reforms. First, there has been a growing influence of parliament in the policy process and therefore of political parties which are often said to be more open to new social risks than trade unions whose core clientele (as well as membership) mainly consists of 'old risk groups', particularly male blue-collar industrial workers (Ebbinghaus 2006; for Switzerland, see also Häusermann et al. 2001: 25–8; for the contribution of corporatism to Switzerland's former liberal welfare state profile, see Trampusch 2008). Secondly, the emergence of new social risks paved the way for a new model of political compromise, combining cutbacks on behalf of the 'old risk groups' (e.g. the elderly) with expansive measures on behalf of 'new risk groups' (e.g. working women, low-skill workers, low-income workers, parents) within a single piece of legislation.

In the *fourth and last phase* of Swiss welfare state reform, which started in the mid-1990s, the increase in coverage of new social risks groups continued, especially in family policy, health insurance, and to some extent in occupational benefits. Women, either as the main providers of informal care or as a large group among low-income and part-time workers, were often at the centre of reform. Yet, overall, the issue of cost containment was still the political priority through-out the 1995–2007 period and dominated social policy reforms. From 1995 onwards, the Swiss constitution has always contained some sort of public deficit 'brake', making the reduction of expenditures (as well as the prevention of new structural budget deficits) mandatory, thereby restricting not only future welfare state change but even furthering welfare state retrenchment. It seems as if the Swiss welfare state had finally 'grown to limits' as socio-economic problem pressure now confronted a mature welfare state.

With regard to the *impact of parties* on Swiss welfare state development, it is clear that in contrast to the other countries analysed here, a clear partisan effect is difficult to detect at the macro level for three reasons. First, the partisan complexion of government remained virtually unchanged between 1970 and 2007. Secondly, all major parties were included in an oversized coalition government. Finally, conventions about cabinet secrecy prevent outside observers acquiring knowledge about decision-making within the Swiss government. This makes it almost impossible to trace policy outputs back to a particular political party.

However, there are two arenas in which partisan effects are observable. One is parliament, the other is direct democracy. The importance of the parliamentary phase within the Swiss decision-making process has strongly increased during the period under review. Hence parties gained influence at the expense of social partners (see also Table 4.3). In the 1970s and 1980s, social partners and health insurance providers had a major impact on policy outcomes by virtue of their inclusion in the then dominant pre-parliamentary phase (Kriesi 1980). It was for the most part in this period that Switzerland moved much closer to the conservative model of welfare. But, as already demonstrated by other studies (e.g. Häusermann et al. 2001, 2002), parliamentary influence in social policy has grown significantly since the 1990s. Expert interviews conducted with members of government, parliament, and administration as well as with repre-sentatives of the social partners offer several explanations for the declining influence of the pre-parliamentary stage within the Swiss decision-making process. On the one hand, the social partners seem to have experienced in-creasing difficulties in reaching compromise solutions in the pre-parliamentary phase, a development which is ascribed to the economic crisis and stagnating wages. On the other hand, experts pointed to a growing partisan polarization in parliament, coupled with rising media influence on and personalization of Swiss parliamentary politics. Finally, some interview respondents suggested that the main cause of increasing parliamentary activism was weaker leadership by the federal government.

In parliament, welfare state reforms (with the exception of family policy) were regularly based on 'modernizing' compromises, exchanging measures benefiting 'new' social risks against cutbacks at the expense of 'old' risks (Bonoli 2004: 178). As in other countries, Social Democrats were the key actors in the accommodation of new social needs (Armingeon 2006: 100, 116; Häusermann 2006: 18). For example, Social Democrats spearheaded the expansion of family policy. The left was sometimes supported by the Christian Democrats, sometimes by the Liberals, and sometimes even by both. Liberal support mainly extended to policies aiming at the better reconciliation of work and family life or the equal treatment of men and women. Although Christian Democrats were generally very much in favour of an accommodation of new social risks, they were less at ease with measures that might weaken traditional role models. In contrast, the conservative SVP was rarely part of such a 'modernizing coalition' which is scarcely surprising given the party's general opposition to further welfare state expansion and its significant following among pensioners (Bonoli 2004: 176).

The political arena in which partisan effects are even more visible is direct democracy (see also Tables 4.4 and 4.5). Of all people's initiatives that were launched in the welfare state policy arena during the period under review, more than 60 per cent were initiated by the political left (including left parties, the Greens, and trade unions). All these initiatives proposed a further expansion of the Swiss welfare state. Examples include attempts to introduce income-related health insurance premiums or a lower and more flexible retirement age. Obviously, the political left used this instrument to compensate for the dominance of right parties in government and parliament and the superior strength of employers vis-à-vis trade unions (see also Linder 2005: 256). That said, all the left people's initiatives that were voted on by the electorate failed. Far fewer initiatives were launched by the political right. The fact that of the three right-wing proposals two were withdrawn (in contrast to only three out of seventeen for the political left) is further evidence of the better accommodation of right interests in the Swiss political system. Pressure groups (e.g. health funds) launched six people's initiatives. Those which were not withdrawn were, however, rejected by the people.

Partisan effects also show up in optional referenda. In contrast to the people's initiative, this instrument of direct democracy was used nearly as frequently by the political right as by the political left (see Table 4.5). Right parties and employers launched referenda mainly to prevent welfare state expansion, although their results were mixed. However, the political right was able to delay the creation of paid maternity leave by defeating two bills at the polls (1987 and 1999). Only in 2004 did the Swiss people finally vote in favour of maternity insurance. The political left — as well as pressure groups — rather used the optional referendum to prevent cutbacks. Left parties and trade unions (to a lesser extent also the political right and pressure groups) even attacked bills that combined welfare state expansion with benefit cutbacks within a single piece of

Table 4.4: People's initiatives in the four social policy areas under scrutiny (1970–2008)

	Number	People's initiatives launched by					
		Left parties, Greens, and trade unions	Of which rejected	Right parties and employers	Of which rejected	Pressure groups	Of which rejected
Launched	26	17		3		6	
Withdrawn	7	3		2		2	
Voted	19	14	14	1	1	4	
Aiming at welfare state expansion	17	14	14	1	1	2	2
Aiming at welfare state retrenchment	1	0		0		1	1
Unclear cases	1					1	

Table 4.5: Optional referenda in the four social policy areas under scrutiny (1970–2008)

	Number	Optional referendum launched by					
		Left parties, Greens, and trade unions	Of which rejected	Right parties and employers	Of which rejected	Pressure groups	Of which rejected
Voted	15	6	2	5	2	4	1
Against welfare state expansion	5	1	1	4	2	0	1
Against welfare state retrenchment	4	2	1	0		2	
Against bills including expansive and restrictive measures	5	3	0	1	0	1	0
Unclear cases	1					1	

legislation. These bills were a typical feature of the 1990s. Examples, such as the so-called 10th reform of public pensions, show that left-wing referenda focused on single cutbacks within an encompassing bill. However, no referendum against such 'balanced reforms' was successful.

Institutionalist accounts also contribute to an explanation of the Swiss case, especially those centring on direct democracy, federalism, and policy feedback. *Direct democracy* was of the utmost importance. First, although none of the many people's initiatives was accepted in the popular vote, some still had indirect effects. Examples can be found in the domain of health insurance, where people's initiatives by trade unions and health funds contributed to an increase and a more targeted use of public grants. Second, the optional referendum also had several important effects. It turned out to be a rather useful tool for blocking both welfare state retrenchment and expansion, as it tends to favour (social policy) solutions close to the status quo. A number of qualifications are appropriate, however. To start with, some programmes appear to be more resilient than others. Take the fact that the only restrictive reform of old-age pensions (the so-called 11th AHV-review) failed in a plebiscite, while only 2 years before similar reform of unemployment insurance survived an optional referendum. The huge popularity of old-age security, especially when compared to benefits in favour of the unemployed, is a feature which is also confirmed in international comparison (Taylor-Gooby 2001: 139; Armingeon 2006: 104–5; Huber and Stephens 2006: 163). What is more, the fact that no optional referendum has been successful against a legal draft combining restrictive with substantial expansive measures seems to demonstrate that such bills allowed the political elite to split the opposition and increased overall support (Bonoli 1997; Moser and Obinger 2007). Lastly, the optional referendum offers dissatisfied political actors a direct influence on welfare state change as federal government and parliament often modify their bills in response to referendum threats. The harmonization of child benefits is one example. Here, referendum threats by Liberals, Conservatives, and employers resulted, *inter alia*, in the exclusion of the self-employed.

To conclude, it has to be mentioned that both instruments of direct democracy have been used much more frequently since the 1970s. In the last three decades, the electorate was called upon to decide on more social policy issues than in the 100 years preceding the first oil shock (Moser and Obinger 2007: 336). The significant growth in the number of optional referenda, in particular, suggests a decreasing effectiveness of Swiss consensus democracy during times of sharpening redistributive conflicts.[22] After all, one important reason for the incorporation of all major political parties and interest groups in the Swiss

---

[22] This interpretation is supported by expert interviews. They also emphasize the more intensive media coverage and a higher professionalization of trade unions and interest groups.

political decision-making process is precisely *to prevent* the use of optional referenda.

Both chambers of parliament accommodated *cantonal interests*, thereby contributing to the path-dependent development of the Swiss welfare state during the period under scrutiny. Moreover, the example of active labour market policies in cantonal unemployment and social assistance shows that cantonal competition may also be a source of innovation as some cantons acted as laboratories, where tested and proven policy solutions often had a demonstrable effect on other cantons (Obinger 1999: 38).

Although welfare state change was often rather gradual and incremental, *'genuine path-dependency'* was restricted to only some policy areas. The main mechanism of path-dependency has been policy pre-emption by cantons. The most obvious example is family policy where initial cantonal predominance resulted in a federal harmonization of child benefits via framework legislation only, setting minimum standards while leaving cantonal competencies largely untouched. A similar phenomenon can be seen in occupational pensions. As in voluntary insurance, employers and pension funds maintained important freedom of action in mandatory insurance.

Finally, Swiss welfare state change in the period from 1970 to 2007 provides several examples of the important role of *new interest groups* created by the welfare state itself (pension funds, health funds, physicians, etc.). Clearly, their influence has been magnified in Switzerland by direct democracy. On the one hand, the optional referendum is an important factor behind their inclusion in the pre-parliamentary phase of the decision-making process. On the other, people's initiatives, referenda, and referendum threats were useful instruments for influencing welfare state reform even further down the road. An especially remarkable example is the successful optional referendum launched by a small unemployment pressure group, since it contradicts the assumption made by authors such as Korpi, Palme, and Pierson that unemployment insurance is not suited for the formation of new influential interest groups 'because unemployment is not an experience all workers expect to share' (Pierson 1994: 166; see also Korpi and Palme 2003: 431–2). It seems as if the strategic opportunities for new interest groups to act depend to a considerable extent on the specific institutional arrangements. Arguably, Switzerland is unique in this respect given the availability of various instruments of direct democracy.

All things considered, the case of Switzerland clearly supports the argument that the *classic theories of comparative welfare state research* contribute to an explanation of welfare state reform even in the 'Silver Age'.

Change was triggered by socio-economic pressures which were then filtered by domestic politics. With regard to the main driving or 'triggering' forces, the emergence and diffusion of new social needs has to be emphasized as has the important role of low economic growth, rising unemployment, public deficits, demographic ageing, and increasing health costs. In the 'laggard' welfare state of Switzerland, these problems actually promoted a marked expansion of both welfare programmes and welfare spending as they uncovered the deficiencies of an 'incomplete' system. Only from the mid-1990s onwards, can we finally speak of a real 'period of austerity'.

Partisan influence has grown since the 1990s when the main locus of decision-making shifted from the pre-parliamentary to the parliamentary phase. For a variety of reasons, the social partners were less capable of generating compromise solutions in 'hard times'. Yet, partisan differences remained and Social and Christian Democrats as well as trade unions continued to be crucial actors not least through the institutions of direct democracy.

Given the nature of the Swiss political system — with its dense structure, the high number of veto players, and strong policy feedbacks — the extent of welfare state transformation in the period from 1970 to 2007 is remarkable. Certainly, most changes proceeded in an incremental and gradual fashion, but not only did these small changes sometimes amount to major transformations, but Switzerland even experienced some quite fundamental reforms. This is particularly true of the third-order changes in labour market policies, health care, and family policy, that is, in three of the four core domains of the welfare state under scrutiny. Arguably, political institutions and policy legacies substantially shaped the politics of social policy reforms as well as its pace, but, even in Switzerland, the *extent* of change was largely the result of power resources and increasing socio-economic problem pressure. At the same time and as argued by the *'new politics'* literature, widespread popular support for a comprehensive welfare state often produced a sort of ratchet effect against a race to the bottom, as exemplified by the failure of several restrictive bills through the plebiscite.

5

Comparative Perspectives

Based on the historical narratives presented in the previous chapters we will now try to provide answers to the research questions raised in the introduction of this volume. We started our enquiry by arguing that small countries are crucial cases for exemplifying the impact of globalization on welfare state change. Given their high level of economic vulnerability and their status of 'rule-takers' rather than 'rule-makers' in a globalized economic and political context, we started from the assumption that these countries have faced particularly strong pressures to adapt their social security arrangements to new exogenous and endogenous challenges. In addition, we argued, in line with Peter Katzenstein (1985), that small countries, due to their small number of decision-makers and the resulting lower decision-making costs, find themselves in a comparatively favourable position to react to such pressures in a swift and flexible way. Given both greater economic vulnerability and greater flexibility in decision-making, we expected rapid and far-reaching policy change.

According to the efficiency thesis in its simplest form, the social policy outcome that is likely to occur under these circumstances is a downward spiral in benefit provision and social expenditure or, more generally, a convergence towards a residual welfare model. By contrast, the 'business as usual' scenario would expect cross-nationally distinct adjustment pathways without convergent outcomes. Our third scenario predicts outcomes falling between these polar developmental trajectories. Outcomes, according to this latter scenario, are likely to be characterized by a supply-side-oriented welfare state transformation, the absence of a 'race to the bottom', and a continuing role for domestic politics.

In order to examine which of these scenarios is nearest the truth, we selected four small countries which at the end of the 'Golden Age' belonged to different welfare regimes. They were also countries which manifested marked variation in their political systems, a factor which we argued should also have an impact on reform outcomes.

5.1 Convergence of welfare states?

5.1.1 Macro-level evidence

Before turning to the comparative qualitative analysis of our four cases, however, we will look at the development of aggregate welfare state indicators including social spending and the replacement rates offered by particular welfare state programmes (see Castles 2004; Allan and Scruggs 2004; Korpi and Palme 2003). Although the approach adopted in this book involves going beyond a comparison of macro-indicators, it is nevertheless worth looking at recent developments of core aggregate welfare state indicators in our countries as compared to a wider universe of cases.

5.1.1.1 SOCIAL EXPENDITURE TRENDS

Public social expenditure as a percentage of GDP, unquestionably the most frequently used indicator of welfare effort, has been going up since 1980 in all but one of the OECD countries, while cross-national differences in spending levels have declined over time (Table 5.1). In all of the four countries examined in this volume, social spending in 2005 exceeded expenditure levels in 1980. This picture of a continuous growth of the welfare state is still more dramatic if social spending per capita and the share of social spending in total government spending are examined. Both indicators went up in all nations listed in Table 5.1 (cf. Obinger and Wagschal 2010). Overall, social expenditure trends are indicative of a convergence to the top (Castles 2004; Starke et al. 2008) or a sort of 'growth to limits' (Flora 1986), a development precisely contrary to that suggested by the efficiency thesis.

It is possible, however, that this expansion of the welfare *state* masks a more profound shift across the entire social welfare sphere, spanning both public and private efforts. If private social protection had also expanded markedly over these years, then it is conceivable that the *relative* importance of the state diminished despite growing public resource inputs. From 1990 onwards, the availability of private spending data in the Social Expenditure Database (OECD 2008a) helps settle this question. The OECD distinguishes between voluntary and mandatory private social expenditure. Voluntary social expenditure includes (a) benefits offered by privately operated programmes which involve redistributive effects and (b) tax-advantaged individual plans or collective support arrangements such as employment-related pension and health plans. Mandatory private spending includes social provision mandated by legislation but which is operated by private actors, notably employers.

Looking at the trends for this data, it is apparent that average levels of private spending have, indeed, increased over time. However, there are important differences compared to public expenditure trends. First, the increase of private spending mainly applies to voluntary expenditure. By contrast, spending on

Table 5.1: Public and private social expenditure, 1980, 1990, and 2005

Country	Gross public			Voluntary spending		Mandatory spending	
	1980	1990	2005	1990	2005	1990	2005
Australia	10.6	13.6	17.1	0.9	2.6	0.0	1.1
Austria	22.5	23.9	27.2	1.1	1.0	1.2	0.9
Belgium	23.5	24.9	26.4	1.6	4.5	0.0	0.0
Canada	13.7	18.1	16.5	3.3	5.5	N.A.	N.A.
Denmark	24.8	25.1	26.9	1.6	2.4	0.5	0.2
Finland	18.0	24.2	26.1	1.1	1.1	N.A.	N.A.
France	20.8	25.1	29.2	1.7	2.6	0.2	0.4
Germany	22.7	22.3	26.7	1.5	1.9	1.6	1.1
Greece	10.2	16.5	20.5	2.1	1.7	N.A.	N.A.
Ireland	16.7	14.9	16.7	1.4	1.3	N.A.	N.A.
Italy	18.0	19.9	25.0	0.5	0.6	3.4	1.5
Japan	10.6	11.4	18.6	N.A.	3.3	0.3	0.5
Netherlands	24.8	25.6	20.9	5.6	7.6	0.4	0.7
New Zealand	17.2	21.8	18.5	0.2	0.4	N.A.	N.A.
Norway	16.9	22.3	21.6	0.7	0.8	1.1	1.3
Portugal	10.2	12.9	23.1[a]	0.7	1.5	0.2	0.4
Spain	15.5	19.9	21.2	0.2	0.5	N.A.	N.A.
Sweden	27.1	30.2	29.4	1.2	2.4	N.A.	0.4
Switzerland	13.5	13.4	20.3	1.0	1.1	4.3	7.3
United Kingdom	16.7	17.0	21.3	4.8	6.3	0.3	0.8
United States	13.1	13.4	15.9	7.1	9.8	0.5	0.3
Mean OECD 21	*17.5*		*22.3*	*1.9*	*2.8*	*1.0*	*1.1*
Range	*16.9*		*13.5*	*6.9*	*9.4*	*4.3*	*7.3*
Standard deviation	*5.3*		*4.3*	*1.9*	*2.5*	*1.3*	*1.8*
Coefficient of variation	*.30*		*.19*	*1.0*	*.90*	*1.3*	*1.6*

Note: [a] = 2004.

Source: OECD (2008a).

private mandatory benefits declined in numerous countries, including Denmark and Austria. Switzerland is an obvious outlier in this respect, with a huge increase in private mandatory expenditure resulting from the introduction of mandatory occupational pensions in the mid-1980s. Second, and more importantly, there is no convergence in private spending since most statistical measures of dispersion increase over time. The rise in private spending was most pronounced in those countries in which private spending already played a prominent role in 1990. Finally, the rise of private spending has not been at the expense of public welfare effort. While the OECD average has slightly grown, the share of public spending as a percentage of total social expenditure has remained more or less stable since 1990 in the four countries focused on by this study (not shown in Table 5.1). This finding is at odds with the notion that globalization triggers a run into privatization and a shift in the public–private mix.

5.1.1.2 BENEFIT LEVELS

Since social expenditure analysis has been strongly criticized for its 'non-theoretical conception' of the welfare state (Korpi and Palme 2003: 426), we look next at the development of cash benefit levels offered by three major welfare state programmes. Replacement rates can be interpreted as a measure of the extent to which social rights are guaranteed by particular welfare states (Esping-Andersen 1990). While criticisms of comparisons based on social spending by Esping-Andersen and other Scandinavian scholars are no longer as appropriate as they once were, given marked improvements in social expenditure data (Castles 2008), it is certainly the case that replacement rates provide much better information about welfare state generosity than social expenditure. Since the replacement rates collected by the *Social Citizenship Indicator Programme* data record are publicly available until 1995 only, we rely here on the *Welfare State Entitlement Database* compiled by Scruggs (2004), which provides information on the net replacement rates offered by pension, health, and unemployment insurance from the early 1970s until 2002 (see Figure 5.1).

One can easily see that the patterns shown in this figure are not consistent with a race to the bottom in social provision. To be sure, benefit retrenchment did occur, but cutbacks have varied greatly across programmes and nations. Figure 5.1 shows that pension benefits remained remarkably stable over time or declined only marginally. However, two important qualifications are necessary. Because pension reforms typically involve long transition periods and take effect in the long run only, it is quite possible that the replacement rates displayed in Figure 5.1 underestimate the real extent of retrenchment. In addition, the most recent and often comprehensive pension reforms are not included in the data record which ends in 2002. Hence, we hesitate to draw any conclusion from this data and postpone the issue of pension retrenchment to later sections.

Cash benefits offered by unemployment and sickness insurance,[1] both areas in which retrenchment can be implemented in the short term (Korpi and Palme 2003), have indeed been subject to quite significant cutbacks. The radical retrenchment episode in New Zealand and the taxation of cash benefits in Denmark clearly show up in the data. By contrast, benefit levels remained by and large stable in the other two countries. Hence, the evidence is not indicative of strong convergence across the board (Allan and Scruggs 2004; Starke et al. 2008). In addition, the story told by Figure 5.1 corroborates the findings of Korpi and Palme (2003) for the long-term OECD member states, who conclude that retrenchment is a real phenomenon but varies significantly across welfare regimes. In line with their findings, we note the strongest cuts were imposed in English-speaking nations (New Zealand) and Nordic countries (Denmark), whereas retrenchment was moderate in continental welfare states such as Austria and Switzerland.

---

[1] Note that sickness cash benefits are non-mandatory in Switzerland.

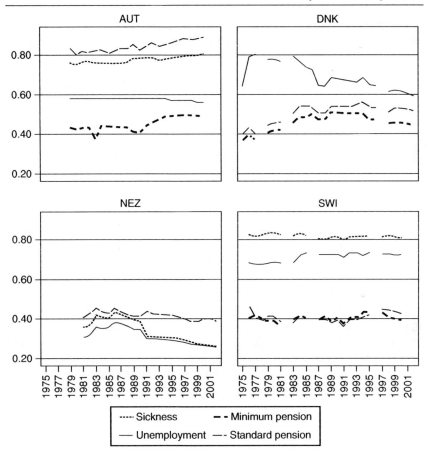

Figure 5.1: Net replacement rates offered by three programmes, *c.* 1975–2002
Note: Replacement rates for singles.
Source: Scruggs (2004).

In sum, turning from social expenditure to benefit generosity does not change the picture depicted so far. While there is sporadic evidence of significant retrenchment, notably in New Zealand, there is no obvious shift towards a race to the bottom. However, the Welfare State Entitlement Database only tells us about a particular segment of the entire benefit spectrum offered by advanced welfare states and only about the two types of model households covered by the Scruggs data set. Family cash benefits and social services, both areas in which according to our case studies expansion has taken place, as well as regulatory social policies are excluded. In addition, age-related cutbacks affecting marginal groups such as the young unemployed are not captured.

249

The absence of clear macro-level evidence of convergence is not sufficient unequivocally to reject the efficiency thesis. It is possible that major but more subtle changes have occurred underneath the level of the aggregate welfare state indicators discussed so far. Based on the evidence summarized in our country studies we now attempt to detect possible ways in which our initially quite distinct welfare states have become more similar over time.

5.1.2 Reform trajectories by policy sector: common trends, but... 'I did it my way'

5.1.2.1 PENSIONS

In the field of pensions there has been a convergence of countries towards multi-pillar pension schemes. However, multi-pillar pensions should not be equated with a retreat of the state or with a shift to 'non-social' pensions. Multi-pillar pensions can rather mean very different things. The significance of public pensions varies, as does the extent to which the government has assured wide coverage of supplementary provision and the extent to which redistribution has been implanted into the other pillars. Hence there are important differences in terms of kinds of state involvement and the redistributive impact of the entire pension arrangements comprising various state and non-state types of provision.

Switzerland is to some extent an outlier as the country had always relied on an informal pension mix consisting of public pensions, occupational pensions, and private saving schemes. Switzerland was thus an 'early bird' that figured prominently in the World Bank's multi-pillar philosophy in pension policy. However, the Swiss multi-pillar system was not deliberately designed but rather an unintended result of early policy pre-emption by private forms of provision and multiple institutional veto points inhibiting the adoption of a public pension scheme (Obinger 1998b; Leimgruber 2008). This fragmented system of provision was eventually restructured and transformed into a formal multi-pillar system in the 1970s and 1980s. The multi-pillar pension system in Denmark is likewise not attributable to a deliberate political decision but rather emerged from political deadlock. The majority of the Danish population was entitled only to a basic public pension in the 1970s. Status preservation for the elderly thus was a major political issue. Given a series of non-decisions at the parliamentary stage, earnings-related pensions were finally negotiated outside the parliamentary arena by the social partners on the basis of collective agreements. In consequence, both labour market pensions and various forms of private provision gained importance since the 1980s.

Pension policy in New Zealand and Austria had been more or less monopolized by the state until the end of the Golden Age. Compared to Denmark and Switzerland, shifts towards a multi-pillar system occurred rather late. Austria moved in this direction only in the early 2000s when severance payment was converted into a second pillar pension and a subsidized voluntary saving scheme was introduced. New Zealand only hesitantly followed suit in 2005 with the introduction of the KiwiSaver, a voluntary but state-subsidized private saving scheme. In both countries, public pensions remain by far the dominant form of provision. However, income support for future generations of pensioners will everywhere be based on a more pronounced mix of public and private pensions.

In respect of first-pillar pension reform, similarities as well as differences characterize national adjustment pathways. What all nations have in common is that early retirement programmes (where they existed), which in the past were often extensively used to mask labour market problems, have been rolled back. In addition, the retirement age, particularly for women, has been raised. Other reforms of public pension schemes have been strongly structured by pre-existing patterns of welfare state financing, with marked differences between social insurance-based systems (Austria and Switzerland) and tax-funded systems (Denmark and New Zealand).

Both Austria and Switzerland introduced pension credits for family and care work and made pension entitlement and benefits more gender-neutral through the introduction of widower's pensions and, in Switzerland, pension-splitting for couples. Moreover, both countries have also changed the pension formula and increased their means-tested minimum pensions. Since public pensions offered very low benefit levels in Switzerland, a new pension formula designed to benefit low-income groups was adopted.[2] In addition, means-tested supplementary benefits for needy retirees, which were not designed to support frail elderly in covering care-related costs, have been expanded in scope. The Austrian development has been more ambiguous. While some specific groups at the margins of the labour market have been given the opportunity to take out public pension insurance (opting-in), atypical employees, and women in particular, have lost out as a consequence of a stronger contribution–benefit nexus, with the benefit calculation now based on the average income earned during lifetime. The only offsetting compensation for these changes was an increase in the means-tested minimum pension and the provision of pension credits for child-raising and care work. In contrast to its western neighbour, Austria's pension system has, traditionally, been strongly occupationally fragmented. In 2005, the government adopted a reform that brought federal civil servants within the ambit of the general pension scheme.

Gender issues and the inclusion of atypical workers were of less relevance in countries with universal and tax-financed public pensions because benefits

---

[2] In addition, eligibility to second-tier pensions was modified with a view to include more atypical jobholders.

were detached from the labour market and marital status. Public pensions nevertheless were a site of reform. Mainly in an effort to reduce expenditure, eligibility for universal pensions was limited. With the introduction of the superannuation surcharge New Zealand adopted a clawback tax to increase targeting of pensions. Under the pressure of the populist New Zealand First Party, however, the surcharge was eventually abolished. Denmark enhanced the income-testing part of the basic pension so that the traditional universal approach in pension policy was rolled back.

When looking at the overall pension mix, we can observe convergence in the sense that most countries have enhanced minimum protection[3] while at the same time the employment-based and actuarial forms of provision gained importance.

5.1.2.2 LABOUR MARKET POLICY

Arguably the most striking parallels can be observed in the field of labour market policy. All countries moved from a mostly passive orientation to activation policies aiming to reduce welfare dependency and to integrate the unemployed into the labour market and society. At the same time, all countries imposed cutbacks of cash benefits and a stricter conditionality for benefit eligibility, reduced benefit duration for the able-bodied unemployed, and deregulated their labour markets and working-time regulations. Public job placement was in some cases decentralized and restructured in an effort to improve efficiency, for example through the establishment of one-stop-shop institutions.

However, there are significant cross-country differences in the timing of reforms, the measures and benefit cutbacks implemented, and the resulting shift in the balance of social rights and duties. In Denmark, New Zealand, and Switzerland, the new instruments of activation were implemented earlier than in most of the large countries. While Denmark responded to the economic crisis of the 1970s mainly with higher cash benefits, employment programmes, and early retirement schemes, the massive labour market crisis in the early 1990s led to an activist turn in labour market policy. The adopted 'flexicurity' approach influenced European employment policy and became a blueprint for labour market reforms in many other countries. New Zealand, in contrast, did not subscribe to this path, but rather relied on radical cutbacks of cash benefits combined with a mainly workfare-based activation strategy. While work tests play a major role in this setting, less emphasis was put on training measures and benefits were low. Switzerland was a latecomer in terms of cash benefits because mandatory unemployment insurance was lacking until the 1970s. When, in the 1970s, the country for the first time

---

[3] Only New Zealand is an outlier in this respect.

in the post-war period experienced significant (albeit low by international standards) unemployment, the government introduced mandatory insurance offering very high replacement rates. This new generous scheme generated a deficit due to mounting unemployment in the early 1990s. This time, however, the government responded with an expansion of active labour market policies. A moderate cutback of cash benefits proposed by the government failed in a referendum. Together with a traditionally weak employment protection, Switzerland therefore implicitly adopted a 'flexicurity' approach in the 1990s. It was not until the 2000s that a first but moderate retrenchment of cash benefits was implemented. As in Switzerland, unemployment remained comparatively low in Austria. However, unlike its neighbour and more in line with Danish practice, Austria relied strongly on labour shedding strategies based on early retirement programmes, higher cash benefits, and its huge public (enterprise) sector to limit unemployment growth in the 1970s and 1980s. However, once the public enterprise sector collapsed in the mid-1980s, and the deficit and public debt went up, cash benefits began to be cut back. However, retrenchment remained moderate as did the expansion of active measures tailored to particular problem groups. Hence passive labour market policy still prevails but has, nevertheless, been subject to reforms. Non-wage labour costs for older unemployed and lower income groups are covered by public funds, whereas quasi-freelancers and the self-employed (opting-in) were included into unemployment insurance. In the very recent past, the government has begun to subscribe to a sort of 'flexicurity' approach. Working-time flexibilization has been combined with the introduction of a minimum wage and a means-tested basic income designed to harmonize the social assistance benefits offered by the *Länder*.

Irrespective of these cross-national differences, it is apparent that labour market policy has been subject to paradigmatic change. Passive schemes have been pushed back and supplemented with a whole battery of activating measures aiming at employability and labour market integration. In a nutshell, the priority has shifted from decommodification to recommodification.

5.1.2.3 FAMILY POLICY

Expansion has been the common trend in family policy, with all the countries introducing new and/or more generous benefits for families. Commonalities in this policy area are the introduction and expansion of paid parental leave schemes, including an extension to fathers,[4] and an expansion of childcare facilities. Austria and Denmark upgraded and remodelled their parental leave schemes, whereas New Zealand and Switzerland introduced such schemes in the early 2000s.

[4] With the exception of Switzerland.

253

Despite these similarities, policy priorities and measures adopted differed. Austria continued to increase the already generous transfer payments and tax deductions. Parental leave was enhanced, extended to fathers and, finally, detached from labour market participation. In addition, measures designed to combine family work and employment were enacted. By contrast, the government only sporadically sought to expand service provision, which, however, is the responsibility of the *Länder*. Family policy in Switzerland was sidelined for decades at the federal level. Policy jurisdiction is even more decentralized than in Austria and led to a fragmented system of cash benefits at the cantonal level. In the 2000s, a harmonization of cantonal cash benefits was achieved and maternity leave was introduced after several attempts had failed in a referendum vote. In a similar vein, increases in service provision proceeded very sluggishly and remained at a comparatively low level.

As in Switzerland, family policy in New Zealand was not part of the post-war welfare state settlement. In the 1970s and early 1980s, there was almost no state intervention in the area and income support to families actually declined. The demise of the wage earners' welfare state reduced the role of the family wage, the benefit for lone parents was cut back, and the universal family benefit, which later on became means-tested, was only sporadically adjusted to inflation. From the mid-1980s onwards, however, this trend was partially reversed and the government also launched initiatives to increase the number and quality of childcare facilities. The 1990s saw an overhaul of income support for families and, in consequence, the end of universalism, since cash benefits henceforth consisted of a benefit for needy families and various tax credits for working families. The generosity of cash benefits was massively expanded in the 2000s. In addition, the government introduced a paid parental leave scheme and adopted several measures to promote institutional childcare.

Denmark, in contrast to all these countries, institutionalized a highly developed system of public childcare facilities from early on, although, initially, leave programmes were of a rather short duration. While both service provision (including later on private kindergartens) and the duration of leave periods were expanded over time, the universal family benefit became income-tested in 1977. However, income-testing was abandoned a decade later. In sum, all four countries made efforts to assist parents to reconcile work and family life, but both the measures used and the extent to which family policy was prioritized varied quite considerably from country to country.

5.1.2.4 HEALTH POLICY

Health reforms were everywhere motivated by considerations of cost containment and strongly preconfigured by problems related peculiar to the institutional make-up of particular national health care systems, which were characterized by a huge diversity in the mid-1970s. More specifically, the countries analysed here represent all the major types of health-care systems distinguished in the literature, that is, a national health service (Denmark and New Zealand), a mainly privately organized liberal health-care system (Switzerland), and a social insurance-based system in Austria. Inefficiencies, such as waiting lists and issues related to the free choice of doctors, guided the reforms in the two countries with a national health service. Switzerland's liberal scheme was confronted with a massive increase in health costs, adverse selection problems, and a low degree of solidarity. Austria had to deal with inefficiencies created by territorially fragmented health-care system, notably in the hospital sector, and with the legacy of an occupationally fragmented health insurance characterized by significant differences in terms of contribution rates, level and duration of cash benefits, and co-payments.

It therefore comes as no surprise that the reforms enacted to cope with these problems differed from country to country. Interestingly, however, and much in line with research carried out by Rothgang et al. (2005), the countries adopted new forms of governance and regulation typically utilized in other health-care systems. Quasi-markets were established in state-run systems, while state intrusion in insurance-based health-care systems and predominantly privately organized health-care systems became more pronounced. Hence the countries relied on a sort of borrowing strength strategy to cope with the peculiar inefficiencies generated by their established health-care systems. Initially, health-care reform in New Zealand was characterized by numerous and often short-lived experiments. With a view to lowering costs and increasing the efficiency of the state-run hospital sector, the approach taken was to establish quasi-markets. By and large, however, this endeavour failed and the country returned to a more centralized, universal, and state-controlled system. The attempt to strengthen competition within a publicly run health-care system was less pronounced in Denmark, but the reforms enacted nevertheless increased the freedom of choice for patients in selecting both hospitals and General Practitioners, and enhanced competition between hospitals. These changes apart, however, the National Health Service systems in both countries remained, by and large, unchanged.

Switzerland introduced mandatory health insurance in 1994 and increased public financing to lower health-related costs for low-income groups and families. Other reforms, however, stuck to the traditional liberal approach, with rises in co-payments and a strengthening of competition among the largely private sickness funds. Austrian policy-makers sought, with varying success, to increase public control over the health-care system on the one hand and to raise private co-payments on the other. While state influence through medical planning powers has been strengthened, markets are still to a very considerable extent crowded-out from the sector. There is neither competition between sickness funds nor an opportunity for the better-off to take out private insurance. Finally, occupationally fragmented differences in terms of cash benefits have been levelled-out to a significant degree and the government introduced a tax-funded universal long-term care benefit in the early 1990s, which, as a side effect, has increased service provision for the frail elderly.

5.1.3 The extent of regime convergence

The programme-related evidence presented in the previous section is indicative of convergent developments. However, important qualifications are in order. While the overarching aims and the design of some programmes became apparently more similar, with moves towards multi-tier and an activist turn in labour market policy as prime examples, there are significant cross-national differences once we go into the programme-specific details. Even though public pensions everywhere were supplemented by a fully funded second pillar, the countries relied on very different instruments and varying degrees of state involvement. By the same token, the activist turn in labour market policy included very different approaches ranging from workfare emphasizing individual duties and responsibilities to active measures aimed at skill formation. Likewise, the common trend to an expansion of family policy was realized with very distinct policy measures. Despite the fact that health-care reforms were characterized by the implantation of new types of regulation the differences between health-care systems did not significantly diminish. Overall we can see that countries followed a common trend 'but did it their way'.

In a final step we now switch to a more holistic perspective. Considering policy change across all sectors, we examine the question of whether there is a convergence of welfare regimes. To begin with, we investigate the implication of the efficiency hypothesis that all advanced welfare states have been forced by mounting competitive pressure to adopt a single line of march in a neo-liberal direction. The findings of the case studies clearly do not support the notion that a liberal welfare system represents the common end point of social policy development in an age of globalization. The case studies rather show that Denmark's welfare state is still dominated by Social Democratic characteristics, while the Austrian welfare state is still imbued with Bismarckian principles. Admittedly, much policy change has occurred and some particular regime traits have been ironed out. One may think of the rollback of universalism in the Danish public pension system and the containment of occupational fragmentation within social insurance in Austria. But these changes do not add up to regime transformations and have, in any case, been, to some extent, counterbalanced by reforms that have further strengthened traditional regime characteristics. Examples include the continued expansion of social services in Denmark and the accentuation of the equivalent principle within Austrian social insurance.

Contrary to the liberal end point thesis, Switzerland, basically a liberal welfare state in the immediate post-war period actually shifted away from a residual welfare state model to one, which, with the exception of health care, is now much more in line with the welfare state model of continental Western Europe. New Zealand is the only country that became more purely liberal over time, mainly through the dismantling of the wage earners' welfare state. Once the various pillars underpinning a 'social policy by other means' (Castles 1989) collapsed, New Zealand was left with a residual system of social protection showing genuine liberal traits which, later on, became even more pronounced.

While there is, thus, no sign of a general shift towards welfare residualism, the far-reaching policy changes highlighted in the case studies, and the regime transitions in Switzerland and New Zealand in particular, demonstrate that the notion of a 'business as usual' scenario is also unwarranted. Our empirical evidence is at odds with the notion of a solely path-dependent development, since all countries, albeit to differing degrees, have departed from the ideal-typical regime characteristics to which their welfare state arrangements bore greatest resemblance in the 1970s. The evidence rather supports the third scenario contending that the 'politics against markets' of the post-war decades has been replaced by a 'politics for markets' centring on efficiency goals and adjustment in the face of growing international competition. This shift towards supply-side-oriented policies is arguably most salient in labour market policy. But even contemporary family and pension policies demonstrate the fact that contemporary welfare states have been reformed with a view to improving market compatibility and of reaping the alleged benefits of market competition. The global turn to private pensions is an example for the latter. Not least amongst the influences leading to the realignment and expansion of family policy is the view that this is the route to a larger increasingly better-educated female labour force.

Although welfare state restructuring has led to some blurring of regimes, there are no signs of any wholesale dismantling of the demarcation lines that have separated welfare state models in the post-war period. This applies particularly to modes of financing, personal coverage, and benefit generosity. To conclude, regime edges are now more blurred but all countries — even New Zealand and Switzerland — still exhibit strong similarities to the welfare state make-up inherited from the past.

5.2 Explanation

These trends are clearly in need of explanation. Our starting hypothesis claimed that politics still matters. This is supported by the absence of a race to the bottom. Yet the convergent trends discussed above indicate that the four countries were exposed to common pressures which may explain the transformation of welfare states. The differences that come into play in the translation of the new supply-side-oriented paradigm into national social policy reforms may be traced to a variety of factors. To what extent the preferences of political actors, institutions, policy legacies, international impacts, and socio-economic problem pressure really account for the cross-national differences and similarities in the national adjustment pathways will be examined in the following sections.

5.2.1 Socio-economic problem pressure

Since the far-reaching changes we described have taken place under very different institutional conditions — both in terms of political systems and welfare state regimes — and were enacted by governments of very different ideological orientation, there is reason to assume that the change in overall course has strong functional causes. Indeed, there is ample evidence that socio-economic problem pressure was the crucial trigger for similar policy changes in all policy sectors examined. All countries had to cope with the repercussions of structural economic change and societal transformation taking effect during the past three decades. The shift to a predominantly service economy entailed lower economic growth, and in consequence, tighter constraints on public revenues, while societal modernization and demographic changes generated mounting social needs and new risk patterns (Pierson 1998).

Labour market reforms are a clear case in point because there is a close correspondence between the occurrence of a labour market crisis and national reform activities. Deindustrialization, technological changes, and ever-increasing exit options for business to relocate business sites overseas lowered the domestic demand for low-skilled labour and led to long-term unemployment and the exclusion of less-skilled workers from the core labour market. In consequence, countries were facing protracted structural labour market problems in the 1990s. Against the backdrop of mounting unemployment and fiscal strains the old tools of demand-side-oriented labour market policy were considered less appropriate and the cost of continuing this course had become higher. Arguably the simplest strategy for reducing costs and at the same time to increase public revenues was to raise the level of labour market participation. Indeed, activation became the magic word from the 1990s onwards. However, a broad set of policy tools for promoting employment is available to policy-makers. Examples include cutbacks of cash benefits and non-wage labour costs, tighter conditionality, the promotion of part-time work, the deregulation of employment protection, in-work-benefits, wage subsides, public employment, family-friendly policies, and efficient job placement. This list is far from being exhaustive. While activation was the common response to structural labour market problems, the choices of policy-makers from this repertoire of options were very different.

With respect to *pensions*, fiscal problems, demographic ageing, and high (projected) returns from capital markets have led governments to move away from single-pillar solutions. Multi-tier pension schemes can be seen as a functional response to all these challenges. At the heart of this response is the idea of risk diversification in terms of the financing mode. Moreover, pension reforms were also driven by gender issues and concerns connected to the spread of atypical jobs, that is, challenges that are also ultimately attributable to societal and economic transformation.

In *family policy*, rising standards in female education and social modernization have led to a significant increase in female participation rates and, in consequence, to a growing demand for policies that help to reconcile work and family life. A family policy centred on the male breadwinner model has not fully disappeared but has lost legitimacy amongst much of the electorate, even though sizeable differences amongst countries still remain (Morgan 2008). In addition, the expansion of family policy has been prompted by a decline in fertility rates, which have everywhere stabilized below the replacement rate, and by new poverty risks connected to structural shifts in family and employment patterns.

In *health care*, technological progress and population ageing have built-up pressure for higher public expenditure. In addition, the 'greying' of the population has increased the demand for long-term care which is typically an age-related risk. Demand for public intrusion in this area also resulted from rising female labour market participation and the erosion of traditional family structures. Under circumstances of fiscal strain, cost containment and cost effectiveness became the leitmotifs for reform and prompted a search for more efficient means to finance and provide care.

It is important to note that these socio-economic pressures differed very appreciably in the four countries. However, since the relationship between the severity of problems and the extent of policy change is relatively loose across the four countries, a more plausible explanation is that problem pressure triggered international ideational shifts which then translated into national shifts in policy mediated by the influence of domestic political actors and institutions.

5.2.2 Policy inheritance of the past

While socio-economic changes have paved the way for a common policy menu, existing national policy patterns shaped national choices. The policy legacy inherited from the past is important for understanding change and stability as it generates positive as well as negative feedback effects. While positive feedback effects are seen to increase policy stability and thus give rise to path-dependent policy development (Pierson 2000), negative feedback effects resulting from existing or past policies may be a crucial trigger for policy change by undermining their political, fiscal, or social foundations (Weaver 2006). The overall argument is, however, that choice for policy-makers is constrained and preconfigured by existing policies. They not only generate distinctive challenges but also make some options more likely than others.

Certainly, our case studies reveal ample evidence that national reform trajectories were foreshadowed by the consequences of past decisions and programme design. *Labour market reform* is a clear case in point in demonstrating that negative feedback effects are important in explaining policy change. The typical response to the oil crises of the 1970s was explicitly or implicitly Keynesian in character. The crisis was mainly seen as a temporary episode, with Denmark and Austria responding with higher cash benefits and contributions as well as with strategies of labour shedding and labour hoarding, while Switzerland introduced mandatory unemployment insurance. All these measures imposed fiscal costs, higher non-wage labour costs, and public indebtedness. The fiscal consequences thereof become more pressing in the context of the structural unemployment and fiscal strain that characterized the 1990s. For example, early retirement programmes designed to cushion labour market problems generated budgetary pressure that subsequently motivated pension reform.

Where *pension reform* is concerned, path-dependency, that is, positive feedback effects, plays an overriding role in Switzerland. Since fully funded occupational pensions were already highly developed in the 1980s, neither a shift towards a Bismarckian regime nor one to a universal and tax-financed pension scheme was politically feasible. The pragmatic choice made was simply to put the existing mixed pension scheme on a formal, that is, constitutional, basis. In Austria, positive and negative feedback effects were more balanced. The sheer size of pay-as-you-go funded public pensions and the well-known double payment problem created strong positive feedback effects. Thus, as in the Swiss case, no paradigmatic reform option was available. However, the huge costs of the extant system (equivalent to 14 per cent of GDP) and the resulting high contribution rate, generous early retirement programmes, population ageing, and problems of legitimacy connected to the occupational fragmentation of the pension system created equally strong negative feedback effects. In the 1980s and 1990s, these challenges were mainly addressed by incremental reforms (Weaver 2006) without bringing them fully under control. In the 2000s, the pension system was eventually restructured by adding two additional tiers on top of the Bismarckian-style public pensions, a policy shift that can best be described as layering (Streeck and Thelen 2005*a*).

Like Bismarckian systems, universal and tax-financed pension systems like those of Denmark and New Zealand face distinctive problems. Equity issues, adverse effects on savings behaviour, and fiscal pressure are examples of negative feedback effects that, as the case studies have shown, motivated policy change. In countries with universal pensions more reform options are available because of the absence of a contribution–benefit nexus and, indeed, these two countries moved in quite different directions.

The Danish basic pension was supplemented by a fully funded labour market pension (ATP) which, however, failed to provide a living standard comparable to that in earlier employment and, in any case, was relevant for only a minority of the population. Hence, earnings-related pensions were high on the agenda from early on, not least with a view to encouraging long-term savings. However, as noted previously, no way could be found through the conflicting interests on this issue to arrive at an acceptable legislative consensus. This void was pre-empted by private as well as by occupational pensions based on collective agreements. Repeated non-decisions fuelled the proliferation of these pension types and created increasing returns as well as new constituencies supporting these pensions. As the Danish case study showed, a point of no return was reached in the late 1980s.

In New Zealand, by contrast, negative feedbacks can be observed. Budgetary pressure was increased by the significant expansion of New Zealand Superannuation under the Muldoon government in the context of an electoral bidding war. Soon, however, this opportunistic expansion backfired when the additional costs became unsustainable in the mid-1980s. The solution adopted was to target the benefits. The political struggle in subsequent periods was mainly about how targeting should be implemented in practice.

It has already been mentioned that *health-care* reforms were strongly driven by the distinctive problems generated by different health-care regimes. For example, the National Health Service countries, Denmark, and New Zealand, suffered from long waiting periods and restricted choice, Austria's social insurance system from the repercussions of occupational and territorial fragmentation, while, in the privately dominated Swiss system, problem pressure resulted from adverse selection and high health-related costs for low-income groups and families. Since many of these problems could not be addressed by a regime's 'within-logic', all countries borrowed from the regulatory tools utilized in other health-care systems. Overall, what was common to all cases was a tinkering with the edges of existing systems rather than any kind of radical shift in system type.

Positive feedback effects are unlikely to occur in *family policy* as the usual suspects for generating them such as adaptive expectations, network effects, or sunk costs (Pierson 2000) are lacking. More plausible is the existence of negative feedbacks. For example, transfer-oriented policies tend to lead to relatively lower fertility and to a lower growth in female employment in cross-national terms. Eventually, governments had to adapt their policies in order to reverse these trends. In fact, this is what we can observe but, as we show in the next section, the reform of family policy was strongly shaped by the political preferences of policy-makers and by the institutional constraints they were facing.

5.2.3 Political parties

Socio-economic problem pressure and policy legacies stimulate and often foreshadow policy change, but these variables still leave a large room for manoeuvre to governments. In fact, policy change cannot be explained without considering political actors and their preferences. Our enquiry has been particularly motivated by the question of the extent to which political parties influence social policy reform in an era of globalization. Based on the case study evidence for Austria, Denmark, and New Zealand, we can conclude that parties, at least in terms of social policy, did matter, while room for manoeuvre in economic policy became ever more restricted. Because of its cabinet stability Switzerland is a special case that requires separate discussion (see below).

In the early 1970s, left governments were in power in Austria, Denmark, and New Zealand. In this period, the New Zealand Labour Party and the Social Democratic single party government in Austria expanded the welfare state under by and large favourable economic circumstances. While the left remained in office in Austria until the early 1980s and, for much of the period, in Denmark, the oil crises of the 1970s were managed by a conservative government in New Zealand.

In economic policy, Denmark, Austria, and New Zealand responded to the crisis with measures based on the dominant Keynesian philosophy of the time, albeit with varying macroeconomic success. The fact that even the conservative Muldoon government in New Zealand practised such policies exemplifies the hegemony of the post-war Keynesian consensus. With respect to welfare state reforms, the second half of the 1970s was a period in which governments attempted to defend the social achievements of the past.

In the mid-1980s, the balance of power turned to the political left in New Zealand, whereas Denmark moved to the right. The left remained in office in Austria but had to share power with the Freedom Party and, after 1987, with the Christian Democrats in a Grand Coalition. But what was ostensibly a shift to the left in New Zealand turned out to be one to the right in the economic policy. Against the backdrop of a deep economic crisis, the Labour government launched one of the most radical programmes of economic restructuring ever seen in an advanced democracy. 'Rogernomics' included deregulation, privatization, and a shift in tax policy from direct to indirect taxation. As a result, New Zealand bid farewell to the idea of domestic defence upon which the post-war wage earners' welfare state had rested and opened up its economy. Industrial relations, the second pillar backing the wage earner's welfare state, by and large survived this neo-liberal turn. In contrast to economic policy, the welfare reforms implemented by Labour were much more cautious and limited. Some retrenchment occurred but its extent was rather moderate compared to what followed under the succeeding conservative government. The approach taken by Labour mainly focused on targeting benefits received by those who were comparatively well off. Examples include the introduction of the Superannuation surcharge, new tax rebates tailored to working families, and the introduction of tax credits for low-income families. While these measures further undermined the universality of the welfare state, they had a Social Democratic imprint as they were tailored to Labour's constituency.

In a manner similar to New Zealand, Denmark stood at the brink of the abyss in economic terms in the early 1980s. But, in contrast to New Zealand, a centre-right government had to cope with the crisis. This government, led by Poul Schlüter, also broke with Keynesianism and changed the style of politics as trade unions were excluded from policy-making. Overall, the political climate became more adversarial culminating in a severe industrial dispute in 1985. While there was a good deal of continuity in social policy, some of the reforms passed mirrored the ideological leanings of the centre-right coalition. The government enacted substantial cutbacks of unemployment benefits for the young unemployed. At the same time, however, active measures were extended. Moreover, ideas borrowed from New Public Management, free choice and private service provision gained importance in the fields of health care and childcare. Family policy received a more conservative flavour.

Again, similar to Denmark and New Zealand, Austria witnessed a turn in economic policy in the mid-1980s against a backdrop of deteriorating economic performance. Unemployment became a real phenomenon and public debt pressing. Both parameters further worsened due to the implosion of the state-owned enterprise sector in the mid-1980s. As a consequence, the Grand Coalition opted from 1987 onwards for a supply-side-oriented course in economic policy comprising tax cuts, debt reduction, and the privatization of state-owned enterprises. However, the welfare state was hardly affected by this policy shift.

In the early 1990s, the balance of power shifted again in different directions in Denmark and New Zealand. Social Democrats resumed office in Denmark in 1993, whereas in New Zealand National took power in 1990. Both countries confronted severe economic crises and double-digit unemployment rates in the early 1990s. Just a few weeks after it was elected, the conservative government led by Jim Bolger in New Zealand launched an attack on the welfare state arguably unrivalled within the OECD world. Virtually all sectors of the welfare state were affected by retrenchment and neo-liberal restructuring. Privatization, workfare, and targeting became the leitmotifs of this strongly ideology-driven assault on the welfare state. In an effort to weaken the unions, the government launched an onslaught on the arbitration system with the consequence that the last pillar of the wage earners' welfare state was dismantled.

In contrast, the Danish centre-left coalition, despite very similar economic problems, started out by attempting to embark on a very different route. At first, a classical Keynesianism was practised, which later, however, was replaced by more mainstream policies emphasizing expenditure and tax cuts. An about-face also occurred in labour market policy and was realized in cooperation with the social partners. Activation was extended but the destination of change was much less workfare-oriented than in New Zealand and was not accompanied by radical reductions in replacement rates. Despite this, the maximum benefit duration for cash benefits was significantly reduced and it was no longer possible to restore eligibility for cash benefits through enrolment in active measures. On the positive side, however, the government expanded the welfare state by improving the coverage of second pillar pensions and by offering a childcare guarantee for virtually all children under six.

Austria was not affected by an economic crisis of a similar extent in the 1990s. Some moderate retrenchment of welfare benefits did occur, but was far outweighed by a significant expansion of family policy and by the introduction of long-term care allowance in 1993. Not surprisingly, the Grand Coalition completely missed its target for reducing public debt when the country joined the European Union in 1995. In order to meet the Maastricht criteria, the government then found it necessary to impose two austerity packages which included cutbacks of several welfare benefits. With the exception of family policy, cutbacks prevailed in the second half of the 1990s and tensions between the government and social partners increased significantly.

At the turn of the new millennium, a change in government occurred in all three countries. While Denmark and Austria moved to the right, with right-wing populist parties as a junior partner in a coalition government, New Zealand again turned to the left. New Zealand's left coalition led by Helen Clark repealed some measures imposed by its conservative predecessor, launched a huge initiative in family policy, modified the workfare-oriented approach in labour market policy by emphasizing social investment, and strengthened the role of the state in health care. Moreover, the government revoked the attack on the unions but without restoring the traditional arbitration regime.

The centre-right governments in Austria and Denmark took office with a view to containing debt, reducing taxes as well as non-wage labour costs, and, at least in the Austrian case, remodelling the welfare state. In order to be able to realize this agenda, both countries departed from the traditional negotiation-based politics style, with trade unions and the opposition bypassed in the decision-making process. Social insurance bodies (Austria) and unemployment insurance (Denmark) were also restructured in a manner that weakened the trade unions. Even though the reforms were certainly less radical than the measures adopted in New Zealand in the 1990s, both governments enacted policies in line with their ideological leanings. Workfare elements in labour market policy were strengthened and, under the slogan of 'free choice', family policy was restructured in a neo-conservative fashion (with the universal child benefit and the 'at home' benefit as major examples). Competition and 'marketization' guided the reforms of the Danish health-care system, whereas the Austrian pension system was transformed into a three-tier system. Early retirement programmes were rolled back and the retirement age was to be increased over the long term. Measures of welfare state expansion were few and far between, and mainly included higher cash benefits for families. When a Grand Coalition in 2007 resumed power in Austria, retrenchment came to a halt and welfare state expansion was back on the agenda, not least due to a revival of corporatism.

As already mentioned, Switzerland is an exceptional case since there has been *de facto* no change in government for decades. In addition, consensus democracy in general and the country's oversized cabinet in particular makes it very difficult to discern the impact of parties on public policy. Nevertheless, the Swiss case study revealed that parties matter. Partisan impacts can be studied in the parliamentary arena which became more important over time. Due to their centrist policy positions, Christian Democrats have played a pivotal role in this arena. However, partisan effects most clearly show up in the post-parliamentary decision-making phase. Where a referendum takes place, parties as well as interest groups of labour and capital are forced to reveal their preferences very visibly. Whereas the populist right and employers opposed welfare state expansion (e.g. the introduction of maternity insurance), bills aiming at retrenchment were attacked by the unions, left parties, and interest groups of welfare beneficiaries. These latter groups have also launched numerous people's initiatives aiming at welfare state expansion.

In sum, all countries, irrespective of partisan complexion of government, made a shift towards supply-side-oriented economic policies. In social policy, by contrast, parties made a difference but in more subtle ways than in the post-war period. The within-case evidence has demonstrated that governments operating under broadly constant institutional conditions have attempted to influence social policy in line with their respective ideological leanings. However, the opportunity to do so was strongly shaped by short-term economic and fiscal circumstances and the type of government. One-party governments were more likely to carry their agenda to completion than multi-party coalitions or minority governments. In a situation of economic crisis, governments of all kinds imposed retrenchment, but the extent varied depending on the partisan complexion of the government. Liberal and secular conservative parties have imposed more significant benefit cutbacks than left parties, with Christian Democrats occupying a position in-between. In addition, the political right has either attempted to bypass the unions in policy-making or deliberately weakened their power resources. No similar attempt was made by governments of the left.

265

Even though partisan differences vanished over time in terms of the meta-strategies and policy priorities that were seen as appropriate for coping with the challenges resulting from the structural changes in society and economy, the translation of common goals such as activation or improving the family–work balance into practice was strongly impacted by political parties. Ideology loomed large in family and labour market policy. While the left is more inclined to policies supporting a dual career model, right parties (and Christian Democrats in particular) opt for higher cash benefits, longer spells of parental leave, and freedom of choice. Where the labour market is concerned, parties of the right retrenched cash benefits more radically than parties of the left. In terms of activation, there are party differences with respect to the balance of duties and social rights, and the choice between workfare-based strategies and more human-capital-oriented types of activation. Partisan differences are less pronounced in pension and health policy. This is not to say that party ideology is irrelevant, but the sheer size of these two programmes makes them a major electoral battleground. With some exceptions, reforms were typically based on broad compromises and often followed patterns emphasized by the 'new politics of the welfare state'. Electoral considerations and vested interests such as doctors and health insurance funds or pressure groups such as Grey Power in New Zealand have significantly influenced reform outcomes. What, nevertheless, has been politically contested in these policy sectors has been the nature of public–private balance in provision, the extent of cost containment, and the associated distributional consequences.

5.2.4 Political institutions

We have already seen that welfare state institutions had a significant impact on national reform trajectories. Based on a cross-national comparison we can also conclude that political institutions played an equally important role in explaining cross-national differences in welfare state restructuring. As one might have expected on the basis of the literature on political institutionalism, veto points, system of interest mediation, and electoral systems turned out to be important factors shaping the room of manoeuvre of political actors, the style of politics, and, in consequence, the extent of policy change. This is most impressively exemplified for the two extreme cases in this respect, namely New Zealand and Switzerland. As we will see, however, it is important to differentiate between the short-term and long-term effects of political institutions on policy change. New Zealand's almost ideal-typical Westminster democracy provided the government with wide-ranging powers and facilitated major policy shifts within a short period of time. Changes in the partisan complexion of the government therefore often went along with policy reversals. Despite frequent policy shifts and an unusually high degree of policy experimentation, the country, nevertheless, quite frequently ended up with policies similar to those it started with decades earlier. Health care is arguably the best example of policy reforms that occurred in such a stop–start manner. In the long-term perspective, however, reform activities oscillated around the long-term trend with little fundamental change taking place as compared to the situation in the mid-1970s. The relevance of political institutions is also shown by the fact that the introduction of PR in 1993 in New Zealand seems to have tamed the amplitude of the pendulum swings, a result predictable in light of the moderation effect associated with coalition government.

In contrast to the striking short-term policy shifts in New Zealand, policy change occurred in an incremental manner in Switzerland. Since the Swiss government is a collegial body consisting of four (currently five) parties, and because cantons and interest organizations are formally incorporated in public policy-making, decision-making is typically negotiation-based and often very protracted. Thus, in order to act in situations requiring quick decisions, the government sometimes had to rely on urgent decrees. Overall, however, the strong fragmentation of power led to gradual policy change rather than to radical policy shifts.[5] Incrementalism is reinforced by the institutions of direct democracy. Swiss policy-makers are always mindful that they operate in the institutional shadow of the (optional) referendum. Averting a referendum is the ultimate goal of Swiss consensus democracy. This is typically achieved by accommodating the interests of the most powerful parties and pressure groups who are able to launch an optional referendum. However, since it has become increasingly difficult to reach compromises in the recent past, because the deteriorating economic situation has hampered logrolling, the number of referendums has increased significantly since the 1990s. The corresponding referendum outcomes underline the *status quo* bias of direct democracy[6] since bills aimed exclusively at welfare state expansion and bills aimed exclusively at retrenchment both faced a high probability of rejection, while all bills that combine benefit cutbacks with measures of welfare state expansion were approved.

However, a series of incremental policy changes in the short run may, nonetheless, add up to a quite significant policy shift over the course of time. Since the mechanism of the referendum as practised in Switzerland in recent decades seems to have constituted an institutional ratchet against welfare state dismantling, the overall direction of policy change has been a creeping welfare state expansion, which ended-up in regime transformation in the long run.

Austria and Denmark are located in between these extremes. Partisan veto players, corporatism, and, in the Danish case, minority governments are the most important factors explaining the incremental and compromised-based adjustment path that has prevailed for much of the period under

---

[5] A few more major changes did occur sporadically in Switzerland as exemplified by the 1994 health reform.

[6] A similar effect can be observed in New Zealand where the people rejected the introduction of a second-tier compulsory savings scheme in 1997.

examination here. It is, thus, hardly surprising that the most far-reaching changes occurred either when corporatism was deliberately suspended by the political right or when a party, like the Austrian Social Democrats in the 1970s, was able to form a single party government. The number of institutional veto players is low in both polities. However, some rulings of the Austrian Constitutional Court had a significant impact on social policy.

5.2.5 And what of the impact of globalization?

The international political economy underwent a profound transformation in the period examined. However, we have seen that these challenges did not unleash a race to the bottom. The question is then whether the far-reaching changes in the social policy we have described are in any way attributable to this transformation. Our answer to this question is mixed. The case studies have clearly shown that many challenges and problems to which welfare state had to respond resulted from structural changes in economy and society, as well as from negative feedback effects of political decisions taken in the past. As Pierson (1998) has correctly noticed, this set of challenges would even in the absence of globalization have led to a restructuring of the welfare state very similar to the patterns observed in our case studies. It would be nonetheless quite wrong to assume that the efficiency thesis is completely irrelevant. While globalization did not engender a race to the bottom, it fuelled a supply-side-oriented transformation of economic and social policies.

To begin with, economic globalization reinforced the challenges and the problem pressures that had built-up as a result of political decisions taken in the past and in the wake of structural changes in society and economy. High levels of public debt accumulated in the past became more difficult to maintain in increasingly open economies. One example is the downgrading of New Zealand's creditworthiness by the Standard & Poor's rating in 1990. It was with reference to this adverse rating that the conservative government justified the radical expenditure cutbacks enacted in subsequent years. In addition, greater exit options for business and capital owners imposed constraints on state revenues and reinforced structural unemployment through the removal of low-skilled jobs to low-wage economies. Economic globalization therefore reinforced economic structural change and undermined the fiscal autonomy of the nation state. These processes and the repercussions of deindustrialization and societal modernization put governments under considerable strain. The uniform response was a fundamental realignment of economic policy. All countries, irrespective of the national distribution of power resources, adopted supply-side-oriented (or even strengthened as did Switzerland) economic policies in the 1980s and, particularly, in the 1990s. Keynesianism practised in Denmark and Austria in the 1970s is, at least as a long-term economic policy strategy, a dead duck at the national level.

Instead, these countries lowered tax rates (while simultaneously broadening the tax base) and reduced regulatory standards in order to create a more business-friendly environment. In addition, debt containment and balanced budgets featured high on the agenda everywhere. The new supply-side-oriented paradigm also affected the welfare state. It is not surprising that the strongest impact can be found in the area of labour market policy which is where economic policy and the welfare state most closely interact.

A corollary of this policy shift was that the strategy of domestic defence became unsustainable at reasonable cost in a markedly changed international economy. What happened in New Zealand was that the high barriers that protected domestic business were removed, and the economy was radically opened up to international competition. It is worth noting that this increased exposure to the world economy did not automatically lead to a shift to the kind of compensation strategy that has been suggested as typical of North West Europe's small open economies.[7]

In general, it seems that even existing strategies of compensation became more difficult to sustain, at least as they had been practised in the immediate post-war period. In contrast to the rationale emphasized by the compensation thesis, we find significant retrenchment in the social protection of the working-age population, notably in respect of unemployment benefits. Moreover, the public sector, another bulwark against the fluctuations of world markets, was significantly restructured. Previously sheltered sectors were opened up to competition and public utilities, and state-owned enterprises, where they existed, were privatized. Austria's huge mixed economy faded away in the aftermath of EU accession, while both New Zealand and Switzerland have retrenched their domestic protectionist bulwarks. In this respect, the Swiss arrangement was similar to New Zealand's post-war political economy. The main difference, however, was that, in New Zealand the agricultural sector supported a largely non-competitive manufacturing sector that was kept behind protective walls, while, in Switzerland, the logic was the other way round. All these domestic types of cross-sectional compensation became less important in the period under review here.

5.3 Small States — big lessons

Comparative welfare state research has traditionally paid most attention to the big steamers. With a few exceptions[8] the yawls floating in the backwash of these steamboats attracted much less interest. In this final section, we take up

[7] But note, if there is a lag in the process, as well there might be, the expansionary reforms of the Clark era might be seen as a modest step in that direction.

[8] Sweden is certainly one of the most studied welfare states. Denmark has recently received a lot of attention, but only in the area of active labour market policy. The same is true for New Zealand and economic reform.

the cudgels for the 'importance of being unimportant' (Armstrong and Read 2002), as we argue that there are big lessons to be drawn from welfare state adaptation in small countries. Five lessons stand out.

The *first* and arguably most important lesson from the adjustment pathways of four small countries is that a generous welfare state and economic openness are still compatible in a world that is characterized by an unprecedented degree of economic and financial integration. The rowing boats floating on an open sea, to take up the quote by Joseph Stiglitz again, though they were broadsided by the waves of globalization, did not capsize. The social policy changes described in the previous section do not support the notion of a dismantling of the welfare state. Retrenchment in some policy sectors, notably unemployment cash benefits, was compensated for, if not overcompensated, by expansion in other areas such as family policy or long-term care. On the whole, there was no rollback of the welfare state across the board and the share of public resources devoted to social affairs is greater than ever before in history. This is remarkable because economic openness has massively increased in all four countries since the mid-1980s (Figure 5.2). Since the welfare state could make it in these small and therefore highly vulnerable countries, we can, by relying on a 'Sinatra inference', draw the powerful conclusion that its chances of survival are very favourable across *all* OECD countries.

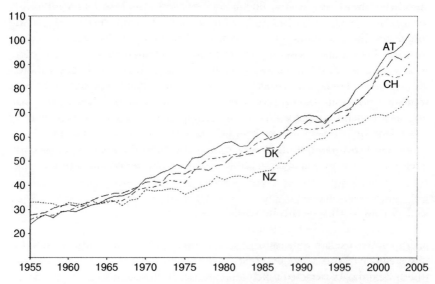

Figure 5.2: Trade openness in Austria, Denmark, New Zealand, and Switzerland, 1955–2004

Notes: Trade openness is measured by the sum of imports and exports as percentage of GDP (at constant prices).

Source: Alan Heston, Robert Summers and Bettina Aten, Penn World Table Version 6.2, Center for International Comparisons of Production, Income and Prices at the University of Pennsylvania, September 2006.

Second, the fact that the welfare state has survived despite a massive increase in economic integration suggests that the effects of increasing economic globalization are by no means all negative. Trade is an important source of economic growth which may generate the fiscal resources necessary for the viability of the welfare state in the long run. As in the past, this requires economic specialization and it seems that our countries have been successful in implementing large-scale structural changes and in occupying new niches in world markets in order to reap the benefits of the international division of labour. Apparently, small nations were able to find an adjustment strategy that could reconcile the economic imperatives generated by globalization with solidarity.

The *third* lesson is that these boats weathered the storms unscathed precisely because they are small in size and thus easy to steer. Once more, small nations were able to turn vice into virtue as they swiftly adjusted their course to changing winds causing economic troubles. More specifically, small boats gathered way because the crew skilfully chose a downwind course by orienting economic and social policies towards a more supply-side-oriented direction. Denmark and New Zealand were affected by threatening economic turbulences in the 1980s and 1990s but managed to avert capsizing by means of significant policy changes which brought them back into calmer waters. The flexibility of small boats is also evident from their role as policy innovators making them exemplary cases of successful welfare state adaptation which, in consequence, featured prominently in the reform agenda heralded by international organizations and the EU. Examples of these innovations include the activist turn in labour market policy and, albeit somewhat unintended in origin, the multi-pillar pension mix in Denmark and Switzerland, as well as the favourable family–work balance practised in Denmark. Other innovations include long-term care allowance and hospice leave in Austria, and even New Zealand's radical reforms in economic and social policy in the 1980s and 1990s must be regarded as rather unprecedented policy experiments.

The danger of being capsized is greatest if the course is reversed by selecting a route against the wind. While domestic defence is an extremely risky endeavour, a strategy of compensation is anything but impossible. It nonetheless requires some adjustments to be sustainable in the open sea. Concepts such as 'flexicurity' demonstrate that solidarity and generous social protection can be successfully combined with the requirements of flexibility in integrated markets.

However, small countries are not alone in their reorientation in economic and social policy. We observe similar welfare state reforms in many countries across the OECD world, that is, also in the big states (see Palier 2009; Palier and Martin 2008; Seeleib-Kaiser 2008; Daguerre 2007; Ellison 2006).

The *fourth* lesson is that the small countries have been more successful in terms of economic performance and it is worth mentioning that this was apparently the case irrespective of the structural make-up of the welfare state. Hence generous welfare states are not only compatible with economic openness but also with economic success. Admittedly, some nations have characteristic

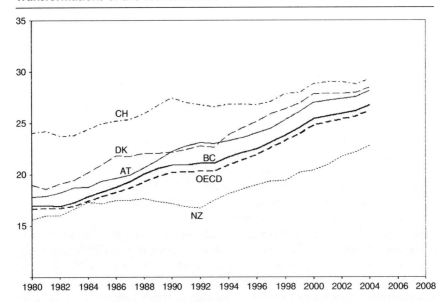

Figure 5.3: Real GDP per capita, 1980–2004

Notes: Real GDP per capita (constant prices: Laspeyres) in 1,000 (USD) and 2000 constant prices. OECD-21 includes: Australia, Austria, Belgium, Canada, Denmark, Finland, France, Germany, Greece, Ireland, Italy, Japan, Netherlands, New Zealand, Norway, Portugal, Spain, Sweden, Switzerland, United Kingdom, USA.
EU-15 includes: Austria, Belgium, Denmark, Finland, France, Germany, Greece, Ireland, Italy, Luxembourg, Netherlands, Portugal, Spain, Sweden, United Kingdom.
BC = Big Countries (Canada, France, Germany, Italy, Japan, Spain, United Kingdom and USA).

Source: Alan Heston, Robert Summers and Bettina Aten, Penn World Table Version 6.2, Center for International Comparisons of Production, Income and Prices at the University of Pennsylvania, September 2006.

economic Achilles heels, but overall they show an above-average economic performance. In the mid-2000s, Denmark, Switzerland, and Austria belonged to the top-ten wealthiest countries in the world and GDP per capita exceeded the average level of wealth in the OECD-21 and the average performance of the eight largest OECD countries[9] (Figure 5.3). By contrast, New Zealand was not able to leave the post-war pattern of poor growth performance behind.

In addition, labour market performance (at least since the 1990s) is much better in our sample compared with the OECD-21 average and the average performance of big countries. The harmonized unemployment rate declined in all four countries below the 5 per cent threshold in the 2000s (Figure 5.4). This exceptional performance is even more striking if the above-average labour market participation rates are taken into account. This holds true for the female as well as the total participation rate (Figures 5.5 and 5.6).

[9] Note that the average of big countries masks important variation within this group. However, only three out of the eight big countries score better on particular indicators. In terms of economic wealth, the United States exceeds all four small countries and outperforms some of them in terms of basic labour market indicators. The United Kingdom shows a very favourable performance with respect to public finances, Japan in terms of total employment.

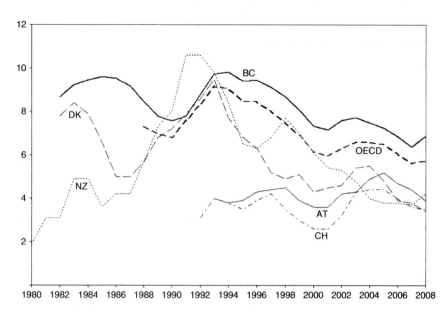

Figure 5.4: Harmonized unemployment rate, 1980–2008

Notes: Number of unemployed persons as a percentage of the civilian labour force. Missing values: OECD-21: Austria (1988–92), Germany (1988–90), Switzerland (1988–91); Big Countries: Germany (1982–90).

Source: OECD Labour Force Statistics.

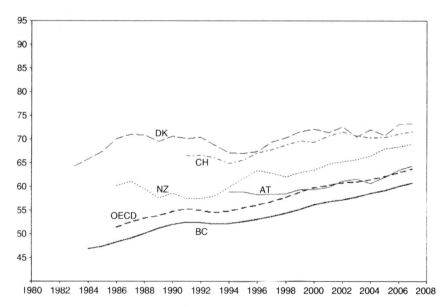

Figure 5.5: Employment rate women, 1983–2007

Notes: Share of women of working age (15 to 64 years) in employment. Missing values OECD-21: Austria (1986–93); Switzerland (1986–90).

Source: OECD Labour Force Statistics.

273

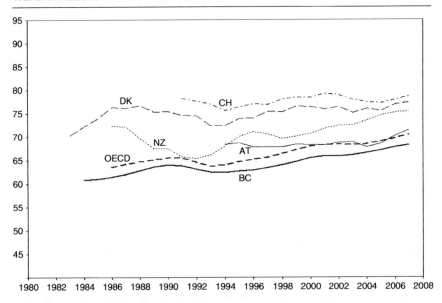

Figure 5.6: Total employment rate, 1983–2007

Notes: Share of persons of working age (15 to 64 years) in employment. Missing values OECD-21: Austria (1986–93); Switzerland (1986–90).

Source: OECD Labour Force Statistics.

Our small countries also exhibit lower levels of public debt (Figure 5.7). While Austria deviated somewhat from the overall trend, our small countries have by and large managed to keep public debt better under control compared to international developments. Overall, small is (still) beautiful. Flexible and quick adjustment to a new international environment was paralleled by a very favourable economic performance.

Yet economic success is certainly not the ultimate goal of the welfare state. If we move on to the theoretical substance of the welfare state, that is, the extent to which redistribution and social rights are secured, we can draw the *fifth* and final big lesson. Inequality has increased in virtually all countries over time (cf. OECD 2008*b*; ILO 2008). With the exception of New Zealand, our countries were also successful with regard to this benchmark (Table 5.2), in the sense that inequality increased less dramatically than in the larger nations of the OECD. Nevertheless, the increase in inequality has also taken place in small countries. Although this has not been part of the subject-matter of this analysis, the trend towards 'growing unequal' (OECD 2008) is presumably strongly connected to the trend towards a supply-side-oriented transformation of social policy identified here. While the efforts to increase market compatibility allowed reaping the benefits of global markets on the one hand, they also uncovered the dark side of markets on the other. Once more,

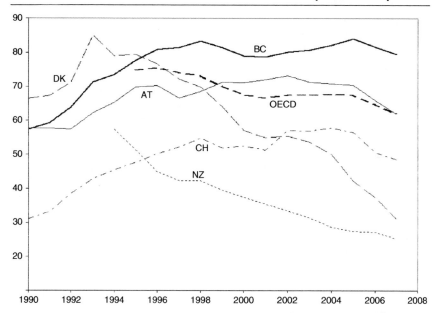

Figure 5.7: Government debt, 1990–2007

Notes: General government gross financial liabilities as a percentage of GDP. Missing values OECD-21: Ireland (1995–7).

Source: OECD Stat (Country statistical profiles 2009).

Table 5.2: Gini coefficient (after taxes and transfers)

	Mid-1980s	Mid-1990s	Mid-2000s
Austria	.24	.24	.27
Denmark	.22	.21	.23
New Zealand	.27	.34	.34
Switzerland	N.A.	N.A.	.28
Canada	.29	.28	.32
Germany	.26	.27	.30
France	.31	.28	.28
Italy	.31	.35	.35
Japan	.30	.32	.32
Spain	.37	.34	.32
United Kingdom	.33	.35	.34
United States	.34	.36	.38
Average small countries	.24	.26	.28
Average big countries	.31	.32	.33

Source: OECD Stat (data set: Income distribution and Poverty).

Table 5.3: Economic outlook for 2010

	Unemployment	Employment rate	Economic growth	Budget deficit	Public debt
	2010	2010	2010	2010	2010
Austria	6.2 (7.9)	71.1	0.2 (−0.1)	−4.2 (−6.1)	79.2
Denmark	4.5 (7.9)	75.7	0.4 (0.1)	−4.8 (−4.1)	51.4
New Zealand	7.5 (7.9)	N.A.	0.5 (0.6)	−4.5 (−5.0)	33.4
Switzerland	4.6 (5.1)	80.1	−0.3 (−0.2)	−1.6 (−2.5)	47.8
EU-15	9.7 (10.8)	65.8[a]	−0.5 (−0.1)	−6.4 (−7.0)	79.3
OECD	9.0 (9.8)	68.6[b]	−0.2 (0.1)	−5.4 (−6.3)	82.0

Notes: Unemployment: unemployment rate as a percentage of total labour force. Budget deficit: general government financial balances as a percentage of GDP. Public debt: general government gross financial liabilities as a percentage of GDP. Employment rates (total): ratio of total employment to the population of working age (all persons of the age 15 to 64 years, 16 to 64 years for Spain).
[a] Sweden excluded.
[b] New Zealand, Sweden, and the United States excluded, projections are not available for these countries due to diverging definitions of the working-age population (New Zealand and United States: 16 years and above; Sweden: 15 to 74 years).
Source: IMF World Economic Outlook, April 2009; in brackets: OECD Economic Outlook No. 85, June 2009.

however, the more generous welfare states in our sample did by far better in taming the rise of inequality.

The question is whether the success story of small states is sustainable. At the time of writing, all advanced democracies are struggling with the repercussions of the deepest economic crisis since the Great Depression. While this massive recession has negatively influenced the fate of millions of people, it is an interesting occurrence for social scientists as it represents a sort of natural experiment which allows for a test of some of the big lessons derived in this section. The years to come will have to show whether small countries will be able to better cope with the crisis than the bigger nations. Some informed guesses can nevertheless be suggested to conclude this volume. Based on our findings we argue that small countries will manage the crisis in a relatively successful way. Even though forecasts by economists should be regarded with utmost suspicion in these days, we present an economic outlook for our small states compiled by reputable international organizations (Table 5.3).

The figures tell an unequivocal story. With the possible single exception of Swiss economic growth rate, all indicators of macroeconomic performance suggest that the four small nations will overcome the crisis much better than the average of the advanced democracies. While there is a great deal of forecast uncertainty, we have every reason to predict that small countries will also weather the current storm.

Bibliography

Abromeit, H. (1992): 'Kontinuität oder "Jekyll-and-Hyde-Politik"': Staatshandeln in der Schweiz und in Großbritannien', in: H. Abromeit and W. W. Pommerehne (eds.): *Staatstätigkeit in der Schweiz*, Bern: Verlag Paul Haupt, 159–92.

Adsera, A. and Boix, C. (2002): 'Trade, Democracy, and the Size of the Public Sector: The Political Underpinnings of Openness', *International Organization*, 56/2, 229–62.

Aebersold, M., Longchamp, C., Tschannen, A., and Ratelband-Pally, S. (2005): 'Romands, Alleinerziehende und Eltern aus der Unterschicht zählen am stärksten auf familienergänzende Kinderbetreuung: Kurzbericht zur Bedürfnisanalyse Familienergänzende Betreuungsangebote im Auftrag der Heilsarmee Schweiz', gfs.bern, http://www.gfsbern.ch/pub/heilsarmee-wik.pdf, 20.12.2005

Alasua, J., Bilbao-Ubillos, J., and Olaskoaga, J. (2007): 'The EU Integration Process and the Convergence of Social Protection Benefits at National Level', *International Journal of Social Welfare*, 16/2, 297–306.

Albæk, E., Eliason, L. C., Nørgaard, A. S., and Schwartz, H. M. (2008): 'Introduction', in: E. Albæk, L. C. Eliason, A. S. Nørgaard, and H. M. Schwartz (eds.): *Crisis, Miracles, and Beyond*, Århus: Århus University Press, 11–31.

Alber, J. (1982): *Vom Armenhaus zum Wohlfahrtsstaat: Analysen zur Entwicklung der Sozialversicherung in Westeuropa*, Frankfurt a. M./New York: Campus.

—— (2002): 'Modernisierung als Peripetie des Sozialstaates?', in: *Berliner Journal für Soziologie*, 12/1, 5–62.

Alesina, A. and Spolaore, E. (2005): *The Size of Nations*, Boston, MA: MIT Press.

Allan, J. P. and Scruggs, L. (2004): 'Political Partisanship and Welfare State Reform in Advanced Industrial Societies', *American Journal of Political Science*, 48, 496–512.

Altvater, E. and Mahnkopf, B. (1999): *Grenzen der Globalisierung: Ökonomie, Ökologie und Politik in der Weltgesellschaft*, Münster: Westfälisches Dampfboot.

Andersen, J. G. (2003): 'The General Election in Denmark, November 2001', *Electoral Studies*, 22, 153–93.

—— (2007): 'Affluence and Welfare State Transformations: Social Policy Change in Denmark: 1993–2007', *CCWS Working Paper*, 55, Aalborg: Aalborg Universitet, Institut for Økonomi, Politik og Forvaltning.

—— (2008): 'From People's Pension to an Equality-Oriented Multipillar System: The Silent Revolution of the Danish Pension System', Centre for Comparative Welfare Studies: Aalborg University. Paper prepared for NOPSA Conference, Tromsø.

277

Bibliography

Andersen, J. G. and Larsen, C. A. (2002): 'Pension Politics and Policy in Denmark and Sweden: Path Dependencies, Policy Style, and Policy Outcome', *CCWS Working Paper*, 27, Aalborg.

Androsch, H. (2005): *Wirtschaft und Gesellschaft: Österreich 1945–2005*, Innsbruck: Studienverlag.

Année Politique Suisse/Schweizerische Politik (APS) (since 1965): *Chronik zur schweizerischen Politik*, Bern: Institut für Politikwissenschaft.

Arbejderbevægelsens Erhvervsråd (2006): *Fordeling og levevilkår*, Copenhagen.

Arbejdsdirektoratet (2003): Benchmarking af arbejdsløshedskasserne 2003, Copenhagen.

——(ed.) (2007): *Arbejdsløshedsforsikringsloven 1907–2007*, Copenhagen.

Arbejdsministeriet (1999): *Arbejdsmarkedsreformerne — ét statusbillede*, Copenhagen.

Armingeon, K. (1996): 'Konkordanz, Sozialpartnerschaft und wohlfahrtsstaatliche Politik in der Schweiz im internationalen Vergleich', in: W. Linder, P. Lanfranchi, and E. R. Weibel (eds.): *Schweizer Eigenart — eigenartige Schweiz: Der Kleinstaat im Kräftefeld der europäischen Integration*, Bern: Verlag Paul Haupt, 69–84.

——(1998): 'The Impact of Globalization on Swiss Policy Making: A Comment', *Swiss Political Science Review*, 4/2, 104–11.

——(1999): 'Swiss Labour Market Policy in Comparative Perspective', in: U. Klöti and K. Yorimoto (eds.): *Institutional Change and Public Policy in Japan and Switzerland*, Zürich: Universität Zürich, Institut für Politikwissenschaft: Abteilung für Internationale Beziehungen, 179–93.

——(2001): 'Institutionalising the Swiss Welfare State', *West European Politics*, 24/2, 145–68.

——(2003): 'Renegotiating the Swiss Welfare State', in: F. van Waarden and G. Lehmbruch (eds.): *Renegotiating the Welfare State. Flexible Adjustment through Corporatist Concertation*, Abingdon/New York: Routledge, 169–88.

——(2006): 'Reconciling Competing Claims of the Welfare State Clientele: The Politics of Old and New Social Risk Coverage in Comparative Perspective', in: K. Armingeon and G. Bonoli (eds.): *The Politics of Post-Industrial Welfare States: Adapting Post-war Social Policies to New Social Risks*, Abingdon/New York: Routledge, 100–22.

——and Bonoli, G. (eds.) (2006): *The Politics of Post-industrial Welfare States: Adapting Post-war Social Policies to New Social Risks*, Abingdon/New York: Routledge.

——and Emmenegger, P. (2007): 'Wirtschaftspolitik in der Schweiz: Erosion eines Modells', in: M. Nollert and H. Scholtz (eds.): *Wirtschaft Schweiz — Ein Sonderfall?*, Zürich: Seismo, 175–207.

Armstrong, H. W. and Read, R. (2002): 'The Importance of Being Unimportant: The Political Economy of Trade and Growth in Small States', in: S. M. Murshed (ed.): *Issues in Positive Political Economy*, London: Routledge, 71–88.

Arter, D. (1999): *Scandinavian Politics Today*, Manchester: Manchester University Press.

Ashton, T. (1999): 'The Health Reforms: To Market and Back?', in: J. Boston, P. Dalziel, and S. St. John (eds.): *Redesigning the Welfare State in New Zealand: Problems, Policies, Prospects*, Auckland: Oxford University Press, 134–53.

——(2005): 'Recent Developments in the Funding and Organisation of the New Zealand Health System', *Australia and New Zealand Health Policy*, 2/9. http://www.anzhealthpolicy.com/consent 12/1/9.

——and St John, S. (2005): *Financing of Long Term Residential Care in New Zealand: Swimming Against the Tide*, Paper presented at the Fifth World Congress of the International Health Economists Association (IHEA), Barcelona, Spain, 11–13 July.

——Cumming J., and McLean, J. (2004): 'Contracting for Health Services in a Public Health System: The New Zealand Experience', *Health Policy*, 69/1, 21–31.

Badelt, C. and Österle, A. (1998): *Grundzüge der Sozialpolitik. Spezieller Teil: Sozialpolitik in Österreich*, Vienna: Manz-Verlag.

Baldwin, P. (1990): *The Politics of Social Solidarity*, Cambridge: Cambridge University Press.

Bale, T. and Bergman, T. (2006): 'Captives No Longer, But Servants Still? Contract Parliamentarism and the New Minority Governance in Sweden and New Zealand', *Government and Opposition*, 41/3, 422–49.

Barnett, R. and Barnett, P. (2004): 'Primary Health Care in New Zealand: Problems and Policy Approaches', *Social Policy Journal of New Zealand*, 21, 49–66.

Barry, M. and Walsh, P. (2007): 'State Intervention and Trade Unions in New Zealand', *Labor Studies Journal*, 31/4, 55–78.

Bauer, T. (1998): *Kinder, Zeit und Geld. Eine Analyse der durch Kinder bewirkten finanziellen und zeitlichen Belastungen von Familien und der staatlichen Unterstützungsleistungen in der Schweiz Mitte der Neunziger Jahre*, Studie im Auftrag der Zentralstelle für Familienfragen des Bundesamtes für Sozialversicherung, BSV, Bern.

Bennett, A. (2002): 'Where the Model Frequently Meets the Road: Combining Statistical, Formal, and Case Study Work', Paper presented at the 2002 APSA Annual Meeting, Boston, MA.

——and Elman, C. (2006): 'Qualitative Research: Recent Developments in Case Study Methods', *Annual Review of Political Science*, 9/1, 455–76.

Bertozzi, F. and Bonvin, J.-M. (2001): 'Wiedereingliederungsmaßnahmen zu Gunsten der Arbeitslosen in der Schweiz: Unterschiedliche lokale Erfahrungen', *Soziale Sicherheit* (CHSS), 1/2001, 39–40.

Beskæftigelsesministeriet (2002): *Handlingsplan for Flere i arbejde*, Beskæftiglesesministeriet, Copenhagen.

Bille, L. (2001): *Fra valgkamp til valgkamp: Dansk partipolitik 1998–2001*, Copenhagen: Jurist- og Økonomforbundets Forlag.

——(2007): 'Denmark', *European Journal of Political Research*, 46/7–8, 938–42.

Binderkrantz, A. (2003): 'Strategies of Influence: How Interest Organizations React to Changes in Parliamentary Influence and Activity', *Scandinavian Political Studies*, 26/4, 287–305.

Bibliography

Bittner, F. (2005): 'Betrachtungen zur Entwicklung der Krankenversicherung', *Soziale Sicherheit*, 9, 373–85.

Blank, R. H. (1994): *New Zealand Health Policy: A Comparative Study*, Auckland: Oxford University Press.

Bock-Schappelwein, J. and Mühlberger, U. (2008): 'Beschäftigungsformen in Österreich: Rechtliche und Quantitative Aspekte', in: *WIFO Monatsberichte*, 12/2008, 941–51.

Bogedan, C. (2005): *Mit Sicherheit besser? Aktivierung und Flexicurity in Dänemark*, ZeS-Arbeitspapier 6/2005.

—— (2008): 'Mehr als Flexicurity: Lehren aus der dänischen Arbeitsmarktpolitik', in: H. Seifert and O. Struck (eds.): *Kontroversen um Effizienz und Sicherheit*. Wiesbaden: VS Verlag für Sozialwissenschaften, 267–85.

—— (2009): 'Zwischen Parlament und Interessenverbänden: Der dänische Wohlfahrtsstaat im Wandel 1973–2006', unpublished PhD thesis, University of Bremen, Bremen.

Boix, C. (1998): *Political Parties, Growth and Equality: Conservative and Social Democratic Economic Strategies in the World Economy*, Cambridge: Cambridge University Press.

Bolger, J. (1990): 'Statement by the Prime Minister', in: J. Bolger, R. Richardson, and W. F. Birch (eds.): *Economic and Social Initiative*, Wellington: New Zealand Government, 3–15.

—— Richardson R., and Birch, W. F. (eds.) (1990): *Economic and Social Initiative*. Wellington: New Zealand Government.

Bollard, A. (1994): 'New Zealand', in: J. Williamson (ed.): *The Political Economy of Policy Reform*, Washington, DC: Institute for International Economics, 73–120.

—— and Mayes, D. (1993): 'Corporatization and Privatization in New Zealand', in: T. Clarke and C. Pitelis (eds.): *The Political Economy of Privatization*, London/New York: Routledge, 308–36.

Bonoli, G. (1997): 'Switzerland: Institutions, Reforms and the Politics of Consensual Retrenchment', in: Jochen Clasen (ed.): *Social Insurance in Europe*, Bristol: The Policy Press, 107–29.

—— (1999): 'La réforme de l'Etat social Suisse: Contraintes institutionnelles et opportunités de changement', *Swiss Political Science Review*, 5/3, 57–77.

—— (2001): 'Political Institutions, Veto Points, and the Process of Welfare State Adaptation', in: P. Pierson (ed.): *The New Politics of the Welfare State*, Oxford: Oxford University Press, 238–64.

—— (2004): 'Switzerland: Negotiating a New Welfare State in a Fragmented Political System', in: P. Taylor-Gooby (ed.): *New Risks, New Welfare: The Transformation of the European Welfare State*, Oxford: Oxford University Press, 157–80.

—— (2005): 'The Politics of the New Social Policies: Providing Coverage Against New Social Risks in Mature Welfare States', *Policy & Politics*, 33/3, 431–49.

—— and Gay-des-Combes, B. (2002): 'Country Report on Switzerland', Project Welfare Reform and the Management of Societal Change, Framework Programme 5 — Improving

Human Potential, http://www.kent.ac.uk/wramsoc/workingpapers/firstyearre-ports/nationalreports/switzerlandcountryreport.pdf, 23 April 2007.

—— and Kato, J. (2004): 'Social Policies in Switzerland and Japan: Managing Change in Liberal-Conservative Welfare States', *Swiss Political Science Review*, 10/3, 211–32.

—— and Mach, A. (2000): 'Switzerland: Adjustment Policies Within Institutional Constraints', in: F. W. Scharpf and V. A. Schmidt (eds.): *Welfare and Work in the Open Economy*, Volume II: Diverse Responses to Common Challenges, Oxford: Oxford University Press, 131–74.

—— —— (2001): 'The Swiss Employment Puzzle', *Swiss Political Science Review*, 7/2, 81–94.

Booth, C. J. (1977): 'The National Party's 1975 Superannuation Policy', in: G. Palmer (ed.): *The Welfare State Today: Social Welfare Policy in New Zealand in the Seventies*, Wellington: Fourth Estate, 72–135.

Borchorst, A. (2006): 'The Public-Private Split Rearticulated: Abolishment of the Danish Daddy Leave, in: A. L. Ellingsæter and A. Leira (eds.): *Politicising Parenthood in Scandinavia*, Bristol: Policy Press, 101–20.

Boston, J. (1987): 'Thatcherism and Rogernomics: Changing the Rules of the Game: Comparisons and Contrasts', *Political Science*, 39/2, 129–52.

—— (1991): 'The Theoretical Underpinnings of Public Sector Reform in New Zealand', in: J. Boston, J. Martin, J. Pallot, and P. Walsh (eds.): *Reshaping the State: New Zealand's Bureaucratic Revolution*, Auckland: Oxford University Press, 1–26.

—— (1992): 'Targeting: Social Assistance for All or Just for the Poor?', in: J. Boston and P. Dalziel (eds.): *The Decent Society? Essays in Response to National's Economic and Social Policies*, Auckland: Oxford University Press, 77–99.

—— (1994*a*): 'Grand Designs and Unpleasant Realities: The Fate of the National Government's Proposals for the Integrated Targeting of Social Assistance', *Political Science*, 46/1, 1–21.

—— (1994*b*): 'The Implications of MMP for Social Policy in New Zealand', *Social Policy Journal of New Zealand*, 3, 2–16.

—— Martin, J., Pallot, J., and Walsh, P. (eds.) (1996): *Public Management: The New Zealand Model*, Melbourne: Oxford University Press.

Brady, D., Beckfield, J., and Seeleib-Kaiser, M. (2006): 'Economic Globalization and the Welfare State in Affluent Democracies: 1975–2001', *American Sociological Review*, 70/4, 921–48.

Breuss, F. (1989): 'Außenwirtschaft', in: H. Abele, E. Nowotny, S. Schleicher, and G. Winckler (eds.): *Handbuch der österreichischen Wirtschaftspolitik*, 3rd Edition, Vienna: Manz, 399–418.

Bryant, J. (2003): 'The Ageing of the New Zealand Population: 1881–2051', *Treasury Working Paper*, 3/27, Wellington: New Zealand Treasury.

Bucher, S. (2000): *Soziale Sicherheit, beitragsunabhängige Sozialleistungen und soziale Vergünstigungen: Eine europarechtliche Untersuchung mit Blick auf schwei-zerische Ergänzungsleistungen und Arbeitslosenhilfen*, Freiburg: Universitätsverlag Freiburg.

Bibliography

Bundesamt für Sozialversicherung (BSV) (2005): 'Aussprache des Bundesrates über den Umwandlungssatz in der Beruflichen Vorsorge', Medienmitteilung vom 16. November 2005, Bern: http://www.bsv.admin.ch/aktuell/presse/2005/d/05111602.htm, 23 November 2005.

——(2006): 'Grundzüge der kantonalen Familienzulagenordnungen', Stand 1. Januar 2006, Bern: http://www.bsv.admin.ch/fam/grundlag/d/grundzuege.pdf, 12 December 2006.

Bundesamt für Statistik (BFS) (2006): 'Teilzeitarbeit in der Schweiz', Neuchâtel: http://www.bfs.admin.ch/bfs/portal/de/index/themen/03/22/publ.Document.80668.pdf, 8 November 2006.

——(ed.) (2007a): *Kantonale Wohnbeihilfen und Arbeitslosenhilfen. Abgrenzungskriterien für die Sozialhilfestatistik und das Inventar der bedarfsabhängigen Sozialleistungen*, Neuchâtel: Bundesamt für Statistik.

——(ed.) (2007b): *Taschenstatistik der Schweiz 2007*, Neuchâtel: Bundesamt für Statistik.

Bundeskanzleramt (1979): *Bericht über die Situation der Familie in Österreich (2. Familienbericht)*, 2 vols., Vienna.

——(2007): Regierungsprogramm 2007–2010: Regierungsprogramm für die XXIII. Gesetzgebungsperiode, Vienna.

Bundesministerium für Gesundheit und Frauen (2004): *Gesundheit und Krankheit in Österreich: Gesundheitsbericht 2004: Berichtszeitraum 1992–2001*, Vienna.

Bundesministerium für Umwelt, Jugend und Familie (ed.) (1999): *Zur Situation von Familie und Familienpolitik in Österreich (4. Österreichischer Familienbericht)*, 2 vols., Vienna.

Bundesrat (1975): 'Botschaft des Bundesrates an die Bundesversammlung betreffend Änderung der Bundesverfassung für eine Neukonzeption der Arbeitslosenversicherung' (3.9.1975), *Bundesblatt*, 127/II (42), 1557–94.

——(1980): 'Botschaft zu einem neuen Bundesgesetz über die obligatorische Arbeitslosenversicherung und die Insolvenzentschädigung' (2.7.1980), *Bundesblatt*, 132/III (42), 489–687.

——(1993a): 'Botschaft zu einem Bundesbeschluss über Maßnahmen in der Arbeitslosenversicherung' (27.1.1993), *Bundesblatt*, 145/I (9), 677–93.

——(1993b): 'Botschaft über die Sanierungsmassnahmen 1993 für den Bundeshaushalt' (4.10.1993), *Bundesblatt*, 145/IV (49), 293–371.

——(1998): 'Botschaft zum Stabilisierungsprogramm 1998' (28.9.1998), *Bundesblatt*, 152/I (1), 4–160.

——(2000): 'Botschaft zur Schuldenbremse' (5.7.2000), *Bundesblatt*, 153/I (35), 4653–726.

——(2001): 'Botschaft zu einem revidierten Arbeitslosenversicherungsgesetz' (28.2.2001), *Bundesblatt*, 153/I (23), 2245–341.

——(2004): 'Botschaft zur Änderung des Bundesgesetzes über die Krankenversicherung (Strategie und dringliche Punkte)' (26.5.2004), Bern: http://www.admin.ch/ch/d/ff/2004/4259.pdf, 13 April 2007.

Bundesversammlung (1975–6): *Amtliches Bulletin der Bundesversammlung: Bundesverfassung (Arbeitslosenversicherung)*, 75.076, Bern: Dokumentationsdienst der Bundesversammlung.

——(1976–7): *Amtliches Bulletin der Bundesversammlung: AHV, 9. Revision*, 76.065, Bern: Dokumentationsdienst der Bundesversammlung.

——(1977–82): *Amtliches Bulletin der Bundesversammlung: Berufliche Vorsorge*, Bundesgesetz, 75.099, Bern: Dokumentationsdienst der Bundesversammlung.

——(1981–2): *Amtliches Bulletin der Bundesversammlung: Arbeitslosenversicherung Bundesgesetz und Arbeitslosenversicherung Übergangsordnung*, 80.048 und 81.009, Bern: Dokumentationsdienst der Bundesversammlung.

——(1985): *AHV/IV: Ergänzungsleistungen, 2. Revision*, 84.090, Bern: Dokumentationsdienst der Bundesversammlung, zusammengestellte Verhandlungen (loose sheets of paper).

——(1991–4): *10. AHV-Revision*, 90.021, Verhandlungsheft, Bern: Parlamentsdienste, Dokumentationszentrale.

——(1997): *Ergänzungsleistungen zu AHV und IV, Bundesgesetz, 3. Revision*, 96.094, Bern: Dokumentationsdienst der Bundesversammlung, zusammengestellte Verhandlungen (loose sheets of paper).

——(1998a): *Amtliches Bulletin der Bundesversammlung*, Wintersession 1998, Nationalrat, Bern: http://www.parlament.ch/Poly/Download amtl_Bulletin/98_12/Nrcn9812.pdf, 18 July 2006.

——(1998b): *Mutterschaftsversicherung*, Bundesgesetz, 97.055, Verhandlungsheft, Bern: Parlamentsdienste, Dokumentationszentrale.

——(2001–3a): *Krankenversicherungsgesetz: Teilrevision (Spitalfinanzierung)*, 00.079, Bern: Dokumentationsdienst der Bundesversammlung, zusammengestellte Verhandlungen (loose sheets of paper).

——(2001–3b): *Parlamentarische Initiative: Revision Erwerbsersatzgesetz: Ausweitung der Erwerbsersatzansprüche auf erwerbstätige Mütter*, 01.426, Verhandlungsheft, Bern: Parlamentsdienste, Dokumentationszentrale.

——(2002–3): *1. BVG-Revision*, 00.027, Verhandlungsheft, Bern: Parlamentsdienste, Dokumentationszentrale.

——(2005–6): *Parlamentarische Initiative Fankhauser Angeline: Leistungen für die Familie*, Bern: http://www.parlament.ch/homepage/do-dossiers-az/do-kinderzulagen.htm, 11 Decenmber 2006.

Burgoon, B. (2001): 'Globalization and Welfare Compensation: Disentangling the Ties that Bind', *International Organization*, 55/3, 509–51.

——(2009): 'Globalization and Backlash: Polanyi's Revenge?', *Review of International Political Economy*, 16/2, 145–77.

Burkhalter, V., Petersen, A., and Pini, F. (1999): 'Le néo-libéralisme comme revendication politique: acteurs et discours dans la Suisse des années 1990', in: A. Mach (ed.): *Globalisation, néo-libéralisme et politiques publiques dans la Suisse des années 1990*, Zürich: Verlag Seismo, 51–104.

Bibliography

Busch A. and Plümper, T. (ed.) (1999): *Nationaler Staat und internationale Wirtschaft*, Baden-Baden: Nomos.

—— and Merkel, W. (1992): 'Staatshandeln in kleinen Staaten: Schweiz und Österreich', in: H. Abromeit and W. W. Pommerehne (eds.): *Staatstätigkeit in der Schweiz*, Bern: Verlag Paul Haupt, 193–219.

Busemeyer, M. (2009): 'From Myth to Reality: Globalisation and Public Spending in OECD Countries Revisited', *European Journal of Political Research*, 48/4, 455–82.

Butschek, F. (1998): *Statistische Reihen zur österreichischen Wirtschaftsgeschichte: Die österreichische Wirtschaft seit der industriellen Revolution*, Vienna: WIFO.

Callister, P. and Galtry, J. (2006): 'Paid Parental Leave in New Zealand: A Short History and Future Policy Options', *Policy Quarterly*, 2/1, 38–46.

Cameron, D. (1978): 'The Expansion of the Public Economy: A Comparative Analysis', *American Political Science Review*, 72/4, 1243–61.

Campbell, I. B. (1996): *Compensation for Personal Injury in New Zealand: Its Rise and Fall*, Auckland: Auckland University Press.

Carigiet, E. and Opielka, M. (2006): 'Einleitung: Deutsche Arbeitnehmer — Schweizer Bürger?', in: E. Carigiet, U. Mäder, M. Opielka, and F. Schulz-Nieswandt (eds.): *Wohlstand durch Gerechtigkeit. Deutschland und die Schweiz im sozialpolitischen Vergleich*, Zürich: Rotpunktverlag, 15–45.

Castles, F. G. (1985): *The Working Class and Welfare: Reflections on the Political Development of the Welfare State in Australia and New Zealand, 1890–1980*, Sydney: Allen & Unwin.

—— (1989): 'Social Protection by Other Means: Australia's Strategy of Coping with External Vulnerability', in: F. G. Castles (ed.): *The Comparative History of Public Policy*, Cambridge: Polity Press, 16–55.

—— (1993): 'Changing Course in Economic Policy: The English-Speaking Nations in the 1980s', in: F. G. Castles (ed.): *Families of Nations: Patterns of Public Policy in Western Democracies*, Aldershot: Dartmouth, 3–34.

—— (1994): 'The Policy Consequences of Proportional Representation: A Sceptical Commentary', *Political Science*, 46/2, 161–71.

—— (1996): 'Needs-Based Strategies of Social Protection in Australia and New Zealand', in: G. Esping-Andersen (ed.): *Welfare States in Transition: National Adaptations in Global Economies*, London: Sage, 88–115.

—— (1998): *Comparative Public Policy: Patterns of Post-war Transformation*, Cheltenham: Edward Elgar.

—— (2001): 'On the Political Economy of Recent Public Sector Development', *Journal of European Social Policy*, 11/3, 195–211.

—— (2003): 'The World Turned Upside Down: Below Replacement Fertility, Changing Preferences and Family-Friendly Public Policy in 21 OECD Countries', *Journal of European Social Policy*, 13, 209–27.

—— (2004): *The Future of the Welfare State: Crisis Myths and Crisis Realities*, Oxford: Oxford University Press.

—— (2008): What Welfare States Do: A Disaggregated Expenditure Approach, *Journal of Social Policy*, 38, 45–62.

——and Mitchell, D. (1993): 'Worlds of Welfare and Families of Nations', in: F. G. Castles (ed.): *Families of Nations: Patterns of Public Policy in Western Democracies*, Aldershot: Dartmouth, 93–128.

——and Obinger, H. (2007): 'Social Expenditure and the Politics of Redistribution', *Journal of European Social Policy*, 17, 206–22.

——and Shirley, I. F. (1996): 'Labour and Social Policy: Gravediggers or Refurbishers of the Welfare State', in: F. G. Castles, R. Gerritsen, and J. Vowles (eds.): *The Great Experiment: Labour Parties and Public Policy Transformation in Australia and New Zealand*, Sydney: Allen & Unwin, 88–106.

——Gerritsen, R., and Vowles, J. (eds.) (1996): *The Great Experiment: Labour Parties and Public Policy Transformation in Australia and New Zealand*, Sydney: Allen & Unwin.

Child Poverty Action Group (2004): *Cut Price Kids: Does the 2004 'Working for Families' Budget Work for Children?*, Auckland: Child Poverty Action Group.

Christensen, J. (1998): *Socialpolitiske strategier 1945–72*, Odense: Universitetsforlaget.

Christl, J. and Potmesil, S. (1984): 'Beschäftigungs- und Arbeitsmarktpolitik in Österreich, *Österreichische Zeitschrift für Politikwissenschaft*, 1984/3, 279–94.

Clark, M. (ed.) (2005): *For the Record: Lange and the Fourth Labour Government*, Wellington: Dunmore Publishing.

Collins, D. B. (1977): 'Formulating Superannuation Policy: The Labour Party Approach', in: G. Palmer (ed.): *The Welfare State Today: Social Welfare Policy in New Zealand in the Seventies*, Wellington: Fourth Estate, 23–71.

Cox, R. H. (1998): 'From Safety Net to Trampoline: Labour Market Activation in the Netherlands and Denmark', *Governance*, 11/4, 397–414.

Cumming, J. and Gribben, B. (2007): *Evaluation of the Primary Health Care Strategy: Practice Data Analysis 2001–2005*, Health Services Research Centre and CBG Health Research Ltd.

Daguerre, A. (2007): *Active Labour Market Policies and Welfare Reform: Europe and the US in Comparative Perspective*, Houndmills: Palgrave.

Dalziel, P. (1992): 'National's Economic Strategy', in: J. Boston and P. Dalziel (eds.): *The Decent Society? Essays in Response to National's Economic and Social Policies*, Auckland: Oxford University Press, 19–38.

——(2001): 'A Third Way for New Zealand?', in: A. Giddens (ed.): *The Global Third Way Debate*, Cambridge: Polity Press, 86–99.

——(2002): 'New Zealand's Economic Reforms: An Assessment', *Review of Political Economy*, 14/1, 31–46.

——and Lattimore, R. (2004): *The New Zealand Macroeconomy*, Oxford: Oxford University Press.

Damgaard, E. (1989): *Who Governs? Parties and Policies in Denmark*, Politikens Sådan fungerer Danmark: Copenhagen.

Danish Regions (2001): *Regional Government in Denmark*, Copenhagen: Amtsrådsforeningen.

Bibliography

Danmarks Statistik (2001): *50-års-oversigten*, Danmarks Statistik.

Davis, P., Gribben, B., Lee, R. L., and McAvoy, B. (1994): 'The Impact of the New Subsidy Regime in General Practice in New Zealand', *Health Policy*, 29/2, 113–25.

Deeks, J. (1990): 'New Tracks, Old Maps: Continuity and Change in New Zealand Labour Relations 1984–1990', *New Zealand Journal of Industrial Relations*, 15/2, 99–116.

Degen, B. (2006): 'Sozialpolitische Geschichte der Schweiz: Soziale Sicherheit für Arbeiterschaft oder esamtbevölkerung?', in: E. Carigiet, U. Mäder, M. Opielka, and F. Schulz-Nieswandt (eds.): *Wohlstand durch Gerechtigkeit. Deutschland und die Schweiz im sozialpolitischen Vergleich*, Zürich: Rotpunktverlag, 47–58.

Delgrande, M. and Linder, W. (1994) VOX: *Analyse der eidgenössischen Abstimmungen vom 4. Dezember 1994*, Bern: Schweizerische Gesellschaft für praktische Sozialforschung, Institut für Politikwissenschaft an der Universität Bern, Forschungsstelle für politische Wissenschaft der Universität Zürich, Département de science politique, Université Genève, VOX Nr.55.

Devlin, N., Maynard, A., and Mays, N. (2001): 'New Zealand's New Health Sector Reforms: Back to the Future?', *BMJ (British Medical Journal)*, 322, 1171–4.

Ditch, J. and Oldfield, N. (1999): 'Social Assistance: Recent Trend and Themes', *Journal of European Social Policy*, 9, 65–76.

Duc, J.-L. (2001): 'L'assurance maternité genevoise', in: Fédération des employés en assurances sociales (FEAS) (ed.): *Aspects de la sécurité sociale*, 3/2001, 25–8.

Due, J. and Madsen, J. S. (2003): *Fra magtkamp til konsensus: Arbejdsmarkedspensionerne og den danske model*, Copenhagen: Jurist- og Økonomiforbundet.

—— —— (2007): 'Det danske Gent-systems storhed — og fald?', in: Arbejdsdirektoratet (ed.): *Arbejdsløshedsforsikringsloven 1907–2007 — udvikling og perspektiver*, Copenhagen: Arbedsdirektoratet, 201–48.

—— ——Jensen, C. S., and Petersen, L. K. (1994): *The Survival of the Danish Model: A Historical Sociological Analysis of the Danish System of Collective Bargaining*, Copenhagen: Jurist- og Økonomforbundets Forlag.

Duncan, G. (2002): 'Workers' Compensation', in: M. Lloyd (ed.): *Occupational Health and Safety in New Zealand: Contemporary Social Research*, Dunedin: Dunmore Press, 19–42.

Eardly, T., Bradshaw, J., Ditch, J., Gough, I., and Whiteford, P. (1996): *Social Assistance in OECD Countries*, Volume 1: Synthesis Report, London: HMSO.

Easterly, W. and Kraay, A. (2000): 'Small States, Small Problems? Income Growth, and Volatility in Small States', *World Development*, 28/11, 2013–27.

Easton, B. (1979): *Social Policy and the Welfare State in New Zealand*, Auckland: Allen & Unwin.

—— (1981): *Pragmatism and Progress: Social Security in the Seventies*, Christchurch: University of Canterbury Press.

—— (1989a): 'The Commercialisation of the New Zealand Economy: From Think Big to Privatisation', in: B. Easton (ed.): *The Making of Rogernomics*, Auckland: Oxford University Press, 114–31.

—— (ed.) (1989*b*): *The Making of Rogernomics*, Auckland: Auckland University Press.

—— (1994): 'Economic and Other Ideas Behind the New Zealand Reforms', *Oxford Review of Economic Policy*, 10/3, 78–94.

—— (1997*a*): *In Stormy Seas: The Post-War New Zealand Economy*, Dunedin: University of Otago Press.

—— (1997*b*): *The Commercialisation of New Zealand*, Auckland: Auckland University Press.

Ebbinghaus, B. (2006): 'Trade Union Movements in Post-Industrial Welfare States. Opening up to New Social Risks?', in: K. Armingeon and G. Bonoli (eds.): *The Politics of Post-Industrial Welfare States: Adapting Post-war Social Policies to New Social Risks*, Abingdon/New York: Routledge, 123–42.

—— and Scheuer, S. (2000): 'Denmark', in: B. Ebbinghaus and J. Visser (eds.): *Trade Unions in Western Europe since 1945*, London: Grove's Dictionaries, 157–99.

Eidgenössische Kommission für Frauenfragen (1992*a*): *Familienexterne Kinderbetreuung Teil 1: Fakten und Empfehlungen*, Bern.

—— (1992*b*): *Familienexterne Kinderbetreuung Teil 2: Hintergründe*, Bern.

Eisenstadt, S. N. (1985): 'Reflections on Centre-Periphery Relations and Small European States', in: R. Alapuro, M. Alestelo, E. Haavio-Mannila and R. Väyrynen (eds.): *Small States in Comparative Perspective*, Oslo: Norwegian University Press.

Ellingsæter, A. L. (1998): 'Dual Breadwinner Societies: Provider Models in the Scandinavian Welfare States', *Acta Sociologica*, 41/1, 59–73.

Ellison, N. (2006): *The Transformation of Welfare States?*, Abingdon/New York: Routledge.

Engeli, I. (2004): 'VOX: Analyse der eidgenössischen Volksabstimmung vom 16. Mai 2004', Bern, Zürich und Genève: Schweizerische Gesellschaft für praktische Sozialforschung, Institut für Politikwissenschaft an der Universität Bern, Forschungsstelle für politische Wissenschaft der Universität Zürich, Département de science politique, Université Genève, VOX Nr.83.

Esping-Andersen, G. (1980): *Social Class, Social Democracy and State Policy. Party Policy and Party Decomposition in Denmark and Sweden*, Copenhagen: New Social Science Monographs.

—— (1985): *Politics Against Markets*, Princeton, NJ: Princeton University Press.

—— (1989): 'The Three Political Economies of the Welfare State', *Canadian Review of Sociology and Anthropology*, 26/1, 10–36.

—— (1990): *The Three Worlds of Welfare Capitalism*, Cambridge: Polity Press.

—— (1996): *Welfare States in Transition: National Adaptations in Global Economies*, London: Sage.

—— (1999): *Social Foundations of Postindustrial Economies*, Oxford: Oxford University Press.

—— Gallie, V., Hemerijck, A., and Myles, J. (eds.) (2002): *Why We Need a New Welfare State*, Oxford: Oxford University Press.

European Observatory on Health Care Systems (2000): *Health Care Systems in Transition: Switzerland*, WHO: Kopenhagen.

European Observatory on Health Care Systems (2001): *Health Care Systems in Transition: New Zealand*, Copenhagen: European Observatory on Health Care Systems.

Evans, L., Grimes, A., and Wilkinson, B. (1996): 'Economic Reform in New Zealand 1984–95: The Pursuit of Efficiency', *Journal of Economic Literature*, 34/4, 1856–902.

Falkner, G. and Treib, O. (2003): 'Die Europäische Union als Herausforderung für die Sozialpolitik der Mitgliedsländer', in: S. Rosenberger and E. Tálos (eds.): *Sozialstaat*, Vienna: Mandelbaum Verlag, 14–27.

Families Commission (2007): *It's About Time: Towards a Parental Leave Policy that Gives New Zealand Families Real Choice*, Wellington: Families Commission.

Farnleitner, J. (1974): *Die paritätische Kommission. Institution und Verfahren*, Eisenstadt: Prugg.

Fink, M. (2006): 'Zwischen „Beschäftigungsrekord" und „Rekordarbeitslosigkeit": Arbeitsmarkt und Arbeitsmarktpolitik unter Schwarz-Blau/Orange', in: E. Tálos (ed.): *Schwarz-Blau: Eine Bilanz des "Neu-Regierens"*, Vienna: LIT Verlag, 170–87.

—— and Tálos, E. (2004): 'Welfare State Retrenchment in Austria: Ignoring the Logic of Blame Avoidance?', in: *Journal of Societal & Social Policy*, 3, 1–21.

Flora, P. (ed.) (1986): *Growth to Limits: The Western European Welfare States Since World War II*, Berlin/New York: de Gruyter.

Flückiger, Y. (1998): 'The Labour Market in Switzerland: The End of a Special Case?', *International Journal of Manpower*, 19/6, 369–95.

Fluder, R. and Salzgeber, R. (2002): 'Zentrumslasten im Sozialbereich', *Soziale Sicherheit* (CHSS), 3/2002, 133–7.

—— and Stremlow, J. (1999): *Armut und Bedürftigkeit. Herausforderungen für das kommunale Sozialwesen*, Bern: Verlag Paul Haupt.

Fougere, G. (2001): 'Transforming Health Sectors: New Logics of Organizing in the New Zealand Health System', *Social Science & Medicine*, 52/8, 1233–42.

Frenzel, M. (2002): *Neue Wege der Sozialdemokratie, Dänemark und Deutschland im Vergleich (1982–2002)*, Wiesbaden: Deutscher Universitätsverlag.

Friisberg, C. (1978): *Socialpolitik i Danmark*, Copenhagen: Gyldendal.

Ganghof, S: (2004): *Wer regiert in der Steuerpolitik? Einkommensteuerreform zwischen internationalem Wettbewerb und nationalen Verteilungskonflikten*, Frankfurt/Main: Campus.

Garrett, G. (1998): *Partisan Politics in the Global Economy*, Cambridge: Cambridge University Press.

—— and Mitchell, D. (2001): 'Globalization, Government Spending and Taxation in the OECD', *European Journal of Political Research*, 39/2, 145–77.

Gärtner, L. (2005): 'Sozialhilfe unter Druck: Zwischen finanziellen Anreizen und Integrationsmaßnahmen', *Soziale Sicherheit* (CHSS), 3/2005, 165–8.

—— (2006): 'Alterssicherung in der Schweiz: Bürger-Grundsicherung und Arbeitnehmer-Vorsorge', in: E. Carigiet, U. Mäder, M. Opielka, and F. Schulz-Nieswandt (eds.): *Wohlstand durch Gerechtigkeit. Deutschland und die Schweiz im sozialpolitischen Vergleich*, Zürich: Rotpunktverlag, 73–88.

Gauld, R. (2001): *Revolving Doors: New Zealand's Health Reforms*, Wellington, NZ: Victoria University of Wellington.

Genser, B. (1989): 'Steuerreform in Österreich', in: H. Abele, E. Nowotny, S. Schleicher, and G. Winckler (eds.): *Handbuch der österreichischen Wirtschaftspolitik*, 3rd Edition, Vienna: Manz, 461–78.

Gerlinger, T. (2003): *Das Schweizer Modell der Krankenversicherung. Zu den Auswirkungen der Reform von 1996*, Veröffentlichungsreihe der Arbeitsgruppe Public Health, Forschungsschwerpunkt Arbeit, Sozialstruktur und Sozialstaat, Wissenschaftszentrum Berlin für Sozialforschung (WZB), Berlin.

Gibson, J. and Le, T. (2008): How Much New Saving Will KiwiSaver Produce?, *Department of Economics Working Paper*, 03/08, Hamilton: University of Waikato.

Gilbert, N. (2002): *Transformation of the Welfare State: The Silent Surrender of Public Responsibility*, Oxford: Oxford University Press.

—— and Gilbert, B. (1989): *The Enabling State: Modern Welfare Capitalism in America*, Oxford: Oxford University Press.

Gill, R. J. (1989): *Inventory of Labour Market Measures, 1970–1989*, New Zealand Department of Labour Occasional Paper Series, Wellington: Department of Labour.

Giriens, P.-Y. and Stauffer, J. (1999): 'Deuxième révision de la loi sur l'assurance chômage: genèse d'un compromis', in: A. Mach (ed.): *Globalisation, néo-libéralisme et politiques publiques dans la Suisse des années 1990*, Zürich: Verlag Seismo, 105–43.

Gisser, R., Reiter, L., Schattovits, H., and Wilk, L. (eds.) (1989): *Lebenswelt Familie (3. Österreichischer Familienbericht)*, Vienna.

Glatzer, M. and Rueschemeyer, D. (2005): *Globalization and the Future of the Welfare State*, Pittsburgh, PA: Univ of Pittsburgh Press.

Goldfinch, S. (1998): 'Remaking New Zealand's Economic Policy: Institutional Elites as Radical Innovators 1984–1993', *Governance*, 11/2, 177–207.

—— (2000): 'Paradigms, Economic Ideas and Institutions in Economic Policy Change: The Case of New Zealand', *Political Science*, 52/1, 1–21.

Goodger, K. (1998): 'Maintaining Sole Parent Families in New Zealand: An Historical Review', *Social Policy Journal of New Zealand*, 10, 122–53.

Goodin, R. E. and Rein, M. (2001): 'Regime on Pillars: Alternative Welfare State Logics and Dynamics', *Public Administration*, 79/3–4, 769–801.

Gould, J. (1982): *The Rake's Progress? The New Zealand Economy Since 1945*, Auckland: Hodder & Stoughton.

Government Programme (2000): Österreich Neu Regieren Zukunft in Herzen Europas, Vienna.

Green, D. G. (1996): *From Welfare State to Civil Society*, Wellington: New Zealand Business Roundtable.

Green-Pedersen, C. (2002): *The Politics of Justification — Party Competition and Welfare-State Retrenchment in Denmark and the Netherlands from 1982 to 1998*, Amsterdam: Amsterdam University Press.

Green-Pedersen, C. (2007): 'Denmark: a "World Bank" Pension System', in: E. Immergut, K. Anderson, and I. Schulze (eds.): *The Handbook of West European Pension Politics*, Oxford: Oxford University Press, 454–95.

Green-Pedersen, C. and Klitgaard, M. B. (2008): 'Im Spannungsfeld von wirtschaftlichjen Sachzwängen und öffentlichen Konservatismus: Das dänische Wohlfahrtssystem', in: S. Klaus, S. Heglich, and U. Bazant (eds.): *Europäische Wohlfahrtssysteme*, Wiesbaden: Verlag für Sozialwissenschaften, 149–68.

———— and Nørgaard, A. S. (2004): *Den danske velfærdsstat: Politiske, sociologiske og institutionelle dynamikker*, Copenhagen: Velfærdskommissionen.

Greve, Bent (1999): *The Changing Universal Welfare Model: The Case of Denmark Towards the 21st Century*, Roskilde: Roskilde Unversity, Department of Social Sciences.

Gustafson, B. (2000): *His Way: A Biography of Robert Muldoon*, Auckland: Auckland University Press.

Ha, E. (2008): 'Globalization, Veto Players and Welfare Spending', *Comparative Political Studies*, 41/6, 783–813.

Hacker, J. S. (2002): *The Divided Welfare State: The Battle over Public and Private Social Benefits in the United States*, Cambridge: Cambridge University Press.

Hall, P. A. (1993): 'Policy Paradigms, Social Learning, and the State: The Case of Economic Policymaking in Britain', *Comparative Politics*, 25/3, 275–96.

—— and Soskice, D. (eds.) (2001): *Varieties of Capitalism: The Institutional Foundations of Comparative Advantage*, Oxford: Oxford University Press.

Hansen, S. K. and Jensen, S. D. (2004): *Spillet om sygehuserne - (re)centralisering af et decentralt velfærdsområde?*, Speciale ved Institut for Statskundskab: Copenhagen Universitet.

Harbridge, R. and P. Walsh (2002): 'Labour Market Reform in New Zealand', in: H. Sarfati and G. Bonoli (eds.): *Labour Market and Social Protection Reforms in International Perspective: Parallel or Converging Tracks?*, Aldershot: Ashgate, 198–220.

Häusermann, S. (2006): 'Changing Coalitions in Social Policy Reforms: The Politics of New Social Needs and Demands', *Journal of European Social Policy*, 16/1, 5–21.

—— Mach, A. and Papadopoulos, Y. (2001): *Social Policy Making in Hard Times: Changing Interactions Between Corporatist and Parliamentary Arenas in Switzerland*, Papier présenté dans le cadre du workshop «Politiques sociales» au congrès annuel de l'Association suisse de science politique à Fribourg, 8.–9.November 2001.

Hawke, G. (2004): 'New Zealand: Developing and Sustaining Economic Liberalization', in: J. Rolfe (ed.): *The Asia-Pacific: A Region in Transition*, Honolulu, HI: Asia-Pacific Center for Security Studies, 239–58.

Hazeldine, T. and J. Quiggin (2006): 'No More Free Beer Tomorrow? Economic Policy and Outcomes in Australia and New Zealand Since 1984', *Australian Journal of Political Science*, 41/2, 145–59.

Hemerijck, A., Unger, B., and Visser, J. (2000): 'Austria, the Netherlands, and Belgium', in: F. W. Scharpf and V. A. Schmidt (eds.): *Welfare and Work in the Open Economy*, Volume II: Diverse Responses to Common Challenges, Oxford: Oxford University Press, 175–263.

Henderson, A. and White, L. A. (2004): 'Shrinking Welfare States? Comparing Maternity Leave Benefits and Child Care Programs in European Union and North American Welfare States 1985–2000', *Journal of European Public Policy*, 11/3, 497–519.

Hernes, H. M. (1987): *Welfare State and Woman Power: Essays in State Feminism*, Oslo: Norwegian University Press.

Higgins, J. (1999): 'From Welfare to Workfare', in: J. Boston, P. Dalziel, and S. St. John (eds.): *Redesigning the Welfare State in New Zealand: Problems, Policies, Prospects*, Oxford: Oxford University Press, 261–77.

Hinrichs, K. (2001): 'Elephants on the Move: Patterns of Public Pension Reform in OECD Countries', in: S. Leibfried (ed.): *Welfare State Futures*, Cambridge: Cambridge University Press, 77–102.

—— (2009): 'Pension Reforms in Europe: Convergence of Old-Age Security Systems?' in: J. H. Petersen and K. Petersen (eds.): *The Politics of Age. Basic Pension Systems in a Comparative and Historical Perspective*, Frankfurt a.M.: Lang, 119–43.

—— and Kangas, O. (2003): 'When Is a Change Big Enough to Be a System Shift? Small System-Shifting Changes in German and Finnish Pension Policies', *Social Policy & Administration*, 37/6, 573–91.

Hirter, H. and Linder, W. (2002): VOX: *Analyse der eidgenössischen Abstimmungen vom 24. November 2002*, Bern, Zürich und Genève: Schweizerische Gesellschaft für praktische Sozialforschung, Institut für Politikwissenschaft an der Universität Bern, Forschungsstelle für politische Wissenschaft der Universität Zürich, Département de science politique, Université Genève, VOX Nr.79.

Hofmarcher, M. M. and Rack, H. (2001): *Health Care Systems in Transition*, Austria: European Observatory on Health Care Systems.

Hofmeister, H. (1981): 'Ein Jahrhundert Sozialversicherung in Österreich', in: P. A. Köhler and H. F. Zacher (eds.): *Ein Jahrhundert Sozialversicherung*, Berlin: Duncker & Humblot, 445–721.

Holstein, E. (2003): *Fyrsten — et portræt af Mogens Lykketoft*, Copenhagen: Aschehoug.

Höpflinger, F. and Wyss, K. (1994): *Am Rande des Sozialstaates. Formen und Funktionen öffentlicher Sozialhilfe im Vergleich*, Bern: Verlag Paul Haupt.

Hopkins, S. and Cumming, J. (2001): 'The Impact of Changes in Private Health Expenditure on New Zealand Households', *Health Policy*, 58/3, 215–29.

Hospital and Related Services Taskforce (1988): *Unshackling the Hospitals: Report of the Hospital and Related Services Taskforce*, Wellington: Hospital and Related Services Taskforce.

Hotz, C., Hugentobler, V., and Radeff, F. (1995): 'Kantonale Sozialhilfe- und Fürsorgegesetzgebungen im Überblick', *Soziale Sicherheit* (CHSS), 4/1995, 219–25.

Howell, B. (2005): 'Restructuring Primary Health Care Markets in New Zealand: From Welfare Benefits to Insurance Markets', *Australia and New Zealand Health Policy*, 2, 20.

Bibliography

Huber, E. and Stephens, J. D. (2001): *Development and Crisis of the Welfare State: Parties and Policies in Global Markets*, Chicago, IL: University of Chicago Press.

Huber, E. and Stephens, J. D. (2006): 'Combating Old and New Social Risks', in: K. Armingeon and G. Bonoli (eds.): *The Politics of Post-Industrial Welfare States: Adapting Post-War Social Policies to New Social Risks*, Abingdon/New York: Routledge, 143–68.

Hughes, J. (2005): 'Lone Parents and Social Security', *Victoria University of Wellington Law Review*, 36/1, 1–44.

Hurrelmann, A., Leibfried, S., Martens, K., and Mayer, P. (eds.) (2007): *Transforming the Golden Age Nation State*, Basingstoke: Palgrave.

ILO (1949): *Systems of Social Security: New Zealand*, Geneva: ILO.

——(2008): *World of Work Report 2008: Income Inequalities in the Age of Financial Globalisation*, Geneva: ILO.

INFRAS, Tassinari Beratungen, Mecop (2005): *Familienergänzende Kinderbetreuung in der Schweiz: Aktuelle und zukünftige Nachfragepotenziale*, Studie im Auftrag des Schweizerischen Nationalfonds, NFP 52, Zürich.

Inland Revenue and Ministry of Social Development (2007): *Receipt of the Working for Families Package: 2007 Update*, Wellington: Centre for Social Research and Evaluation, Inland Revenue.

Iversen, T. and Cusack T. (2000): 'The Causes of Welfare State Expansion: Deindustrialization or Globalization?', in: *World Politics*, 52, 313–49.

——and Wren, A. (1998): 'Equality, Employment, and Budgetary Restraint. The Trilemma of the Service Economy', *World Politics*, 50, 507–46.

Jacobs, K. and Barnett, P. (2000): 'Policy Transfer and Policy Learning: A Study of the 1991 New Zealand Health Services Taskforce', *Governance*, 13/2, 185–213.

Jacobsson, K. (2003): *Trying to Reform the 'Best Pupils in Class'? The OMC in Sweden and Denmark*, Draft paper prepared for the workshop on the Open Method of Coordination, Florence.

Jaggi, M (2000): 'Der Bundesrat befürwortet eine gesamtschweizerische Regelung der Familienzulagen', *Soziale Sicherheit* (CHSS), 4/2000, 211–14.

——(2006): 'Bundesgesetz über die Familienzulagen vom Parlament angenommen', *Soziale Sicherheit* (CHSS), 3/2006, 149–52.

James, C. (1992): *New Territory: The Transformation of New Zealand 1984–92*, Wellington: Bridget Williams Books.

——(2005): 'What Made the Revolution?', in: M. Clark (ed.): *For the Record: Lange and the Fourth Labour Government*, Wellington: Dunmore Publishing, 18–24.

Janssen, J. (2001): New Zealand's Fiscal Policy Framework: Experience and Evolution, *NZ Treasury Working Papers*, Wellington: NZ Treasury.

Jegher, A. (1999): *Bundesversammlung und Gesetzgebung: Der Einfluss von institutionellen, politischen und inhaltlichen Faktoren auf die Gesetzgebungstätigkeit der Eidgenössischen Räte*, Bern: Verlag Paul Haupt.

Jesson, B. (1989): *Fragments of Labour: The Story Behind the Labour Government*, Auckland: Penguin.

—— (1993): 'Towards a Schumpeterian Workfare State: Remarks on a Postfordist Political Economy', *Studies in Political Economy*, 40, 7–39.

—— (2002): *The Future of the Capitalist State*, Cambridge: Polity.

Johansen, L. N. (1986): 'Denmark', in: Flora, P. (ed.): *Growth to Limits: The Western European Welfare States Since World War II*, Berlin/New York: de Gruyter, 294–381.

Johnson, N. (2005): *Working for Families in New Zealand: Some Early Lessons*, Wellington: Fulbright Foundation, New Zealand.

Jonasen, V. (2006): 'Dansk Socialpolitik 1708–2006', download: http://webfiler.dsh-aa.dk/publikationer/Viggo%20Jonasen/Dansk%20Socialpolitik/dir.asp

Jones, S. R. H. (1999): 'Government Policy and Industry Structure in New Zealand: 1900–1970', *Australian Economic History Review*, 39/3, 191–212.

Jørgensen, H. (2002): *Consensus, Cooperation and Conflict — The Policy Making Process in Denmark*, Cheltenham: Edward Elgar.

Kaiser, A. (1997): 'Types of Democracy: From Classical to New Institutionalism', *Journal of Theoretical Politics*, 9/4, 419–44.

Kappel, R. (1998): 'Die Schweiz im Prozess der Globalisierung: Einige Aspekte aus der Sicht der Ökonomie', *Swiss Political Science Review*, 4/2, 96–104.

Karlhofer, F. (1999): 'Verbände: Organisation, Mitgliederintegration, Regierbarkeit', in: F. Karlhofer and E. Tálos (eds.): *Zukunft der Sozialpartnerschaft: Veränderungsdynamik und Reformbedarf*, Vienna: Signum Verlag, 15–46.

—— and Tálos, E. (1996): *Sozialpartnerschaft und EU: Integrationsdynamik und Handlungsrahmen der österreichischen Sozialpartnerschaft*, Vienna: WUV.

—— —— (eds.) (2005): *Sozialpartnerschaft: Österreichische und Europäische Perspektiven*, Vienna: LIT.

—— —— (2006): 'Sozialpartnerschaft am Abstieg', in: E. Tálos (ed.): *Schwarz-Blau: Eine Bilanz des 'Neu-Regierens'*, Vienna: LIT Verlag, 102–16.

Katzenstein, P. J. (1980): 'Capitalism in One Country? Switzerland in the International Economy', *International Organisation*, 34/4, 507–40.

—— (1985): *Small States in World Markets: Industrial Policy in Europe*, Ithaca, NY: Cornell University Press.

—— (2003): 'Small States and Small States Revisited', *New Political Economy*, 8/1, 9–30.

Kaufmann, F-X. (1997): *Herausforderungen des Sozialstaates*, Frankfurt: Suhrkamp.

Kehrli, C. and Knöpfel, C. (2006): *Handbuch Armut in der Schweiz*, Luzern: Caritas-Verlag.

Kelsey, J. (1997): *The New Zealand Experiment: A World Model for Structural Adjustment?*, Auckland: Auckland University Press and Bridget Williams Books.

Khol, A. (2001): *Die Wende ist geglückt: Der schwarz-blaue Marsch durch die Wüste Gobi*, Vienna: Molden.

Kirchgässner, G. (2005): 'Sustainable Fiscal Policy in a Federal State: The Swiss Example', *Swiss Political Science Review*, 11/4, 19–46.

Kittel, B. and Obinger, H. (2003): 'Political Parties, Institutions, and the Dynamics of Social Expenditure in Times of Austerity', *Journal of European Public Policy*, 10/1, 20–45.

Bibliography

Klitgaard, M. B. (2004): 'At beskytte et politisk våben. Når Socialdemokratiet de-kollektiviserer den universelle velfærdsstat', PhD-afhandling, Institut for Økonomi, Politik & Forvaltning: Aalborg Universitet.

Knöpfel, C. (2002): 'Interinstitutionelle Zusammenarbeit in der Sozialpolitik', *Soziale Sicherheit* (CHSS), 4/2002, 198–202.

Kohr, L. (1957): *The Breakdown of Nations*, London: Routledge & Kegan Paul.

Koopman-Boyden, P. G. (1990): 'Social Policy: Has There Been One?', in: M. Holland and J. Boston (eds.): *The Fourth Labour Government*, Auckland: Oxford University Press, 213–31.

—— and Scott, C. D. (1984): *The Family and Government Policy in New Zealand*, Sydney: Allen & Unwin.

Korpi, W. (1983): *The Democratic Class Struggle*, London: Routledge.

—— (2002): *Velfærdsstat og socialt medborgerskab: Danmark i et komparativt perspektiv, 1930–1995*, Århus: Århus University Press.

—— and Palme, J. (2003): 'New Politics and Class Politics in the Context of Austerity and Globalization: Welfare State Regress in 18 Countries, 1975–95', *The American Political Science Review*, 97/3, 425–46.

Kreisky, E. and Löffler, M. (2003): 'Staat und Familie: Ideologie und Realität eines Verhältnisses', *Österreichische Zeitschrift für Politikwissenschaft*, 32, 375–88.

Kriechbaumer, R. (2006): *Die Ära Kreisky*, Vienna: Böhlau.

Kriesi, H. (1980): *Entscheidungsstrukturen und Entscheidungsprozesse in der Schweizer Politik*, Frankfurt a.M./New York: Campus Verlag.

Kurzer, P. (1993): *Business and Banking: Political Change and Economic Integration in Western Europe*, Ithaca, NY: University of Cornell Press.

Kuznets, S. (1963): Economic Growth of Small Nations; in: E. A. Robinson (ed.): *Economic Consequences of the Size of Nations*, London: Macmillan.

Kvist, J. (1999): 'Welfare Reform in the Nordic Countries in the 1990s: Using Fuzzy-Set Theory to Assess Conformity to Ideal Types', *Journal of European Social Policy*, 9/3, 231–52.

—— (2000): 'Activating Welfare States. Scandinavian Experiences in the 1990s', The Danish National Institute of Social Research, *Working Paper*, 7/2000, Copenhagen.

—— (2003): 'A Danish Welfare Miracle? Policies and Outcomes in the 1990s', *Scandinavian Journal of Public Health*, 31/4, 241–5.

—— and Ploug, N. (2008): 'Small Steps, Big Change? Continuity and Change in the Danish Social Security System', in: E. Albæk, L. C. Eliason, A. S. Nørgaard, and H. M. Schwartz (eds.): *Crisis, Miracles, and Beyond*, Århus: Århus University Press, 171–200.

Langager, K. (1997): 'Indsatsen over for de forsikrede ledige. Evaluering af arbejds-markedsreformen I', Socialforskningsinstituttet rapport, 97/20, Copenhagen.

Lattimore, R. and Wooding, P. (1996): 'International Trade', in: B. Silverstone, A. Bollard, and R. Lattimore (eds.): *A Study of Economic Reform: The Case of New Zealand*, Amsterdam: Elsevier, 315–53.

Lauber, V. and Pesendorfer, D. (2006): 'Wirtschafts- und Finanzpolitik', in: H. Dachs, P. Gerlich, H. Kramer, V. Lauber, W. C. Müller, and E. Tálos (eds.): *Politik in Österreich: Das Handbuch*, Vienna: Manz, 607–23.

Laugesen, M. (2005): 'Why Some Market Reforms Lack Legitimacy in Health Care', *Journal of Health Politics, Policy and Law*, 30/6, 1065–100.

Lehner, F. (1992): 'Phänomen Schweiz: Aufstieg und kein Niedergang?', in: H. Abromeit and W. W. Pommerehne (eds.): *Staatstätigkeit in der Schweiz*, Bern: Verlag Paul Haupt, 283–303.

Leibfried, S. (2005): 'Social Policy: Left to the Judges and the Markets?', in: H. Wallace, W. Wallace, and Mark Pollack (eds.): *Policy-Making in the European Union*, Oxford: Oxford University Press, 243–78.

—— and Zürn, M. (eds.) (2005): *Transformations of the State?*, Cambridge: Cambridge University Press.

Leimgruber, M. (2008): *Solidarity Without the State? Business and the Shaping of the Swiss Welfare State, 1890–2000*, Cambridge: Cambridge University Press.

Leira, A. (2006): 'Parenthood Change and Policy Reform in Scandinavia, 1970s–2000s', in: A. L. Ellingsæter and A. Leira (eds.): *Politicising Parenthood in Scandinavia*, Bristol: Policy Press, 27–51.

Leu, R., Burri, S., and Priester, T. (1997): *Lebensqualität und Armut in der Schweiz*, Bern: Verlag Paul Haupt.

Leutwiler, F. (ed.) (1991): *Schweizerische Wirtschaftspolitik im internationalen Wettbewerb: Ein ordnungspolitisches Programm*, Zürich: Orell Füssli.

Lewis, J. (1995): 'Gender, Family and the Study of Welfare "Regimes"', *FREIA Working Paper*, Aalborg University 17.

Lijphart, A. (1987): 'The Demise of the Last Westminster System? Comments on the Report of New Zealand's Royal Commission on the Electoral System', *Electoral Studies*, 6/2, 97–103.

Lindbeck, A. (1997): 'The Swedish Experiment', *Journal of Economic Literature*, 35/3, 1273–319.

Linke-Sonderegger, M. (2009): *Aktivierung statt passive Leistung: Der Wandel der dänischen Arbeitsmarktpolitik seit 1990*, Frankfurt: Campus.

Lunt, N. (2009): 'The Rise of a "Social Development" Agenda in New Zealand', *International Journal of Social Welfare*, 18/1, 3–12.

Maarse, H. and Paulus, A. (2003): 'Has Solidarity Survived? A Comparative Analysis of the Effect of Social Health Insurance Reform in Four European Countries', *Journal of Health Politics, Policy and Law*, 28/4, 585–614.

McAllister, I. and Vowles, J. (1994): 'The Rise of New Politics and Market Liberalism in Australia and New Zealand', *British Journal of Political Science*, 24/3, 381–402.

McClure, M. (1998): *A Civilised Community: A History of Social Security in New Zealand 1898–1998*, Auckland/Wellington: Auckland University Press/Department of Internal Affairs, Historical Branch.

Bibliography

McClure, M. (2003): 'A Decade of Confusion: The Differing Directions of Social Security and Accident Compensation 1969–1979', *Victoria University of Wellington Law Review*, 34/2, 269–77.

Mach, A. (1998): 'Quelles réponses politiques face à la globalisation et à la construction européenne ? Illustration à partir de la révision de la loi suisse sur les cartels', *Swiss Political Science Review*, 4/2, 25–49.

—— (1999): 'Présentation générale et contexte socio-économique des années 1990', in : A. Mach (ed.): *Globalisation, néo-libéralisme et politiques publiques dans la Suisse des années 1990*, Zürich: Verlag Seismo, 11–50.

—— Häusermann, S., and Papadopoulos, Y. (2003): 'Economic Regulatory Reforms in Switzerland: Adjustment Without European Integration, or How Rigidities Become Flexible', *Journal of European Public Policy*, 10/2, 301–18.

Mackay, R. (1995): 'Foodbank Demand and Supplementary Assistance Programmes: A Research and Policy Case Study', *Social Policy Journal of New Zealand*, 5, 129–41.

—— (2003): 'Remaking the Welfare State in New Zealand', in: N. Gilbert and R. A. Van Voorhis (eds.): *Changing Patterns of Social Protection*, New Brunswick, NJ/London: Transaction Publishers, 75–118.

Mäder, A. and Neff, U. (1990): *Vom Bittgang zum Recht. Zur Garantie des sozialen Existenzminimums in der schweizerischen Fürsorge*, 2nd edition, Bern: Verlag Paul Haupt.

Maderthaner, W., Mattl, S., Musner, L., and Penz, O. (2004): *Die Ära Kreisky und ihre Folgen: Fordismus und Postfordismus in Österreich*, Vienna: Löcker.

Madsen, P. K. (2006): 'How Can It Possibly Fly? The Paradox of a Dynamic Labour Market in a Scandinavian Welfare State', in: J. L. Campbell, J. A. Hall, and O. K. Pedersen (eds.): *National Identity and the Varieties of Capitalism: The Danish Experience*, Montreal et. al.: MacGill-Queens, 321–55.

Maeder, C. and Nadai, E. (2004): *Organisierte Armut: Sozialhilfe aus wissenssoziologischer Sicht*, Konstanz: UVK Verlagsgesellschaft GmbH.

Mailand, M. (2008): 'The Uneven Impact of the European Employment Strategy on Member States' Employment Policies: A Comparative Analysis', *Journal of European Social Policy*, 18/4, 353–65.

—— (2009): 'Perspektiven des skandinavischen Korporatismus: Dänemark und Norwegen im Vergleich', *WSI Mitteilungen*, 1/2009, 17–24.

Mairhuber, I. (2000): *Die Regulierung des Geschlechterverhältnisses im Sozialstaat Österreich: Traditionen, Wandel und feministische Umbauoptionen*, Frankfurt a. M.: Lang.

Manow, P. (1999): 'Sozialstaatliche Kompensation außenwirtschaftlicher Öffnung?', in: A. Busch and T. Plümper (eds.): *Nationaler Staat und internationale Wirtschaft*, Baden-Baden: Nomos, 197–222.

Marterbauer, M. (2005): 'Veränderte Rahmenbedingungen und Präferenzen in der Wirtschaftspolitik', in: F. Karlhofer and E. Tálos (eds.): *Sozialpartnerschaft: Österreichische und Europäische Perspektiven*, Vienna: LIT, 57–78.

May, H. (2002): 'Aotearoa-New Zealand: An Overview of History, Policy, and Curriculum', *McGill Journal of Education*, 37/1, 19–36.

Meade, A. and Podmore, V. N. (2002): 'Early Childhood Education Policy Co-ordination under the Auspices of the Department/Ministry of Education: A Case Study of New Zealand', *Early Childhood and Family Policy Series*, 1, UNESCO.

Michalski, A. and Cheyne, C. (2008): 'The European Union and New Zealand: Converging Approaches to the Knowledge-Based Economy?', *Journal of European Public Policy*, 15/7, 1087–106.

Miller, K. E. (1996): *Friends and Rivals: Coalition Politics in Denmark, 1901–1995*, Lanham: University Press of America.

Ministry of Social Development (2001): *Pathways to Opportunity: From Social Welfare to Social Development*, Wellington: Ministry of Social Development.

—— (2004): *New Zealand Families Today*, Wellington: Ministry of Social Development.

—— (2005): *Briefing to the Incoming Minister: Leading Social Development in New Zealand*, Wellington: Ministry of Social Development.

Mishra, R. (2004): 'Social Protection By Other Means: Can It Survive Globalization?', in: P. Kennett (ed.): *A Handbook of Comparative Social Policy*, Cheltenham: Edward Elgar, 68–88.

Mitchell, L. (2005): 'Policy Shifts in Early Childhood Education: Past Lessons, New Directions', in: J. Codd and K. Sullivan (eds.): *Education Policy Directions in Aotearoa New Zealand*, Southbank Victoria: Thomson/Dunmore Press, 175–98.

Montanari, I. and Palme, J. (2004): 'Convergence Pressures and Responses: Recent Social Insurance Developments in Modern Welfare States', Paper presented at the ESPAnet Conference in Oxford, 9–11 September.

Mørch, S. (2001): *24 Statsministre*, Copenhagen: Gyldendal.

Morgan, K. J. (2008): 'The Political Path to a Dual-Earner/Dual-Carer Society: Pitfalls and Possibilities', *Politics & Society*, 36/3, 403–20.

Moser, J. (2003): 'Die Sozialpolitik der Schweizer Kantone im Vergleich — oder die Kunst, so viel wie möglich selbst und so wenig wie möglich gemeinsam zu entscheiden', Diplomarbeit an der Universität Bremen.

—— (2008): *Der schweizerische Wohlfahrtsstaat. Zum Ausbau des sozialen Sicherungssystems 1975–2005*, Frankfurt a. M./New York: Campus.

—— and Obinger, H. (2007): 'Schlaraffenland auf Erden? Auswirkungen von Volksentscheiden auf die Sozialpolitik', in: M. Freitag and U. Wagschal (eds.): *Direkte Demokratie: Bestandsaufnahmen und Wirkungen im Vergleich*, Münster/Hamburg: Lit-Verlag.

Mosler, R. (2004): 'Wie viel Reform braucht die Krankenversicherung?', in: O. Meggeneder (ed.): *Reformbedarf und Reformwirklichkeit des österreichischen Gesundheitswesens: Was sagt die Wissenschaft dazu?*, Frankfurt a. M.: Mabuse, 129–47.

Mulgan, R. (1990): 'The Changing Electoral Mandate', in: M. Holland and J. Boston (eds.): *The Fourth Labour Government: Politics and Policy in New Zealand*, Auckland: Oxford University Press, 11–21.

Mulgan, R. (1995): 'The Democratic Failure of Single-Party Government: The New Zealand Experience', *Australian Journal of Political Science*, 30/1, 82–96.

Müller, W. C. (1988): 'Die neue große Koalition in Österreich', *Österreichische Zeitschrift für Politikwissenschaft*, 1988/4, 321–47.

—— (2006): 'Die Österreichische Volkspartei', in: H. Dachs, P. Gerlich, H. Kramer, V. Lauber, W. C. Müller, and E. Tálos (eds.): *Politik in Österreich: Das Handbuch*, Vienna: Manz, 341–63.

—— and Jenny, M. (2004): '"Business as Usual" mit getauschten Rollen oder Konflikt- statt Konsensdemokratie?', *Österreichische Zeitschrift für Politikwissenschaft*, 33, 309–26.

Murphy, L. (2003): 'To the Market and Back: Housing Policy and State Housing in New Zealand', *GeoJournal*, 59/2, 119–26.

Mydans, S. (2007): 'Across Cultures, English Is the Word', *New York Herald Tribune*, April 9. Available at http://www.nytimes.com/2007/04/09/world/asia/09iht-eng-lede.1.5198685.html

Myles, J. and Quadagno, J. (2002): 'Political Theories of the Welfare State', *Social Service Review*, 76/1, 34–57.

Nagel, J. H. (1998): 'Social Choice in a Pluralitarian Democracy: The Politics of Market Liberalization in New Zealand', *British Journal of Political Science*, 28/2, 223–67.

—— (2000): 'Expanding the Spectrum of *Democracies*: Reflections on Proportional Representation in New Zealand', in: M. M. L. Crepaz, T. A. Koelble, and D. Wilsford (eds.): *Democracy and Institutions: The Life Work of Arend Lijphart*, Ann Arbor, MI: University of Michigan Press, 113–125.

Nannestad, P. (1991): *Danish Design or British Disease? Danish Economic Crisis Policy 1974–1979 in Comparative Perspective*, Århus: Århus University Press.

—— and Green-Pedersen, C. (2008): 'Keeping the Bumblebee Flying: Economic Policy in the Welfare State of Denmark, 1973–99', in: E. Albæk, L. C. Eliason, A. S. Nørgaard, and H. M. Schwartz (eds.): *Crisis, Miracles, and Beyond*, Århus: Århus University Press, 33–74.

Narr, W.-D. and Schubert, A. (1994): *Weltökonomie: Die Misere der Politik*, Frankfurt: Suhrkamp.

Neidhart, L. (1970): *Plebiszit und pluralitäre Demokratie: Eine Analyse der Funktion des schweizerischen Gesetzesreferendums*, Bern: Francke.

New Zealand Planning Council (1979): *The Welfare State? Social Policy in the 1980s*, Wellington: New Zealand Planning Council.

—— (1990): *Who Gets What? The Distribution of Income and Wealth in New Zealand*, Wellington: New Zealand Planning Council.

New Zealand Superannuation Fund (2006): *Annual Report 2006*, Wellington: New Zealand Superannuation Fund.

New Zealand Treasury (1984): *Economic Management*, Wellington: New Zealand Treasury.

—— (1987): *Government Management: Brief to the Incoming Government*, Wellington: New Zealand Treasury.

—— (2001): 'Towards an Inclusive Economy', *Treasury Working Paper*, 01/15, Wellington: New Zealand Treasury.

—— (2003): *Fiscal Impacts of Population Ageing in New Zealand: Report to the Periodic Report Group*, Wellington: New Zealand Treasury.

—— (2007): *KiwiSaver - Questions and Answers*, Wellington: New Zealand Treasury.

Nikolai, R. (2005): 'Die Arbeitsmarkt- und Beschäftigungspolitik in der Schweiz — Die Schweiz als Erfolgsmodell?', *Swiss Political Science Review*, 11/3, 193–97.

Nolan, P. (2002): 'New Zealand's Family Assistance Tax Credits: Evolution and Operation', *New Zealand Treasury Working Paper*, 02/16, Wellington: New Zealand Treasury.

Nowotny, E. (1986): 'Die Wirtschaftspolitik in Österreich seit 1970', in: E. Fröschl and H. Zoitl (eds.): *Der österreichische Weg 1970–1985*, Vienna: Europa Verlag, 37–59.

Obinger, H. (1998a): 'Federalism, Direct Democracy, and Welfare State Development in Switzerland', *Journal of Public Policy*, 18/3, 241–63.

—— (1998b): *Politische Institutionen und Sozialpolitik in der Schweiz: Der Einfluß von Nebenregierungen auf Struktur und Entwicklungsdynamik des schweizerischen Sozialstaates*, Frankfurt a. M.: Peter Lang.

—— (1998c): 'Soziale Sicherung in der Schweiz', in: E. Tálos (ed.): *Soziale Sicherung im Wandel: Österreich und seine Nachbarstaaten*, Vienna: Böhlau Verlag, 31–102.

—— (1999): 'Minimum Income in Switzerland', *Journal of European Social Policy Research*, 9, 29–47.

—— (2000): 'Wohlfahrtsstaat Schweiz: Vom Nachzügler zum Vorbild?', in: H. Obinger and U. Wagschal (eds.): *Der gezügelte Wohlfahrtsstaat: Sozialpolitik in reichen Industrienationen*, Frankfurt a. M./New York: Campus, 245–82.

—— (2001): 'Vetospieler und Staatstätigkeit in Österreich: Wirtschafts- und sozialpolitische Reformchancen für die neue ÖVP/FPÖ-Koalition', *Zeitschrift für Parlamentsfragen*, 32, 360–86.

—— (2006): 'Wir sind Voesterreicher': Bilanz der ÖVP/FPÖ-Privatisierungspolitik', in: E. Tálos (ed.): *Schwarz-Blau: Eine Bilanz des Neu-Regierens*, Vienna: LIT, 154–69.

—— (2009): 'Sozialpolitische Bilanz der Großen Koalition in Österreich', in: H. Obinger and E. Rieger (eds.): *Wohlfahrtstaatlichkeit in entwickelten Demokratien*, Frankfurt a. M./New York: Campus, 347–74.

—— and Tálos, E. (2006): *Sozialstaat Österreich zwischen Kontinuität und Umbau: Eine Bilanz der ÖVP/FPÖ/BZÖ-Koalition*, Wiesbaden: Verlag für Sozialwissenschaften.

—— —— (2010): 'Janus-Faced Developments in a Prototypical Bismarckian Welfare State: Welfare Reforms in Austria Since the 1970s', in: B. Palier (ed.): *A Long Good-Bye to Bismarck? The Politics of Welfare Reforms in Continental Europe*, Amsterdam: Amsterdam University Press, forthcoming.

—— and Wagschal, U. (2000): 'Von Pionieren und Nachzüglern — Eine Einleitung', in: H. Obinger and U. Wagschal (eds.): *Der gezügelte Wohlfahrtsstaat: Sozialpolitik in reichen Industrienationen*, Frankfurt a. M./New York: Campus, 7–21.

Obinger, H. and Wagschal, U. (2010): 'Social Expenditure and Revenues', in: F. G. Castles, S. Leibfried, J. Lewis, H. Obinger, and C. Pierson (eds.): *The Oxford Handbook of the Welfare State*, Oxford: Oxford University Press, forthcoming.

——Armingeon, K., Bonoli, G., and Bertozzi, F. (2005): 'Switzerland: The Marriage of Direct Democracy and Federalism', in: H. Obinger, S. Leibfried, and F. G. Castles (eds.): *Federalism and the Welfare State: New World and European Experiences*, Cambridge: Cambridge University Press, 263–304.

OECD (1988): *Reforming Public Pensions*, Paris: OECD.

——(1993): 'Private Pensions in OECD Countries: New Zealand', *OECD Social Policy Studies*, 11, Paris: OECD.

——(1994): *Labour Force Statistics 1972–1992*, Paris: OECD.

——(1999): *The Battle Against Exclusion: Social Assistance in Canada and Switzerland*, Paris: OECD.

——(2000): *OECD Economic Surveys: Switzerland*, Paris: OECD.

——(2002): *Babies and Bosses: Reconciling Work and Family*, Volume I: Australia, Denmark and the Netherlands, Paris: OECD.

——(2004*a*): *Babies and Bosses: Reconciling Work and Family Life*, Volume III: New Zealand, Portugal and Switzerland, Paris: OECD.

——(2004*b*): *Labour Force Statistics 1983–2003*, Paris: OECD.

——(2005): *Economic Survey: New Zealand*, Paris: OECD.

——(2006*a*): *Revenue Statistics 1965–2005*, Paris: OECD.

——(2006*b*): *Employment Outlook*, Paris: OECD.

——(2006*c*): *Social Expenditure Database*, Paris: OECD.

——(2007*a*): *Pensions at a Glance*, Paris: OECD.

——(2007*b*): *Economic Surveys: Austria*, Paris: OECD.

——(2007*c*): *Babies and Bosses: Reconciling Work and Family, A Synthesis of Findings for OECD Countries*, Paris: OECD.

——(2007*d*): *Revenue Statistics 1965–2006*, Paris: OECD.

——(2008*a*): *Social Expenditure Database*, Paris: OECD.

——(2008*b*): *Growing Unequal? Income Distribution and Poverty in OECD Countries*, Paris: OECD.

——(2009*a*): *Taxing Wages 2007–2008*, Paris: OECD.

——(2009*b*) *OECD Family Database*, Paris: OECD.

——(2009*c*): *Pensions at a Glance 2009: Retirement-Income Systems in OECD Countries*, Paris: OECD.

Oesch, D. (2007): 'Weniger Koordination, mehr Markt? Kollektive Arbeitsbeziehungen und Neokorporatismus in der Schweiz seit 1990', *Swiss Political Science Review*, 13/3, 337–68.

Ohmae, K. (1995): *The End of the Nation State: The Rise of Regional Economies*, London: HarperCollins.

Overbye, E. (1997): 'Mainstream Pattern, Deviant Cases: The New Zealand and Danish Pension Systems in an International Context', *Journal of European Social Policy*, 7/2, 101–17.

Palier, B. (2006): 'The Politics of Reforms in Bismarckian Welfare Systems', in: *Revue Française des Affaires Sociales*, 1, 47–72.

—— (ed.) (2010): *A Long Good-Bye to Bismarck? The Politics of Welfare Reforms in Continental Europe*, Amsterdam: Amsterdam University Press.

—— and Martin, C. (eds.) (2008): *Reforming the Bismarckian Welfare Systems*, Malden/ Oxford/Carlton: Blackwell.

Palmer, G. (1987): *Unbridled Power: An Interpretation of New Zealand's Constitution & Government*, Auckland: Oxford University Press.

Pedersen, J. H. (2007): 'Et rids af udviklingen i det danske arbejdsløshedsforsikrings-systemfra 1907 til 2007 — belyst ved centrale lovinitiativer og beslutninger', in: Arbejdsdirektoratet (ed.): *Arbejdsløshedsforsikringsloven 1907–2007: udvikling og perspektiver*, 67–104.

Pelinka, A. (1993): *Die Kleine Koalition: SPÖ-FPÖ*, Vienna: Böhlau.

—— (1998): *Austria: Out of the Shadow of the Past*, Boulder, CO: Westview Press.

Periodic Report Group (1997): *1997 Retirement Income Report: A Review of the Current Framework*, Wellington: Retirement Incomes Policies Periodic Report Group.

—— (2003): *Retirement Income Report 2003*, Wellington: Retirement Incomes Policies Periodic Report Group.

Perry, B. (2004): 'Working for Families: The Impact on Child Poverty', *Social Policy Journal of New Zealand*, 22, 19–54.

Perspektivplanlægning (1971): 'Redegørelse fra den af regeringen i november 1968 nedsatte arbejdsgruppe', Copenhagen: Finansministeriet.

Petersen, J. H. (1985): *Den danske alderdomsforsørgelseslovgivnings udvikling I. Oprindelse*, Odense: Odense Universitetsvorlaget.

Petersen, K. (1998): *Legitimität und Krise — Die politische Geschichte des dänischen Wohlfahrtsstaates 1945–1973*, Berlin: A. Spitz.

Pfau-Effinger, B. (2006): 'Gender und Care im Vergleich Deutschland–Schweiz: Care im Wandel des wohlfahrtsstaatlichen Solidaritätsmodells', in: E. Carigiet, U. Mäder, M. Opielka, and F. Schulz-Nieswandt (eds.): *Wohlstand durch Gerechtigkeit: Deutschland und die Schweiz im sozialpolitischen Vergleich*, Zürich: Rotpunktverlag, 239–51.

Pierson, P. (1994): *Dismantling the Welfare State? Reagan, Thatcher, and the Politics of Retrenchment*, Cambridge: Cambridge University Press.

—— (1996): 'The New Politics of the Welfare State', *World Politics*, 48/2, 143–79.

—— (1998): 'Irresistible Forces, Immovable Objects: Post-industrial Welfare States Confront Permanent Austerity', *Journal of European Public Policy*, 5/4, 539–60.

—— (2000): 'Increasing Returns, Path Dependence, and the Study of Politics', *American Political Science Review*, 94/2, 251–67.

—— (ed.) (2001): *The New Politics of the Welfare State*, Oxford: Oxford University Press.

—— (2004): *Politics in Time. History, Institutions, and Social Analysis*, Princeton, NJ: Princeton University Press.

Ploug, N. (2003): 'The Recalibration of the Danish Old-Age Pension System', *International Social Security Review*, 56/2, 65–80.

——Reib, J., Sidenius, N. C., and Winter, S. (1992): *A-kasserne og de ledige*, Copenhagen: Socialkommissionens Sekretariat.

Podder, N. and Chatterjee, S. (2002): 'Sharing the National Cake in Post Reform New Zealand: Income Inequality Trends in Terms of Income Sources', *Journal of Public Economics*, 86/1, 1–27.

Potrafke, N. (2007): 'Social Expenditure as a Political Cue Ball? OECD Countries Under Examination', *DIW Berlin Discussion Papers*, 676.

Preston, D. (1997): 'The Compulsory Retirement Savings Scheme Referendum of 1997', *Social Policy Journal of New Zealand*, 9, 138–50.

——(2004): *Retirement Income in New Zealand: The Historical Context [Updated Version]*, Wellington: Office of the Retirement Commissioner.

Pury, D. de, Hauser, H., and Schmid, B. (1995): *Mut zum Aufbruch: Eine wirtschaftspolitische Agenda für die Schweiz*, Zürich: Orell Füssli.

Pylkkänen, E. and Smith, N. (2003): 'Career Interruptions Due to Parental Leave: A Comparative Study of Denmark and Sweden', *OECD Social, Employment and Migration Working Papers*, 1, Paris: OECD.

Queisser, M. and Whitehouse, E. (2003): 'Individual Choice in Social Protection: The Case of Swiss Pensions', *OECD Social, Employment and Migration Working Papers*, 11, 3–50.

Quiggin, J. (1998): 'Social Democracy and Market Reform in Australia and New Zealand', *Oxford Review of Economic Policy*, 14/1, 76–95.

Ray, R. (2008): *A Detailed Look at Parental Leave Policies in 21 OECD Countries*, Washington, DC.: Center for Economic and Policy Research.

Richardson, R. (1995): *Making a Difference*, Christchurch: Shoal Bay Press.

Richter, A. (2002): 'Alles neu? Sozialhilfe-Gesetzesrevisionen in den Kantonen', *SozialAktuell*, 34/11, 21–4.

Rieger, E. and Leibfried, S. (2003): *Limits to Globalization. Welfare States and the World Economy*, Cambridge: Polity.

Robinson, E. A. (ed.) (1963): *Economic Consequences of the Size of Nations*, London: Macmillan.

Rodrik, D. (1997): *Has Globalization Gone Too Far?*, Washington, DC: Institute for International Economics.

——(1998): 'Why Do More Open Economies Have Bigger Governments?', *Journal of Political Economy*, 106/5, 997–1032.

Rokkan, S. (1994): 'Die Entstehung und Entwicklung der nordeuropäischen Demokratien', in: F. U. Pappi and H. Schmidt (eds.): *Parteien, Parlamente und Wahlen in Skandinavien*, Frankfurt a. M.: Campus, 30–55.

Ross, F. (1997): 'Cutting Public Expenditure in Advanced Industrial Democracies: The Importance of Blame Avoidance', *Governance*, 10/2, 175–200.

——(2000): 'Beyond Left and Right: The New Partisan Politics of Welfare', *Governance*, 13/2, 155–83.

Rothgang, H., Cacace M., Grimmeisen, S., and Wendt, C. (2005): 'The Changing Role of the State in OECD Health Care Systems', in: S. Leibfried and M. Zürn (eds.): *Transformations of the State?*, Cambridge: Cambridge University Press, 187–212.

Rothschild, K. W. (1985): 'Felix Austria? Zur Evaluierung der Ökonomie und Politik in der Wirtschaftskrise', *Österreichische Zeitschrift für Politikwissenschaft*, 1985/3, 261–74.

——(1989): 'Ereignisse und Reaktionen: Reflexionen über die österreichische Wirtschaftspolitik', in: H. Abele, E. Nowotny, S. Schleicher, and G. Winckler (eds.): *Handbuch der österreichischen Wirtschaftspolitik*, 3rd edition, Vienna: Manz, 113–24.

Rothstein, B. (2000): 'The Future of the Universal Welfare State: An Institutional Approach', in: S. Kuhnle (ed.): *Survival of the European Welfare State*, London: Routledge, 217–33.

Royal Commission of Inquiry into Social Security (1972): *Social Security in New Zealand: Report of the Royal Commission of Inquiry*, Wellington: Royal Commission of Inquiry into Social Security.

Ruder, R. (1999): 'Working Poor und Sozialhilfe', *Soziale Sicherheit* (CHSS), 3/2001, 123–5.

Sager, F., Ledermann, S., Zollinger, L., and Vatter, A. (2003): 'Familienpolitik auf Bundesebene', Bern: unpublished manuscript.

St John, S. (1992): 'National Superannuation: Or How Not to Make Policy', in: J. Boston and P. Dalziel (eds.): *The Decent Society? Essays in Response to National's Economic and Social Policies*, Auckland: Oxford University Press, 126–45.

——(1999): 'Accident Compensation in New Zealand: A Fairer Scheme?', in: J. Boston, P. Dalziel, and S. St John (eds.): *Redesigning the Welfare State in New Zealand: Problems, Policies, Prospects*, Auckland: Oxford University Press, 154–76.

——(2001): 'Financial Assistance for the Young: New Zealand's Incoherent Welfare State', Policy Discussion Paper, 25, Auckland: University of Auckland.

——(2004): *Financial Assistance for the Young: 1986–2008*, Discussion Paper Series Auckland: Department of Economics, University of Auckland.

——(2005a): *New Zealand's Financial Assistance for Poor Children: Lessons for Other Countries?*, Paper presented at the 2005 Social Policy Conference, 26–29 June, University of Bath, UK.

——(2005b): 'Retirement Incomes in New Zealand', *The Economic and Labour Relations Review*, 15/2, 217–39.

Scharpf, F. W. (1987): *Sozialdemokratische Krisenpolitik in Europa*, Frankfurt a. M./ New York: Campus.

——(1997): *Games Real Actors Play: Actor-Centered Institutionalism in Policy Research*, Boulder, CO: Westview Press.

——(2000): 'The Viability of Advanced Welfare States in the International Economy: Vulnerabilities and Options', *Journal of European Public Policy*, 7, 190–228.

303

Scharpf, F. W. and Schmidt, V. A. (eds.) (2000): *Welfare and Work in the Open Economy: Diverse Responses to Common Challenges*, 2 vols., Oxford: Oxford University Press.

Scheve, K. and Slaughter, M. J. (2004): 'Economic Insecurity and the Globalization of Production', *American Journal of Political Science*, 48/4, 662–74.

——and Slaughter, M. J. (2006): 'Public Opinion, International Economic Integration, and the Welfare State', in: P. Bardhan, S. Bowles, and M. Wallerstein (eds.): *Globalization and Egalitarian Redistribution*, Princeton, NJ: Princeton University Press, 217–60.

Schmidt, M. G. (1992): 'Politische und soziale Grundlagen der Vollbeschäftigung in der Schweiz', in: H. Abromeit and W. W. Pommerehne (eds.): *Staatstätigkeit in der Schweiz*, Bern: Haupt, 249–62.

——(1995): 'Vollbeschäftigung und Arbeitslosigkeit in der Schweiz: Vom Sonderweg zum Normalfall', *Politische Vierteljahresschrift*, 36/1, 35–48.

——(2005): *Sozialpolitik in Deutschland: Historische Entwicklung und internationaler Vergleich*, Opladen: Leske + Budrich.

——Ostheim, T., Siegel, N. A., and Zohlnhöfer, R. (eds.) (2007): *Der Wohlfahrtsstaat*, Wiesbaden: VS Verlag.

Schmidt-Hansen, U. and Kaspersen, L. B. (2004): 'The Relative Stability of Consensualism: Preliminary Results from Studies of the Political Decision-Making Process in Denmark', Amsterdam: Smallcons Project, The Danish Contribution to Workpackage 4.

Schoen, C., Osborn, R. Huynh, P. T., Doty, M., Davis, K., Zapert, K., and Peugh, J. (2004): 'Primary Care and Health System Performance: Adults' Experiences in Five Countries', *Health Affairs*, 4, 487–503.

Schumacher, E. F. (1973): *Small Is Beautiful: A Study of Economics as if People Mattered*, London: Blond & Briggs.

Schwartz, H. (1994): 'Small States in Big Trouble. State Reorganization in Australia, Denmark, New Zealand and Sweden in the 1980s', *World Politics*, 46, 527–55.

——(2000): 'Internationalization and Two Liberal Welfare States: Australia and New Zealand', in: F. W. Scharpf and V. A. Schmidt (eds.): *Welfare and Work in the Open Economy*, Volume II: Diverse Responses to Common Challenges, Oxford: Oxford University Press, 69–130.

Schwartz, H. M. (2001): 'The Danish "Miracle": Luck, Pluck, or Stuck?', *Comparative Political Studies*, 34/2, 131–155.

Schweizerische Konferenz für Sozialhilfe (SKOS) (2007): 'Zusammenfassung: Sozialhilfe, Steuern und Einkommen in der Schweiz', http://www.skos.ch/store/pdf_d/publikationen/Sozialhilfe_Steuern_Einkommen_Zusammenfassung.pdf, 22 November 2007.

Scott, C. D. (1994): 'Reform of the New Zealand Health Care System', *Health Policy*, 29/1, 25–40.

——Fougere, G., and Marwick, J. (1986): *Choices for Health Care: Report of the Health Benefits Review*, Wellington: Health Benefits Review.

Scruggs, L. (2004): *Welfare State Entitlements Data Set, Version 1.1*, Storrs, CT: University of Connecticut.

—— and Allan, J. (2006): 'Welfare-State Decommodification in 18 OECD Countries: A Replication and Revision', *Journal of European Social Policy*, 16/1, 55–72.

—— —— (2008): 'Social Stratification and Welfare Regimes for the Twenty-First Century: Revisiting The Three Worlds of Welfare Capitalism', *World Politics*, 60/4, 642–64.

Seeleib-Kaiser, M. (ed.) (2008): *Welfare State Transformations*, Basingstoke: Palgrave.

—— van Dyk, S., and Roggenkamp, M. (2008): *Party Politics and Social Welfare: Comparing Christian and Social Democracy in Austria, Germany and the Netherlands*, Cheltenham/Northampton: Edward Elgar.

Serdült, U. (1995): *VOX: Analyse der eidgenössischen Abstimmungen vom 25. Juni 1995*, Bern, Zürich und Genève: Schweizerische Gesellschaft für praktische Sozialforschung, Institut für Politikwissenschaft an der Universität Bern, Forschungsstelle für politische Wissenschaft der Universität Zürich, Département de science politique, Université Genève, VOX Nr.57.

Shipley, J. (1991): *Social Assistance: Welfare That Works*, Wellington: New Zealand Government.

Shirley, I. F., Koopman-Boyden, P. G., Pool, I., and St John, S. (1997): 'Family Change and Family Policies: New Zealand', in: S. B. Kamerman and A. J. Kahn (eds.): *Family Change and Family Policies in Great Britain, Canada, New Zealand, and the United States*, Oxford: Clarendon Press, 207–304.

Siebert, H. (2000): *Zum Paradigma des Standortwettbewerbs*, Tübingen: Mohr.

Siegel N. A. (2002): *Baustelle Sozialpolitik*, Frankfurt a.M./New York: Campus.

Silverstone, B, Bollard, A., and Lattimore, R. (eds.) (1996): *A Study of Economic Reform: The Case of New Zealand*, Amsterdam: Elsevier.

Sinclair, K. (1991): *A History of New Zealand*, Auckland: Penguin.

Sinn, H.-W. (2002): 'EU Enlargement and the Future of the Welfare State', *Scottish Journal of Political Economy*, 49/1, 104–15.

Skocpol, T. and Amenta, E. (1986): 'States and Social Policy', *Annual Review of Sociology*, 12, 131–57.

Sommer, J. H. (1978): *Das Ringen um soziale Sicherheit in der Schweiz: Eine politisch-ö konomische Analyse der Ursprünge, Entwicklungen und Perspektiven sozialer Sicherung im Widerstreit zwischen Gruppeninteressen und volkswirtschaftlicher Tragbarkeit*, Diessenhofen: Rüegger.

SPÖ (1982): *Der österreichische Weg aus der Weltwirtschaftskrise: Ein Jahr Wirtschaftsprogramm der SPÖ: Eine Bilanz*, Vienna: Verlag der SPÖ.

Starke, P. (2006): 'The Politics of Welfare State Retrenchment: A Literature Review', *Social Policy & Administration*, 40/1, 104–20.

—— (2008): *Radical Welfare State Retrenchment: A Comparative Analysis*, Houndmills, Basingstoke: Palgrave Macmillan.

—— Obinger, H., and Castles, F. G. (2008): 'Convergence Towards Where? In What Ways, If Any, Are Welfare States Becoming More Similar?' *Journal of European Public Policy*, 15/7, 975–1000.

305

Statistics New Zealand (2006a): 'Demographic Aspects of New Zealand's Ageing Population. Wellington: Statistics New Zealand', http://www.stats.govt.nz/NR/rdonlyres/DFB087B8-8425-466F-A1C2-ACE92D12C4ED/0/NZsAgeingPopulation. pdf, retrieved 21 March 2007.

——(2006b): *Long-Term Data Series*, Wellington: Statistics New Zealand, http://www. stats.govt.nz/tables/ltds/default.htm, retrieved 21 March 2007.

Statistik Austria (2002): *Krippen, Kindergärten & Horte (Kindertagesheime)*, Vienna.

Stephens, R. (1993): 'Radical Tax Reform in New Zealand', *Fiscal Studies*, 14/3, 45–63.

——(2000): 'The Social Impact of Reform: Poverty in Aotearoa/New Zealand', *Social Policy & Administration*, 34/1, 64–86.

——(2003): 'The Level of Financial Assistance to Families with Dependent Children: A Comparative Analysis', *Social Policy Journal of New Zealand*, 20, 173–96.

——(2005): 'Horizontal Equity for Disabled People: Incapacity from Accident or Illness', *Victoria University of Wellington Law Review*, 35/4, 783–800.

——and Bradshaw, J. (1995): 'The Generosity of Financial Assistance to Families with Dependent Children: An Eighteen Country Comparison', *Social Policy Journal of New Zealand*, 5, 53–75.

Stiefel, D. (2006): 'Die österreichische Wirtschaft seit 1950', in: H. Dachs, P. Gerlich, H. Kramer, V. Lauber, W. C. Müller, and E. Tálos (eds.): *Politik in Österreich: Das Handbuch*, Vienna: Manz, 64–81.

Strange, S. (1996): *The Retreat of the State: The Diffusion of Power in World Economy*, Cambridge: Cambridge University Press.

Streeck, W. and Thelen, K. (2005a): *Beyond Continuity: Institutional Change in Advanced Political Economies*, Oxford: Oxford University Press.

————(2005b): 'Introduction: Institutional Change in Advanced Political Economies', in: W. Streeck and K. Thelen (eds.): *Beyond Continuity: Institutional Change in Advanced Political Economies*, Oxford: Oxford University Press, 1–39.

Strohmeier, R. and Knöpfel, C. (2005): 'Was heißt soziale Integration? Öffentliche Sozialhilfe zwischen Anspruch und Realität', Diskussionspapier 14, Luzern: Caritas-Verlag.

Strøm, K. (1990): *Minority Government and Majority Rule*, Cambridge: Cambridge University Press.

Stummvoll, G. (1977): 'Der Sozialstaat am Scheideweg', in: *Die Industrie*, No 25.02.1977, 1–7.

Sunstein, C. R. and Thaler, R. H. (2003): 'Libertarian Paternalism Is Not an Oxymoron', *University of Chicago Law Review*, 70/4, 1159–202.

Swank, D. (2002): *Global Capital, Political Institutions, and Policy Change in Developed Welfare States*, Cambridge: Cambridge University Press.

——(2005): 'Globalisation, Domestic Politics, and Welfare State Retrenchment in Capitalist Societies', *Social Policy & Society*, 4/2, 183–95.

Tálos, E. (1981): *Staatliche Sozialpolitik in Österreich: Rekonstruktion und Analyse*, Vienna: Verlag für Gesellschaftskritik.

——(1986): 'Sozialpolitik in Österreich seit 1970', in: E. Fröschl and H. Zoitl (eds.): *Der österreichische Weg 1970–1985*, Vienna: Europa Verlag, 93–114.

—— (1987): 'Arbeitslosigkeit und beschäftigungspolitische Steuerung', in: E. Tálos (ed.): *Arbeitslosigkeit*, Vienna: Verlag für Gesellschaftskritik, 91–166.

—— (1999): 'Atypische Beschäftigung in Österreich', in: E. Tálos (ed.): *Atypische Beschäftigung: Internationale Trends und sozialstaatliche Regelungen*, Vienna: Manz, 252–84.

—— (2000): 'Sozialpolitik in der "Ostmark"', in: E. Tálos (ed.): *NS-Herrschaft in Österreich*, Vienna: öbv & hpt, 376–408.

—— (2005*a*): *Vom Siegeszug zum Rückzug: Sozialstaat Österreich 1945–2005*, Innsbruck: Studienverlag.

—— (2005*b*): 'Vom Vorzeige- zum Auslaufmodell? Österreichs Sozialpartnerschaft 1945 bis 2005', in: F. Karlhofer and E. Tálos (eds.): *Sozialpartnerschaft: Österreichische und Europäische Perspektiven*, Vienna: LIT-Verlag, 185–216.

—— (2008): *Sozialpartnerschaft. Ein zentraler Gestaltungsfaktor in der Zweiten Republik*, Innsbruck: Studienverlag.

—— and Badelt, C. (1999): 'The Welfare State Between New Stimuli and New Pressures: Austrian Social Policy and the EU', *Journal of European Social Policy*, 9, 351–361.

—— and Kittel, B. (1999): *Gesetzgebung in Österreich: Netzwerke, Akteure und Interaktionen in politischen Entscheidungsprozessen*, Vienna: WUV.

—— and Wörister, K. (1994): *Soziale Sicherung im Sozialstaat Österreich*, Baden-Baden: Nomos.

—— —— (1998): 'Soziale Sicherung in Österreich', in: Emmerich Tálos (ed.): *Soziale Sicherung im Wandel*, Vienna/Cologne/Weimar: Böhlau, 209–88.

Tanaka, S. (2005): 'Parental Leave and Child Health across OECD Countries', *The Economic Journal*, 115/501, F7–F28.

Tanzi, V. (2002): 'Globalization and the Future of Social Protection', *Scottish Journal of Political Economy*, 49/1, 116–27.

Taylor-Gooby, P. (2001): 'Sustaining Welfare in Hard Times: Who Will Foot the Bill?', *Journal of European Social Policy*, 11/2, 133–47.

—— (2002): 'The Silver Age of the Welfare State: Perspectives on Resilience', *Journal of Social Policy*, 31/4, 597–621.

—— (ed.) (2004): *New Risks, New Welfare: The Transformation of the European Welfare State*, Oxford: Oxford University Press.

Tecklenburg, U. (1997): 'Die neuen kantonalen Sozialhilfe-Modelle: Leistungen und Gegenleistungen', *Soziale Sicherheit* (CHSS), 1/1997, 15–18.

Thomson, D. (1998): 'Taking the Long View on Pensions', *New Zealand Journal of History*, 32/2, 93–120.

Torfing, J. (1999): 'Workfare with Welfare: Recent Reforms of the Danish Welfare State', *Journal of European Social Policy*, 9/1, 5–28.

Trampusch, C. (2008): 'Von einem liberalen zu einem post-liberalen Wohlfahrtsstaat: Der Wandel der gewerkschaftlichen Sozialpolitik in der Schweiz', *Swiss Political Science Review*, 14/1, 49–84.

Tsebelis, G. (1995): 'Decision-Making in Political Systems: Veto Players in Presidentialism, Parliamentarism, Multicameralism and Multipartyism', *British Journal of Political Science*, 25/3, 289–325.

—— (2002): *Veto Players: How Political Institutions Work*, Princeton, NJ: Princeton University Press.

Twain, M. (1880): 'The Awful German Language', in: M. Twain, *A Tramp Abroad*, Hartford: American Publishing Company and London, Chatto & Windus. Appendix D. Available also at http://www.crossmyt.com/ hc/linghebr/awfgrmlg. html

Udredningsudvalget Sekretariatet (1992): *Rapport fra Udredningsudvalget om arbejdsmarkedets strukturproblemer*, Copenhagen.

Unger, B. (2001): 'Österreichische Beschäftigungs- und Sozialpolitik von 1970 bis 2000', *Zeitschrift für Sozialreform*, 47, 340–61.

—— and Heitzmann, K. (2003): 'The Adjustment Path of the Austrian Welfare State: Back to Bismarck?', *Journal of European Social Policy*, 13, 371–87.

UNICEF (2005): *Child Poverty in Rich Countries 2005*, Florence: UNICEF Innocenti Research Centre.

Upton, S. (1991): *Your Health and the Public Health*, Wellington: GP Print.

Velfærdskommissionen (2005): *Fremtidens velfærd - vores valg*, Copenhagen.

Vowles, J., Banducci, S. A., and Karp, J. A. (2006): 'Forecasting and Evaluating the Consequences of Electoral Change in New Zealand', *Acta Politica*, 41/3, 267–84.

VOX (1978): *VOX: Analyse der eidgenössischen Abstimmung vom 26. Februar 1978*, Bern, Zürich und Genève: Schweizerische Gesellschaft für praktische Sozialforschung, Institut für Politikwissenschaft an der Universität Bern, Forschungsstelle für politische Wissenschaft der Universität Zürich, Département de science politique, Université Genève, VOX Nr. 5.

—— (1987): *VOX: Analyse der eidgenössischen Abstimmung vom 6. Dezember 1987*, Bern, Zürich und Genève: Schweizerische Gesellschaft für praktische Sozialforschung, Institut für Politikwissenschaft an der Universität Bern, Forschungsstelle für politische Wissenschaft der Universität Zürich, Département de science politique, Université Genève, VOX Nr. 34.

—— (1988): *VOX: Analyse der eidgenössischen Abstimmung vom 12. Juni 1988*, Bern, Zürich und Genève: Schweizerische Gesellschaft für praktische Sozialforschung, Institut für Politikwissenschaft an der Universität Bern, Forschungsstelle für politische Wissenschaft der Universität Zürich, Département de science politique, Université Genève, VOX Nr. 35.

Vrangbæk, K. (1999): *Markedsorientering i sygehussektoren? Opkomst, udformning og konsekvenser af frit sygehusvalg*, Copenhagen: Institute of Political Science, Dissertation.

—— (2001): *Ingeniørarbejde, hundeslagsmål eller hovedløs høne? - Ventetidsgarantier til sygehusbehandling*, Århus: Århus University Press.

—— and Østergren, K. (2004): 'The Introduction of Choice in Scandinavian Hospital Systems: Arguments and Policy Processes in the Danish and the Norwegian Case', Stein Rokkan Centre for Social Studies, *Working Paper*, 5–2004, University of Bergen.

—— and Christiansen, T. (2005): 'Health Policy in Denmark: Leaving the Decentralized Welfare Path?', *Journal of Health Politics*, 30/1–2, 29–52.

Vranitzky, F. (2004): *Politische Erinnerungen*, Vienna: Zsolnay.

Wagschal, U., Ganser, D., and Rentsch, H. (2002): *Der Alleingang: Die Schweiz 10 Jahre nach dem EWR-Nein*, Zürich: Orell Füssli.

Waldegrave, C. and Frater, P. (1991): *National Government Budgets of the First Year in Office: A Social Assessment*, Wellington: The Family Centre and Business and Economic Research Ltd.

Weaver, R. K. (2002): 'New Zealand: The Supreme Political Football', *CRR Working Paper*, 2002–12, Chestnut Hill, MA: Center for Retirement Research at Boston College.

—— (2006): 'Paths and Forks or Chutes and Ladders? Negative Feedbacks and Policy Regime Change', Paper presented at the McMaster University conference on 'Private Pensions and Income Security in Old Age: An Uncertain Future', Hamilton, Ontario, 16 October.

Wecker, R. (2006): 'Gender und Care in der Schweiz: Traditionen und Veränderungen', in E. Carigiet, U. Mäder, M. Opielka, and F. Schulz-Nieswandt (eds.): *Wohlstand durch Gerechtigkeit. Deutschland und die Schweiz im sozialpolitischen Vergleich*, Zürich: Rotpunktverlag, 227–38.

Wendt, C. (2003): *Krankenversicherung oder Gesundheitsvorsorge? Gesundheitssysteme im Vergleich*, Wiesbaden: Westdeutscher Verlag.

Werner, H. (2002): 'Arbeitsmarkt Schweiz — ein noch wenig beachtetes Erfolgsmodell', IAB Kurzbericht, 9, Nürnberg: http://doku.iab.de/kurzber/2002/kb0902.pdf, 28 March 2007.

Wicki, M. (2001): 'Soziale Sicherung in der Schweiz: Ein europäischer Sonderfall', in: K. Kraus and T. Geisen (eds.): *Sozialstaat in Europa: Geschichte, Entwicklung, Perspektiven*, Westdeutscher Verlag: Opladen, 249–72.

Winckler, G. (1988): 'Der Austrokeynesianismus und sein Ende', *Österreichische Zeitschrift für Politikwissenschaft*, 1988/3, 221–30.

Wolffers, F. (1993): *Grundriss des Sozialhilferechts: Eine Einführung in die Fürsorgegesetzgebung von Bund und Kantonen*, Bern: Verlag Paul Haupt.

World Bank (1994): *Averting the Old Age Crisis: Policies to Protect the Old and Promote Growth*, New York: World Bank Policy Research Report.

—— (2006): *Doing Business 2007: How to Reform*, Washington, DC: World Bank.

Wyss, K. (1997): *Massnahmen zur sozialen und beruflichen Integration von Langzeitarbeitslosen bezw. SozialhilfeempfängerInnen*, SKOS, Bern.

—— and Ruder, R. (1999): 'Integrationsmaßnahmen zur Bekämpfung der Langzeiterwerbslosigkeit: Starke Segmentierung', *Soziale Sicherheit* (CHSS), 5/1999, 239–45.

Yoo, K. and de Serres, A. (2004): 'Tax Treatment of Private Pension Savings in OECD Countries and the Net Tax Cost per Unit of Contribution to Tax-Favoured Schemes', *OECD Economics Department Working Paper*, 406, Paris: OECD.

Ziniel, G. (2003): 'Selbstbehalte im Gesundheitswesen — ein gescheitertes Experiment?', *Soziale Sicherheit*, 9/2003, 404–8.

Zohlnhöfer, R. (2009): *Globalisierung der Wirtschaft und finanzpolitische Anpassungsreaktionen in Westeuropa*, Baden-Baden: Nomos.

Index

Index

Index